PI

Plato's *Symposium* is an exceptionally multi-layered dialogue. At once a historical document, a philosophical drama that enacts abstract ideas in an often light-hearted way, and a literary masterpiece, it has exerted an influence that goes well beyond the confines of philosophy. The essays in this volume, by leading scholars, offer detailed analyses of all parts of the work, focusing on the central and much-debated theme of *erōs* or 'human desire' – which can refer to both physical desire and desire for happiness. They reveal thematic continuities between the prologue and the various speeches as well as between the speeches themselves, and present a rich collection of contrasting yet complementary readings of Diotima's speech. The volume will be invaluable for classicists and philosophers alike, and for all who are interested in one of Plato's most fascinating and challenging dialogues.

PIERRE DESTRÉE is Associate Research Professor in Philosophy at the University of Louvain. He has co-edited several volumes on ancient ethics, politics, and aesthetics, including *The Cambridge Companion to Aristotle's Politics* (Cambridge 2013).

ZINA GIANNOPOULOU is Associate Professor in Classics at the University of California, Irvine. Her publications include *Plato's* Theaetetus *as a Second Apology* (2013).

CAMBRIDGE CRITICAL GUIDES

Recent titles in this series:

Mill's *On Liberty*
EDITED BY C. L. TEN

Kant's *Idea for a Universal History with a Cosmopolitan Aim*
EDITED BY AMÉLIE OKSENBERG RORTY AND JAMES SCHMIDT

Kant's *Groundwork of the Metaphysics of Morals*
EDITED BY JENS TIMMERMANN

Kant's *Critique of Practical Reason*
EDITED BY ANDREWS REATH AND JENS TIMMERMANN

Wittgenstein's *Philosophical Investigations*
EDITED BY ARIF AHMED

Kierkegaard's *Concluding Unscientific Postscript*
EDITED BY RICK ANTHONY FURTAK

Plato's *Republic*
EDITED BY MARK L. MCPHERRAN

Plato's *Laws*
EDITED BY CHRISTOPHER BOBONICH

Spinoza's *Theological-Political Treatise*
EDITED BY YITZHAK Y. MELAMED AND MICHAEL A. ROSENTHAL

Aristotle's *Nicomachean Ethics*
EDITED BY JON MILLER

Kant's *Metaphysics of Morals*
EDITED BY LARA DENIS

Nietzsche's *On the Genealogy of Morality*
EDITED BY SIMON MAY

Kant's *Observations and Remarks*
EDITED BY RICHARD VELKLEY AND SUSAN SHELL

Augustine's *City of God*
EDITED BY JAMES WETZEL

Descartes' *Meditations*
EDITED BY KAREN DETLEFSEN

Kant's *Religion within the Boundaries of Mere Reason*
EDITED BY GORDON MICHALSON

Kant's *Lectures on Anthropology*
EDITED BY ALIX COHEN

Kierkegaard's *Fear and Trembling*
EDITED BY DANIEL CONWAY

Kant's *Lectures on Ethics*
EDITED BY LARA DENIS AND OLIVER SENSEN

Aristotle's *Physics*
EDITED BY MARISKA LEUNISSEN

Aristotle's *Politics*
EDITED BY THORNTON LOCKWOOD AND THANASSIS SAMARAS

Aquinas's *Disputed Questions on Evil*
EDITED BY M. V. DOUGHERTY

Plato's *Symposium*
EDITED BY PIERRE DESTRÉE AND ZINA GIANNOPOULOU

PLATO'S *Symposium*

A Critical Guide

EDITED BY

PIERRE DESTRÉE

Université Catholique de Louvain

ZINA GIANNOPOULOU

University of California, Irvine

CAMBRIDGE
UNIVERSITY PRESS

CAMBRIDGE
UNIVERSITY PRESS

University Printing House, Cambridge CB2 8BS, United Kingdom

One Liberty Plaza, 20th Floor, New York, NY 10006, USA

477 Williamstown Road, Port Melbourne, VIC 3207, Australia

314-321, 3rd Floor, Plot 3, Splendor Forum, Jasola District Centre, New Delhi - 110025, India

79 Anson Road, #06-04/06, Singapore 079906

Cambridge University Press is part of the University of Cambridge.

It furthers the University's mission by disseminating knowledge in the pursuit of education, learning and research at the highest international levels of excellence.

www.cambridge.org
Information on this title: www.cambridge.org/9781107525696
DOI: 10.1017/9781316273166

First published 2017
First paperback edition 2018

A catalogue record for this publication is available from the British Library

Library of Congress Cataloging in Publication data
NAMES: Destrée, Pierre, editor. | Giannopoulou, Zina, editor.
TITLE: Plato's Symposium : a critical guide / edited by Pierre Destrée, Université Catholique de Louvain, Zina Giannopoulou, University of California, Irvine.
DESCRIPTION: Cambridge, United Kingdom ; New York, NY : Cambridge University Press, 2017. |
SERIES: Cambridge critical guides | Includes bibliographical references and index.
IDENTIFIERS: LCCN 2016047802 | ISBN 9781107110052 (hardback : alk. paper)
SUBJECTS: LCSH: Plato. Symposium.
CLASSIFICATION: LCC B385 .P53 2017 | DDC 184–dc23 LC record available at https://lccn.loc.gov/2016047802

ISBN 978-1-107-11005-2 Hardback
ISBN 978-1-107-52569-6 Paperback

Contents

Contributors

PIERRE DESTRÉE is Associate Research Professor in Philosophy at the University of Louvain (Louvain-la-Neuve, Belgium). He is the author of numerous articles in Greek philosophy (esp. on Plato and Aristotle). He has edited several volumes, including *Akrasia in Greek Philosophy* (with Ch. Bobonich; 2007), *Plato and the Poets* (with F.-G. Herrmann; 2011), *Plato and Myth* (with C. Collobert and F. Gonzalez; 2012), *The Cambridge Companion to Aristotle's Politics* (with M. Deslauriers; 2013), and *The Blackwell Companion to Ancient Aesthetics* (with P. Murray; 2015).

RADCLIFFE G. EDMONDS III is Paul Shorey Professor of Greek at Bryn Mawr College. He is the author of *Myths of the Underworld Journey: Plato, Aristophanes, and the "Orphic" Gold Tablets* (2004) and *Redefining Ancient Orphism: A Study in Greek Religion* (2013). He has edited *The Orphic Gold Tablets and Greek Religion: Further Along the Path* (2011).

ZINA GIANNOPOULOU is Associate Professor of Classics at the University of California, Irvine. She is the author of *Plato's* Theaetetus *as a Second Apology* (2013) and the editor of *Philosophers on Film: Mulholland Drive* (2013). She is the author of numerous articles on Plato, Homer, and the reception of philosophy, epic, and tragedy in the literature and film of the twentieth and the twenty-first century.

FRANCISCO J. GONZALEZ is Professor of Philosophy at the University of Ottawa. He is the author of *Dialectic and Dialogue: Plato's Practice of Philosophical Inquiry* (1998) and *A Question of Dialogue: Plato and Heidegger* (2009). He has edited *The Third Way: New Directions in Platonic Studies* (1995) and *Plato and Myth* (with C. Collobert and P. Destrée; 2012).

RICHARD KRAUT is Charles and Emma Morrison Professor in the Humanities at Northwestern University. He is the author of *What is Good and Why: The Ethics of Well-Being* (2007) and *Against Absolute Goodness* (2011). His historical studies include *Socrates and the State* (1984), *Aristotle on the Human Good* (1989), *Aristotle Politics Books VII and VIII* (1997), *Aristotle: Political Philosophy* (2002), and *How to Read Plato* (2008). He is the editor of *The Cambridge Companion to Plato* (1992), *Plato's Republic: Critical Essays* (1997), and *The Blackwell Guide to Aristotle's Nicomachean Ethics* (2006).

ANDREA NIGHTINGALE is Professor of Classics at Stanford University. She is the author of *Genres in Dialogue: Plato and the Construct of Philosophy* (1995), *Spectacles of Truth in Classical Greek Philosophy: Theoria in its Cultural Context* (2004), and *Once out of Nature: Augustine on Time and the Body* (2011). She has edited *Ancient Models of Mind: Studies in Human and Divine Rationality* (with D. Sedley; 2010).

SUZANNE OBDRZALEK is Associate Professor in Philosophy at Claremont McKenna College. She is the author of several articles on Plato and the Stoics.

ANTHONY W. PRICE is Professor of Philosophy at Birkbeck, University of London. His books include *Love and Friendship in Plato and Aristotle* (1989, reprinted with an Afterword 1997), *Mental Conflict* (1995), *Contextuality in Practical Reason* (2008), and *Virtue and Reason in Plato and Aristotle* (2011).

JEREMY REID is a graduate teaching assistant in Philosophy at the University of Arizona, Tucson.

DAVID SEDLEY is Emeritus Laurence Professor of Ancient Philosophy at the University of Cambridge. His books include *The Hellenistic Philosophers* (with A.A. Long; 1987), *Lucretius and the Transformation of Greek Wisdom* (1998), *Plato's Cratylus* (2003), *The Midwife of Platonism: Text and Subtext in Plato's Theaetetus* (2004), and *Creationism and its Critics in Antiquity* (from his 2004 Sather Lectures at the University of California, Berkeley; 2007).

F.C.C. SHEFFIELD is Director of Studies in Philosophy at Christ's College, University of Cambridge. She is the author of *Plato's Symposium: The Ethics of Desire* (2006). She has edited *Plato's Symposium: Issues in Interpretation and Reception* (with J. Lesher and D. Nails; 2006), and *The Routledge Companion to Ancient Philosophy* (with J. Warren; 2013). She has also edited a translation of Plato's *Symposium*, with introduction and critical notes for the series *Cambridge Texts in the History of Philosophy* (2008).

CHRISTOPHER SHIELDS is Shuster Professor of Philosophy at the University of Notre Dame. He is the author of *Order in Multiplicity: Homonymy in the Philosophy of Aristotle* (1999), *Classical Philosophy: A Contemporary Introduction* (2003), *The Philosophy of Thomas Aquinas* (with R. Pasnau; 2003), and *Aristotle* (2007). He has edited *The Blackwell Guide to Ancient Philosophy* (2002) and *The Oxford Handbook of Aristotle* (2012).

FRANCO V. TRIVIGNO is Professor of Philosophy at the University of Oslo. He is the author of numerous articles on Plato and on Virtue Ethics.

Introduction

Pierre Destrée and Zina Giannopoulou

The *Symposium* is one of Plato's most admired and widely read dialogues. At once a philosophical drama that enacts abstract ideas in a lighthearted and often humorous way, and a literary masterpiece, it has exerted an influence that extends well beyond the confines of philosophy. At a banquet in honor of the young tragic poet Agathon who has just won his first prize for a tragedy, six speakers – Phaedrus, Pausanias, Eryximachus, Aristophanes, Agathon and Socrates – propose competing accounts of *erōs*, and a drunken Alcibiades offers a dazzling encomium of Socrates as impersonating *erōs*. The speeches cover all aspects of desire, from the physical to the metaphysical, from pederasty to love of Beauty, so that the *Symposium* is the most comprehensive treatment of *erōs* in the Platonic corpus. And since *erōs* may, and probably should, also be understood as a metaphor of philosophical research, the *Symposium* is at the very core of Plato's reflection on philosophical method. Moreover, since Beauty can, and perhaps should, be taken as a metaphor for the human good, i.e. happiness, the *Symposium* must also be read within Plato's eudaimonistic perspective. The *Symposium* is thus at the center of Plato's work. Yet as the continuous flow of literature shows, this is one of the most difficult Platonic dialogues.

The difficulties are of various kinds. Perhaps the most obvious and thorniest is the importance of each speech and the relation(s) among them. The structure of the dialogue seems relatively uncontroversial and yet it generates puzzles. The introductory material with its intricate narrative structure and parade of narrators may seem a mere anteroom to the inner chambers, but it is unclear how it connects with them. The first four speeches are meant to serve as a kind of prelude to Diotima's speech, which is followed by Alcibiades' speech, itself a kind of follow-up to Diotima's. It thus seems that Diotima's account constitutes the core of the dialogue against which all the other speeches of the *Symposium* must be evaluated. But how exactly? What sort of prelude are the first four speeches supposed to be? Are they offering radically mistaken views on *erōs*? Or are they rather first answers – or perhaps *endoxa*, as Aristotle might have called them – that need to be refined or properly rechanneled? More specifically, what role is each of the first speeches supposed to play in the broader structure of the dialogue? And how are the speeches linked to one another? In particular, the first two (Phaedrus' and Pausanias') sound rather serious, while the following two (Eryximachus' and Aristophanes') are meant to be funny, at least up to a point. But up to what point? Does Eryximachus defend a proper thesis about *erōs* or is his rather pompous speech meant to be a sheer parody? If it is a parody, what is its object? What of Aristophanes' speech, one of the most artfully composed speeches of the dialogue with its marvelous tale on the origin of sexual *erōs*? Is it just a piece of comic and philosophically empty entertainment or is it meant to convey a more sophisticated message – perhaps a sort of "warning" before we get Diotima's message (where Aristophanes' speech is explicitly referred to)? And how about Alcibiades' speech, which is strikingly different in tone from the rest of the speeches – it is, among other things, a jealousy scene that combines a eulogy with harsh criticisms of Socrates? What is it supposed to add to Diotima's speech? From a literary perspective, it may be seen as a satyric drama (as Socrates calls it), which follows Diotima's account, an arguably "tragic" speech due to its elevated tone. Indeed, some parts of Alcibiades' speech have been seen as parodying Diotima's presentation – for example, the so-called seduction scene, which unmistakably parodies the description of the ascent. But is the speech simply parodic? Or is it rather meant to serve as a confirmation of points developed by Diotima, as a profound modification of them, or even as a deep rejection of them?

If we now turn to Socrates' speech, we see that its first part develops a typically Socratic elenchos of what Agathon has just said in his eulogy of *erōs* that paves the way to the rather different presentation of *erōs* by Diotima. Agathon's speech has usually been neglected, if not completely dismissed, as if he were solely the host of this philosophical gathering. But if so, why does Plato make Socrates refute him first, the Socrates who confesses to have held the very opinions Agathon has just passionately defended? Finally, Diotima's speech, the Platonic core of the dialogue, remains deeply puzzling. What does the philosophical conception of *erōs* exactly amount to? What does this repeated expression "begetting in beauty" mean? Or what sort of immortality does Diotima have in mind when she has Socrates admit that *erōs* ultimately amounts to the desire for immortality? How are we to take the conclusion of her description of the highest mysteries of *erōs* according to which contemplation of Beauty is the very moment that makes life "worth living for a human being" (211d)?

All the essays collected in this volume are original studies of the *Symposium*, which shed new light on the dialogue's artistic and philosophical richness. Almost all of them in various ways relate their particular topic of inquiry to Diotima's account of *erōs*. This approach stresses the dialogue's unity by showing that the introduction and the speeches prior to Diotima's are not independent accounts of desire but anticipate Diotima's speech – its themes, images, and metaphysical concerns. Another feature of this volume is the engagement of many of its essays with the apparent tension between, on the one hand, mortality and human fallibility, and, on the other, divinization or the process of becoming as much like god as possible by gazing at Beauty. Sometimes this engagement leads to intertextual readings between the *Symposium* and other dialogues, while at other times it invites reflection on the local meaning and possible resolution of this tension, as well as its intellectual and ethical implications for human life. Yet another feature of this volume is that some of its essays give different answers to similar questions and thereby point up the irresoluble complexity of the dialogue. For example, does Aristophanes' speech offer a pessimistic account of *erōs* as an irrational urge incapable of being satisfied or an optimistic one by alluding to our original spherical nature and thus to our godlikeness? Does Diotima defend the ideal of a contemplative life or that of a perfect ethical-*cum*-political life? Does Plato hold that human *eudaimonia* is the ultimate standard for a good life or that such a standard must be of a higher level?

In Chapter 1, "Narrative Temporalities and Models of Desire," Zina Giannopoulou looks at the preface in light of Diotima's speech. She divides the passage into two parts, the frame (172a–174a) and the prologue (174a–175c), and examines primarily their use of time and its philosophical implications. Giannopoulou argues that frame and prologue use time antithetically, and that this use of time prefigures philosophical ideas of Diotima's account of *erōs*. The frame's regressive temporality subtends a possessive model of *erōs* that receives emphasis in the first part of Diotima's speech (204d–206a) and treats the object of desire as something to be had. By contrast, the prologue's progressive temporality supports a procreative model of desire that prevails in the second part of Diotima's speech (206b–212a) and is especially potent in the notion of "begetting in beauty" (206b).

Jeremy Reid's intertextual reading in Chapter 2, "Unfamiliar Voices: Harmonizing the Non-Socratic Speeches and Plato's Psychology," highlights parallels between the speeches prior to Diotima's and the goals of the early education in the *Republic*. Reid argues that in both dialogues, Plato is concerned with educating people through (1) activating and cultivating spirited motivations; (2) becoming lawful and taking virtue as a goal; (3) harmonizing the opposing forces in their soul; and (4) minimizing the appetites and making them orderly – features that are prominently defended in, respectively, Phaedrus', Pausanias', Eryximachus', and Aristophanes' speeches. In the *Republic* this moral education is necessary for intellectual ascent, and in the *Symposium* training our character adequately is necessary for climbing the ladder of love. The importance of this moral education is dramatized at the end of the *Symposium* through Agathon's amicable refutation by Socrates on the one hand, and the drunken entrance of Alcibiades on the other.

The next four chapters focus on the three main speeches that serve as prelude to Diotima's. In Chapter 3, "A Doctor's Folly: Diagnosing the Speech of Eryximachus," Franco Trivigno sets out to (1) formulate the different senses in which the speech may be considered serious; (2) examine which senses of serious are compatible with comedy; (3) establish criteria for what would count as comic; and (4) articulate a philosophical justification for the use of comedy. Trivigno argues that Eryximachus' speech plays two distinct roles in the dialogue: it is intended by Plato both to advance the level of discourse on *erōs* beyond what was presented by the previous two speakers and to expose Eryximachus as a pretender to philosophical wisdom. The speech may also be connected to Diotima's account: insofar as it instantiates a higher level on the ladder of love, it presents a serious position that is "on the way" toward appropriately philosophical *erōs*; insofar as it offers a physicalist view of the universe, it presents a rival to Diotima's philosophical vision.

In Chapter 4, "Aristophanic Tragedy," Suzanne Obdrzalek counters two common readings of Aristophanes' speech: instead of seeing it as a comic fable of little philosophical merit, she contends that it advances a view of *erōs* as a state of lack and a corresponding desire for completion, which is the starting point for Diotima's subsequent analysis; and instead of regarding it as an appealing and even romantic treatment of love, she argues that it contains a profoundly pessimistic account of *erōs*: far from being an appreciative response to the individuality of the beloved, Aristophanic *erōs* is an irrational urge incapable of satisfaction. This irrationality precludes Aristophanes' lovers from achieving the partial satisfaction of erotic desire that is open to their Socratic counterparts through their relationship to the Forms.

By contrast, in Chapter 5, "Divinization," David Sedley reads Aristophanes' celebrated tale of human origins as a comic debasement of Plato's own account of human origins in the *Timaeus*. This connection does not require dating the *Timaeus* before the *Symposium*. Rather, it requires that we recognize that the *Timaeus* includes a cosmologically inflected synopsis of Plato's philosophical system, all or much of whose content will have been the shared property of the Academy even before it found its way into the dialogues. Sedley locates further Timaean themes in the *Symposium*. In particular, since Plato invites us to contrast Diotima's lesson in erotics favorably with that of Aristophanes, we can read her culminating description of human immortalization in light of the *Timaeus*' account of human immortalization. The upshot of this analysis is that if the Timaean account is fundamentally intellectualist, it provides further backing for an already plausible reading of Diotima's speech in similarly intellectualist terms.

In Chapter 6, "Why Agathon's Beauty Matters," Francisco Gonzalez rehabilitates philosophically Agathon's speech by claiming that it introduces various points to which Socrates' own speech will prove indebted, notably the attempt to define the nature of *erōs*. Yet Socrates' critique of Agathon targets what the latter admits to be the purely playful parts of his speech and assumes an opposition between beauty and goodness in the context of *erōs* that Socrates' speech will bring into question. The reason is that the beauty promoted by the poet is not so easy to separate from the goodness pursued by the philosopher. The critique must therefore be qualified by Socrates' wish at the end to praise Agathon. Though this wish is frustrated, Agathon is the last one to stay awake in discussion with Socrates. The kinship between Socrates and Agathon thus proves much closer than it is usually taken to be.

Foregrounding Diotima's speech, in Chapter 7, "*Erōs* and the Pursuit of Form," Frisbee Sheffield examines the nature and structure of erotic desire in an attempt to explain why *erōs* is a uniquely appropriate term to characterize the philosopher's pursuit of Forms, appearing most strongly in dialogues where Forms feature prominently. She makes a fourfold argument. First, *erōs* involves an evaluative judgment of its object as *kalon* or *agathon* in some respect, and the object in question is desired under that description. Second, the mode of valuing involved in *erōs* is one in which one attends to the object in its ideal state. Third, objects pursued with *erōs* are desired as goods whose pursuit we consider, above all else, to make life worth living. Finally, the asymmetry, lack of reciprocity, and characteristically "reproductive" action of this desire make *erōs* a uniquely appropriate term with which to characterize action for the sake of an end perceived to be of supreme value and divine.

Since philosophical *erōs* is linked with eternal Forms and the divine, it is only natural, if for us rather obscure, that *erōs* must also be thought to be the desire of something eternal and divine – the desire of immortality. In Chapter 8, "The Mortal Soul and Immortal Happiness," Andrea Nightingale examines flux and change as characteristics of the soul. Diotima places great weight on the changing and fluctuating soul, using discourse that we associate with the body and the realm of becoming. These changing and finite humans desire ongoing goodness and immortality. However, mortals can achieve immortality only through genesis – by "giving birth" to new things that will carry on one's lineage after they die (207d). These offspring may be children, poems, laws, or (in the case of the philosophers) virtues, fine discourses, and ideas (210d). We have, then, a theory that features a fluctuating and finite soul that can nonetheless contemplate the everlasting Forms. Can a soul that dwells in the realm of becoming grasp and apprehend Being? If we reject this position, then we must ask (again) whether Diotima's account is truly Platonic. If not, then how do we interpret her speech?

In Chapter 9, "A Fetish for Fixity?", Christopher Shields adopts a similar starting point while targeting Plato's ideal for humans in the *Symposium* "to see Beauty absolute, pure, unmixed" (211e), which associates the mortal viewer with the divine and invites him to become immortal as much as is humanly possible. Against this ideal Shields lodges a familiar criticism: why should creatures who live and love in a world of change and impermanence embrace a conception of the culmination of human life that may seem to them not its apotheosis but rather its abnegation? He responds that the criticism is valid only within a partial and decontextualized understanding of Plato's motivation for characterizing the ascent toward Beauty. Once its roots in Plato's ideal of a process of *homoiōsis theōi* – a being made like unto god – are appreciated, the criticism gives way to the perfectly legitimate, albeit less stinging question: why should humans wish to become like god?

In Chapter 10, "Generating in Beauty for the Sake of Immortality: Personal Love and the Goals of the Lover," Anthony Price concludes the series of chapters devoted exclusively to Diotima by posing two questions about how best to interpret the contribution to the *Symposium* that Socrates pretends to derive from Diotima: (1) within the Lesser Mysteries, is the *erōs* that is being defined and characterized, with appeal to the notion of "generation in beauty," a generic *erōs* that is equivalent to Socratic desire in general or a specific *erōs* that is erotic in our sense? (2) Within the Greater Mysteries, is interpersonal *erōs* maintained or supplanted? Price claims that neither answer to (1) is unproblematic but argues that either can be reconciled with the text while both leave open the interesting questions. In answer to (2), he concedes that there are radical shifts of focus but concludes that it is most likely that interpersonal *erōs* has a continuing role in, eventually, making the lover worthy of "becoming dear to the gods and, if any man can, immortal himself also" (212a).

Diotima's Greater Mysteries with their emphasis on immortality are followed by the unexpected arrival of Alcibiades, a man notorious for his mortal desires and the profanation of the mysteries. In Chapter 11, "Alcibiades the Profane: Images of the Mysteries," Radcliffe Edmonds reads the final episode of the drunken Alcibiades from the point of view of mystery rituals. He argues that Plato deploys the imagery of mystery rituals and the idea of Alcibiades as a profaner of mysteries to provide at least a partial answer to the problem of the spectacular failure of Alcibiades. Far from being fundamentally unfit for philosophy, Alcibiades engaged in his weird relation with Socrates precisely because he was, as a brilliant youth full of potential, able to perceive the beauty in Socrates. But because he failed to understand that the beauty he perceived was not a possession of Socrates (or even something that could be possessed), he tried to take possession of that beauty for himself, just as he tried to appropriate the Mysteries of Eleusis for himself. Thus, Alcibiades's speech is first of all to be read as the description of a total misunderstanding of what philosophical mysteries should consist in.

Yet as Pierre Destrée argues in Chapter 12, "How Does Contemplation Make you Happy? An Ethical Reading of Diotima's Speech," Alcibiades' speech can also shed more positive light on Diotima's. Threading together the practice of virtue and godlikeness, Destrée focuses on Diotima's final words: the man who is contemplating the Beautiful "will give birth not to mere images of virtue but to true virtue, because it is not an image that he is grasping but the truth. And when he has given birth to and nurtured true virtue it is possible for him to be loved by the gods and to become, if any human can, immortal himself" (212a). What does this "virtue" amount to? And what might it mean to "become immortal" in this context? Destrée argues that contemplation of the Beautiful is the cause of the virtue – i.e. moral virtues – and that happiness essentially consists in the practice of such virtues. Alcibiades' speech confirms this point by emphasizing the moral education Socrates is supposed to give him and the moral virtues Socrates himself displays, both resulting from his contemplation of the Beautiful. Becoming "loved by the gods" is the expected consequence of such a virtuous life, while "becoming oneself immortal" refers to that virtuous life: thanks to the contemplation and the *mathēma* of the Beautiful, true virtue, which makes perfect *eudaimonia*, can be enjoyed forever.

Eudaimonia is one of the key words in Plato's philosophy and lies at the center of the *Symposium*. Yet Richard Kraut boldly asks in the last chapter, "Eudaimonism and Platonic *erōs*," whether Plato is a eudaimonist. That is, does he hold that one ought to have a single ultimate goal that informs one's life, namely one's own *eudaimonia* (and no one else's)? It is widely held that this is Plato's guiding assumption not only in the *Symposium* but also in many other dialogues. But eudaimonism, Kraut counters, conflicts with the deepest idea that guides Plato's ethical thought, i.e. that one should live one's life in response to something superior to oneself. Eudaimonism says that nothing should be of more importance to a human being than his or her own good, whereas Plato thinks that each of us is of little importance when compared with what is outside us – the polis, the cosmos, the gods, the Forms. The policy of always acting for the sake of one's happiness will never lead one astray – that is the grain of truth in eudaimonism. But that does not make one's happiness the most valuable object there is; it is not the ultimate standard of good practical reasoning.

CHAPTER I

Narrative Temporalities and Models of Desire

Zina Giannopoulou

That Plato's *Symposium* is at once a literary masterpiece and an extraordinarily rich piece of philosophy is a truism acknowledged by most studies of the dialogue.[1] The philosophical potential of its intricate composition, as well as its use of banter, setting and colorful parade of characters, has received much fruitful scrutiny.[2] In this chapter, I aim to revive and, hopefully, enrich this truism by looking closely at the dialogue's frame and prologue, terms I shall explain momentarily, from the viewpoint of their treatment of time. Along the way, I shall discuss the dialogue's narrative structure and use of character insofar as these topics impinge upon matters of temporality. The Platonic frame has been variously seen as a register of the temporal distance between the dramatic present and the past, a marker of the dialogue's fictionality, a sign of playfulness, and an indication of the gap between the perceptible realm and the realm of the Forms.[3] In his stimulating study of the frame of the *Symposium*, Halperin argues that the dialogue's framing "stag[es] the erotics of narrativity . . . [it] reveals narrative as both an expression and an object of desire—a means of gratifying the desire it incites and of renewing the desire it gratifies" (1992: 106). On this reading, the narrators of the frame are negative exempla, lovers of the claims made by others, most of all by Socrates, as opposed to lovers of the philosophical life. But since these narrators are also "sites of textual inscription," their narrative "manages to contain and transmit wisdom, to reproduce itself repeatedly and accurately" (1992: 111). The elaborate narrative structure of the *Symposium* thus illustrates the

[1] See, for example, Halperin 1992: 121: "the *Symposium* . . . remains beyond dispute the finest work of fiction, of prose literature, to survive from the Classical Period."

[2] See, especially, Osborne 1994 and Corrigan and Glazov-Corrigan 2004: 7–42.

[3] For the frame as an indicator of temporal distance see Bacon 1959: 417–8 and Clay 1992: 117, 124–5; as suggestive of the fictional nature of the account see Krentz 1983: 33; as an example of Platonic *paideia* see Krentz 1983: 43; and as an indication of the gap between the phenomena and the Forms see Johnson 1998. For a general study of the Platonic frame see Burnyeat 1998 and Morgan 2004.

"self-regenerating tradition of storytelling" and transmits wisdom by "manifest[ing] and dramatiz[ing] the workings of *erōs*" (1992: 102).

This chapter shares Halperin's interest in narrative but focuses on time as a principle of narrative structure in the frame and the prologue. My objective is twofold, contextual and broad. Contextually, I argue that time is used antithetically in these two parts, and broadly I show that this antithetical use of time prefigures philosophical ideas of Diotima's account of *erōs*.[4] Before I elaborate on my argument, I should explain my use of the terms "frame" and "prologue." Collectively, these two terms refer to the exchanges from the first word of the dialogue to the moment when Socrates arrives alone at Agathon's banquet. Specifically, by "frame" I mean a set of two exchanges: (1) the exchange in the dramatic present between Apollodorus and an unnamed friend and member of an equally unnamed group of friends, some wealthy businessmen (cf. 173c6); and (2) the recollected exchange, nested within (1), between Apollodorus and Glaucon (172a1–174a2).[5] By "prologue" I mean the opening scene of the dialogue proper, the reported conversation between Aristodemus and Socrates on their way to Agathon's party, ending with Socrates' arrival "in the middle of the dinner" (174a3–175c6).[6]

The particulars of these two parts are well known, and so a summary will suffice. In the frame, Apollodorus, a recent convert of Socrates, has just been asked, apparently, to tell the story of Agathon's victory party, which he relayed to another acquaintance, Glaucon, two days before. In his report of this earlier exchange, Apollodorus says that Glaucon had obtained the story of Agathon's party from a fellow who had heard it from Phoenix, but this fellow "hadn't anything clear to say on the subject" (172b4–5). So garbled was this man's report that Glaucon was under the impression that Apollodorus had been present at the symposium. Apollodorus, however, did not attend the party, which took place many years before the conversation he is currently engaged in, but can recapitulate the narrative handed down to him by Aristodemus, a devoted follower of Socrates who did attend. It is this account that Apollodorus narrated to Glaucon the other day and is going to narrate once again to his

[4] For "the literary interweaving—or method of 'responsions,'" whereby earlier passages are related to later ones see Bury 1973: xx. Cf. Rowe 1999: 243 and Blondell 2006.

[5] Here and throughout, I use the terms "recollection" and "recollected" interchangeably with "memorization" and "memorized," respectively. Often "recollection" serves as shorthand for "recollected account."

[6] On the dialogue's prologue and the overall frame see Bury 1932: xv–xxii, Rowe 1998: 3–5, and Halperin 1992.

unnamed friends in the dramatic present. The account begins with a prologue, the exchange between Aristodemus and Socrates. There we learn that Socrates has made himself beautiful in order to attend Agathon's party and invites Aristodemus to join him. On the way, he gets lost in thought and falls behind, which causes Aristodemus to arrive alone at the party. When he arrives, he is warmly invited in, and the assembled guests start eating, while Socrates makes his entrance a little later and takes his place on Agathon's couch.

In the following two parts of this chapter, I argue that in the frame and the prologue Plato uses time antithetically, and that this use of time validates two different models of desire. In Part 1, I contend that the frame, both in the unfolding of its narrative and in the arrangement of its material, is regressive. The brief reference to the present in the first line yields to the reproduction of a conversation of two days before, and the subsequent return to the present is followed by the report of speeches made in the distant past, itself a replica of the conversation of two days before. Although the frame unfolds forward – the pages follow one another, and with each line we get closer to the desired account – it takes us backward, one layer at a time. The fact that, as we shall see, the exchange in the dramatic present is structurally and thematically similar to the conversation of two days before, as well as the use of character in the frame (especially Apollodorus), reinforces this part's regressive temporality. In short, in the frame, the present leads to the past and mirrors the past. This narrative use of time subtends a possessive or acquisitive model of *erōs* that treats the object of desire as something to be had.

In Part 2, I turn to the prologue and show that it is progressive with respect both to its narrative arc and the composition of its episodes: the present leads to the future by breaking with the past and creating something new out of material supplied by the past. Apollodorus and his friend[7] give way to Socrates and Aristodemus, and the dynamic of this interaction poses a new set of intellectual and ethical considerations. The progressive use of time in the prologue supports the procreative model of desire echoed in Diotima's idea of "begetting in beauty" (206b7–8). The possessive and the procreative models of *erōs* reflect the notions of sexual appetite and desire, respectively, whereby appetite aims at "achieving terminal gratification, usually by means of possessing some object in the world," while desire "is aroused by a perception of value in things and so neither

[7] I use the singular "friend" to refer to the person with whom Apollodorus exchanges words in the frame.

terminates in nor is fully consummated by the possession of any concrete entity" (Halperin 1985: 170). They also receive emphasis in two different parts of Diotima's speech (204d1–206a12 and 206b1–208b6) in the order in which they appear in the frame and the prologue. If this order is not only sequential but also normative (the procreative model both succeeds and is superior to the possessive), Diotima's "ladder of love" becomes, from a narrative standpoint, a set of two steps: the lower step or the possessive model of desire, and the higher step or the procreative model of desire. This interpretation reflects James Richardson's aphorism: "Desire's most seductive promise is not pleasure but change, not that you might possess your object but that you might become the one who belongs with it" (2001: 4).

1. The Frame

As the answer to an unstated question, the first line of the frame places the reader *in medias res* of an ongoing conversation: "I believe I'm not unrehearsed (*dokō moi . . . ouk ameletētos einai*) in relation to what you people are asking about" (172a1–2).[8] An answer presupposes a question, and so the present gestures to the past. The frame thus begins in the present ("I believe I'm not unrehearsed") and immediately switches to the past first by alluding to moments earlier ("what you people are asking about") and then by recording a recollection of an even earlier exchange that contains both the phantom question and its answer. As a narrative construct, Apollodorus' recollection is built out of the following five blocks:

(1) *The request* ("*the what,*" *172a2–b3*): a man, whose name is at first withheld and later revealed to be Glaucon, has been looking for Apollodorus in order to hear the speeches on *erōs* made by Agathon's guests ("I wanted to ask you what they said about love" [172b2–3]). (1) registers a lack couched as a question – the same as the unstated question implied in the first line of the frame – that needs an answer. In its need of an answer it has a progressive thrust, which, as we shall see in the next block, is short-lived.
(2) *The author* ("*the who,*" *172b3–c6*): the reporter of the account is Apollodorus, a better source of information than Glaucon's earlier informant due to his recent "companionship" (*synousia*, 172b7,

[8] All translations come from Rowe 1998 with occasional modifications. I return to the term *meletē* at the end of this section.

c1; cf. c5) with Socrates ("it's not yet three years that I've been spending time with Socrates and have made it my business each day to know everything he is saying and doing" [172c5–6]). (2) is regressive insofar as it establishes an earlier, anonymous line of transmission in order to stress the superiority of Apollodorus' version of the account.

(3) *Self- and other-reproach* ("*the why*," *173a1–3*): in his pre-Socratic days Apollodorus was as wretched as Glaucon is at this very moment. (3) looks to the past from the vantage of the present: a currently enlightened Apollodorus reproaches his former unphilosophical life and his interlocutors for leading it: "I simply rushed around this way and that, thinking I was achieving something; in fact, I was a more miserable figure than anyone you might care to mention—just like you now: I thought anything was a greater priority than doing philosophy"). Self- and other-awareness – specifically, a negative appraisal of self and others – results from Socratic *synousia* and is a necessary condition for moral improvement.

(4) *The author* ("*the who again*," *173a3–b6*): Aristodemus, an eyewitness to the banquet, is the source of Apollodorus' account. He was a "small man who always went barefoot" (173b2) and a lover of Socrates. Apollodorus checked some of the details with Socrates, the Ur-author, who confirmed Aristodemus' version of the account. In its concern with authorship, both proximate and ultimate (Aristodemus and Socrates), and in its emphasis on the epistemic reliability of the official account, (4) echoes (2) and reinforces its regressive slant.

(5) *The request* ("*the what again*," *173b6–8*): Apollodorus' recollection ends as it began with (5) reiterating Glaucon's request in (1): "'Then why not tell me?' he said" (173b6–7). The recollection thus folds upon itself: (5) repeats (1), and (4) mirrors (2).

At the end of his recollection, Apollodorus moves to the present with an allusion to the first line of the frame: "so we went on together as he proposed and had our talk about the subject, with the result that—as I said at the beginning (*hoper archomenos eipon*)—I'm not unrehearsed (*ouk ameletētōs echō*)" (173b9–c1). Ring-composition thus characterizes not only Apollodorus' recollection but also the text around it, namely, the first line of the frame and the transition from the recollection to the dramatic present. This layering of two narrative levels of ring-composition gives the frame a decidedly regressive spin. One and a half pages into the dialogue, we have made no narrative progress since we still lack the speeches alluded to in the first line of the frame. Instead, we have digressed into Apollodorus' recollection, which is meant to explain his readiness to give the account requested in the first line. This digression is at the same time a regression both temporally, as a recast of the events of two days before, and formally/thematically, as the aforementioned structure of the recollection shows. Curiously, and importantly for my argument, the conversation in the dramatic present is also built out of the same five blocks as the recollection:

(1′) *The request* ("*the what,*" *173c1–2*): the speeches are to be given once again, a repetition marked by the use of the conjunction *kai* ("too"): "So if I'm to tell you people, too, well, then, that's what I must do."

(2′) *The author* ("*the who,*" *173c1–2*): in the conditional that constitutes (1′) only the protasis, "So if I'm to tell you people, too," is the actual first building block because it implies the request that Apollodorus tell the story once again to those present. The apodosis ("that's what I must do"), however, calls attention to the speaker or reporter, Apollodorus, who is well positioned to meet the request, given his prior rehearsal of the speeches.[9]

(3′) *Self- and other-reproach* ("*the why,*" *173c2–d3*): Apollodorus knows that his interlocutors are bad and shares their low opinion of him. Yet he delights in philosophical conversations, even if he is only a listener and regardless of the benefit he reaps from them: "In fact, quite apart from thinking I benefit from [telling you the speech], I myself get an amazing amount of pleasure from any talking I do, or hear others doing, about philosophy; other sorts of talking, especially your rich businessmen's talk, bores me, and I pity you who are my friends because you think you're achieving something when you're achieving nothing. Maybe you in your turn suppose I'm in a wretched state, and I think what you think is true; however, I don't just think you are, *I know* you are" (173c2–d3).

(4′) *The author* ("*the who again,*" *173d4–e4*): the friend quips that Apollodorus "always speaks ill" (173d5; cf. d6, d9) of himself and others, except Socrates, and wonders whether he is really a suitable reporter or is in fact mad. Apollodorus, tongue-in-cheek, admits that he is "a maniac and off his head" (*mainomai kai parapaiō*), whereupon the friend agrees to set aside this worry, thus settling on Apollodorus as an appropriate source of information.

[9] The speaker is foregrounded in *egōge* (173c2).

(5′) *The request* (*"the what again," 173e4–6*): having accepted that Apollodorus is fit for the task, the friend repeats his request: "What about doing just what I was asking you to do, and telling us what they said?" (173e5–6). As in the recollection, so here (5′) repeats (1′), and (4′) mirrors (2′).

Apollodorus undertakes to meet the request by telling the whole thing "from the beginning in the way that man [sc. Aristodemus] told it to [him]" (174a1–2). From now on, his audience will be given the speeches as Glaucon was given them two days previously and as Aristodemus narrated them to Apollodorus at some earlier time. The end of the frame thus harks back to the past and registers that what is to follow has already taken place both as an event (speeches at Agathon's party) and as reports of that event.

The architectural symmetry of the frame – the formal and thematic parallels between its two exchanges – suspends the temporal flow of the narrative and turns the present into an elaborate déjà-vu. The present recycles the past, and the future, the much-anticipated report of the speeches, has already occurred. Insofar as the future is experienced as a recast of the past, the narrative is trapped in a kind of static mobility: things proceed backward while remaining the same. Both the recollected exchange and the conversation in the dramatic present belong to the same overarching narrative, the frame, which starts with the readiness to tell the speeches (first line) and ends with their telling (the prologue and the speeches). One might expect the movement between these two points to be straight and forward, but it is backward in three ways: (1) from the readiness to tell the speeches to the explanation of the readiness to tell them (the report of the speeches to Glaucon two days prior); (2) from the explanation of the readiness to tell them to the reprise of the readiness to tell them; and (3) from the reprise of the readiness to tell them to the actual report, which was first given by Aristodemus at some time in the past, then repeated in part by Socrates, and finally repeated in full by Apollodorus. The present yields to the past, then re-emerges as a recast of that past, and finally recedes into a prior past never to reappear (as is well known, the term "frame" is a heuristic misnomer since Apollodorus and his friends do not resume their exchange at the end of the dialogue). The pervasive mood is nostalgia for the past couched as the desire to commemorate it by repeating it over and over again in a stable pattern of narrative transmission. The feeling of nostalgia is reinforced by the frame's lack of formal closure, which leaves things, literally, in the past, with Agathon's guests and Agathon himself having fallen asleep, and Socrates leaving the party and proceeding to have a regular day before going home in the evening to rest. Since Apollodorus' tale is a report, as shown by his frequent use of *inquit* formulas ("he said" [*phanai*] or "he said that he said" [*ephē phanai*]) and quotation marks, it registers at least a duality of viewpoints and thus stresses the distance between narrator(s) and characters, or between the present and the past. At the same time, however, it strives to elide that distance by purporting to be a most reliable source of information, a verbal image or reproduction of a past event.[10]

The use of character in the frame reinforces its regressive temporality. The characters are either the same as those of two days earlier (Apollodorus) or bear some resemblance to them. The anonymous friend, for example, recalls Glaucon to whom Apollodorus at first refers generically as "someone I know" (*tōn oun gnōrimōn tis*, 172a3) – in contrast to the emphatic use of Apollodorus' name in the next line, "Hey, you, the man from Phalerum! I mean you, Apollodorus" (172a4–5) – and whom he identifies by name halfway through (172c3).[11] Also, the catalyst for the exchanges is the same: a man desires to listen to speeches and seeks out the person who can meet his desire. The labor is divided between the haves and the have-nots, a division illustrated by making the latter follow the former: one man goes ahead, the other follows and, in a spatial analogue of the retrospective temporality of the frame, the follower makes the leader stop and look back so as to converse with him. Eventually, two of them proceed together, the leader giving the follower the requested speech. This narrative situation dramatizes the erotic urging by showing how a have-not strives to have.

It might be tempting to see Apollodorus as an incarnation of *Erōs*, a being portrayed as a leader in the dialogue. In Aristophanes' speech, *Erōs* is the *hēgemōn* and *stratēgos* (193b1), and in Agathon's he is a leader and teacher (197a), the *hēgemōn* we should all follow (197d–e). For Phaedrus, *Erōs* instills a sense of shame that should lead us (178c; cf. 210a6–7, c7, e3, 211c1).[12] This reading gains support from Apollodorus' role as narrator, the intermediary between, on the one hand, Socrates and the priestess Diotima who possess wisdom and, on the other, the anonymous friend and Glaucon who lack wisdom and wish to acquire it. It also recalls *Erōs*' intermediate status between the immortal and the mortal realms (202e3–203a1). An alternative reading of Apollodorus is possible; however,

[10] On this feature see Halperin 1992: 106.

[11] Note also the placelessness of the exchanges in the frame: Apollodorus' encounters are presented as journeys from out of town into town, always in-between and in motion.

[12] See Blondell 2006: 151 n. 16.

one that takes into account the narrative elements of the frame (temporality, structure, and use of character) and views him as a parodic incarnation of Poros who can, at best, beget *erōs* of the lowest kind (of the first rung in Diotima's *scala amoris*) in his encounters with the Peniae of the frame, the anonymous friend and Glaucon. So read the frame of the *Symposium* stages two episodes of erotic failure by Platonic standards and enacts some of the conditions that make intellectual *synousia* philosophically barren and ineffectual.

Apollodorus' "resource" is a memorized account, whereas his unnamed acquaintance and Glaucon lack this *poros* and thus represent Penia. In Socrates' account of *Erōs*' heritage, Penia initiates the interaction with the drunken and slumbering Poros, probably on account of her awareness of her lack and the desire to fill it – after all, "one does not desire what one does not think one needs" (204a6–7). Penia is a mortal barred from dining with the gods, whereas Poros, who is implicitly described as a god (203b2–3), joins the feast of the gods and lies in Zeus' garden (203b5–7). In the frame, Apollodorus' resourceless interlocutors instigate the exchanges with their resourceful friend and obtain the speeches by repeatedly asking for them. This recalls Penia's scheming to have a child by Poros (203b7). Finally, although Apollodorus checks parts of his account with the almost divine Socrates, the unnamed friend and Glaucon have had only approximations to the truth, second- and third-hand reports. Poros and Penia thus seem to map nicely onto Apollodorus and his unnamed friend/Glaucon, respectively, but the offspring of these *synousiai* are importantly dissimilar. As the child of Poros and Penia *Erōs* oscillates between plenty and lack, the resourceful and the needy, but the psychic offspring of Apollodorus and his interlocutors is deemed accurate and fixed, the best available version of the speeches. Recall that obtaining this version is Apollodorus' loftiest ambition: his elaborate "process of authentication" (Rowe 1998: 3) and "documentary anxiety" (Halperin 1992: 108) produce an account that is more reliable than the garbled report of the intermediary between Phoenix and Glaucon. After all, Apollodorus is importuned *because* of his meticulous gathering of data whereby he fixes the previously unstable report into a new account that purports to be as faithful a verbal image of the original event as possible.[13] Although the narrative transmission of the speeches *over time* (diachronic perspective)

[13] There are hints of inaccuracy: neither Aristodemus nor Apollodorus can recall the speeches verbatim (178a), Aristodemus omits some speeches altogether (180c) and, as he falls asleep at the end, he misses most of the final arguments (223c–d).

"enacts the very processes of loss and renewal, of emptying and filling . . . processes [that are] familiar and characteristic effects of *erōs*" (Halperin 1992: 102), Apollodorus' narrative *in time* (synchronic perspective), i.e. the account he has already delivered and is going to redeliver, poses as the best reproduction of speeches given elsewhere – at Agathon's house – and at another time – many years previously.

Apollodorus' synchronic attitude to his narrative shows that there is and can be no *erōs* between him and his interlocutors since, as Diotima says, *erōs* achieves its ends by means of procreation, the continual production of something new or young to replace what is old and dying (207d2–3, 208b1–2). In procreation, the pregnant lover generates a physical or mental fetus in his *synousia* with a beautiful beloved, but Apollodorus' fetus in the dramatic present is the same as the one generated two days earlier and the one composed at an even earlier time; his procreation is recreation. For him process and product merge into each other: the process of memorizing the speeches and having given them has already yielded the product. Going over the product repeats the process and redelivers the product, so that, paradoxically, an already born fetus is born again. The thematic and structural similarities between the recollected exchange and the conversation in the dramatic present underscore the repetitive or mechanical aspect of Apollodorus' delivery. Apollodorus-*qua*-Poros has already begotten what each successive act of verbal generation requires him to beget.

His "creative sameness" can be usefully compared with the sameness attributed to him by the unnamed friend.[14] Recall that the latter says that Apollodorus is "always the same" because he always scolds himself and others except Socrates. His disparaging attitude recalls Socrates' critical stance toward himself and others but also differs from it. As Andrea Nightingale says, ". . . when [Apollodorus] reviles his companions, he fails to emulate the philosopher's ironic handling of others. [He], in short, opts for invective instead of irony" (1995: 118). His lack of irony may explain to some extent his relatively little ethical progress three years into the relationship with Socrates, and his unnamed friend, an ethically worse fellow who responds off-handedly and nonchalantly to Apollodorus' rebuke of his life, shows no interest in self-improvement.[15] The encounter

[14] Insofar as sameness is a divine attribute, Apollodorus' sameness may be taken to support the parodic association with the divine Poros.

[15] The unnamed friend meets Apollodorus' thrice-leveled critique with the words: "It's not worth quarrelling about these things now, Apollodorus" (173e4).

between two persons of whom one is confessedly wretched, and the other unobjectionably more wretched, cannot be erotic on Diotima's understanding of *erōs*. The function of *erōs* is to "give birth in beauty" (206b7–8; cf. 209c2–3), where beauty acts as midwife to childbirth (206d1), but the unnamed friend is neither physically beautiful (at least not explicitly since he is devoid of physical traits) nor psychically "beautiful and noble and naturally well-endowed" (209b6).[16] In his presence, Apollodorus can at best re-beget a mental fetus already begotten, not bring forth a new one. Contrast this "recycled fetus" with the speech generated in the encounter between Diotima and Socrates. If we construe Diotima as the plentiful Poros and Socrates as the lacking Penia, we can see why their spiritual *synousia* should have engendered a *logos* of unique beauty, an image of excellence: the impoverished Socrates is beautiful because he is possessed, supra-personally, by a philosophical *erōs* for truth and, interpersonally, by an *erōs* for the beauty of Diotima's soul. There is no evidence of this kind of *erōs* in Apollodorus' exchanges with his interlocutors in the frame.[17]

At this point, I should pick up an earlier thread and distinguish two stages in Apollodorus' career as reporter of Agathon's banquet: a productive stage (what I previously called a diachronic perspective), which has come to an end by the time of the exchanges in the frame and which looms large in building blocks (2) and (4) with their emphasis on the pre-Apollodorus line of transmission; and a rehearsal stage (what I previously called a synchronic perspective), which dominates the exchanges in the frame and which features prominently in building blocks (2′) and (4′) with their stress on Apollodorus-*qua*-reporter. In her account of *erōs*, Diotima mentions two requirements that a living being must meet in order to survive over time: there must be (1) another new thing which replaces the old (*heteron neon*, 207d6) and (2) which is qualitatively similar to the old thing (*hoion auto ēn*, 208b2). Only at the productive, pre-frame stage does Apollodorus meet both requirements as best as possible, given that he was absent from the banquet. His scrupulous attempts to record

[16] Apollodorus pays scant attention to his interlocutors' lives. His only complaint is that they, like himself in the past, rush around and are miserable in their un-philosophical lives (173a). For the connections between talking to a more or less unknown audience and oratory see Halperin 1992: 109–10.

[17] It is worth noting that at the end of the frame and right before the narration proper Apollodorus says that he will "try to tell" it "from the beginning, in the way Aristodemus told it to him" (173e7–174a2). The reference at the end of the frame to one of the authors of the speeches stresses both the oldness of the tale and Apollodorus' secondary role to its transmission.

the speeches, combined with the awareness that his report is incomplete (178a), suggest that his account is both "another new thing, which replaces the old" and a new thing that is "qualitatively similar to the old thing." By contrast, at the rehearsal stage of the frame, Apollodorus meets Diotima's requirements in an attenuated manner. His repetition of the speeches nods at Diotima's first requirement (it satisfies it in the strictly temporal sense that if a report is delivered both at an earlier and at a later time, the latter version is "a new thing that replaces the old") and radicalizes her second requirement (the later report is not just qualitatively similar to but exactly the same as the earlier one). The distinction between the procreative and the rehearsal stage is important given that only the former stage observes an important fact about human things, that "none of [them] is ever the same in any individual, but some are coming into existence, others passing away" (207e3–5).

Yet we need to be careful not to overestimate Apollodorus' *erōs* in the procreative stage because it seems to lack another ingredient of Diotima's erotic diet. According to the priestess, the object of *erōs* is the good (*kalon* or *agathon*) and is desired as such (201a8–10, b6–7, c4–5, 202d1–3, 206a11–12), but Apollodorus' relentless quest for an accurate account serves as a substitute for, or even sublimation of, his *erōs* of Socrates whose daily words and deeds he takes great care to record.[18] Upon scrutiny, Apollodorus' zeal has little, if anything, to do with an understanding of the good encapsulated by Socrates' words. Although he derives "extraordinary pleasure" from making[19] or hearing speeches about philosophy, a pleasure he feels "quite apart from thinking that he benefits from them" (173c3–4), there is no evidence that this "intellectual pleasure" stems from a deep appreciation of the quality of Socrates' account by which he has himself improved as a human being – quite the opposite, if his admission of his current *kakodaimonia* (173d2) is to be taken seriously.[20] His pleasure evinces an erotic hunger that, on the basis

[18] One might object that Apollodorus perceives the speeches he has been able to recall as "worth remembering" (178a4), a term that seems to bestow value on them. See Sheffield 2006: 107 n. 36. This is plausible but uncertain. It is just as plausible to say that the reasons for which he deemed the speeches "worth of remembrance" were, for example, their being rumored as such (*doxa*), the social and intellectual prominence of the speakers, the colorful touches of most of the speeches, the spectacular and memorable entry of one of the speakers (Alcibiades), none of which proves that Apollodorus perceives the speeches as something good.

[19] Note the ambiguity of the phrase "to make speeches" (*logous poieisthai*): is Apollodorus making speeches with his own resources, or is he making, i.e. putting together and delivering, the speeches of others? His attitude in the frame supports the latter view.

[20] Similarly, the unnamed friend, as well as Glaucon, fails to recognize – at least explicitly – that the desired speeches are something good. His fascination with them evinces a gossip-like curiosity about

of his life thus far, is likely to remain just that, a hunger, and, moreover, one that will not be sated by philosophical nourishment. We could, if we so wished, envision a happy scenario for Apollodorus, a philosophical life awaiting him in the future, but in that case we would also have to envision an Apollodorus fit for that life, a man who does not only listen to and record speeches but also inquires about and ponders what he hears.

Our Apollodorus emerges from the frame as the exact antithesis of that man: he is a lover of speeches-*qua*-bodies who desires a particular instantiation of Beauty, i.e. Socrates, and a particular instantiation of beautiful progeny, the *logoi* at Agathon's banquet.[21] The problem here is not only that his love for the particular makes it unlikely that he will appreciate Beauty in its abstract generality, but also that in his fixation on speeches that he has memorize as accurately as possible he has confused categorically distinct entities, the seemingly stable particular with the truly stable Form (211a1–b5).[22] From this point of view, Apollodorus is not unlike Alcibiades, a lover of Socrates' body with only a tenuous glimpse of the beauty of his soul, which, try as he might, he cannot really appreciate and unfailingly desire. The two men's erotic failure, placed at opposite ends of the *Symposium*, can be seen as a "frame" along thematic rather than formal criteria.

Apollodorus' *erōs* of a fixed, memorized account favors a possessive model of desire echoed in Diotima's account of *Erōs*. Osborne divides Diotima's account into two parts: in the first part (204d–206a), the priestess emphasizes the desire to possess, while in the second part (206b–212a) she stresses the notion of "begetting in the beautiful," thereby moving from *possessing* the beautiful to *gazing* on beauty and goodness, with the need to possess becoming a need to possess immortality in order to gaze forever on the beautiful itself (cf. 206e8–207a2). Osborne thinks that Diotima intends to drive a "wedge between the desire to possess and what constitutes true love," or between possession of good things and "a vision of unfailing beauty" (1994: 102). On this reading, Apollodorus' *erōs* of the speeches falls into the first part of Diotima's account,

speeches made when "Agathon and Socrates and Alcibiades got together" (172a7–8) rather than the desire to hear them *qua* good.

21 Cf. Nussbaum 1986: 168: "Socrates' pupils, inspired by personal love, tend not to follow his advice. Instead of ascending to an equal regard for all instances of value they, like Alcibiades, remain lovers of the particulars of personal history." Cf. Sheffield 2006: 204.

22 For the ironies generated by Plato's use of the written medium to celebrate oral transmission see Halperin 1992: 107.

where the lover desires to possess *the good things forever* and by possessing them to be happy (204e2–205a1). But again, when we attribute to Apollodorus the desire to possess the good forever, we need to be wary of how we use the notions of "the good" and immortality. In his case, the good is the preservation and accurate transmission of a memorized *logos* engendered by others, and immortality is the span of his very mortal life, unless he is lucky enough to find as conscientious commemorators and recorders of his report in others as he himself is of Socrates' account.[23]

How about immortality construed as possessing the speeches forever? Here it might be helpful to look at Apollodorus' use of *meletē* ("care," "study," or "practice"), a rhetorical term that means to "con over" a speech or part.[24] In the second part of Diotima's account, the term is used in relation to the preservation of knowledge (*epistēmē*, 208a2–6): *meletē* preserves knowledge by creating it anew and preventing it from dissipating through forgetfulness. Does Apollodorus' *meletē* preserve knowledge? It certainly preserves something–as Socrates' follower and lover of his *logoi*, Apollodorus staves off oblivion of the speeches by memorizing them and through *meletē* "puts back a fresh memory in place of what went away" (208a5–6; cf. 172a1, 173c2). But does it preserve *knowledge*? Halperin thinks that it does, claiming that "Apollodorus' series of nested narratives exemplifies ... the procreative labor of *meletē*: only by means of that ongoing oral tradition has the *knowledge* of what was said and done at Agathon's victory party been preserved ... and thus been saved from dissolution in the endless cycles of becoming" (1992: 102; emphasis added). In light of my discussion thus far, it is clear that Apollodorus' *meletē* does not preserve "knowledge" but other people's words, which can but need not engender knowledge in their recipient(s). Apollodorus himself, one of the recipients of Aristodemus'/Socrates' reports, can be said neither to know nor to understand a narrative that he has merely pieced together and to whose foreign origin he calls attention in the frame and in the narrative by means of *inquit* formulas. His *meletē* preserves words and conveys ideas generated by others so that we, readers of the *Symposium*, might come to know them by engaging in the rigorous intellectual work necessary for acquiring and preserving knowledge. The best example in the dialogue

[23] A seemingly obvious objection is that Plato fits this bill beautifully. However, Plato is the extradiegetic reporter/author, whereas Apollodorus is the proximate diegetic reporter/author. Pointedly, the other proximate diegetic reporter/author (Phoenix) failed to obtain a reliable reporter of his version of the account.

[24] Bury 1973: 1. *Meletē* is a common rhetorical term for memorization (cf. *Phdr.* 228b). For a discussion see Halperin 1992: 102.

of this kind of work is the relationship between Diotima and Socrates, which is cashed out as a relationship between a teacher and her student (204d2, 206b6), and to which, I believe, the exchanges in the frame serve as foils.

A final and not unrelated issue is that Apollodorus does not seem to entertain the possibility that he might have forgotten material between one rehearsal and the next. Having labored to put together the best account of the speeches, he treats his product as fixed, not as subject to change and decay, which govern the world of becoming. He thus behaves like a mortal Poros, assured of his "fullness" and unperturbed by self-doubt, despite the fact that he is a mortal utterly dependent on the fallible mechanism of memory. Even though he admits that "Aristodemus . . . didn't remember everything each person said" and concedes that he, Apollodorus, did not "remember everything [Aristodemus] told him; but what he remembered best and the people who seemed to say something worth remembering" (178a1–4), he never as much as suspect that his own memory may have lapsed. In his case, *meletē* is reduced to the care or labor of "going-over" a fixed text, like rewinding a DVD, an act that lacks the energetic searching and investigative spirit of the attempt to preserve something valuable and fragile that can and often does get lost.

2. The Prologue

Whereas the frame is retrospective, the prologue stresses novelty by breaking with the past and/or being future-directed. This temporal shift is accompanied by a change in the narrative voice: Apollodorus cedes his place to Aristodemus, the original narrator of the tale, but from time to time he calls attention to his own narrative mediation by means of indirect discourse (e.g. 178a2, 185c5, 198a1, 199c2, 223b8, 223d1). Given that Apollodorus succeeds Aristodemus in the transmission of the speeches, his use of indirect discourse signals the future of the past – the retellings (by Apollodorus) of the telling (by Aristodemus) of the story. Since this future also coincides, from the vantage of the current narration, with the past of two days previously and with the dramatic present, it registers a move away from the Ur-past of the speeches toward their current retelling. This forward thrust or future-directionality of the prologue makes good narrative sense given that we are *about to* hear the speeches as they unfold *over time*, in their narrative progression from the beginning to the end.

The prologue's break with the past is visually marked by Socrates' unusual physical appearance. Socrates chances upon Aristodemus "bathed and wearing his fine sandals, both things he rarely did" (174a3–4). He has taken care of his looks so that his beauty can match Agathon's when he arrives at the latter's house (174a6). Socrates has beautified himself in anticipation of an encounter with a handsome man, an encounter he could have had the day before but postponed because "he was afraid of the crowds" (174a7). Unlike Apollodorus who repeats himself, Socrates acts once by choosing the best time for action: he is about to do (in the imminent future) what he refused to do (in the recent past). He also amends the past by inviting the previously uninvited Aristodemus to join him to the party. His invitation counters custom with innovation since, traditionally, the host invites his guests; guests can invite neither themselves nor other guests. Note that Aristodemus couches his acceptance of the invitation as *agreement with Socrates* ("Whatever you say," 174b2) and a little later asks Socrates for a "defense" of his attending the banquet "because *I* shan't admit that I came uninvited–I shall say it was you who invited me" (174c8–d1).[25] Finally, although Socrates says that he will help Aristodemus find an excuse for his presence at the banquet ("As we two go together further along the way, we'll work out what we'll say," 174d2–3), he lets his friend show up alone, having to do the excusing by himself. In all these cases, planned or spontaneous actions violate past agreements or conflict with established notions of self and social etiquette; they are ways of adapting the accepted and familiar to the contingencies of the present. They are also creative activities, which produce something new (physical appearance, attending a party, inviting an uninvited guest) through interactions between Socrates and his mental states (his anticipation of dining with Agathon and fear of crowds), as well as between Socrates and another person (Aristodemus, although even this interaction can be construed as taking place between Socrates and what he thinks is the right thing to do under the circumstances: it must have seemed rude and uncaring not to take poor Aristodemus with him). Contrast Apollodorus' creative paralysis, the result of a reverential attitude to the past – a memorized account and pre-established views about his unidentified friends – that he seems unwilling or incapable of revising.

Socrates' critical stance to the past manifests itself most acutely in his reception of the proverb "Good men go uninvited to an inferior man's feast." Instead of quoting the proverb, he assumes knowledge of it and proceeds to emend it: "Well then," said Socrates, "follow me, and we'll

[25] His passivity and proneness to imitate others have been widely noted. See, e.g., Blondell 2002: 102 ff. and Sheffield 2006: 13. For the idea of symposiastic exclusivity see Stehle 1997: 218.

make a mess of the proverb by changing it: now it'll turn out to be good men's feasts that "good men go to of their own accord" (174b3–5). By failing to cite a proverb that he alters, Socrates asserts the primacy of the present over the authority of the past. It is as if the past offers him, in the present, the stimulus for its critical reappraisal; the contingencies of application supersede veneration. But also, to the extent that his change of the proverb will be confirmed or disconfirmed in the future, the present looks to what lies ahead.

This temporal orientation receives support from Socrates' reference to the greatest figure of authority of his time, Homer, and his use of the proverb in *Iliad* 10.222–226. At first, it seems that Homer's re-reading of the proverb is meant to serve as endorsement of Socrates' own emendation of it, evidence in Homer of a kindred, "brothers-in-arms" spirit, but things are more complicated than that. After Socrates has given his version of the proverb, he says, ". . . it looks as if Homer didn't just make a mess of this proverb but did criminal damage to it (*ou monon diaptheirai alla kai hubrisai*, 174b6): after making Agamemnon an exceptionally good man when it comes to warfare, and Menelaus a 'soft spear-fighter,' when Agamemnon is sacrificing and laying on a feast Homer had Menelaus come uninvited to the banquet, an inferior to his superior's" (174b–c). Homer's *hubris* or violation consists in his turning the proverb on its head by switching the positions of subject and object: whereas the proverb has good men going uninvited to an inferior man's feast, Homer has an inferior man going uninvited to his superior's feast. Homer alters the proverb by inverting its meaning, Socrates alters it (*metabalontes*, 174b4) by expanding its meaning.

Two things are noteworthy here, given the concerns of this essay: (1) Socrates works *with* the proverb rather than *against* it. His interaction with it is an instance of spiritual begetting that generates a new version of the proverb to replace the old one yet a remnant of the old version (the subject) remains in the new one. Aristodemus, on the other hand, like Apollodorus in the frame, begets nothing and simply agrees with Homer since he, too, is "a person of no consequence going uninvited to the feast of a man of accomplishment" (174c3–4). (2) Socrates' version succeeds both the original proverb and the Homeric variant. This temporal ordering yields the following mini-narrative: Socrates delves into the past, retrieves a proverb from it, begets a new version of the proverb, delves again into the past, retrieves Homer's variant of the proverb, criticizes it and by implication finds his own version superior to Homer's, and finally opens up his version for testing in the future.

Things change constantly: the past affords two different items for inspection, and the present accommodates two different interventions on the past, one generative, the other critical, while the narrative as a whole looks forward. By contrast, in the frame, the present mirrors the past, and the overall temporality is regressive.

The ability to change in the present what is supplied by the past with a view to engendering something new in the future is also evident in Socrates' "lurking solipsistically in doorways."[26] On their walk to Agathon's house, Socrates "wrapped up somehow in his own thoughts" (174d5) is left behind, which causes Aristodemus to make a solo appearance at the party. A concerned Agathon inquires after Socrates' whereabouts, and a slave reports that Socrates will not move from the neighbor's doorway where he is standing. Agathon asks that the slave not leave Socrates alone until he comes into the house, but Aristodemus intervenes: "You mustn't do that! Leave him there. This is one of his ways; sometimes he just goes off, it doesn't matter where, and just stands there. He'll come presently, that's my guess. So don't disturb him. Leave him there" (175b1–3). By falling behind, Socrates breaks his earlier agreement with Aristodemus and does so on his own initiative and without warning. This sudden change has ramifications for the future as it forces[27] the previously dependent Aristodemus to speak up in front of everyone – he becomes, in fact, so bold as to issue three orders/requests to Agathon (175b1, twice at b3) – and to repeat his earlier excuse for his unexpected appearance.[28] Socrates changes the past and thereby catalyzes the future, whereas Aristodemus meets the needs of the future by rehashing the past. Here we see once again two different attitudes to time: Socrates looks forward, while Aristodemus looks backward. Socrates' falling behind his road-companion illustrates this difference – the two men, literally, do not walk together – and his procreative capacity is suggested by his "being wrapped up in thought." If thinking is a speech made to oneself, a form of internal address or self-communion, Socrates may be said to "withdraw into immobile seclusion to 'endure' his intellectual labor."[29] His creative

[26] I borrow the phrase from Blondell 2006: 150.

[27] Note that Socrates "orders" (*keleuein*, or, less strongly, "requests") Aristodemus to go without him (174d5).

[28] Aristodemus lacks autonomy as he blames *Socrates* for making him go to Agathon's house uninvited. What matters, for my purposes, is that he rehashes at a later time the excuse he announced at an earlier time.

[29] Montiglio 2005: 172 draws a comparison between Odysseus and Socrates on the basis of Alcibiades' description of Socrates during the siege at Potidaea.

work, his "poetry," echoes John Stuart Mill, "Poetry is feeling, confessing itself to itself in moments of solitude" (Mill, Gibbs, and Lytton 1897: 208).[30] His physical stillness may be said to minimize his engagement with the phenomenal world and assist his contemplation of Forms – if that is, in fact, what Socrates is doing on the porch. One might also see in his abiding tendency to go off and stand still an allusion to the eternal world of Forms.

Whatever we make of these suggestions, one thing is clear: Socrates' interaction with Aristodemus shows his predilection for a procreative model of desire, one that foregrounds the idea of creative begetting, which, as stated earlier, becomes prevalent in the second part of Diotima's analysis (206b–212a). There we learn that the purpose of *erōs* is "giving birth in beauty" (*tokos en kalōi*, 206b7–8) and that "*erōs* is not of the beautiful, but of procreation and giving birth in the beautiful" (*ou tou kalou ho erōs alla tēs gennēseōs kai tou tokou en tōi kalōi*, 206e2–5). Socrates begets ideas not in the beauty of a beloved (Aristodemus seems disappointing in that regard), but in the beauty of other ideas – be they proverbs, which *qua* distillations of traditional wisdom resemble customs, or Homer's offspring, whose beauty and immortality Diotima extols (209d1–4), or his own thoughts, which remain tantalizingly opaque. The progressive thrust of the prologue, both as a whole and in the arrangement of its episodes, lends narrative support to the model of desire as creative begetting. Ruby Blondell may be right to see the Socrates of the *Symposium* "more or less plausibly as occupying all of the steps on the 'ladder of love,'" but the Socrates of the prologue can best be placed, I believe, somewhere in the middle, definitely above the first and below the last rung. This position recalls *Erōs*' intermediate status between mortals and immortals, and Socrates' role as guide of others from the first to the last rung. For mere mortals that is no mean achievement.[31]

[30] Socrates is a poet not only in the literal sense of the word, a "maker" or "creator," but also in the sense that his creation, his variant, competes with that of the most venerable poet, Homer.

[31] I presented various versions of this chapter in Athens, Bologna, Chicago, Irvine, Lake Tahoe, London, Louvain, Paris, and Portland. For insightful comments I thank warmly Adam Phillips, Andrea Nightingale, David Halperin, David Sedley, Dimitris Lignadis, Eric Brown, Françoise Meltzer, Helen Vendler, Karen Bassi, and Yannis Houvardas. The seed of my ideas was sown a few years ago in Villa Maistros in Skopelos – thanks, Marc.

CHAPTER 2

Unfamiliar Voices: Harmonizing the Non-Socratic Speeches and Plato's Psychology

Jeremy Reid

While the *Symposium* is often praised as a literary masterpiece, the logic of its overall construction remains a deep puzzle. Why are *these* seven speeches singled out from the other speeches delivered that night, and why are they taken to be the ones "worth remembering" (178a)? Why do they proceed in the order that they do, and what is the relationship between what Socrates says and what everybody else says? These questions cause the *Symposium* to be a curious and problematic text: what are we to make of Plato speaking with all these unfamiliar voices?

Here I will explore the thesis that the first four speeches of the *Symposium* are propaedeutic for philosophy. I argue that the concerns raised in the early speeches highlight features of Plato's psychology and aspects of his education program that are more fully developed in the *Republic*. As the *Republic* also contains a philosophical ascent, the upshot for this reading of the *Symposium* is that we can see consistency across these dialogues insofar as both ascent passages are preceded by discussions that reflect concerns about education and character. In particular, Plato highlights four psychological features that are necessary for the soul to make progress on the ascent: firstly, it must have strong spirited capacities; secondly, it must be lawful and aim at virtue; thirdly, its various opposing elements must be harmonized; finally, its appetites must be minimized and orderly.[1] I contend that these four goals of education correspond to the first four speeches of the *Symposium* and that philosophical progress will not be possible without these psychic qualities.

[1] Plato has grouped these phenomena according to a tripartite schema in the *Republic*, which might suggest that the psychology implicit in the *Symposium* must also be tripartite, but the evidence for such a claim, though suggestive, is underdetermined. See Brickhouse and Smith 2012 for how Socratic psychology accounts for the appetites and passions, and Sheffield 2006: Appendix.

The division of the speeches into a group of four and a group of three is suggested by the text. Before beginning his encomium, Agathon reflects on the previous speeches:

> All those who have spoken before me did not so much celebrate the god [*Erōs*] as congratulate human beings on the good things that come to them from the god. But who it is who gave these gifts, what he is like (*hopoios de tis*) – no one has spoken about that.[2] (194e)

What unifies the early speeches is that they discuss the effects of *erōs* rather than its nature. Socrates approves of Agathon's observation (199c, 201d–e) and Diotima's speech is in part structured around this distinction between the nature of *erōs* and its effects (206b). I contend that the effects for which each of the early speakers praise *Erōs* are related to goals of Plato's education program in the *Republic*; thus, we are benefitted by *Erōs* insofar as his effects improve our soul. For each of the early speeches, I will first highlight features of the account of education and psychology in the *Republic*, and then show how these relate to the characterization of the speakers and the content of their speeches. I will end by suggesting how we might understand the characterization of Agathon and Alcibiades in light of this discussion of education: Agathon shows potential for philosophy whereas Alcibiades serves as a warning for those who attempt philosophy without a harmonized soul.[3] So with this general structure in mind, let us turn now to the propaedeutic thesis and consider whether the same psychological concerns that shape the discussion of education in the *Republic* are present in the *Symposium*.

1. Phaedrus and Spirited Motivations

The Guardians of Kallipolis receive an extensive education designed to develop their characters and prepare them for dialectic. Plato's education program is notoriously demanding and only a small number of the Guardians will complete all the stages that qualify them to be

[2] All translations are from Cooper 1997, with modifications.

[3] This division of the dialogue's speeches is fruitful for understanding the unity of the last three speeches. What Agathon says about *erōs*' nature is *false* and he is promptly refuted, suggesting a state of *ignorance*; Socrates, having learned from Diotima, provides a true account of *erōs*' nature, its powers, activities, and effects such that one gains understanding, leading us up the ascent to the Forms and thus the grounds of *knowledge*; Alcibiades swears that he'll only tell the truth and asks Socrates to correct him if he says anything that is false, but he shows the characteristic instability of those with *untethered true beliefs*, vacillating between the views of the many and what Socrates told him.

philosopher-rulers. In the *Republic*, education promotes virtue and character virtue is explained (partly) in terms of the tripartite soul and the relations between its elements. Much of the discussion of education reflects Plato's novel introduction of the spirited or *thumoeidic* part of the soul, explaining its nature, objects, characteristic activities, and correlative character types.

The Guardians need to be educated to have a strong spirited part so that they can become courageous (375a–b, 386a, 395c, 399a–b, 410d, 429b–430b). When the spirited part is strong, the Guardians will have a reliable sense of shame and honor. Socrates tells us that they will feel shame at shameful things and shameful actions, which will prevent them from associating with such objects or acting in such ways (378b–c, 395e–396a). Moreover, Guardians will be taught to honor the gods and their parents (386a). Because they are taught that the gods honor virtue in this life and in the afterlife, they will be unafraid of death and Hades (386b, 387d). Their strong desire for honor and love of the fine (*kalon*) will cause them to aim at noble actions, victory, and honor, especially honor from warfare and military prowess (440c–d, 549a, 581b). This makes the Guardians the best fighters, and causes them to preserve the prescriptions of reason in the face of pain, trial, and temptation (442b–c).

In the *Symposium*, Phaedrus is characterized in spirited terms and his speech is replete with thumoeidic content.[4] Firstly, he is introduced as being indignant that the god *Erōs* has not received sufficient honor and so wants to hear encomia to him (177a–c). Elsewhere in the Platonic corpus, Phaedrus is characterized as being particularly eager to hear speeches from famous orators though he is an amateur himself (*Phdr.* 228a–c; *Prot.* 315c). This corresponds to the timocratic, spirit-ruled youth in the decline of Kallipolis, who would "love to listen to speeches and arguments, though he's by no means a rhetorician" (548e). Thus while Phaedrus' characterization is thin, the descriptions we do have suggest he has a spirited nature.

This characterization is confirmed by the content of his sparse and short speech. Phaedrus starts the proceedings by praising the guidance that *erōs* provides: *Erōs* instills an especially strong sense of shame for shameful things and love-of-honor for fine things in the lover and the beloved (178d). The idea is that those in love cannot bear the thought of being thought ill of by the person whom they love and this stops them from doing shameful things. Love, then, can act as a safeguard against our

[4] Hobbs 2000: 251–2, Wilburn 2015: 22n38.

excessive or bad inclinations. However, *erōs* also inspires lovers to do great and honorable things, which make lovers the best and most courageous fighters (179a–b). Furthermore, gods honor lovers who do great deeds for love and punish those who do not – this is why Alcestis and Achilles are rewarded and Orpheus, made soft by his kithara playing, is punished (179b–180b).[5]

Phaedrus' speech is easy to pass over quickly, but it is striking how many times shame and honor feature in the speech; moreover, there is a strong emphasis on acts of courage and military prowess, especially in his use of the Theban Band (178e–179b) and Achilles (179e–180a). Phaedrus also highlights the motivational force that *erōs* provides in the performance of great deeds for others (178e–180a). He thus concludes that "of the gods, *erōs* is the most ancient, most honorable, and most powerful for the acquisition of virtue and happiness for men" (180b). It is notable though that we have no reason to think that Phaedrus' conception of virtue extends beyond courage or that his conception of happiness extends beyond receiving honor. His conception of value is thus limited by spirited concerns. Stepping back, the point of Phaedrus' speech is that *erōs* effectively engages and develops spirited capacities: few things can make us more ashamed of our bad behavior than the disappointment or disapproval of our lover, and few things motivate us to do great and wonderful deeds more than love. Thus, *Erōs* benefits us by activating and fostering these psychological forces.

Because the *Republic* makes it clear that spirit ought to be fostered, the effects Phaedrus praises improve our character along this dimension. This needn't entail that taking a lover is just as good as the education system of Kallipolis for developing spirit, but it provides grounds for thinking that what Phaedrus details is an image or imitation of the ideal education.[6] Lovers do not always reliably or perfectly cultivate our spirited capacities, but they do often improve and activate them – and in noticing this, Phaedrus is right to think that *Erōs* benefits us.

2. Pausanias and Lawfulness

It is unsurprising that for the education system in Kallipolis to work, its prescriptions have to be followed strictly. But it is notable that the

[5] For the natural antagonism between spirited types and musical training (especially the deleterious effects of stringed instruments) see *Rep.* 399d–e, 549b.

[6] For the early speakers as "shadow lovers" who provide images of virtue and happiness, see Sheffield 2006: chapter 7.

education system is repeatedly described in terms of laws or conventions (*nomoi*) and that the Guardians take these to be an authoritative guide to how they should think, feel, and act (at least in the early stages of their education).[7] Even in childhood games and in musical practices, there is to be no innovation or anything done against the established order so that lawfulness can be firmly established in the Guardians (424b–425a). Plato is explicit that strict lawfulness is necessary for education to work (427a). Indeed, lawfulness is the *goal* of education: Socrates says that education in music and gymnastics was for "nothing other than this," namely, the inculcation of the laws, so that the Guardians "would absorb the laws in the finest way possible, just like a dye" (430a). Just as a well-prepared wool will absorb a dye so thoroughly that "no amount of washing... can remove it," the Guardians are to internalize the laws completely and permanently that they preserve it through "such extremely effective detergents as pleasure, pain, fear, and desire" (429c–430b).

The emphasis on lawfulness in the discussion of the early education is further confirmed in later passages. The decline of Kallipolis is characterized repeatedly in terms of a breakdown of the established laws at each stage (546d, 550d, 572c–d, 574e), where rulers "[run] away from the law like boys from their father" (548b). Socrates also describes good pleasures and desires as lawful (571b) and bad ones as lawless (572b). Law is further connected with the prescriptions of reason in that "whatever is most distant from reason [is] also most distant from law and order" (587a). Law is called a kind of external reason that establishes a constitution in the soul, fostering the best part in it and acting as the ally of everyone (590d). Law also works together with reason to fight against the desires and reactions of the lower part of the soul, especially grief and pleasure (604a–c). Finally, there is evidence suggesting that law's influence extends well into philosophical education: Socrates says that only the most steadfast in preserving what law had laid down are fit for dialectic (537c–d) and that dialectic has received a bad reputation because of those who do it badly now, on account of their filling it with lawlessness (537e–539a). Cultivating lawfulness is thus an integral part of Platonic education.[8]

[7] Annas 2010, 2013 and forthcoming; Lane 2013.

[8] Becoming lawful may be important in the development of *reason*. Law reliably gives citizens true beliefs about how they ought to act (*Stat.* 300b), and deferring to law and to what is conventionally believed is better than thinking you know something when you don't (*Phdr.* 230a). This explains

Returning to the *Symposium*, after some other speeches that Aristodemus couldn't remember (180c), Pausanias continues by elaborating on the theme of *erōs* as an important motivational and educational tool, but criticizes Phaedrus for not distinguishing between two types of *erōs*: one of which leads us well and produces beneficial dispositions in us, the other of which does not (181a). Pausanias subsequently separates Common and Heavenly Love (180d). His main point throughout the speech is that Athenian laws and conventions allow lovers to love rightly and that what divides the two kinds of *erōs* is that heavenly love is *lawful*. Pausanias says that only Heavenly *Erōs* should be praised because only Heavenly *Erōs* benefits lovers and produces praiseworthy actions. He claims that one cannot determine in the abstract which actions are good and which bad because what matters is whether the action is done "finely and rightly" (181a). But what makes an action right and fine is its being lawful. Thus good lovers act lawfully and bad lovers act hubristically.[9]

Indeed, Pausanias' focus on the importance of law has prompted one commentator to call him a "legal pedant."[10] Notice how Pausanias condemns those filled with Common *Erōs*:

> All they care about is doing it. Whether they do it finely or not is of no concern. That is why they do whatever comes their way, sometimes good, sometimes bad; and which one it is, is incidental to their purpose (181b).

These lovers behave indiscriminately as they have no consistent guide; rather, they are led by whatever happens to strike them – that is, depending on how things appear to them. This reliance on appearances could in turn lead them to ignore the limits determining what they ought and ought not to do. Now compare these lovers with those filled with Heavenly *Erōs*, who are not subject to the hubris of Common *Erōs* (181c). Heavenly lovers recognize the limits on the actions they might perform and these limits are determined by law. While Pausanias thinks Athenian laws are basically good, good men make further laws for themselves to fill in the gaps and loopholes (181e). This language of self-legislation bears strong similarities to the *Republic*, where Socrates says that it is not fitting to legislate every tiny detail for good men, as they will "easily find out for themselves whatever needs to be legislated about such things" (425d–e).[11]

why lawfulness is necessary for beginning dialectic – it provides the best set of beliefs and intellectual humility from which to start investigation. See also Annas forthcoming.

9 See Dover 1989: 34–39 for the relationship between *hubris* and law. 10 Sheffield 2006: 222.

11 Glaucon agrees, *provided the people are already lawful*. This gives us a clue to the underdeveloped characterization of Pausanias.

Thus, good lovers understand their actions in terms of law, are guided by law, and act willingly in accordance with it, whereas bad lovers are prone to transgress the law and need to be forced to follow it (181e–182a). In that sense, law determines what actions are shameful and honorable, what is to be done and what is not to be done.

It may be objected that in the *Republic* citizens are not obeying just *any* laws, but *good* laws – laws that aim at virtue in accordance with what is actually good and honorable, whereas Pausanias is talking about ordinary laws. But Pausanias thinks that Athenian and Spartan laws do in fact meet this higher standard and that is what justifies them. His defense of Athenian and Spartan laws has a Goldilocks structure: Elis and Boeotia are too hot in approving the taking of a lover in every case; Ionia and Persia are too cold in always considering it disgraceful; but Athens and Sparta get it just right in having complex laws, not always condemning nor always praising the taking of a lover (182a–183d). Moreover, the Athenian laws "are designed to separate the wheat from the chaff, the proper love from the vile" (184a) in that ultimately they "provide for only one honorable way of taking a man as a lover" (184c). Thus Athenian laws result in honorable behavior and are a good standard for what is honorable.

Pausanias ends his speech by defending that Athenian laws are good because they approve of subjection (*douleia*) for the sake of wisdom and virtue:[12]

> If someone decides to put himself at another's disposal because he thinks that this will make him better with respect to some wisdom or in any other part of virtue (*kata sophian tina ē kata allo hotioun meros aretēs*), we approve of his voluntary subjection (*ethelodouleia*): we consider it neither shameful nor servile… When an older lover and a young man come together and each obeys the principle appropriate to him – when the lover realizes that he is justified in doing anything for a loved one who grants him favors, and when the young man understands that he is justified in performing any service for a lover who can make him wise and virtuous – and when the lover *is* able to help the young man become wiser and better, and the young man *is* eager to be taught and improved by his lover – then, and only then, when these two principles coincide absolutely, it is fine for a young man to accept a lover. (184c–e)

The pursuit of virtue determines when it is honorable to take a lover and this pursuit is so important that even if one of the parties is deceived about the character of their partner, their desire is of such a noble kind that

[12] This may seem shocking, but see *Euthd.* 282b; *Crit.* 50e; *Leg.* 698a5–701c4, 715d, 762e.

their actions are still honorable (185a–b). The cultivation of the soul thus has pride of place for Pausanias and its goal is wisdom and virtue.[13] Thus, because Athenian laws aim at this goal, lawful Athenian lovers act well and finely.

Pausanias' speech, therefore, focuses on *lawfulness* and *the establishment of virtue as a goal.* An important part of this conception is that lawful lovers are not merely guided by whatever appearances happen to strike them and deference to the law allows them to act well.[14] Thus I contend that the moral to take from Pausanias' speech is that heavenly *erōs* benefits lovers by leading them to aim at wisdom and virtue in accordance with the law. Of course, Pausanias' own account of virtue and the role of reason looks thin and instrumental insofar as it results in what we might call "right action" but right action lacking a substantive philosophical justification. In that sense, like Phaedrus, he still only presents an image or imitation of the ideal education program, and Athenian laws will be in practice less beneficial than the laws of Kallipolis. But Pausanias has also expanded on Phaedrus' conception of virtue by making reference to wisdom, even if it is unclear whether he has more to say about what virtue and wisdom consist in. So, on the one hand, perhaps Pausanias does not help us much in moving beyond lawfulness itself as the standard of virtue, and maybe his lovers could only ever attain conventional virtue, participating in it "through habit and without philosophy" (*Rep.* 619c).[15] On the other hand, insofar as he encourages lovers to be lawful *for the sake of* their aspirations to wisdom and virtue, there is no reason why their pursuit might not lead them beyond where Pausanias can guide them. At any rate, Pausanias' account is one which evidently needs to be supplemented, but lawfulness is an important stage in the development of character for Plato, and it confers substantial psychological benefits in the course of education.

3. Eryximachus and Harmonizing Opposites

In order to ensure that they do not become dominated by their spirited natures, the musical education of the Guardians also aims at bringing about a love of order and a harmony in their souls. This helps to make the

[13] Sheffield 2006: 6, 18–20.

[14] Cf. Moss 2008, Carone 2001, and Ganson 2009 on reason as measuring appearances.

[15] Lawfulness might have been all that some thought virtue was (*Prot.* 326d–e).

soul-parts an integrated whole, with the various potentially opposing elements working together as one.

Socrates is explicit that the education program is designed to harmonize the opposing gentle and spirited natures in the Guardians (375b–c, 410e–411a).[16] When this happens correctly, the harmony generated is primarily what moderation (*sōphrosunē*) consists in (389d, 430e, 431e–432a, 442c, 443d–e, 591c–d); specifically, moderation is a kind of agreement (*homonoia*) between the parts of the soul (432a). Certain kinds of music produce moderation insofar as they exemplify these harmonies and establish order in the soul (399a–400e). Musical education also causes the Guardians to love harmonious things wherever they find them and to hate disorderly and unharmonious things (402d). Socrates describes this in terms of love: "The right kind of love," he says, "is by nature the love of order (*kosmiou*) and beauty that has been moderated by education in music and poetry... [and] the right kind of love has nothing mad or licentious (*akolasias*) about it" (403a). This love of harmony also informs how the Guardians act, as actions that destroy the harmony of the soul are unjust and that actions that preserve it are just (443e).

Importantly, the *Republic* conception of psychic harmony is associated with medicine and natural science. Glaucon concedes that the justice of the soul and its harmony are goods in themselves when Socrates points out that this state is a kind of health (444d). Moreover, in motivating the goodness of psychic harmony, Socrates appeals to the fact that the *technai* aim at the harmony, grace, and rhythm that develop "in accordance with an intelligent plan" (400e–401a). He goes on to claim that "our bodily nature is full of [these qualities], as are the natures of all growing things, for in all of these there is grace and gracelessness. And gracelessness, bad rhythm, and disharmony are akin to bad words and bad character, while their opposites are akin to and are imitations of the opposite, a moderate and good character" (401a). This is why training in music and poetry is so important for cultivating a harmonized soul: through noticing when "something has been omitted from a thing and when it hasn't been finely crafted or finely made by nature," the Guardians will come to form a conception of harmony and order, and then use that to inform their own actions (401d–402a). Just as they will notice when a note is missing from a musical chord, they will notice deficiencies in the city and soul that need counter-balancing. Socrates explains the theoretical basis for this when he says that "excessive action in one direction usually sets up a reaction in

[16] Cf. *Stat.* 306a–311c.

the opposite direction. This happens in seasons, in plants, in bodies, and last but not least, in constitutions" (563e). Thus this conception of health and the harmonizing of opposites is a crucial piece of the *Republic's* argument, and its psychological import grounds much of the education program.

Eryximachus' characterization and speech in the *Symposium* share many similarities on these points. Firstly, he is a doctor, so we should be alert to the parallels between his concerns about bodily health and those in the *Republic*. Furthermore, Eryximachus acts as a kind of doctor for Agathon's symposium in that he keeps order and prevents the party from declining into intemperance at a number of points: he is the one who recommends that the guests should refrain from heavy thinking in light of the previous night's excesses (176c–d), and then suggests that they send away the flute girl so that they can spend the night listening to speeches (176e–177e); when Aristophanes gets the hiccups and disrupts the order of the speeches, Eryximachus both remedies Aristophanes' health and takes his place as speaker (185c–e); finally, when an already drunken Alcibiades starts to drink still more, Eryximachus is the one who chastises his impropriety and suggests that he give an encomium to Socrates instead (214b–e).[17] The resident doctor thus wards off intemperance and maintains order in the *Symposium*.

Eryximachus' speech begins by expanding on Pausanias' distinction between Common and Heavenly *Erōs*, explaining that both forms of love not only occur with respect to human souls (*psuchais*) but also occur with respect to animals and plants and in all the things that are (186a). Beginning with the human body, Eryximachus claims that in healthy and diseased constitutions, there are different forms of *erōs*: unhealthy *erōs* comes from a constitution which is dissimilar (*anomoion*), which generates a desire and love for things which are themselves dissimilar (186b–c). The knowledge and skill of the doctor consists in knowing what ought to be "encouraged and gratified" for the sake of health, and what ought to be "frustrated and rebuffed" (186c). Specifically, Eryximachus says that a physician's job is to make the opposites in the body friends (*phila*), and share love (*eran*) and agreement (*homonoian*), where the harmonized opposites are hot and cold, bitter and sweet, wet and dry, and everything else like this (186d–e). Already this is similar to the *Republic*'s conception of health in that it involves generating agreement and harmony between opposing elements.

[17] See Edelstein 1945.

Eryximachus then seems to commit a baffling *non sequitur* by saying that in the same way that medicine is guided by love, so too are gymnastics, farming, poetry, and music (187a). He later claims that love also controls the seasons (188a), astronomy (188b), and divination (188c–d). Although this expansion of the theory has been the target of criticism (and Eryximachus probably does claim more than he can justify), each of these fields includes examples of generating harmony between opposites.[18] Because the music analogy is most fully explained, let us start there.

The passage begins by quoting Heraclitus: "being at variance with itself is in agreement with itself. . . like the attunement of a bow or a lyre."[19] Eryximachus interprets Heraclitus to mean that "an expert musician creates a harmony by resolving the prior discord between high and low notes" (187a–b). In music, as soon as a note moves from the tonic, a kind of dissonance is created – but music isn't about avoiding such dissonances so much as shaping these dissonances into an orderly whole. So too with rhythm (187c): music and poetry do not avoid fast and slow rhythms, but order them systematically. Eryximachus' point is not that we should pull the high and low notes into a less extreme middle pitch, or fast and slow rhythms into a homogeneous *andante* – that wouldn't make sense of his examples – his claim is that the various opposites need to be ordered so that harmony and agreement between them are created, both synchronically and diachronically (187c).

Eryximachus then discusses the effects of music on audiences and performers, which further emphasizes the connection between musical structures and the desires in those habitually exposed to them (187c–d). This interpretation goes some way in explaining his other applications: firstly, the doctor is able to show how appetites can be gratified without slipping into intemperance (*akolasias*) or disease (*nosos*), by drawing attention to the various opposites in diet (hot/cold, dry/wet, sweet/bitter) and regulating the excess of one through the supplementation of the other (187e). His point is this: given the kind of being that we are, we are going to experience appetites, bodily lacks and excesses – what's important is that we satisfy them in an orderly way that leads to a healthy state. Similarly, when the seasons are governed by the good kind of *erōs*, they are balanced and in harmony, causing plants and animals to be in good health, whereas the bad kind of *erōs* in seasons kills and destroys living things through extreme conditions and disease (188a–b). Presumably this also explains the

[18] See Sheffield 2006: 21–22 and Trivigno, Chapter 3 in this volume.

[19] Cf. "stretching and relaxing" and "slackening and loosening" the soul (*Rep.* 411e, 441e, 590b).

earlier reference to the two kinds of *erōs* being relevant for the skill of farming: farmers must know how to counterbalance the natural excesses of the weather and seasons. Eryximachus' extension of this theory to astronomy is puzzling, but plausibly the idea is that orderly heavenly motions cause orderly seasons and disorderly heavenly motions cause disorderly seasons, so he is pointing to a higher cause (188b). Finally, Eryximachus applies the theory to divination in urging us to gratify the orderly kind of love with respect to the gods (188c). This also need not be as overreaching as it seems, considering that much of Greek religious practice was about performing the right kind of ceremonies at the right times in order to establish friendship and harmony between gods and mortals.

Eryximachus' speech thus bears strong resemblances to the passages on psychic harmony and health in the *Republic* insofar as it endorses a picture of health that consists in the harmonization of opposites, and in that it gives an explanation of unhealthy love for bad things in terms of its being caused by an unhealthy and out-of-balanced subject. There are, however, two notable limits to Eryximachus' speech. Firstly, in the *Republic*, psychic health explains bodily health and is thus prior to it (408d–e). Eryximachus seems to leave open the possibility that, for example, a bodily remedy will bring about the good kind of *erōs* in a person and change their desires. Plato is more careful in the *Republic* as he has a richer psychological account to explain how bad desires come about. Secondly, Eryximachus claims that *everything that is* partakes in or is governed by *erōs* (186b). That all things partake in opposites might be true of most sensible particulars, but certainly not of everything that *is* – the obvious counterexample being the Forms. Therefore Eryximachus' speech oversteps with respect to metaphysics, though its implicit materialism might be appropriate for explanations in Platonic physics.

At any rate, the claims Eryximachus makes about how *Erōs* benefits us by bringing about harmony between our opposing elements are in accordance with Plato's view of education. The establishment of psychic harmony will allow us to gratify our appetites in an orderly fashion and will draw us towards the right objects for our psychic and bodily health. So if Eryximachus is right that *Erōs* improves us by bringing about harmony between the opposing elements in us, such a result would be an image or imitation of the moderation instilled by the education program of Kallipolis, improving our body and soul with respect to their health and integrity.[20]

[20] This reading may help us understand why the order of speeches is wrong (185c–d). Eryximachus makes a number of references to the appetites, but Plato has not yet given us an adequate description of the appetites, so Eryximachus' speech relies on conceptual resources that have not

4. Aristophanes and the Appetites

Though not introduced until late in *Republic* IV (437b), the appetitive part of the soul lurks threateningly throughout the earlier discussion of education: the Guardians of Kallipolis are not allowed to own property, accrue money, or even touch gold and silver (417a); the Homeric epics are purged of references to Achilles loving money and suggestions that virtue consists in finding effective means to acquire tripods (390e–391e); the juicy passages about Zeus' sexual exploits are likewise swiftly athetized (390b–c), and even the passages on feasting and drinking are removed, lest young people think that this behavior is consistent with moderation (390a–c). Plato is explicit that excessive pleasures and appetites are incompatible with moderation and virtue, and are closely connected with violence (*hubris*) and licentiousness (*akolasia; Rep.* 403a, 408b, 431b, 560e, 572c; *Phdr.* 238a, 250e, 253e, 254e, 255e, 256c; *Gorg.* 493b–494a, 505b, 507e, 525a). These measures are thus designed to keep the appetites as small and restrained as possible. We learn more about the appetites and how they are corrupted in *Republic* VIII–IX. Before Kallipolis' decline, appetitive desires are weak and few in the citizens, and are limited to necessary and natural objects (558d–561c, 571b–d). This result is attributed to the education system acting in conjunction with the laws (571b). But once the characters of the rulers worsen and the laws are changed, new appetites arise in the city, and fulfilling these appetites eventually becomes the sole object of pursuit for the tyrant, who is controlled by a "violent crowd of desires" (572d–575a).[21]

Before returning to the *Symposium*, it is worthwhile to explore briefly what an appetite is in the *Republic*. In Book IV, we are told that each appetite is a desire for a natural object (437e), which is pleasant when satisfied. Plato is clear that the natural object is desired *as* the natural object and not as the natural object *plus* goodness or some other modifier (438a–439d). Furthermore, what is most one's own (*oikeion*) is also most pleasant:

> Can't we confidently assert that those desires of even the money-loving and honor-loving parts that follow knowledge and argument and pursue with their help those pleasures that reason approves will attain the truest

yet been provided. Hence, his speech comes one too early. The given order heightens the dramatic arc and tempo of the work by putting the amateur speech-makers before the experts, but, strictly speaking, their *logical* content requires that Aristophanes comes before Eryximachus.

[21] Wilburn 2014.

> pleasures possible for them, because they follow truth, and the ones that are most their own (*oikeias*), if indeed what is best for each thing is most its own (*oikeiotaton*)? (586e)

Plato uses this claim to argue that because the pleasures of the rational part of the soul are the most *oikeion*, they are also the most pleasant (586d–588a). Moreover, it is important that *all* of the parts of the soul do best with respect to their own *oikeion* objects and thus their own pleasures when they are guided by reason, because the pleasures pursued when reason rules are true and the most *oikeion*; that is to say, appetite and spirit are both better off when they are guided by reason, *even on their own terms*. Thus, there is a strong connection between Plato's conception of the appetites, desire, the *oikeion*, and pleasure in the *Republic*.

It is fitting for Aristophanes to speak about the appetites in the *Symposium*. For Plato's subject is *erōs*, and sexual desire is an important species of *erōs*. So to set the scene, Aristophanes responds to Eryximachus' speech by making a crude joke: if he was returned to health from his hiccups by sneezing, then is the orderly sort of love in the body created by the same sort of thing that a sneeze is (189a)?[22] The mockery rests on an oversimplification: the diseased state of *erōs* is just an excess of semen – get rid of that and health is returned. We have been prepared for such baseness though: Aristophanes needs no introduction regarding the content of his comedies, but even in the dialogue he is said to "think of nothing but Dionysus and Aphrodite" (177e), is singled out for his particularly excessive drinking the night before (176b), and gets the hiccups because he "probably stuffed himself again" (185c) which causes him to speak out of order. Aristophanes, then, is a paradigm of the disorderly appetitive character.

This reading is supported by how Aristophanes starts his speech, which has as its stated topic human nature (*phusis*) and what happened to it (its *pathēmata*). Plato can never resist a pun and this one is especially good: on the one hand, Aristophanes' speech is about how we used to be spherical conjoined humanoids who were split into two by the gods, thus creating our needy nature and desire to be united with our other halves; on the other hand, *pathēmata* is one of Plato's terms for the appetites (*Rep.* 439d, *Tim.* 69c–d), and *phusis* has valences regarding sex and genitalia.[23] Thus, Aristophanes basically announces that his subject is sex and appetitive desire, and I contend that we should read the speech

[22] Specifically, by certain sounds and itchings. Greeks used itching, scratching, tickling as euphemisms for masturbation and sexual lust. See Dover 1989: 99, 123, 137.

[23] See LSJ "*phusis*," section VII; Henderson 1991.

on these two levels throughout: in particular, we should understand the humanoids as a metaphor for the appetites and the gods as a metaphor for reason.

Things used to be different, Aristophanes tells us. Human beings were once spherical conjoined pairs (189e–190a) and we came as either a pair of males, a pair of females, or an androgynous combo (190b). We rolled around from place to place, our spherical motion imitating that of the heavens. These original humans were no mean things: they were so strong and ambitious that they tried to overthrow Olympus – the paradigm of hubris – and the story about the Giants was really about them (190b–c). But Zeus and the gods could not simply destroy these humanoids as they were required for worship and sacrifice (nourishment), but neither could they "let them run riot," so they came up with a plan "to stop their misbehaving" (*akolasia*, 190c, cf. 187e). Zeus then cut all the humans in two and Apollo rearranged their features (190d–191a). But this caused yet more problems as the humans only desired to embrace their other halves, so they neglected to eat and eventually died (191a–b, cf. *Phdr.* 259b–c). Zeus solved this problem by moving the genitals and inventing sex, so that after orgasm "they could stop embracing, return to their jobs, and look after their other needs in life" (191c–d).

Erōs then, according to Aristophanes, is the desire to re-unite ourselves with our natural other half and the desire is (momentarily and partially) fulfilled by achieving orgasm with one's partner. This would be much the same point as the joke from the start of the passage, but there's more to it than that, as even for Aristophanes *erōs* is about more than satisfying sexual desire (192c–d). Sex is an expression of wanting to become unified with our original halves, but it falls short. If Hephaestus were to offer to put us back together with our lover, none of us would refuse such an offer as it is *that* which we have always desired (*epethumei*, 192d–e). "'Love' is the name for the desire and pursuit of the whole" (*tou holou oun tēi epithumiai kai diōxei erōs onoma*, 192e–193a). This is why we should take a lover: it is the fulfillment of our natural desire to be whole again (193c). The desire for wholeness is likely to be frustrated in these bodies – "Love does the best it can for the time being: he draws us towards what belongs to us" (*eis to oikeion agōn*, 193d) – but if we are pious, we will perhaps be restored to our original nature.

Notice that Aristophanes' preferred word for desire is *epithumein*, and recall that, in the *Phaedrus*, *Republic*, and *Gorgias*, the appetites are frequently described as intemperate (*akolastos*) and hubristic; similarly, in the decline of Kallipolis, the appetites seek to overthrow the rule of reason in the soul just as the humanoids seek to overthrow the gods (*Phdr.* 253e–254e; *Rep.* 442a–b, 444b; *Tim.* 91b). Moreover, an appetite is a lack with a natural and *oikeion* object which it desires; in the myth we were cut in half and were not happy until we found that which made us whole, and so too our appetites are each continually unhappy until they find satisfaction in their desired object. But it is the nature of appetites not to stay satisfied for long: our bodies are continually depleting and even the satisfaction of sex is taken as only a rough approximation of its true desire, which is total fusion with its *oikeion* object. Compare Plato's point about appetitive desires always being in flux: even the satisfaction from eating and drinking is only momentary, as the process of filling or emptying never ends in these bodies (*Rep.* 585e–586a; *Gorg.* 493d–494b). We do, however, need the appetites to continue living.[24]

But how does Aristophanes' speech give us a picture of the *education* of the appetites? How does *Erōs* benefit us with respect to that part of the soul? Firstly, we know that the appetites are needy but also that they have tunnel-vision: each appetite can only care about one thing, its natural *oikeion* object (recall *Rep.* 439a–b). Given the hubristic nature of the appetites and their pretensions to overthrow the gods, Aristophanes says we need to be careful to "keep order before the gods" lest we be "split in two again" (193a). Thus the gods should be treated with reverence so that humans can be made whole, "and we will [be made whole again], if Love is our guide and commander. Let no one work against him" (193b). Aristophanes might here be hinting at the same lessons from the *Phaedrus* and the *Republic* that the appetites need to be guided and restrained by something external to themselves to remain in a good state. Because the appetites cannot co-ordinate their efforts themselves and are naturally prone to excess, limit has to be placed on them and deliberation done for them by a superior faculty (*Rep.* 432a, 444a–b, 586e); for example, in *Republic* IX, the democratic man uses reason to determine the greatest compossible set of his desires he can fulfill (561b–c). Moreover, increasing the number of desires competing for different objects would cause more frustration and pain

[24] See Obdrzalek in this volume for the claim that Aristophanes' humanoids work at a low-grade cognitive level, as they lack *logos* and cannot express what they want. For the appetites lacking *logos*, see Ganson 2009 and Moss 2008. Plato is careful in his choice of evaluative language: Aristophanes speaks of what makes us (our appetites) happy (*eudaimōn*, 193c–d), but says nothing about the relationship between the *oikeion* and the good. This may be why he objects to Socrates' criticisms (205e, 212c): as there *is* an important relationship between the *oikeion* and the good.

in the appetitive part of the soul, especially as the desires became stronger and harder to fulfill. Plato thus urges us to restrain our appetites to those that are natural and necessary so that the appetitive part of the soul remains orderly (571b, 589b).[25]

But why think that this subordination of the appetites to reason and spirit leads to the appetites being fulfilled and made whole? Well, for one, the appetites have no internal way of resolving conflict. If somebody is hungry but also wants sex, there is no way for the appetites to adjudicate this dispute on their own terms: each object is *oikeion* but they might not both be honorable or good. Another way we might think about Plato's point here is that the appetites aren't capable of determining the details of what they really want and this ends up making them worse and more intense; for example, our hunger for pastries only ends up making us sick and hungrier later because it cannot distinguish between the food it really needs and the food it wants. Thus the appetites individually and collectively have a better chance of getting fulfilled if they submit to reason. Of course, we cannot hope to have our desires completely fulfilled all the time, but perhaps that is why Aristophanes concludes by saying that love "does that best that can be done for the time being: he draws us towards what belongs to us" (193d). This reading makes a bizarre speech stranger still, but I contend that the appetitive references are too numerous to be merely accidental, especially when put into the mouth of Aristophanes.

5. Agathon and Alcibiades: Having a Soul Fit for the Ascent

If this reading of the early speeches is promising, then both the *Republic* and the *Symposium* contain discussions of education before the ascent. Why? The *Republic* seems to suggest that the education system will implant something like *demotic* virtue into the Guardians (429c–430c, 522a).[26] Elsewhere, Plato raises the possibility that lower-grade character virtue can be found in people who were not raised in a perfect education system (*Rep*. 619c; *Phd*. 68d–69c, 82a–b). Perhaps in the *Symposium* too, then, the beneficial effects detailed in the early speeches would (when taken collectively) result in demotic virtue in a person, improving the soul in various ways but without philosophy. Thus, I will end by suggesting that cultivating demotic virtue and improving one's soul along these four dimensions is necessary as a propaedeutic for the ascent.

[25] Cf. Brennan 2012: 104–6. [26] Vasiliou 2012.

The early education of the Guardians ends in love of beautiful boys, but, just as in the *Symposium* ascent, they quickly move beyond bodies in their love of beauty (403b–d). Thus, early education gets us to the bottom of the ladder in both dialogues, and, as Socrates states, "a naturally virtuous person, when educated, will in time acquire knowledge of both virtue and vice. And it is someone like that who becomes wise, in my view, and not the bad person" (*Rep.* 409d–e). Education prepares the soul for philosophy and one cannot make progress on the ascent without a harmonized soul.

In the *Republic*, Plato's explanation for why unjust souls cannot make philosophical progress is that their *erōs* is channeled away from philosophy and directed towards lower ends (485d–e). This prevents the soul from moving to and focusing on higher objects, as lower desires drag the sight of reason down like "leaden weights" to focus on base sensible particulars (518e–519b, 572a). The prime example of this phenomenon of being dragged from philosophy by spirited and appetitive desires is Alcibiades (490e–495b).[27] Only those with just souls have the necessary psychic stability to keep their erotic resources channeled consistently towards reason's desires, leaving it free to do philosophy and contemplate intelligible objects.

While I cannot defend this fully, the later speeches of the *Symposium* can be seen as dramatizing the relationship between character and philosophical progress. Agathon claims to speak about the nature of *erōs*, but almost everything he says about *erōs* is false insofar as he attributes to *Erōs* the qualities that *Erōs* in fact desires; he is thus refuted by Socrates.[28] But notice how smoothly the refutation goes: Agathon is not angry that he is being corrected by Socrates and he graciously admits that he didn't know what he was talking about (201b). Indeed, Agathon's refutation is one of the least antagonistic in the Platonic dialogues. His grace in responding to refutation may give us a reason to think that the real reason Socrates is flirting with Agathon is not (just) because he is physically beautiful, but because he has a beautiful soul and shows potential for philosophy (*Gorg.* 458a–b; *Tht.* 151b–d). Note that Socrates puns at the start of the dialogue that they are going to a

[27] Wilburn 2015.

[28] Note Agathon's *method of inquiry* is correct and shows his potential for philosophy (Sedley 2006), but he doesn't know what *erōs* is. There is another conceit here, as not only is Agathon Pausanias' beloved (rather than lover) but his name means "Good," so Plato makes Good ignorant of *erōs*.

good man's house (174a–b), and, given that Agathon is Pausanias' *eromenos*, this characterization of Agathon may further bolster the thesis that *Erōs* has beneficial effects on the soul.

On the other hand, consider the drunk and disorderly Alcibiades. Alcibiades has heard Socrates' *logoi* and says that their effect is like being possessed by a divine spirit or being intoxicated (215c–e). But Alcibiades finds them *upsetting* insofar as they make him radically re-evaluate his values, feeling as though his life "was no better than the most miserable slave's" (215e). Socrates causes Alcibiades to say that "all that matters is just what I most neglect: my personal shortcomings, which cry out for the closest attention" (216a). But rather than embracing these truths, Alcibiades refuses to listen and runs off, as if he were being drawn into impending doom by the sweet sounds of the Sirens (216a). Indeed, he says he wants Socrates to die but also knows that he cannot live without him, so torn up and confused is he over this man (216c). Socrates makes Alcibiades feel shame in the way Phaedrus detailed, but it is transitory in that Alcibiades only feels it when he is around Socrates. Alcibiades cannot prove Socrates wrong, yet goes back to his old ways "in [his] desire to please the crowd" the moment he leaves Socrates' side (216b). Alcibiades is occasionally purged of his false beliefs but he somehow doesn't *get* Socrates' point and cannot sustain a character change once he is pressured by the crowd. When Alcibiades is with Socrates he says that "nothing is more important to me than becoming the best man I can be" (218d), but these values do not remain fixed in his soul.

Alcibiades' changing ways are contrasted with Socrates' steadfast virtue. Socrates is surrounded by beautiful boys but considers their beauty, along with their fame and wealth, "beneath contempt" (216d–e), and resists Alcibiades' advances (217a–219c). To Socrates' temperance, Alcibiades praises his bravery (219e–221d), and says that his arguments are "worthy of a god, bursting with figures of virtue inside... of the greatest importance for anyone who wants to become a good man *(kalōi kagathōi)*" (222a). The dialogue closes with Socrates arguing till dawn and then going off to the Lyceum to "spend the rest of the day just as he always did," while the other guests rested (223d). Socrates is totally dedicated to philosophy in a way that Alcibiades clearly is not, which is why only Socrates can make philosophical progress. Alcibiades cares about philosophy while Socrates is around, but Socrates, barely human and quasi-divine, continues his lifestyle through rain, cold, and snow, and when everybody else needs to sleep.

Philosophy without erotic dedication can do more harm than good, and those with conflict between different motivations in their soul will not make progress on the ascent. Alcibiades embodies this: he hates being corrected, despite recognizing the truth that Socrates reveals to him (cf. *Rep*. 476d). Thus while Alcibiades can speak the truth, he does not love it and he does not live in accordance with it. He does not have the kind of soul necessary for grounding a complete commitment to philosophy. Only those with souls as stable as Socrates can move up the ascent.[29]

[29] Thanks to Pierre Destrée, Radcliffe Edmonds, Zina Giannopoulou, David Halperin, Emily Hulme, Noelle Lopez, M.M. McCabe, Jessica Moss, Alexander Nehamas, Suzanne Obdrzalek, Anthony Price, Frisbee Sheffield, Nick Smith, Franco Trivigno, and Paul Woodruff for their comments on earlier drafts of this chapter. Special thanks are due to Julia Annas, Tom Hercules Davies, Rachana Kamtekar, and Josh Wilburn for their extensive help and detailed comments at numerous points during the course of this project. I am also grateful to audiences at the Society for Ancient Greek Philosophy Annual Meeting at Fordham University, Oct. 2014, and the Princeton Graduate Philosophy Colloquia.

CHAPTER 3

A Doctor's Folly: Diagnosing the Speech of Eryximachus

Franco V. Trivigno

Scholarly opinion is sharply divided concerning the value and interest of the speech of Eryximachus in Plato's *Symposium*. Until Edelstein's vociferous challenge to the position in 1945, there was a consensus in the literature that the speech was meant by Plato to be a comic send-up of Eryximachus, exposing him as a pretentious and self-absorbed pedant.[1] In more recent times, some scholars have worked to rehabilitate the speech and, with it, its speaker, as the serious expression of an interesting and valued medical expert.[2] The passages in which Eryximachus appears in the dialogue have thus been interpreted as having been penned either with satirical malice or with admiration and respect. In this chapter, I present a defense of the older consensus that the speech is satirical.

As it stands, the debate has fuzzy parameters: interpreters on the one side have not clearly formulated what is supposed to be serious about the speech, while those on the other have explained neither what exactly is comic about the speech nor what its larger role or significance is. The debate has also been hampered by an implicit fallacy of false dilemma: either the speech is comic – an *ad hominem* interlude that can be safely ignored – or it is serious – the sober pronouncements of an exemplary physician that demand our attention. I impose some structure on the debate (1) by formulating the different senses in which the speech may be considered serious; (2) by examining which senses of serious are compatible with comedy; (3) by establishing criteria for what would count as comic; and (4) by articulating a philosophical justification for the use of comedy. In my view, the reason that Eryximachus' speech has been

[1] Edelstein 1945. See e.g. Gildersleeve 1887, 1888; Bury 1909; Robin 1929; Wilamovitz 1929; and Friedlander 1930. Taylor 1926 was an exception to this trend.

[2] The most prominent rehabilitators are Konstan and Young-Bruehl 1982; Rowe 1999; McPherran 2006. For an opposing view, see Levin 2009.

the subject of so much disagreement is that it plays two distinct roles in the dialogue: it is intended by Plato both to advance the level of discourse on *erōs* beyond what is presented by the previous two speakers and to expose Eryximachus – and indeed medicine in general – as a pretender to philosophical wisdom.

1. The Facts: A Brief Overview of the Eryximachus Scene (185e6–189c1)

I want to begin by providing a short summary and outline of the Eryximachus scene, which I take to encompass the speech itself (185e6–188e4) and the two brief conversations with Aristophanes that surround it (185c4–e5; 188e4–189c1). I divide the speech itself into the following sections:

1. The scope of Love (185e6–186b2)
2. Medicine and the nature of Love (186b2–e3)
3. Love and the other crafts (186e4–188d3)
   a. Music (187a1–e6)
   b. Astronomy (188a1–b6)
   c. Divination (188b6–d3)
4. Conclusion (188d4–e4)

In the first interlude (185c4–e5), it is Aristophanes' turn to speak but, since he has an attack of the hiccups, he asks Eryximachus "either [to] take his turn or [to] cure him" (185d2–3). Eryximachus advises Aristophanes to try three remedies (holding his breath, gargling and sneezing) and gives his own speech on love.

In Part 1 (185e6–186b2), Eryximachus takes over Pausanias' idea that there are two kinds of love – a good or noble kind of love and a bad or base kind of love. However, he criticizes the narrowness of Pausanias' speech in focusing on human desire and greatly expands the scope of love to encompass animals, plants, and indeed everything in the universe, including "both human and divine matters" (186b2).[3]

In Part 2 (186b2–e3), Eryximachus uses the case of the human body to explicate the nature of love and its relation to knowledge or science. The view about love consists of the following claims:[4]

[3] Translations are from Nehamas and Woodruff 1989, with some minor corrections.

[4] While McPherran 2006: 75 repeats Rowe's formulation of the main points of this section (1999: 56), I have chosen to make a fresh start, mainly because I think that Rowe (and thus McPherran) leave

(1) "The nature (*phusis*) of bodies is such that they contain a double love" (186b4)
(2) Healthy and diseased bodies are different and "desire and love (*epithumei kai erai*) different things" (186b4–7)
(3) Thus, healthy [good] love and diseased [bad] love are different (186b7–8).
(4) "It is noble and necessary to gratify the good and healthy love in each body, and it is shameful to gratify and necessary to frustrate the bad and diseased love" (186c2–4)
(5) "Medicine is. . .the science of the loves [desires] of the body for repletion and depletion" (186c5–7)
(6) The doctor's task is "to diagnose healthy and unhealthy love" and most importantly, "to transform diseased loves [desires] into healthy ones, to implant healthy love [desire] where it is absent and remove diseased love [desire] where it is present" (186c7–d5)
(7) "For (*gar*) it is necessary [for the doctor] to be able to make the most hostile things in the body friends (*phila*) and to make them love one another (*eran allēlōn*)" (186d5–6)
(8) These "most hostile things are what are most opposite, like hot and cold, bitter and sweet, wet and dry, and all other such things" (186d6–e1)
(9) "Asclepius, the founding father of medicine, established science when he first learned how to implant concord and love (*erōta* . . . *kai homonoian*) among such opposites" (186e1–2)

Since it is a matter of some interpretive controversy regarding how exactly to take these claims, I offer them here only as "the facts" and I will hold off addressing interpretive questions for now. The core question is whether and how they can be understood as comprising a coherent view, since (2) to (6) seem to conceptualize love in terms of an agent's *desire*, while (7) to (9) seem to conceptualize love in terms of *friendship*, or concord, between opposites.

In Part 3 (186e4–188d3), the longest part of the speech, Eryximachus elaborates his view, showing the role and power of love in other areas (gymnastics, farming, music, astronomy and divination), subject to the relevant science and known by the relevant practitioner.

Eryximachus begins by providing an analysis of music (187a1–e6). Critically appropriating a fragment of Heraclitus, he claims that, "from a prior discord between high and low, a later agreement is established by the

out of their summaries what I take to be a central claim, what I label as (5). My inclusion of this point is not really an interpretive issue, since it is directly stated in the text, but it bears on interpretive issues, as I will later show.

musical science" (187a8–b2), and that this agreement is what "harmony" is (187b4); similarly, from a prior discord of fast and slow, a later agreement is established, and this is rhythm (187b7–c2). Music "implants concord and love for one another" in these opposites (187c3–4), such that "music is the science of loves concerning harmony and rhythm" (187c4–5). Though there is no double love in the structure of music, it does exist in the effects of music on its audience, that is, in education, or *paideia* (187c5–d4). Eryximachus claims that, with such music, "it is necessary to gratify orderly humans (in such a way that those who are not yet orderly are likely to become more orderly) and to preserve the [good] love of these men" (187d4–7). Love for the music of the "noble, heavenly Muse" must be protected, whereas the music of the "common, vulgar Muse" must be used only with great caution (187d7–e3).

Reiterating that love is found in "all areas" (187e8) and requires a knowledgeable practitioner to tend to it, Eryximachus extends his analysis to astronomy (188a1–b6), claiming that the "seasons of the year" are also comprised of opposites – hot and cold, wet and dry– and that when these are controlled by "orderly love, they possess harmony and a temperate mixture" (188a1–5); when this happens, the weather is mild, there is a good crop yield, all living things thrive, and nothing is harmed (*adikēsen*). However, when the "hubristic love" is in control, the opposites are "greedy and disorderly toward each other" (188b3–4), and this leads to "much destruction and harm" (188a7–b3). Eryximachus ends by defining "astronomy" as "the science of the loves concerning the movements of the stars and the seasons of the year" (188b4–6).

Eryximachus gives a brief account of divination (188b6–d3), which he defines as "the craftsman of friendship (*philias*) between gods and humans through its knowledge of the human loves which concern divine law (*themin*) and piety" (188c7–d3).

In Part 4 (188d4–e2), Eryximachus completes his speech, emphasizing the "great power of love" especially when "directed, in temperance and justice, toward goods, whether in heaven or on earth: happiness and good fortune, the bonds of human society, concord with the gods above are all among his gifts" (188d4–9).

In the second interlude (188e2–189c1), Aristophanes, whose hiccups have been cured, claims that it required sneezing, and playfully mocks Eryximachus' speech by suggesting that the successful use of the sneeze treatment seems to undermine the idea that love involves a kind of harmony or concord. Eryximachus warns Aristophanes not to make himself vulnerable to similar mockery, and the latter retracts his joke.

2. Symptoms of the Serious Eryximachus

The arguments for taking Eryximachus and his speech seriously revolve around roughly five claims, which I will assess in this section. Eryximachus is thought to be a serious figure in five senses: he is important, self-aware, authoritative, coherent and insightful. If he is indeed aptly described as such, then we should certainly pay attention to what he says.

(a) Important

Eryximachus is said to be a serious figure in that he plays an important role in the proceedings of the symposium.[5] He serves as *symposiarch*, sending away the flute-girl, proposing that they converse instead, and suggesting the topic of Love on Phaedrus' behalf (176d–177e); either Eryximachus (189a–c, 193d, 194a, 198a–b) or Phaedrus is addressed in between the speeches, confirming his role in the proceedings; his expertise as a doctor is acknowledged by the others (176d, 185d, 189a, 214b); and he persuades Alcibiades to give a speech in praise of Socrates, instead of allowing the party to descend immediately into drunken revelry (214a–c).

It is undeniable that Eryximachus plays an important role in the events of the dialogue and that his status as doctor gives him a certain standing within the group. That said, being important to the proceedings and having a certain standing within the group hardly rule out his being self-important and thus subject to comic ridicule.[6] For example, Protagoras and Callicles are clearly portrayed as important in these senses, and this does not rule out their being subject to derision and ridicule. Indeed, it would seem odd for Plato to subject to ridicule someone who was not taken to be important.

(b) Self-aware

Second, Eryximachus is described as employing "self-conscious humour" (Rowe 1999: 62); "as entering into the general light-hearted sympotic spirit of things by speaking as bombastically as he does" (McPherran 2006: 77);[7] and the speech is described as being "fanciful and whimsical," "meant to

[5] Edelstein 1945: 94–7; Rowe 1998: 147; McPherran 2006: 72.

[6] Dover, e.g., recognizes both that Eryximachus acts as *symposiarch* (1980: 11) and that the speech is meant to ridicule him (1980: 105)

[7] See also Taylor 1926: 217.

amuse himself" (Edelstein 1945: 88) and "festive and self-knowing in its overfullness" (Hunter 2004: 54). At least three pieces of evidence have been adduced in this regard: the ideas that the farmer and trainer are guided by *Love* (186e);[8] the analysis of musical education (187c–d),[9] and Eryximachus' mild reaction to Aristophanes' mocking him (189a–b).[10] The idea here seems to be that, in these comic moments, Eryximachus is self-aware and being funny on purpose.

The claim that Eryximachus is good-humored and self-aware is a bit trickier to deal with, since this strategy seeks to turn any potentially comic moments at his expense into evidence against his ridiculousness. Once Eryximachus is let in on the joke, the joke cannot be at his expense.[11] If, as I have argued elsewhere, self-ignorance is at the core of the ridiculous and central to Plato's characterization of certain figures as imposters, then it will be difficult for Eryximachus both to be self-aware and a subject for ridicule.[12] It is much harder to sort the evidence on this question, since much of it depends on reading the tone of the Greek: for example, whereas Dover reads Eryximachus' response to Aristophanes' mocking as "authoritarian" (1980, *ad loc.*), Edelstein sees it as "sarcasm" (1945: 89). Are the mention of farming and gymnastics meant to be tongue-in-cheek, or are they signs of his ridiculous overreach? I will address these questions directly later in the paper.

(c) *Authoritative*

Eryximachus' speech exemplifies the medical thinking of the period, as can be attested by the numerous resonances with the Hippocratic corpus.[13] His speech is thus "serious" in the sense of being authoritative within the domain of medicine and an accurate or honest representation of the medical literature. This is not to say that the literature is uniform, or taken to be uniform by Plato – indeed some of the authors are debating each other about core issues in medicine. However, as many scholars have noted, the speech resonates with many passages from the medical literature. To give an exhaustive list would be tedious and unnecessary, but here is a partial list:

[8] Edelstein 1945: 88. [9] Rowe 1999: 60–2. [10] Edelstein 1945: 89.

[11] Both Hunter (2004: 54) and McPherran (2006: 76–7) affirm both that the speech is a parody and that Eryximachus is self-consciously being bombastic, but neither explains how exactly that is supposed to work. I will address this kind of position later in the chapter.

[12] See Trivigno 2012; Trivigno 2016, and my discussion below.

[13] Edelstein 1945: 85–7, 90–1; Craik 2001; McPherran 2006: 76–7; Levin 2009; Hunter 2004: 54–7.

Theme	Text
Healthy vs. diseased appetites	*De vetere medicina* 20
Epistemic priority of medicine	*De victu* 1.3–10; *De flatibus* 1–5, *De vetere medicina* 20
"Emptying" and "filling"	*De flatibus* 1, *De natura hominis* 9, *De victu* 1.2
Opposites, hot and cold, wet and dry	*De vetere medicina* 14, 16, *De victu* 1.4, 11
Presocratics, esp. Heraclitus	*De vetere medicina* 20, *De victu* 1.5, 11, *De alimento*
Musical harmony	*De victu* 1.8, 18
Cooking as a *technē*	*De victu* 1.18
Concern with climate and health	*De aeribus aquis locis, De victu* 1.2

As Hunter notes, "some of the basic ideas of the speech – mixture, the harmonization of opposites, the alternation of excess and deficiency – are among the most staple tropes of medicine" (2004: 56). More broadly, we might say that there is a common commitment to an empirical methodology and a physicalist ontology, that is, to a concern with *physis*, as traditionally conceived. Material, bodily phenomena are basic, and need to be assessed and treated with physical interventions. Any interpretation of the speech must take the fact of the Hippocratic background into account.

Nearly all commentators agree that Eryximachus represents the medical type.[14] But even if Edelstein is right to see Eryximachus as "a historically correct picture of a medical man of that time" (1945: 91), this does not necessarily weigh against seeing him as a target for ridicule. Indeed, if Plato intends to satirize Eryximachus, it is not necessarily (or even likely) out of a particular hostility toward the man but rather to what he represents – that is, medicine as a methodological rival to philosophy. If this is so, then satire or parody would demand that he bear the hallmarks of the medical type.

(d) Coherent

Eryximachus' speech can be understood as presenting a logically consistent and interesting, i.e. serious, position on *erōs*.[15] These defenders of Eryximachus are arguing, in particular, against Dover who charges that Eryximachus "runs together (1) the contrast between good desires or tendencies and bad desires or tendencies and (2) the contrast between

[14] Edelstein 1945: 91; McPherran 2006: 74; Levin 2009: 277.
[15] Konstan and Young-Bruehl 1982; Rowe 1999; McPherran 2006.

the good consequences of reconciling opposites and the bad consequences of failure to reconcile opposites" (1980: *ad loc.*) and those who take the speech (and perhaps all the pre-Socrates speeches) to contain, as it were, the seeds of their own destruction. Konstan and Young-Bruehl were the first to give sustained attention to this problem; on their view, Eryximachus does not conflate two senses of *eros* – he rather makes a distinction between love as "*epithumia* (desire)" and love as "*philia* (concord)" that he holds to consistently throughout his speech (1982: 40). Thus, they disarm Dover's criticism making Eryximachus consistent at that level. Rowe goes further and attributes to Eryximachus "a *single* 'kind of love'" (1999: 56), and interprets possible instances of the second kind, that is, love as friendship, in terms of the first, that is, love as desire (1999: 58).

Pace Konstan and Young-Bruehl, who claim that their "analysis of Eryximachus' argument points to a degree of systematic exposition and intellectual rigor in the speech that is incompatible with sheer parody" (1982: 40), I do not think that the consistency of Eryximachus' conception of love would by itself provide any general evidence against reading the speech as satirical or parodic. Even granting its consistency, one might still locate the parody elsewhere, that is to say, one might see its comic features emerge in other aspects or parts of the speech. Of course, one way to present the speech as parodic or to satire Eryximachus might be to give him a speech that was internally inconsistent or logically incoherent, but this is surely not the only way. One can have a coherent but *false* and even positively pernicious view, and that could form the basis for the parody or satire.

(e) Insightful

Last, Eryximachus' speech is a clear advance on the previous speeches and anticipates at least some of Diotima's claims. McPherran makes the most of such resonances, claiming that Eryximachus formulates "a Platonically-acceptable theory of physical Nature," agrees that "true physicians must be philosophers" (2006: 80) and himself represents or at least prefigures Plato's "ideal physician" (2006: 93). This is the strongest claim of seriousness, since the claim is that what Eryximachus presents is true, or at least thought to be true by Plato.

Even if the speech is an advance on the previous ones and there are resonances with what Diotima says, this does not imply that Plato does not take a critical stance towards the speech nor that he does not wish to portray Eryximachus as foolish. If the speech is, for example, superior to those of Pausanias and Phaedrus, this is still consistent with Plato rejecting it. That said, if it turns out that the position advocated by

Eryximachus is *true*, then this will be hard to square with the interpretation of the speech as comic. I will return to this issue at the end of the chapter.

All of the preceding senses of "serious" attributed to Eryximachus or his speech –important, self-aware, authoritative, coherent and insightful – are meant to imply that his speech is serious in the sense of "worthy of interpretive attention." There is a kind of argument here: the premises characterize Eryximachus and his speech, and the conclusion concerns how we interpreters should respond. There are two things to notice about this argument: first, were its premises all true, Eryximachus would be wholly unique amongst interlocutors in having so high a standing in the dialogue – indeed, he would be a rival, in Plato's eyes, to Socrates. Second, it seems to rely on an unstated assumption that, if Eryximachus and his speech were comic, they would be unworthy of interpretive attention. In my view, the speech may be worthy of interpretive attention *precisely because* it shows him and medicine to be, in some sense, ridiculous. We are thus not required to regard the speech merely as a "comic interlude" (2006: 72),[16] since I think that properly understanding the comedy will be seriously informative, that is, it will give some content to a philosophically inspired criticism of medicine. Thus, to see comedy in the speech is not simply to "dismiss" it as philosophically uninteresting.

To sum up, the one sense of "serious" that is potentially inconsistent with the idea of comic presentation – serious as in self-aware – already takes comic content for granted, since it is in light of his alleged joking that Eryximachus is claimed to be self-aware. The only kind of seriousness that seems to rule out entirely treating the speech as comic is the strongest formulation of serious as insightful, that is, the claim that the speech is simply true. Thus, most of the claims to seriousness are actually compatible with the idea that Eryximachus is ridiculous and that his speech is comic. In the next section, I will set out some principles whereby one can determine whether and in what sense Eryximachus' speech may be comic.

3. Definitions and Methodological Considerations

Before assessing the evidence, I think it prudent to provide some working definitions, so that it is clear what I mean when I use terms like satire and parody, and to make some methodological remarks about how to go

[16] Cf. Levin 2009: 275–6.

about identifying these in the context of a Platonic dialogue. I propose the following:

> *Satire*, primarily aimed at persons, involves the use of humor, irony, exaggeration, or ridicule to expose and criticize a character's stupidity or vices.
> *Parody*, primarily aimed at texts, methodologies, or genres, involves the use of a distorted imitation that exaggerates some feature that is prominent in the original, often in order to undermine a text, methodology or genre's claim to authority.

The question of whether Plato is employing comic devices cannot be made to hang on whether or not we twenty-first-century scholars laugh at or are amused by the relevant text. Much of the debate currently seems to be stuck at the level of the interpreter's subjective reactions, but these cannot be taken as decisive evidence for Plato's intentions. However, at least three kinds of independent evidence may be adduced: first, we may look to Old and Middle Comedy to see whether some figure or device can be seen as the historical antecedent. This would provide some evidence that Plato's audience would have experienced the figure or trope as comic. Second, we may seek some philosophical grounds for understanding how Plato might have viewed his own use of comedy. This would provide some principled way of determining whether comedy would be the appropriate idiom. Last, we may seek to see whether there are some signals in the text that might suggest a comic context. This would help to provide some evidence that Plato's audience would have been prepared to experience the figure or trope as comic.

In *The Origin of Attic Comedy*, Francis Cornford mentions the doctor, or physician, as an instance of the comic imposter, or *alazōn*, a standard figure from Old Comedy, and the imposter motif may be considered a form of *satire*. The imposter is, in general, a pretender to certain advantages whom the comedy regards as a kind of parasite (Cornford 1961: 122).[17] This general figure of the imposter has a professorial variety, what Cornford calls the "Learned Doctor," which encompasses intellectuals of all stripes, including poets, sophists, mathematicians, doctors and philosophers, etc. and of which Socrates in the *Clouds* is a prime example.[18] The figure has some generic features: he proclaims himself to be wise; is self-important and pedantic, using specialized or technical jargon;

[17] See also MacDowell 1990; Diggle 2004. Cf. Arist. *EN* 1108a20–22; 1127a13–b32; *EE* 1124a24–25; Theophr. *Char.* 23; pseudo-Pl. *Def.* 416a10–11.

[18] For an account of the different imposter types, see Cornford 1961: 134–46.

and he aims at earning money; but his knowledge is exposed as fraudulent or useless. Though we only have two brief references to doctors in Aristophanes – *Birds* l. 584 and *Wealth* ll. 407–9 – in which doctors are treated as imposters seeking to get rich, we know of two Middle Comedies entitled *Iatros*, or *The Doctor* (by Antiphanes and Aristophon), and we have a fragmentary scene from Alexis (fr.142). In addition, we know of two New Comedies, entitled *The Doctor* (by Philemon and Theophilus), and there is a doctor scene in Menander's *The Shield* (*Aspis*). The tradition continues into Roman Comedy: Plautus wrote a lost play called *Parasitus Medicus*, or *The Parasite Doctor*, and there is an extended doctor scene in his *The Brothers Menaechmus* (ll. 889–956). So it is safe to say that the doctor is a stock figure from comedy, and there is a tradition within the comedy of Plato's time of portraying the doctor as a self-important, pedantic quack. If Eryximachus is portrayed in ways that evoke the stock figure, then we will be on secure historical grounds in thinking of him as comic.

As to philosophical grounds for the use of comedy, Plato gives us, in the *Philebus*, some resources for what his practice of comedy might look like. There, Socrates defines *to geloion*, the "laughable," as a lack of self-knowledge, most commonly instantiated as a pretension to virtue and wisdom (48c–e). As I have argued elsewhere, this account is amenable to the comic practice of portraying certain characters as imposters, though there will of course be some differences.[19] In Plato, we should expect to find comic devices aimed at those figures and methodologies that lay claim to moral or epistemic authority and expertise. Indeed, we might expect certain figures to be representatives of methodological rivals to philosophy that purport to have a universal scope and a systematic content, i.e. offer some rival vision of the whole. Thus, if we have grounds to think that Plato regarded his character, Eryximachus, as a self-ignorant pretender to wisdom, the latter will, by this standard, be both laughable and the proper subject for a comedy, and it would then be proper for us to take him as such. Further, if we take him to be ridiculed qua representative of medicine, then we will be justified in seeing Plato making a critical point against medicine's methodology or epistemic ambition.

The last methodological point concerns the presence or absence of certain cues indicating to the reader that a comic figure or scene is occurring or about to occur. It would seem peculiar of Plato as a writer to insert something comic into his text without signaling it in some way.

[19] See Trivigno 2012; Trivigno 2016.

The absence of such cues would make it difficult for readers to understand that they should expect something comic and thus would seem to provide fairly strong evidence against taking a scene or figure to be comic. Therefore, if we find that there are cues indicating a comic context, then we will at least be on safer grounds in regarding Eryximachus and his speech as comic.

4. Symptoms of the Comic Eryximachus

In this section, I will focus primarily on the Eryximachus scene, but I will also touch on at least some of the other scenes in which Eryximachus speaks. I proceed by first considering whether there are comic cues from the context indicating that we should take his speech as parodic. Then I will examine the speech itself to see whether it is plausible to attribute to its speaker the features of the comic imposter. Last, I will consider whether we have reason to think that Plato regarded his character, Eryximachus, as a self-ignorant pretender to wisdom.

4.1. Comic Context

I have included the two brief conversations with Aristophanes that surround the speech (185c4–e5; 188e4–189c1) in my account of the Eryximachus scene because it is in these passages, if anywhere, that we should look for comic cues. Many commentators have noticed these scenes and provided some interpretation of them, but, for the most part, they have been used to say something about either Aristophanes or Plato's self-conscious ordering of the speeches. But few commentators have seen them as significantly bearing on the speech of Eryximachus.

The mere presence of Aristophanes, the master of Old Comedy, in these scenes might be enough to signal a comic context. But the scenes themselves are also comic in nature: in the first, Aristophanes is portrayed as having the hiccups, and Apollodorus speculates that he might have "stuffed himself again" (185c6); in the latter, Aristophanes is found making a joke and laughing. Further, the scenes are comic in ways that essentially involve Eryximachus. In the first, he is called upon as the expert on bodily conditions to provide a medical remedy for the hiccups. This might involve a pun on his name: "Eryximachus" literally means "fighter of belching." Eryximachus provides three remedies, holding one's breath, gargling and sneezing, and we may detect some self-importance in the doctor's suggestion that the hiccups might be "extremely severe" (185e1, e3).[20] The second comic scene is clearly at the expense of Eryximachus: Aristophanes wryly remarks, "It makes me wonder whether the 'orderly sort of Love' in the body calls for the sounds and itchings that constitute a sneeze, because the hiccups stopped immediately when I applied the Sneeze treatment" (189a3–6). Hunter rightly points out that we are meant to "sympathize with Aristophanes' evident amusement" (2004: 54). Eryximachus warns Aristophanes that the former "may be forced to be on his guard lest [Aristophanes] say something funny" (189a8–b2). Aristophanes laughs at this and rescinds his joke, but clarifies that saying something "funny (*geloia*)" would not be a problem – he is a comedian after all – so much as saying something "ridiculous (*katagelasta*)" (189b6–7). While Aristophanes certainly has his own speech in mind, a possible implication here is the thought that Eryximachus' speech was ridiculous, and, indeed, that Aristophanes' own joke was funny precisely because what Eryximachus said was ridiculous.

In these two scenes, Eryximachus plays the straight man to Aristophanes' more comic figure, but the joke is, in the end, at the straight man's expense. I should also like to point out one final contextual consideration: during the course of Eryximachus' speech, we are to imagine that Aristophanes is in the background hiccupping for much of it, trying to hold his breath for some time until he breaks out into hiccups again, then trying to gargle for some time until he breaks out into hiccups again, until he finally sneezes. We have every reason to think that this is happening during the speech and, since Aristophanes clearly knows what Eryximachus said, there is no reason to think that Aristophanes has retired elsewhere to do so.

4.2. *Eryximachus as Imposter*

The generic features of the medical imposter are the following: (a) he represents himself as possessing wisdom; (b) he is pedantic, using specialized and technical medical jargon; and (c) he primarily aims at earning money; but (d) his medical knowledge or wisdom is exposed as fraudulent or useless. Since there is no trace of the third feature (c) here in the *Symposium*, I will set it aside.

[20] See Dover 1966: *ad loc.*

(a) Self-representation as Wise

It is, of course, no surprise that Eryximachus thinks of himself as possessing knowledge, since he is a doctor. Whenever he appears in the dialogue, either he or someone else makes reference to his medical expertise, and his own speech makes repeated reference to medicine. Not only do we find many references to his discipline, Eryximachus regards the knowledge one gains "from medicine" (186a7) as providing a paradigm for understanding the entire universe.[21] That is, Eryximachus takes himself to have an understanding of universal relevance, one that ranges over "both human and divine matters" (186b2; cp. 187e). The other forms of knowledge he mentions, gymnastics, farming, music, astronomy and divination, already cover a very wide range: the human body, the earth, music and education, the heavens and the gods.[22] He thinks of medicine as a supreme knowledge, a kind of higher order *technē* that provides the standard for the other sciences. Those others, modeled on medicine, are said to consist in the knowledge of effects of love concerning the relevant opposites and to share a common methodology, namely, establishing the right kind of love and effecting a harmony between the opposites. Eryximachus' knowledge of the human body and its physical processes puts him, he thinks, in a unique epistemic position that enables him to see all this.

In short, Eryximachus thinks that to possess medical knowledge makes him, not merely a doctor, but a wise man who possesses a knowledge of universal scope, systematic content, and consistent methodology. He sets himself apart and above, not only poets like Agathon and Aristophanes, but natural philosophers like Heraclitus. Eryximachus ends his speech by claiming "not to have omitted anything willingly" (188e1–2) and even Edelstein admits that claim "betray[s] [Eryximachus'] belief in his own wisdom and superiority" (1945: 91).

(b) Technical and Pedantic Use of Language

Eryximachus uses quite a bit medical and technical jargon: as we saw, he twice refers to the hiccups as potentially "extremely severe" (185e1, e3), and he continues his repetitive technical ways in the opening of the speech, using knowledge, or knowledge words, an astonishing number of times. He uses "medicine (*iatros*)" and cognates no fewer than six times within a

[21] Robin writes, "La médecine est....l'art des arts, celui qui donne le secret de tous les autres" (1929: LII).

[22] Edelstein acknowledges that the scope claim seems to indicate "a rather ludicrous pride in the importance of the medical art" (1945: 89), and McPherran points to this aspect of the speech as clearly parody (2006: 76–7).

single Stephanus (186a7, b3, c3, c5, d1, e3). If this were not sufficient for comic accumulation – a classic strategy for parody – then, in addition, he employs other knowledge-words an additional eight times over that same span (186b1, b3, c5, c6, c7, d4, d5, e1). Eryximachus is also made to use the rare superlative adjectival form, *iatrikōtatos*, meaning "most doctorly" (186d1).

Given the list of parallels to the Hippocratic corpus I gave earlier, it is clear that the speech is full of medical jargon and terminology: "emptying and filling," "opposites," "hot and cold," "wet and dry," etc. He may be showing off in his technical uses of musical terminology in his definitions of "harmony" and "rhythm" and of meteorological phenomena, with his reference to "both frost and hail and blights" (188b3).

In addition, we have Eryximachus' interpretation of Heraclitus's aphorism (187a–c), "being at variance with itself is in agreement with itself like the attunement of a bow or a lyre," which quarrels with the details of formulation in a way pretty nearly universally acknowledged to rely on an incorrect reading. The doctor treats Heraclitus pedantically, as though the latter needed a wise doctor to express himself, claiming that Heraclitus' "mode of expression certainly leaves much to be desired" (187a4) and that, taken at face value, the claim is "patently absurd" (187a6–7). Eryximachus reveals his lack of understanding of the philosophical point of the saying, never mind the enigmatic nature of Heraclitean aphorisms. His insistent insertion of "later" and "prior" (187b1; cf. 187c1) to modify pre-harmonic states and emphasize the asynchronic nature of the phenomenon are ham-handed and clearly *mal apropos.*[23]

(d) Knowledge and/or Wisdom Exposed as Useless and/or Fraudulent

Before elaborating on this feature of the imposter, it will be worthwhile to pause and to make two important distinctions: first, between Eryximachus' (I) knowledge of medicine, narrowly speaking, and (II) his alleged wisdom, that is, his knowledge beyond medicine, and second, between (1) exposing someone's knowledge as useless and (2) exposing it as fraudulent, or nonexistent. To anticipate, on my reading, Eryximachus' medical knowledge is exposed as useless *in a certain sense* (I–1), and his alleged wisdom is exposed as fraudulent (II–2). There are two moments in the dialogue

[23] Nehamas and Woodruff 1989: *ad loc.* Rowe acknowledges that the interpretation is flawed, but thinks that Eryximachus is being tongue-in-cheek (1999: 62 n. 34). See the extensive discussion of this passage in Levin 2009: 290–8.

when the *value* of Eryximachus' medical knowledge is called into question: at the very beginning of the dialogue and in the middle of his speech.

When we first see Eryximachus in the dialogue, he is giving advice based on his medical knowledge: he says, "If one thing is absolutely clear from medicine, it is this, that inebriation is bad for everyone" (177c8–d2). It is worth noting that nearly everyone at the party, including Eryximachus, engaged in heavy drinking the night before, and what explains their refraining this evening is not Eryximachus' medical advice, nor even the fact that the lot of them are hung over – it is, rather, the fact that Agathon "is not up to drinking heavily" (177b6–8). Eryximachus proclaims this to be "a lucky stroke (*Hermaion*)!" for the light drinkers, including himself and Phaedrus (176c1–2). Further, after Eryximachus declares drinking to be bad, he continues: "I myself would never wish—if I could help it anyway—to drink heavily, nor would I advise another to do so, especially when one has a hangover" (176d2–4). Eryximachus thus admits that he doesn't always take his own advice, and, as we know, most of the participants, including Agathon and Socrates, do drink heavily after the arrival of Alcibiades. Last, Eryximachus also mentions that Socrates, who is immune to the effects of alcohol, is an exception to his proclamations on drinking (176c3–5), and this suggests that medical advice, dedicated as it is to the maintenance of the body, is useless for a philosopher.

It is in light of this passage and its implications that we should understand the force of Eryximachus' discussion of "a serious issue" in medicine, one that is parallel to the difficulty of "enjoying the pleasures of the vulgar Muse" without "slipping into debauchery" (187e2–3). This issue is, in Eryximachus' own words, "how properly to manage the desires related to the craft of fine cooking (*tais peri tēn opsopoiikēn technēn epithumiais*), so that one may enjoy its pleasure without becoming ill" (187e4–6). There are several things to notice here: first, this is the only practical medical issue he raises in his speech, and it seems rather trivial, especially when compared with the grand claims about education, astronomy and divination that surround it;[24] second, this may be another implicit pun on the name of Eryximachus; third, it continues the tendency in the speech to pile up knowledge-terms and it seems pompous to refer to "prepared food" via such an elaborate locution; fourth, classifying cooking as a *technē*, at

[24] This is not to deny that nutrition formed an important part of medicine as conceived by fifth- and fourth-century practitioners. But cf. the critical remarks about this aspect of medicine in *Rep.* 406c–408b.

best, reveals an unreflective epistemology;[25] fifth, and perhaps most significantly, it suggests that the medical art is really about *bodily pleasure* – the focus on filling and emptying in the speech seems to confirm this (cp. the accounts of pleasure in the *Gorgias* and *Philebus*), and one might further add that his advice on drinking earlier in the dialogue resulted in each person drinking "as much as he wants" (176e5) or "according to pleasure (*pros hēdonēn*)" (176e3). Thus, in raising this issue, Eryximachus seems unwittingly to undermine the value of his medical knowledge.

It is not, then, that Plato wants to deny that Eryximachus has medical knowledge. Indeed, he does manage to cure Aristophanes' hiccups, though the disjunctive nature of the prescription perhaps suggests that medicine lacks precision.[26] The core point is that this knowledge is only useful for one who cares about the body and filling and emptying it.[27] From the philosopher's perspective, these are trivial concerns – in the *Symposium*, Socrates is presented as perfectly indifferent to whether he abstains from drinking or drinks heavily, whether he enjoys a big feast or does not eat for days, whether he has weather-appropriate clothing and shoes or not, whether he sleeps or does not sleep. What possible use could Eryximachus' advice be for him? This is, of course, a modification of Old Comedy's use of imposter motif, which takes the common man as its standard, but one would not expect Plato to slavishly follow Aristophanes.

4.3. *Eryximachus' Speech as a Parody of Medical Discourse*

If the preceding is correct, then it already provides a good deal of evidence in favor of taking the speech as a parody. Recall that parody, as I defined it, targets "a text, methodology or genre." In this case, it seems clear that the medical texts of the Hippocratic corpus are a relevant target, along with the methodology that they seem to endorse, and the genre of medical display speeches, of which some of the Hippocratic texts are arguably examples.[28] The proponents of the serious approach have done all of the work in finding the relevant Hippocratic texts, such that it would be hard to deny

[25] See Levin 2009: 299–301. In the *Gorgias*, fine cooking is classified quite emphatically as an *empeiria* and not a *technē* (462d–e).

[26] Cf. *Phil.*, in which medicine, along with music, is classified as an *empeiria* (55e–56b).

[27] Cf. *Rep.*, in which certain applications of medicine are associated with "excessive care of the body" (407b5–6).

[28] Jouanna 1984; Hunter 2004: 53–4; McPherran 2006: 76–7. Hunter makes "the medical profession and its theorizing" (2004: 54) the target of the parody, while McPherran identifies it as "high-flying medical rhetoric" (2006: 76–7).

that the speech is an imitation of them. I would like to pick out two ways in which the parody amplifies, goes beyond, or exceeds its target and what kind of criticism we might discern from the parody. To anticipate, I suggest that the parody targets medical methodology, insofar as it purports to a more general relevance, that is, to have implications beyond medicine, narrowly construed. In short, the parody focuses its critique on the alleged *scope* of medical knowledge.

First, what I describe previously as Eryximachus' pedantic use of language functions also, within the speech, as a parodic accumulation. Such linguistic accumulations are often employed to reveal that the target discourse is nothing but the repetition of high-flown terminology. Eryximachus is demanding by repetition, precisely what the arguments of the Hippocratic *De Arte* try to accomplish, namely that the status of *technē* be firmly established for medicine, but his repetitions extend well beyond references to medicine, and indeed, there are knowledge terms all over the place. The parodic point seems to be – not that medicine is not really a kind of knowledge – but rather that medicine thinks it contains more knowledge than it really does. Indeed, Eryximachus goes beyond what actual medical authors seemed to want to claim. We might, in particular, pick out *De Victu* 1.11–24 as being especially genial in this regard, since it too foregrounds medicine as a preeminent *technē* with special insight into the other crafts: "[T]hough the crafts they employ are like the nature of the human being, they do not know it" (I.11).[29] Since medicine knows the nature of the human being, it better understands those other crafts: divination, iron-work, shoemaking, carpentry, building, music, cooking, basket-weaving, etc. The basic strategy of Eryximachus is the same as the author of *De Victu* in that medicine possesses a structural insight that gives it a special epistemic status. However, Eryximachus goes beyond *De Victu*'s author in the case of music and divination, and with the inclusion of astronomy. The Hippocratic author restricted himself, in the first case, to the sounds made by musical instruments (I.18), and in the second, to forms of divination that do not involve the gods (I.12). Eryximachus extends his analyses to include both musical education and "friendship between gods and humans" (188d1),[30] and he includes astronomy, which seems

[29] Translations of the Hippocratic texts are from the Loeb editions with some emendations: Jones 1923 and 1931.

[30] There may be historical irony at work in Eryximachus' inclusion of divination: Eryximachus was denounced as having taken part in the mutilation of the herms (Andocides, *On the Mysteries* 1.35), that is, the defacement of the faces (Thuc. 6.27) and genitals (Ar. *Ly.* 1093–4) of the statues of

to lack a practical function – how can one "doctor" the heavens? Thus, he extends his epistemic authority even further, making the Hippocratic author look modest by comparison.

Second, connected to medicine's epistemic authority is a methodological focus on bodies and an ontological point about the priority of bodies, or physical nature. Connected to this is an understanding of human nature in terms of the human body. The fundamental point is that medicine emerges as a rival to philosophy both on the nature of the whole and on the nature of human being. One might recall here the passage in the *Phaedrus* in which understanding the body is made dependent on understanding the whole (270c). As I understand that claim, it is meant to subordinate medicine to philosophy. Consider *De vetere medicina*'s take on debates within medicine:

> [My] view is, first, that all that philosophers or physicians have said or written on natural science no more pertains to medicine than to painting. I also hold that clear knowledge about natural science can be acquired from medicine and from no other source, and that one can attain this knowledge when medicine itself has been properly comprehended, but till then it is quite impossible – I mean to possess this information, what man is, by what causes he is made, and similar points accurately. (20.1–14)

Like Eryximachus, the Hippocratic author seeks to displace philosophy as the proper route to understanding human nature and sets up medicine as the appropriate methodology for investigation into nature in general. Eryximachus goes even further than the ambitions voiced here and in *De Victu*, since he wants his epistemic authority to encompass the gods as well. That is, this Hippocratic author wants to restrict investigation into those physical matters that may affect humans – the scope here is limited, whereas that of Eryximachus seems unlimited. Eryximachus' move amplifies the actual epistemic ambitions of medicine into a domain that seems virtually impossible for the empirical medical methodology (and physicalist ontology) to get a foothold.

I would like to end this section by reflecting on how Aristophanes' comment on Eryximachus' speech seems to confirm my reading. To repeat, Aristophanes said, "It makes me wonder whether the 'orderly sort of Love' in the body calls for the sounds and itchings that constitute a sneeze, because the hiccups stopped immediately when I applied the Sneeze

Hermes in the city. Plato's audience would likely have been aware of this and perhaps found his remarks evocative. That Plato has Eryximachus exclaim "*Hermaion*!" (176c1) earlier in the dialogue may serve to confirm this line of thinking.

treatment" (189a3–6). The violent and disorderly cure for the hiccups stand as a counterexample to Eryximachus' grand theory – who better than Aristophanes to deliver a mundane yet fatal blow to the epistemic pretensions of the doctor? It is as though Aristophanes said, "Your remedy works, dear doctor, but it shows that your theorizing is bullshit."

4.4 A Diagnosis

If the preceding analyses are on target, then we have seen sufficient number of symptoms that we may diagnose Eryximachus with self-ignorant foolishness. He has craft-knowledge, and indeed, he may even be good at it, but he greatly overvalues his own knowledge both by thinking it to be more important than it actually is and by thinking it gives him a grander insight into, or vision of, the whole. He suffers from the same flaw as those craftsmen described in the *Apology*: "each of them, because of his success at his craft, thought himself very wise in other more important pursuits, and the error of this overshadowed the wisdom that he had" (22d6–8). Eryximachus' encomium to Love turns out to be an encomium to medicine, and thus an encomium to himself.[31] Thus, I think it is safe to conclude that Plato regarded his character, Eryximachus, as a self-ignorant pretender to wisdom, who is both laughable and the proper subject for a comedy. Given that Eryximachus is a representative of certain medical theorists of his time, the criticism seems to hold of a certain type who believes that medicine holds the key to wisdom. Part of the point seems to be to show that the ambitions of medicine's empirical methodology in understanding the whole – including human nature – are misguided. Thus, Plato is serious about making Eryximachus ridiculous, since he embodies a seriously ridiculous flaw, self-ignorance, that is characteristic of practitioners of medicine at the time. We should pay attention to Eryximachus and his speech because it is comic and has comic content not in spite of its being comic.

One might object that I have not adduced decisive textual evidence against the reading of Eryximachus as *self-aware* and intentionally comic. This objection accepts that the speech is comic but insists that Eryximachus is its "author" not its target; in short, it denies that Eryximachus is an imposter but accepts that the speech is a parody. Indeed, even on my view, Eryximachus lacks one hallmark of the imposter, namely, the concern to make money. Nevertheless, I think the weight of the evidence as I have

[31] Cf. Hunter 2004: 56.

presented it seems to be squarely in favor of the thesis that Eryximachus is an unintentionally, rather than intentionally, comic figure. That said, even if I conceded, for the sake of argument, that Eryximachus delivers the parody of medical discourse willfully, as it were, the core philosophical upshot of my position remains, since the speech still functions as critique of the epistemic ambitions of medicine.

5. Conclusion: Eryximachus, Diotima and the Order of the Speeches

In this conclusion, I want very briefly to situate Eryximachus' speech in relation to the order of the speeches, and to Diotima's speech in particular. Here, I come back to the questions of whether Eryximachus' speech contradicts itself in its presentation of love and whether it formulates a Platonically acceptable theory of Nature, that is, to what extent the speech really is *coherent* and *insightful*.

It is clear that Eryximachus' speech is an advance on those of Pausanias and Phaedrus. Their focus on individual love between humans seems to correlate with the initial rung on the ladder – "one body" – whereas Eryximachus' generalizing move seems to get us to the next step: "all bodies" (210a–b).[32] Further, Eryximachus' emphasis on "knowledge" is an advance on Pausanias' reliance on "custom" – this is also verified by the ordering of the ladder of love (210c–d). This is not necessarily to "place" Eryximachus anywhere on the ladder, but rather to show that his concerns are appropriate to a higher rung than those of his predecessors.

It seems equally clear that Eryximachus' speech is not to be taken as seriously as those of Aristophanes and Agathon. Socrates provides a direct refutation of Agathon and an indirect one (via Diotima) of Aristophanes, but he provides no such attention to Eryximachus.[33] One way to see the dialectic between the speeches of Eryximachus, Aristophanes and Agathon is as follows: whereas Eryximachus makes love do double duty, both as the thing wanting (the desire) and the thing wanted (the aim), Aristophanes restricts love to the thing wanting (the desire), while Agathon makes love the thing wanted (the aim). Aristophanes and Agathon both see that these must be separated, and while Aristophanes is right about the desire but

[32] Cf. McPherran 2006: 74.

[33] Socrates does say that Eryximachus "competed well" (194a1–2), but this can hardly mean that he made true claims, as McPherran seems to want (2006: 77 n. 17), since he is even more effusive about Agathon's speech (198a6, b2–3) before very quickly exposing it as incoherent. It does mean, as Edelstein rightly points out, that the doctor's speech was not the worst (1945: 94).

wrong about the aim and Agathon is right about the aim but wrong about the desire, it seems that Eryximachus is wrong about both. This way of looking at the progression lends some support to the idea that Eryximachus is (wrongly) conflating or confusing the aim and the desire in his account of love. Thus, in my view, despite the ingenious reconstructions provided by Konstan and Young-Bruehl and by Rowe, Dover's criticism of incoherence still stands.[34]

We might say that the problem is precisely that Eryximachus remains stuck at the level of the body. He begins with *phusis*, and his analysis cannot escape the parameters set by this. It is thus highly unclear how to fit Eryximachus' passing mention of the soul at the beginning (186a) and brief talk of virtue, happiness and goods at the end (188d) into the physicalist framework he articulates. The medical writers do not deny the existence of soul but rather give it a physical basis: in *De Victu* I.7, for example, it is claimed that "soul consists in a blend of fire and water" (cp. I.25). It is hard to see how Eryximachus would avoid some such account of soul, and thus it is hard to see how Plato could endorse this view of nature. McPherran, who sees the view of nature as Platonically acceptable, admits that the picture is physicalist (2006: 87), but he cannot have it both ways. If physicalist reading of the speech is correct, then Eryximachus would be wholly concerned with bodies and what Diotima derides as "mortal nonsense" (211e3). I am therefore inclined to accept the opinion of Gildersleeve, who considered the idea of identifying Eryximachus with Plato himself to be "as monstrous a theory in [his] eyes, as if Shakespeare had been supposed to identify himself with Malvolio" (1909: 110).

[34] Konstan and Young-Bruehl do not provide compelling evidence to indicate that Eryximachus *self-consciously* marks the distinction between the two kinds of love. Rowe's solution involves attributing love (desire) exclusively to the opposites (1999: 56–7), a move that ignores 186c5–7, where Eryximachus quite directly attributes them to the body – this is what I label as (5) above, and given the centrality of the claim –it is the definition of medicine – it is hard to see how one gets around it.

CHAPTER 4

Aristophanic Tragedy

Suzanne Obdrzalek

1. Introduction

At the close of the *Symposium*, we are left with a striking image. All the other symposiasts have departed or fallen asleep, and only three are left, Agathon, Aristophanes and Socrates, seated side by side, drinking wine from a common cup, while Socrates attempts to prove to the comic poet and the tragedian that the truly skillful dramatist should be a master of both arts. The reader cannot help but wonder what we are to make of this stricture – should it somehow inform how we read the speeches of both playwrights? In fact, Aristophanes frames his speech on both ends with warnings not to take it as pure comedy (189b3–7, 193b6–7, 193d7–8). Of course, foreswearing comic intent is a standard trick in the comic's arsenal; Aristophanes' speech, with its grotesque depictions of the various transmogrifications of the human body, is not without comic appeal. But in this chapter, I want to suggest that we take Aristophanes' warnings seriously, that beneath its comic veneer lies an account of the human condition that is both tragic and philosophically rich.[1]

The significance of Aristophanes' speech to the dialogue is highlighted by various means. In the first place, given that the *Symposium* self-consciously emphasizes the ordering of its speeches, Aristophanes' merits attention due to his disruptive role. When it is his turn to speak, Aristophanes is overcome by the hiccups, and Eryximachus is forced to take his place;

[1] In claiming that Aristophanes' speech is tragic, I do not mean to suggest that it belongs to the genre, tragedy. Indeed, following Dover 1966: 41–5 and Kurke 2011: 310–11, I believe that, stylistically, its greatest affinities lie with fable. Rather, I mean that it is tragic in a broad sense – it portrays us as unable to achieve happiness due to our lacking understanding of our own natures and the nature of happiness. In attributing this broad sense of the tragic to Plato, I follow Halliwell 1996 and Trivigno 2009: 93. I also do not mean to deny the extent to which Aristophanes' speech is comic. Though Aristophanes' speech is not stylistically linked to his comedies, it is deeply humorous, particularly in how it reduces the romantic pretensions of love and sex to a series of grotesque bodily contortions. In calling Aristophanes' speech tragic, my intention is to highlight the fact that its core message is pessimistic, a fact that is typically overlooked by interpreters.

as a result, he is placed in a triumvirate with Agathon and Socrates. This grouping is mirrored at the close of the dialogue, when Aristophanes, Agathon and Socrates are left drinking together, replicating the order of their speeches, and suggesting that they should be understood in relation to one another. The significance of Aristophanes' speech is further emphasized by various anachronistic cross-references that Plato establishes between his speech and Socrates'. In his speech, Aristophanes compares the condition of his divided humans to that of the Arcadians (193a2–3); this comparison is jarring because it refers to the events of 385 BC, whereas the dramatic date of the dialogue is 416 BC, thirty-one years earlier. One might dismiss this as a mere slip on Plato's part, were it not for the fact that Diotima is said to be a woman of Mantinea, one of the Arcadian cities divided by the Spartans. Diotima, in turn, famously makes a further anachronistic reference when she opposes Aristophanes' account of love, though, supposedly, her speech was delivered to Socrates before the actual symposium (205d10–206a1). All these details suggest that Plato wishes to emphasize that Aristophanes' speech stands in a crucial relation to Socrates'.

Modern responses to Aristophanes' speech tend to fall into two groups. According to the first, Aristophanes' speech contains nothing of philosophical significance; according to the second, Aristophanes' speech alone proposes an appealing, and even true account of love. On behalf of the first camp, Guthrie, for example, refers to the speech as "comic burlesque" (1975: 384); Taylor describes it as a piece of Pantagruelism, its purposes solely humorous and dramatic (1936: 209, 219); and, more recently, Rowe has suggested that it is meant as an "imaginative but otherwise useless aetiology of sexual intercourse" (1998: 9).[2] To turn to the second camp, though Nussbaum acknowledges the pessimism of Aristophanes' speech, she also claims that it is unique in emphasizing the significance of human individuals as love-objects to be valued for their own sakes (1986: 173–4). Against these two interpretive strategies, I want to advance two claims. Against the first, I shall argue that Aristophanes' speech is of the utmost philosophical significance to the dialogue. In his speech, he sets forth a view of *erōs* as a state of lack and a corresponding desire for completion, which is the starting-point for Diotima's subsequent analysis. Against the second, I shall propose that Aristophanes' speech contains a pessimistic account of love. *Erōs*, for Aristophanes, is not the appreciation of another person as a unique and irreplaceable individual; rather, it is an irrational urge, incapable of satisfaction.

[2] See also Destrée 2015: 364–5 and Hunter 2004: 70.

In the first part of my chapter, I shall offer a close reading of the initial physical transformations undergone by Aristophanes' humans. I shall argue that these offer an account of human nature as incomplete, an account that is later adopted by Socrates. In the second part of my chapter, I shall examine the various solutions Aristophanes considers for the human predicament. I shall argue that within Aristophanes' speech, Plato subtly indicates that these are all futile.[3] In the third part of my chapter, I shall ask what, non-metaphorically, is Plato's objection to the pursuit of wholeness through union with one's other half. I shall argue that the problem with Aristophanic love is that it is irrational. It is this very irrationality that precludes Aristophanes' lovers from achieving the partial satisfaction of erotic desire that is open to their Socratic counterparts.

2. Aristophanes on Human Nature

To turn to Aristophanes' speech, he begins by observing that humans did not always possess their current form (189d5–190b5). There were originally three kinds of humans: male-male, female-female and male-female composites. These proto-humans were round in shape, resembling two persons joined at the midline. They had two arms, two legs and one set of sex organs on each side. Their two faces, the same in every way, were adorned with four ears, and faced opposite directions on a common head, placed on a rounded neck. Possessed of great pride and ambition, these men attempted to scale the heavens in order to attack the gods (190b5–c1). The Olympians were hard-pressed to find a solution; they could not let this threat go unchecked, but, being dependent upon human worship, the gods could not afford to kill their would-be usurpers. At last, Zeus found an ingenious solution. He would split the humans in half, thereby disabling their strength, while increasing his number of worshippers. Having

[3] In what follows, I argue that Plato views Aristophanic *erōs* as problematic. Though he presents some of his concerns directly, placing them in Diotima's mouth, he presents others indirectly, weaving them into the details of Aristophanes' speech. Before I proceed, it will be helpful to clarify why I believe that Plato adopts this second, indirect, strategy. To answer this, we should ask ourselves what we are to make of the argumentative structure of the *Symposium* as a whole. Suppose that Plato most fully endorses Socrates' speech. In that case, what are we to make of his inclusion of the other speeches? Like many interpreters, I believe the reason Plato includes the earlier speeches is twofold: on the one hand, he wants to present a variety of commonly held views about love, while on the other, he wants to critique certain aspects of these views. Were this an ordinary Socratic dialogue, this critique would be enacted via the *elenchos*, and, indeed, Agathon's speech, coming directly before Socrates', is subject to elenctic cross-examination. But given the sympotic setting, direct cross-examination is not an option for the others. Instead, Plato inserts subtle markers into the speeches themselves, as well as into the dialogue as a whole, to indicate his objections.

sliced them in half, Zeus commanded Apollo to bunch their skin together to form a navel and to turn their heads to face their scars (190c1–191a5).

Deprived of their original other halves, the half-men would weave their limbs together, and, unable to eat or drink, would soon perish. Taking pity on their pathetic state, Zeus came up with a new plan. He ordered Apollo to relocate their genitals to the fronts of their bodies so that they might have intercourse. If the embrace happened between a man and a woman, they would have offspring, while if it occurred between two men, they would have the satisfaction of intercourse, and could cease embracing and look after their other needs (191b5–c8).

As each of us is the matching half of a human whole, our desire for partners of the same or opposite sex can be explained by the nature of our original whole (191d3–192a2). When humans find their matching halves, they are struck from their senses with a feeling of belonging. Though they finish their lives together, none is able to say what he wants from the other. However, should Hephaestus offer to weld them together, none would refuse. He would achieve what he had always wanted, to melt with his other half and become one (192b5–e9). The name given to this longing is *erōs*. Should we be friendly to *Erōs*, eventually he may restore us; should we quarrel with him, we risk being split in half again (192e10–193b6).

The first thing to observe about Aristophanes' speech is that it opens with an analysis of human nature; its analysis of *erōs* emerges from and is dependent on this account of human nature. Throughout the speech, we see a contrast developed between two senses of human nature: our ancient nature, which represents a state of wholeness to aspire to, and our current nature, one that is debilitated as a result of the transformations we have undergone. What, then, was our ancient nature, the nature of the original circle-men? Three things are striking. First, Aristophanes emphasizes their circularity: they are round, their back and ribs form a circle, they move by rolling, their round shape resembles their heavenly parents and so forth. Second, Aristophanes highlights their complete symmetry: every bodily part is mirrored across the circle-men's axis; their faces are identical; indeed, the only difference between the two halves is their genitalia, and this difference only holds for the hermaphroditic pairs. Third, their primary characteristic is that they are strong, outwardly directed and ambitious.

What about our current nature? Where the circle-men were strong and ambitious, our central characteristic, according to this myth, is that we are weak. Their circularity signified a kind of perfection and self-containment: they were round because they resembled their parents, who were heavenly bodies; in the *Timaeus* Plato states that the sphere is the most perfect shape (33b1–7). By contrast, we are circles that are thwarted, cut in two. In his speech, Aristophanes compares our state to that of a sliced egg (190e1–2); this image is poignant, suggesting that our genesis from the circle-men is a sort of perverse anti-birth at the hands of the gods. The portrayal of the gods in the myth is not flattering either. Where Diotima portrays them as self-sufficient and free of desires (202c6–d5), Aristophanes' deities are dependent on human acknowledgment (190c3–5). Their treatment of humans, in turn, is far from philanthropic. Ironically, it is Apollo, the god of healing, who twists our heads so that we are made forever aware of the wound inflicted on us by the gods (190e2–191a5). It should be noted that there was no physical necessity for our heads to be turned towards our scars; in fact, if our heads had been left facing outward, then it would have been unnecessary to later move our genitals. It appears that Apollo's primary motive is spite, and that Aristophanes' intention is to draw attention to the bleakness of our current condition.

The pessimism of Aristophanes' account comes to a cusp at 191a5–b5, where he describes how the half-men intertwine themselves and, unwilling to detach, waste away. One detail is striking: when the now half-humans weave themselves together, they embrace, face-to-face. But this is no replica of their original condition. Their original condition was outward-facing; they now turn inwards. This physical disanalogy mirrors the complete transformation of their natures: the circle-men were outwardly directed, bold and ambitious; the half-men are inwardly directed, sickly and inactive. This inversion also suggests that the half-men may not even be trying to regain their original nature. Aristophanes writes that their longing for their original nature caused them to interweave their limbs in a debilitating embrace. But if they wished to resume the closest proxy to their original condition, they should stand back-to-back, facing outwards, ready to take on the world. In turning inwards, the half-men respond to their yearning for wholeness not by trying to replicate the state of wholeness, but by turning away from the world and losing themselves in the embrace. In fact, it is not even clear that it is their unique other halves that they seek to embrace. Aristophanes write that if one half dies before the other, the survivor will find another with whom to enmesh himself; his language even implies an indiscriminateness of sexual orientation – "whether the half was from a whole woman . . . or a man" (191b3–5). The humans do not appear to seek their unique other halves; instead, they stumble from one partner to the next, pursuing any embrace that will blunt their sense of longing.

Let us pause and take stock. What is Aristophanes' view of human nature? Our central feature is that we are incomplete; this gives rise to the desire for completion. The desire for completion, in turn, causes us to seek to embrace another – either as a futile means to regaining our original state or as an attempt to forget our yearning for completion. Human nature and the *erōs* it gives rise to are centrally characterized through imagery of sickness; Aristophanes later writes that *erōs* is inborn in man, trying to heal human nature (191c8–d3).

Aristophanes' characterization of human nature, though dark, is psychologically compelling. Many people are subject at times to an inchoate sense of lack. This can give rise to a search for meaning, which many individuals make one of their central life-projects. Though this might take the form of religious devotion, altruistic endeavors or intellectual exploration, for many, the search for meaning is expressed in the attempt to find someone to love. We are so much in the grips of an Aristophanic way of thinking about love, that the expression "my other half" is commonly used to denote one's spouse, and popular fiction and film depict true love as encountering the one person who is, as it were, made for you. The sense that there is another person who is uniquely suited to you, and who could make you complete, is ubiquitous.

This account of human nature as incomplete, and of *erōs* as the desire for completion, stands at the heart of Socrates' speech. In questioning Agathon, Socrates' central point is that *erōs* is a desire, and hence must be the desire for something, specifically for what the lover lacks (200e8–9). Socrates further develops this characterization of *erōs* as grounded in incompleteness when he presents *Erōs* as a spirit and not a god, precisely because *Erōs* does not possess, but desires, the beautiful and the good (202d1–e1).[4] Socrates goes on to maintain that *erōs*, understood as the desire for the beautiful and the good, characterizes all humans (205a5–7); if this desire is grounded in lack, then the implication is that human nature is, at its core, incomplete. In what follows, Socrates gives a more rigorous presentation of the source of our incompleteness. According to Socrates, humans are in a constant state of decay; nothing about us is stable, from our physical constitution to our beliefs. As a result, we are incapable of true immortality, but must seek a mortal proxy thereof, through reproduction. It is this constant perishing which gives rise to *erōs*, the desire to surmount

[4] This is further reflected in the myth of Poros and Penia (203b1–204b7), where, in naming Penia, poverty, *Erōs*' mother, Socrates emphasizes its origins in need, and where he describes *Erōs* as poor, homeless and needy.

our mortality via reproduction (207c9–208b6). Significantly, in this context, Socrates, echoing Aristophanes, refers to *erōs* as a sickness (207a7–b1). Socrates' analysis of the human sense of lack is more fully worked out than Aristophanes'; rather than relying on myth, he points to a specific feature of human nature, mortality, which is its source. However, the insight is the same, that *erōs* arises from a sense of lack endemic to human nature.

3. Aristophanes' Pessimism

According to my interpretation, Aristophanes' speech is fundamentally tragic. However, if our sense of incompleteness can be surmounted, if *erōs* can, in fact, make us whole again, then it would turn out to be optimistic. In the next section of my chapter, I shall turn to the two solutions to *erōs* that Aristophanes considers, sex and union with one's other half. I shall argue that Plato subtly indicates that neither of these is satisfactory, either because they do not offer us true completion, or because what they aim at is impossible.

Let us begin with Aristophanes' presentation of sex. According to Aristophanes, when Zeus saw us wasting away, he moved our genitals to the fronts of our bodies so that we would be capable of interior reproduction and, as a result, of detaching from one another (191b5–c8). The details of our physical transformations merit closer scrutiny. Why, exactly, does Zeus need to relocate our genitals to the fronts of our bodies? If the need is for our heads and genitals to face the same direction, then an alternative would have been for Zeus to untwist our heads back to their original orientation; he does not do so because of the need for us to remain aware of our wounded natures. Perhaps if we were not aware of our wounded state, we would cease to feel incomplete and hence to waste away. But this gives rise to a further question: why do our genitals need to be relocated for us to be capable of intercourse? We can find an answer to this question if we look more closely at Aristophanes' language. He writes that Zeus moved our genitals "so that at the same as the interweaving embrace (*en tēi sumplokēi*), if a man happened upon a woman, they would have intercourse and the race would be reproduced, while if a man happened upon a man, they might have the satisfaction of intercourse" (191c4–7). Intercourse occurs at the same time as the *sumplokē*, the interweaving embrace. In the preceding passage, the humans died because, throwing their arms around one another and interweaving themselves (*sumplekomenoi allēlois*), they would not abandon one another (191a5–b1). Thus, the reason the humans' genitals have to be relocated to the fronts of their bodies is that they are not willing to abandon the face-to-face embrace in order to copulate; Zeus therefore has to make it possible for them to copulate within this embrace. Intercourse functions as a continuation of the embrace, but in such a manner that we are able to subsequently abandon it. But if the embrace does not, in fact, recreate our original position, then neither does intercourse.

The way in which Aristophanes presents sex is disconcerting; he writes that it enabled the humans to "stop embracing and turn to their work and look after the rest of their lives" (191c7–8). Sex does not resolve their sense of incompleteness by making them one. Rather, it enables them to stop caring that they are incomplete so that they can let go of one another and get on with their lives. It represents a palliative and not a cure. But it is not even certain that this palliative will succeed. Aristophanes writes, "Whenever the lover of boys or anyone else meets his other half, then they are wondrously struck from their senses by affection, love and belonging, not wishing to be apart from one another for even a moment" (192b5–c2). So it turns out that we are back to where we started – what we really want is to be united with our other halves, and once we achieve this, we will not willingly detach. Aristophanes raises the supposed solution of sex to show that it is a non-starter. People in the grips of *erōs* do typically long for sex with their beloveds, as though this would offer them true union; what Aristophanes reveals is that this gets them nowhere. In the imagery of his myth, when the halves engage in intercourse, they remain inwardly directed inversions of their original selves; more fundamentally, they remain insurmountably separate – though they become physically closer, they still do not become one. Aristophanes goes on to explicitly reject intercourse as the object of *erōs*: "no one would think that the union of sex is [what the lovers desire]" (192c4–5).[5]

[5] Hooper argues for an opposing interpretation, on which Aristophanes' point is that sex is indeed the solution to *erōs*, since it enables us to temporarily lose the absurd desire for unity (2013: 577–9). Against Hooper, if Aristophanes did take sex to be the solution to *erōs*, precisely because it enables us to lose the desire for unity, then it is unlikely that, immediately after discussing sex, he would go on to state that sex is not what the lovers truly want (192c4–7), to define *erōs* as the pursuit of wholeness (192e10–193a1), and to conclude with a rousing call to worship the gods in order that they may someday reunite us (193a7–d5). Perhaps one might maintain that even if Aristophanes does not consider sex a solution, he ought to. If sex can temporarily dampen our longing for unity, then so much the better. While I am sympathetic to this position, I do not take it to constitute an argument against my reading of Aristophanes' speech, but rather an argument against the speech, as I have interpreted it. It is also worth noting that this objection accepts Aristophanes' diagnosis of our predicament, but proposes that, since it is insoluble, we are best off distracting ourselves. But if his diagnosis of our predicament is correct, then perhaps there is something worthwhile in facing it head-on, even if this results in a sense of dissatisfaction.

What, then, is the object of *erōs*? Complete union with the beloved. However, the details of his story create significant doubts as to whether this is achievable.[6] In the first place, it is not clear how we might go about finding our other halves. How would we even know what they look like? In his myth, Aristophanes specifies that the heads are positioned in opposite directions on a joint neck (190a1–2); they are therefore physically incapable of seeing one another. Perhaps we could recognize our other halves because they would possess features we lack. However, in his myth, Aristophanes lays great emphasis on the complete symmetricality of the two halves. His use of the image of the tally (*sumbolon*, 191d3–4) suggests that they might recognize one another by some brute physical fit. But the image of the egg cut by a hair (190e1–2) pulls us in the opposite direction, suggesting that the cut is smooth, not jagged. At any rate, Apollo has so reworked our bodies that there is no hope of preserving an original cut line, nor, for that matter, of recognizing one's original other half in his mutilated descendent. Even if we could find our other halves, it is uncertain whether we could become whole. Our bodies have been so mutilated that it is not clear that we could ever resume our original configuration. Non-metaphorically, Aristophanes' suggestion is that even if there is one person in the universe who can complete you, it is not clear how you would go about finding this person, nor how you could become unified with him.

Suppose, though, that we could achieve full unification with our other halves – would this be a desirable outcome? On the one hand, insofar as *erōs* is the desire to become complete, and insofar as we believe that this can only be achieved by union with another person, then it does seem that the fullest expression of this would be to be completely conjoined with that other person. But this solution is, at the same time, horrifying. And Aristophanes deliberately presents this solution as problematic. It is Hephaestus who offers to weld us (192d3). Lest we miss the mythical reference, in the very next speech, Agathon refers to the tale of Hephaestus punishing Aphrodite and Ares by ensnaring them in the midst of their embrace, forcing them to remain entwined for all the gods to see (196d1–2). Complete union with the beloved might, in some sense, represent the culmination of erotic longing, but even imagining this state reveals that it is far from desirable; this suggests that the longing of *erōs* cannot be resolved by romantic love of another individual.

[6] See also Benardete 1993: 51-5 and Nussbaum 1986: 174–6.

4. Plato's Critique of Aristophanes

Thus far, I have made the case that Plato subtly indicates that the proposed solutions to *erōs* – intercourse and union with the beloved – are unsatisfactory. In the next section of my chapter, I would like to raise the following question: what philosophical issue does Plato have with Aristophanes' treatment of love? My response will proceed in two stages. In the first, I will argue that Plato objects to Aristophanes because Aristophanes treats human nature and *erōs* as irrational. In the second, I will argue that Plato objects to Aristophanes because he assigns the wrong object to *erōs* – union with a human beloved, rather than contemplation of Forms. These are not unconnected: since Aristophanes' circle-men are irrational, it is impossible for them to transform their love of persons into love of Forms.

Let us begin with Aristophanes' portrayal of human nature and *erōs* as irrational. Dramatically, this irrationality is first presented in the person of Aristophanes. He is depicted as someone who is unable to speak due to a ridiculous and involuntary bodily convulsion, the hiccups. At the conclusion of Socrates' speech, Aristophanes attempts to respond, but is again prevented from speaking due to the noisiness of the incoming revelers (212c4–7). Just as Aristophanes is rendered mute, so are his half-men. They are not presented as speaking; this speechlessness is reflective of a deeper ignorance – they do not know what they want.[7] When they first meet, the halves are described as struck from their senses (*ekplēttontai*, 192b5–c1). Though they finish their lives together, they cannot say what they want from one another (192c2–4). They do not wish for sex, but for something else, but are unable to say what it is (192c4–d2). When Hephaestus asks them what they desire, they are dumbstruck (*aporountas*, 192d2–5). Aristophanes repeats three times between 192c and 192e that the lovers are unable to say what they want and, in the end, it is Hephaestus who supplies the answer for them – union with their other halves (192d5).

[7] The one exception to this is 192c7–d2, where Plato writes, "But the soul of each clearly wishes for something else, but is not able to say what, but it has a dim presentiment of what it wishes for and *ainittetai*." *Ainittetai* is standardly translated as "talks in riddles" (Rowe 1998; see also Nehamas and Woodruff 1989, and Howatson and Sheffield 2008). However, as Dover notes, it can also mean to express oneself elusively or incompletely (1980: 119). To talk in riddles would suggest that Aristophanes' half-men know what they want but conceal it, a possibility ruled out by Plato's repeated statements that they cannot say what they want. At any rate, for my purposes, the significant point is that they appear to be speaking incoherently, in a manner that reflects their inability to articulate what they actually want.

But even here, they do not reply; instead, Aristophanes observes to his audience that no one would refuse such an offer (192e5–6).

Thus, the first sense in which Aristophanes' humans are irrational is that they are unable to articulate what they want. Their *erōs* resembles a blind urge or a bodily ache – they engage in semi-purposive activity in order to alleviate it, blundering about in search of a mate, but are not sure what they are pursuing, nor what they will achieve once they secure it. They resemble the animals caught in the grips of *erōs* that Diotima describes at 207b6–c1: whereas humans, she claims, protect their young due to reasoning, in the case of animals, we must seek another explanation, their instinctual drive for reproductive immortality.

Now it is clear that Aristophanes' humans do have a goal that they pursue: reunification with their other halves. But even if they were able to articulate this goal, there would remain a further source of irrationality: they fail to connect it to the good. This causes Diotima to object:

> There is a certain story according to which lovers are those who seek their other halves. But my story says that *erōs* is not of the half or the whole, unless, my friend, it turns out to be good. For men are even willing to cut off their own hands and feet if it seems to them that they are bad. I do not think that anyone cherishes what is his own, unless he calls the good his own and the bad another's. (205d10–206e7)

Diotima's objection is susceptible to two different interpretations. Her objection could be that all *erōs* is of what is in fact good. This interpretation is supported by her initial formulation of the objection: "*erōs* is not of the half or the whole, unless … it turns out to be good." On this interpretation, Diotima's concern is that what Aristophanes' humans desire, their other halves, is not in fact good. In what follows, I will argue that Diotima objects to Aristophanes on precisely these grounds. However, the second half of her objection suggests another interpretation. Here, she focuses on how things appear to the agent: "... men are even willing to cut off their own hands and feet if it seems to them that they are bad." This suggests that, just as it is possible for a man to cut off his limb when it is not in fact sick, but merely seems such to him, so it is possible for someone to love what merely appears good to him. That Diotima takes *erōs* to be of the perceived good is further suggested by her discussion of honor-lovers at 208c2–e1. Here, she observes that we would be astonished by their irrationality if we did not bear in mind "how terribly they are affected by *erōs* for making a name for themselves and for 'laying up immortal glory for all time.'" Given Plato's treatment of honor-lovers in other dialogues, it is doubtful that he takes their goal to be genuinely good; nonetheless, he still treats their desire for glory as *erōs*. On this interpretation, Diotima's issue with Aristophanes is that his portrayal of *erōs* does not make reference to the perceived good of the agent. His humans pursue completion *tout court*, independently of, and indeed lacking any conception of, its connection to the good. Literally, what they desire is to regain their original configuration by being fused with their other halves. But it is not clear why this should offer them completion in any desirable sense: after all, we do not yearn to be reunited with our toenail clippings. Non-metaphorically, what Aristophanes' humans desire is a state of wholeness, where they are unable to articulate what this wholeness would consist in and why it is desirable. In treating *erōs* as a blind urge, one that does not aim at the good, Aristophanes perhaps seeks to build upon popular portrayals of *erōs* as a form of madness, one that is both beyond the reach of reason and, as a result, immune to rational assessment. But it is precisely this portrayal of *erōs* that Diotima rejects, when she treats it as the desire for the good, which ultimately aims at a philosophical grasp of Forms.

Thus far, I have argued that Plato takes issue with Aristophanes' speech because he portrays human nature as irrational, both because his humans cannot articulate what they want and because they are unable to articulate why the sort of completion they pursue is good. The way in which Socrates portrays Diotima functions as a carefully crafted rebuke to Aristophanes' characterization of human nature as irrational. As I noted earlier, Socrates specifies that Diotima is a woman from Mantinea, thereby linking Diotima to Aristophanes' half-men, who have been cut in half like the Arcadians (201d2). But Diotima, though a Mantinean, differs fundamentally from Aristophanes' humans. Where they are mute, she gives the central speech of the dialogue; where they are in a state of *aporia*, she is wise; where they are sick, she is a healer; where they are alienated from the gods, she knows just which sacrifices to make to appease them. In investing Diotima with these attributes, Socrates is suggesting that humans are not as irrational as Aristophanes makes out; our rational capacities, in turn, offer us the hope that our erotic longing can somehow be healed.

To discover how this healing can be effected, we must turn to the second aspect of Plato's critique of Aristophanes: Aristophanes assigns the wrong object to *erōs*. This concern is expressed in Diotima's second, implicit, critique of Aristophanes, when she states:

> There, if anywhere in life . . . should a person live, beholding the beautiful itself. If ever you see it, it won't occur to you to compare it to gold or clothing or beautiful boys or youths who, if you see them now, strike you from your senses, and make you and many others eager to always see and

> be with your beloved, if it were possible, not eating or drinking, but only seeing and being with them. But how would it be if someone got to see the beautiful itself, absolute, pure, unmixed, not polluted by human flesh and colors and any other great mortal nonsense, but if he could see the divine beauty, one in form. (211d1–e4)

Diotima's language here is deliberately reminiscent of Aristophanes'. She refers to boys who strike you from your senses – the same verb, *ekplēttein*, is used by Aristophanes when he writes that, should one find his other half, he would be struck from his senses (192b5–c2). Diotima describes these boys as making you eager to be with them, not eating or drinking; Aristophanes' men die of hunger, because they are not willing to detach (191a5–b1). So Diotima appears to explicitly contrast her solution to *erōs* with Aristophanes'. The central difference lies in its object: Aristophanic love is directed at mere humans, Diotimic love ultimately at Forms.[8]

On a surface level, the difficulty with Aristophanic love is that its aim, complete union with the beloved, is one that cannot possibly be secured. In the language of Aristophanes' myth, this could only ever be achieved by an act of god, by the complete transformation of our physical natures. As things stand, the best we can hope for is to embrace or copulate with a beloved; clearly, this will not make us into one person, nor make us whole. The other person will always remain separate. His thoughts and feelings can never be directly or fully known to you. His experience will always be different from yours. Even if you find your other half, the risk remains that your romance will dissolve or that you will lose your beloved to death. But even if one could achieve full union with the beloved, a further difficulty remains: unless we subscribe to Aristophanes' myth, there is no reason to think that this should offer us completion. For Plato, the sense in which we are incomplete is that we are mortal and imperfect. Romantic union with another does not promise to make us complete in this sense.

But it is not just that romantic love could not possibly make us complete; Plato's doubts run deeper than that. If *erōs* is the desire to be complete, and hence to be a being that is not dependent or lacking in any way, then this desire is surely one that cannot be fully satisfied. In Diotima's speech, Plato suggests that we are beings who are incomplete. We are subject to constant perishing, and cannot achieve the true form of

[8] On my interpretation, Plato holds that Forms are the proper object of *erōs*, that persons are less worthy of love than Forms, and that love of persons that does not give rise to love of Forms is problematic. However, my interpretation does not require that the lover of the ascent cease to love persons altogether upon completing the ascent, nor that he see persons as having no value. For further defense of this intellectualist reading of the ascent, see Obdrzalek 2010.

immortality – everlasting changelessness – which pertains to the gods (207c9–208b6). The closest we can come to possessing the good forever is to grasp a truly good object – the Form of beauty – but this grasp is merely intellectual and does not constitute full possession; it makes us virtuous, but our virtue is a merely mortal form of perfection.[9]

Why should the fact that Diotimic love aims at Forms offer a better solution to *erōs*, conceived of as the desire for completion? Here, we might pause to ask ourselves what a fully complete, non-dependent object would be. Not a human, I have suggested. In fact, such an object would be a Form. Plato describes the Form of beauty as eternally existing, not waxing or waning – it achieves the true immortality which we mimic via reproduction (211a1– b5). The Form is not in relation to anything and not affected by anything – it is without any sources of dependence or deficiency. It exists by itself with itself, one in form and always; surely this is what it would be to be perfect, complete and non-dependent. We cannot ever become such. However, if we spend our lives contemplating such perfect, complete objects, we become as perfect and complete as a human can be. We see this in how Socrates is presented. On the surface, he appears to be erotic: he pretends to be forever in a tizzy over beautiful boys such as Agathon and Alcibiades. However, as Alcibiades notes, Socrates is in fact unaffected by male beauty: he remains utterly impassive when Alcibiades does his best to seduce him. Similarly, Socrates is someone who is beyond being affected by hunger, thirst, cold or fear. Twice in the dialogue, we hear of how he stands, in a state of complete detachment from this world, absorbed in contemplation (175b1–3, 220c3–d5). In a certain sense, Socrates remains erotic – a lover of Forms – but this does not fill him with a sense of dependency and incompleteness. This is what we are offered should we achieve a philosophical grasp of Forms.[10]

[9] In this way, Diotima's speech, as well as Aristophanes', reflects a tragic outlook. (I owe this observation to Franco Trivigno.) However, as I shall argue, Diotima's speech is not as pessimistic as Aristophanes'. While she holds that human nature is not fully perfectible, she does allow that we are rational and that we can achieve a partial form of completion through our (imperfect) relationship to the Forms.

[10] This raises the question of what degree of understanding of the Forms Socrates has achieved. The textual evidence is unclear. On the one hand, in the opening of the dialogue, Socrates describes his wisdom as "inferior and debatable, existing as if in a dream" (175e2–4). But shortly thereafter, he claims that he knows nothing but *ta erōtika* (things concerning love, 177d7–8). Later, though, he declares that he was mistaken to call himself an expert concerning *ta erōtika* (198c5–d3); while his statement appears ironic, it creates further confusion regarding his degree of initiation into *ta erōtika*. Finally, before commencing the ascent, Diotima expresses doubts as to whether Socrates can be initiated into the highest *erōtika* (210a1–2). My sense is that Socrates has achieved at least a partial glimpse of the Forms, but that he is unable to sustain it; Plato therefore portrays him as both

Aristophanes' speech leaves us with the following puzzle: why are the Aristophanic lovers stuck attempting to lose themselves in a destructive embrace, while their Socratic counterparts are able to find at least partial fulfillment through their relationship to the Forms? Both begin by falling for a person, or at least a body; why, then, are only the Socratic lovers able to transcend? The kind of love that Socrates employs as his starting point in the spiritual ascent must be of a very different nature than the love described by Aristophanes. But where exactly does the Aristophanic conception differ from the Socratic?

Here, we should turn to a puzzling feature of Aristophanes' account. Given that he portrays the lovers as seeking their other halves, we might expect him to highlight the differences between them, each possessing unique features that make him the other's complement. Instead, his emphasis is on their complete symmetry: their faces are exactly alike (189e7–190a1), and their bodies identical, with the exception of the genitalia of the hermaphroditic pairs. He compares them to halves of apples and of eggs (190d7–e2).[11] Aristophanes never presents one half as loving another for his virtues or even his quirks – indeed, he never tells us what they love in each other beyond their belonging to one another. This feature of Aristophanes' account, I suggest, follows from his portrayal of his humans as irrational. They pursue completion as such, understanding it in purely physical-historical terms, independently of its connection to the good. But in that case, they cannot be said to love their other half for any of his qualities beyond the fact that he is their other half;[12] they fail to love their other half because his goodness and beauty offer them a path to securing the good. In Diotima's speech, what makes the spiritual ascent possible is that the lover responds to the beauty of his beloved's body. As a result, he is able to generalize – to see that all beautiful bodies are alike, to abstract – to value bodily beauty as such, and to ascend – to respond to other forms of beauty, such as beauty of souls or laws. Aristophanes' lovers, on the other hand, do not respond to the beauty or goodness of their beloveds. It is this feature of Aristophanic love that makes it immune

ignorant and knowldegeable of *ta erōtika*, and as cycling in and out of contemplative trances. Thus, I do not mean to suggest that Socrates has achieved a full and permanent understanding of the Forms; even if he had achieved this, this would not ensure him *eternal* possession of the good. Rather, I take Plato's intention to be to portray the way in which a life spent in even an imperfect relationship to the Forms offers Socrates fulfillment.

11 The one exception to this is 191d3–4, where Aristophanes compares them to tallies.

12 Note that the quality of being one's other half has the peculiar feature that, by definition, it has only one instantiation; it is therefore not susceptible to the generalizing move that we see in the ascent, where one recognizes that the beauty of all bodies is akin and comes to love all beautiful bodies.

to Vlastos' (1981) worry about replaceability, but the flip side is that it ceases to be love of the individual *qua* individual; instead it is just the yearning for wholeness. In the ascent, Socrates' lover starts by gazing upon his beloved and ends up gazing at the Forms. The difficulty with Aristophanes' lovers is that, pressed against one another, their limbs interwoven, they are unable to see one another. Love at its best requires that one recognize the separateness of the beloved so that one can really see him; this is impossible if one is completely preoccupied with one's own incompleteness.

5. Response to Dover and Nussbaum

We are now in a position to see how Dover and Nussbaum have misunderstood the significance of Aristophanes' speech. In his article, "Aristophanes' Speech in Plato's *Symposium*," Dover draws a distinction between sexual desire and preference (1966: 48–9). Sexual desire is a response to objectively desirable qualities. Preference, by contrast, can be felt for someone who is not conspicuous for objectively desirable qualities and is therefore unshaken by the availability of a more objectively desirable partner. According to Dover, the form of *erōs* that Aristophanes describes corresponds to preference, not sexual desire (49). Nussbaum offers a complementary reading of Aristophanes' speech in *The Fragility of Goodness*. She proposes that Aristophanes' speech offers us "much of what Vlastos wanted from an account of love" (1986: 173). Vlastos famously objects to Plato's treatment of love in the *Symposium* because it holds that we love others only insofar as they instantiate valuable properties; as a consequence, it fails to be love of whole persons, and it is subject to the transferability of affection. Nussbaum argues that Aristophanes' speech is intended to function as a counter to Diotima's because its analysis of *erōs* invokes just those features that Vlastos found lacking in Diotima's. Nussbaum maintains that Aristophanes treats love as a response to whole persons, "entire beings, thoroughly embodied, with all their idiosyncrasies, flaws and even faults" (173). Such love is non-transferrable, since "the individual is loved not only as a whole, but also as a unique and irreplaceable whole" (173). Both Dover and Nussbaum treat Aristophanes' model of *erōs* as a more realistic and attractive depiction of interpersonal love than Socrates'.

Before we can consider whether Nussbaum and Dover capture Aristophanes' model of *erōs*, we must first get clear on what model they are attributing to him. Both authors emphasize that Aristophanic *erōs* is not a response to objectively desirable qualities; Nussbaum adds that it is a response to the whole person, including his idiosyncrasies and flaws. On this model, *erōs* is a response to the entire set of qualities that make up the individual, warts and all; this set of qualities is peculiar to the beloved, thereby securing the non-transferability of affection. But this characterization of *erōs* gives rise to the question of what it is about this set of qualities that occasions *erōs*. One compelling response might be that we find this set of qualities to be better than any other that we have encountered. But this would return us to the model of *erōs* as a response to objective value, to which they claim that Aristophanes offers an alternative. But if the lover does not respond to the value of the beloved's set of qualities, then why does he love precisely that person? And can this response even be called love?

Whatever we make of this model of *erōs*, it is not what we are offered in Aristophanes' speech. We do get some version of it in Alcibiades' speech, when he presents Socrates to us in all his idiosyncratic glory – he loves Socrates not just for his wisdom, but also for his slovenliness and his penchant for dowdy examples. Arguably, Plato intends this to show us the risks of Diotima's *scala amoris* – one might become so caught up in an individual in his particularity that one becomes unable to ascend to better examples of beauty. But Aristophanes' speech does not present us with anything along these lines. Where Alcibiades offers us a vivid and poignant depiction of his beloved Socrates, Aristophanes tells us nothing about why the halves are lovable to one another, beyond their role in enabling the return to wholeness. Within the myth, the quality which occasions love is simply the physical-historical quality of being one's other half. When we demythologize Aristophanes, his idea may be that it doesn't really matter what qualities the beloved possesses; it is simply his being designated your beloved that makes him lovable. On the one hand, this does secure us some of what Vlastos was looking for: the other is loved as a concrete particular, and not as a congeries of valuable qualities; furthermore, this love could not possibly be felt for anyone else. But it brings with it attendant moral risks. From Plato's perspective, the risk is that the lover does not even get to the first rung of his ladder of love – he cannot even be said to love a *beautiful* body. From our perspective, there is a concern that this form of love does not involve the recognition of the beloved; it is not a response to "the individual in all the uniqueness and integrity of his or her individuality."[13] Furthermore, far from desiring to benefit the beloved for

[13] Vlastos 1981: 31; cf. Nussbaum 1986: 173–4.

his own sake, the Aristophanic lover treats him as a means to his own pursuit of wholeness. Perhaps one might respond that this complaint is inapt – if Aristophanic lovers truly are halves of the same whole, then they cannot be viewed as using one another in seeking to become reattached.[14] But this brings us to our final concern: insofar as Aristophanes' lovers aim at subsuming their beloveds within themselves, they cannot be said to respect the individuality and autonomy of their beloveds.

6. Conclusion

In this chapter, I have argued for two theses. First, that Aristophanes' speech is of the utmost philosophical significance in relation to Socrates'. Second, that despite its comic veneer, it is fundamentally tragic. In mythic form, it articulates a view of human nature as incomplete. It proposes that this sense of incompleteness lies at the heart of *erōs*. It expresses the common hope that we can achieve completion through interpersonal love. And, finally, it demonstrates the futility of this hope. Thus, on the one hand, it articulates a view of human nature and of the problem posed by *erōs* with which Plato agrees. And on the other hand, Plato uses it to express his view that interpersonal love cannot make us whole, thus opening the way to his proposal that love of Forms alone can offer us a mortal form of completion.[15]

[14] I owe this objection to Rachel Barney and Jennifer Whiting. For an alternate response, see Ludwig 2002: 56.

[15] I would like to express my gratitude to Pierre Destrée and Zina Giannopoulou for inviting me to contribute this chapter, as well as for their hospitality at the workshop they held at the Université Catholique de Louvain. I am also indebted to audiences at Northwestern University, U. C. Berkeley, U.C. Riverside, the University of Toronto, and at the International Plato Symposium in Pisa; to Franco Trivigno and Nick Smith for serving as commentators; and to Yahei Kanayama and Frisbee Sheffield for their written comments.

CHAPTER 5

Divinization

David Sedley

1. Aristophanes' Story of Human Origins

Prominent among the many delights that emerge from Plato's *Symposium* is the raunchily funny speech of Aristophanes,[1] in which the comic poet narrates an aetiological fable to account for the phenomenon of love. First, a very brief summary. Originally, he explains, we were spherical beings. We were equipped with four hands, four legs, two sets of genitals, two faces, and so on. Although we were able to walk upright, we were at our nimblest when we rolled around at high speed, combining the advantages of spherical shape with the use of no fewer than eight limbs to propel ourselves in any direction. We came in three kinds: some were all male, some all female, and some androgynous. The all-male beings were the offspring of the Sun, the all-female ones the offspring of the Earth, and the androgynous ones the offspring of the Moon. And, says Aristophanes, it was from those parents that they inherited their spherical shape (190a–b):[2]

> The reason for their being three in kind, and for what kinds those were, is that the male kind originated as offspring of the Sun, and the female kind as offspring of the Earth, while the kind that shares in both was the offspring of the Moon, because the Moon shares in both. The roundness of both of them and their gait were due to their resemblance to their parents.

We can be reasonably confident that those three cosmic spheres are being viewed as divinities, since the description of living things as their "offspring" implies that they are themselves to be conceived as *living*

I am grateful to Frisbee Sheffield, Robert Wardy and Zina Giannopoulou for helpful comments on a first draft. Naturally they should not be assumed to agree with everything I say.

[1] *Symp.* 189c2–193d5.

[2] They and their parents were alike "round": *stroggulos*, 189e6; *peripherēs*, 190b3. For *stroggulos* used to indicate a "spherical" (not just horizontally "circular") earth in Plato, cf. *Phd.* 97e1. Like English "round," these terms are not limited to spheres, but there can be little doubt that "spherical" is intended here, given that the shape is one shared by Sun, Moon and Earth.

parents, not as inert lumps of matter. This tacit acknowledgement of spherical divinities will prove important later on.

So powerful were those ancestors of ours that they launched an abortive attack on the gods themselves. As a punishment, and to diminish their power, the gods cut them in half, condemning them thereafter to walk upright on two legs, with the added threat (fortunately not yet fulfilled) that if they still did not behave themselves they would be cut in half again, and left to hop around on just one leg. The two-legged beings have never stopped pining for their missing other half, and they have made it their goal to find it and reunite themselves with it. Thus love, both heterosexual and homosexual, originated out of a desire to return to the wholeness of our superior ancestors – to our "original nature" (*archaia phusis*), as Aristophanes repeatedly calls it – by achieving which we can acquire supreme happiness (*megistē eudaimonia*, 189d1, cf. 193c3, d5).

Now the origin of this fable is unknown.[3] It is generally assumed that Plato himself was its inventor, but the alternative possibility has remained that the idea was supplied by the real Aristophanes. The story's brilliance alone cannot settle the authorship, given the equal brilliance of both contenders. Nevertheless, I hope in the course of this study to resolve any doubts, and to assign the authorship confidently to Plato. For it seems to have gone unnoticed that the aetiological fable is a tragi-comic perversion of the creation story told by the eponymous speaker in Plato's *Timaeus*.

The *Timaeus* will play a pivotal role in what follows, and will take up what may seem a disproportionate amount of the space, but for good reasons.

2. Timaeus' Story of Human Origins

In Timaeus' narrative we meet a hierarchy of divinities in which a supreme creator-god brings into being a spherical created-god. Plato's creator-god, the Demiurge or "Craftsman," cannot himself be said to have any geometrical form. He is a pure intelligence who imposes form on pre-existing space or matter, without himself becoming immanent in it. But the god that he creates is, quite simply, the world, bounded by its own outermost envelope, the heaven. And the world is a superlatively good, intelligent and– most relevant to the present context – *spherical* being. This

[3] Aristophanes does in fact claim Homeric authority for it (190b7–8), citing as an actual reference to this episode (see Dover 1980: 115, cf. Rowe 1998: 154) *Odyssey* 11.305–20 on Otus and Ephialtes (explicitly called human at *Iliad* 5.385–91), who piled Ossa on Olympus and Pelion on Ossa in their assault on heaven; but of course none of the details are drawn from Homer or from any other known source.

world-god was the culmination of a long theological tradition. When Plato called it a "happy god" (*Tim.* 34b8–9, quoted in note 22), he was placing himself in line of descent from Empedocles, whose own cosmos undergoes a cycle of change, culminating periodically in a single blissfully happy spherical god, appropriately known as Sphairos.[4]

That tradition itself relied partly on an empirical datum supplied by astronomy, that mathematically speaking the rotation of the fixed stars around us – to all appearances the world's outer envelope – is that of a perfect sphere. What Plato adds to that evidence is four explicit reasons for the spherical shape of this world-god.

(1) Inclusiveness (33b2–4). A world is by its very nature an all-inclusive structure, being a living thing designed to contain all living things. The most appropriate shape for it is therefore the most all-inclusive, the shape that is such as to contain all other shapes. And that shape is the sphere.
(2) The beauty of symmetry (33b5–7). The sphere is the one perfectly symmetrical solid, the shape "most like itself." And the Demiurge took the view that "like is ten thousand times more beautiful than unlike."
(3) Self-sufficiency (33b7–34a7). The complete absence of irregularities at the world's outer boundary, an absence that makes it a perfect sphere, is explained by the lack of need for external limbs or organs. In creating the world-god, the Demiurge had already made the well-reasoned decision to use up all the available matter on a single world, rather than leave any outside it that might later pose a threat (33a), or on whose supply it might depend, thus compromising its total independence (33d). Given too that Plato does not fully distinguish space from matter, it must be assumed that not even any space (as we might conceive it) remained outside. Hence the world, living creature though it was, did not need eyes or ears, there being nothing outside for it to see or hear. Similarly, it had no need of the equivalent of a mouth, or for excretory organs, its entire food supply being internal and endlessly recycled. Nor did it need external limbs to protect it from external threats, because there were none.
(4) Rotation (33d5–34a7). On the one hand the world-god needed to be in motion, above all in order that there should be time, because time is dependent on the regular rotations of the great celestial clock. On the other hand, it was inappropriate for this divine being to have to travel from place to place, so it was not given legs and feet. And,

[4] Empedocles B27–9 DK.

correspondingly, instead of being assigned any of the six varieties of rectilinear motion – motion forward, backwards, leftwards, rightwards, upwards or downwards – it was given the seventh and best kind, rotation. The advantage of rotation was that it can be done on the spot, without going anywhere, and can continue eternally, as a clock should do. Strictly, one might object, the outer part of the world could have rotated on the spot even if it had been, say, cylindrical or conical. But its spherical shape, already fully determined on other grounds, was further confirmed by its simultaneous circular rotations on *two different axes* (34b10–36d7). That is, the world's soul was constructed out of two criss-crossing circles at its periphery, corresponding roughly to the celestial equator and the ecliptic. Setting aside their mathematical details, suffice it to say that the rotation of these two celestial circles accounts both for the main astronomical phenomena, and at the same time for the world-god's thoughts. When we look up at, and come to understand, the mathematically complex rotations around us of the stars, sun, moon and planets, we are quite literally watching the world-god *thinking*. Moreover, the individual heavenly bodies – Sun, Moon, planets and fixed stars – are themselves all spherical divinities, and they are not only carried round the heaven in their daily and annual orbits: each of them, as it does so, also spins perpetually on its own axis (40a–b). One reason for this is that in Plato's view the thinking proper to the intellect concerns eternal entities and eternal truths, and is therefore itself potentially eternal. Only circular motion has the capacity to remain eternally the same. Therefore, the eternal rotations of the numerous heavenly bodies are the visible aspect of their exercise of intelligence. At the geometrical center of the heaven lies the earth, itself a sphere. Plato's hint that it too is in motion (40b–c) probably reflects his assumption that, despite the lack of astronomical evidence, it too *must* rotate in order to be a thinking entity, as its celestial relatives are.

Why then can't we ourselves be spheres, and enjoy that same intellectual fulfilment? In a sense, spheres is just what we are. When the gods created mankind, according to Timaeus, in the first stage of their creation humans were merely heads. The approximately spherical human head, our "most divine" part (44d5), imperfectly mimics the perfectly spherical heaven. It was designed to house the individual human rational soul, itself a less pure version of the divine world soul. Thus, inside our round heads the proper motions of our rational souls, when our intellects are fully functional, is a miniature version of the perfect rotations that the world soul enjoys. To that extent, the intellectually fulfilled human being is, albeit imperfectly, godlike.

In origin or essence, then, we *are* spheres. The reason why we could not retain our simple sphericity is merely practical. As Timaeus carefully explains (44d–45a), a spherical head trying all by itself to roll around from place to place and deal with the necessities of life would have little chance of survival. Once stuck in a hollow, for example, it would never get moving again. So to enable human beings to live a life long enough to bring with it a realistic prospect of intellectual progress, the gods who made us appended a variety of additional equipment: the neck, the trunk, the legs and arms – indeed, a complete transport, nutrition and defence system, corresponding to the very appendages that the world sphere itself had been spared, thanks to its complete self-sufficiency. And this added substructure brought with it a set of new obstacles to the smooth functioning of our brains, above all in the form of bodily appetites, which violently disrupt the intellectual endeavours going on up above in our heads. Hence the task of re-establishing the dominance of the intellect within the human body is a difficult and protracted one, to which only philosophers can aspire. The highest achievement of a human life, Timaeus explains (90a–d), is to succeed in identifying the core of your being with the intellect, located in the head, setting aside the lower psychological drives, housed in the heart and gut. The implicit advice is: stop thinking of yourself as the entire amalgam of body and soul parts; identify yourself instead exclusively with the spherical thinking-hub perched on top of this rather complex vehicle. By doing so, you can concentrate on restoring the circular motions in your head to match those of the world soul, and hope to achieve a truly godlike existence, to the extent that that is possible for a human being (90c, quoted below, p. 100).

3. The Two Stories Compared

In the light of this radical defamiliarisation of the human body, consider the multiple parallelisms between Aristophanes' story about our origins and the Platonic doctrine about those same origins.

According to Plato, human beings originated as imperfect spheres – namely heads. This sphericity was a divine characteristic, thanks to the way the human head imitated the spherical form of the divine and supremely intelligent cosmos itself, a form already shared by all its divine major components: Earth, Sun, Moon, planets and fixed stars. Indeed, it was this spherical shape that made it possible for human beings to think godlike thoughts, and in time to recover their own godlikeness.

According to Aristophanes too, by clear implication, human beings originated as imperfect spheres, although in this case not heads alone but biologically complete organisms. As in the *Timaeus*, this spherical form was implicitly a divine attribute, since it was inherited from all three of their parents, the Sun, Earth and Moon (190b).

Thus, in both stories alike not only is sphericity the divine shape *par excellence*, but human beings, as offshoots of divinity, originally inherited it. Again according to both stories, we have forfeited our divine sphericity. In the *Timaeus*, we have compromised our essential sphericity by having to acquire asymmetric appendages for the sake of survival in the material world, appendages which make it harder for us to use our intellects properly. In Aristophanes' story, we have compromised our sphericity by misusing it in a bid to equal the gods.

Notice how the two parallel aetiologies play off traditional anthropomorphism against the mathematically more rational conception of gods as spherical beings. At 40d5 Timaeus' account of scientific theology – which is tantamount to the mathematics of celestial rotations – comes to an abrupt end, to be followed (40d6–41a3) by a sketchy genealogy of the traditional Greek pantheon, culminating in the births of Zeus, Hera and their siblings, and the offspring of these. Timaeus makes it clear that this is a distinct class of gods, whose reality he endorses by reverentially (and without a trace of the irony often alleged here) respecting the authority of the early theogonic poets regarding their births, even though no scientific account of them is or ever could be available. Thus the scientific theology of intelligent spheres and the traditional myths about more or less anthropomorphic gods sit alongside one another,[5] each finding its own place in the theological hierarchy, although we are left in little doubt as to the greater cosmic significance and intelligibility of the former, spherical pantheon.

In Aristophanes' story, the situation is comically reversed.[6] The gods who exercised their ingenuity to put our unruly ancestors in their place sound like the Olympians of Homer and Hesiod, the all-too-human divine family recalled by Plato elsewhere in his myths, for example in those of the *Gorgias* and *Protagoras*, who in their attempts to regulate the human race are driven sometimes by bafflement (190c), sometimes by pity (191b), and so on. In Aristophanes' story these anthropomorphized gods resemble the mathematically ideal divinities of Timaeus' cosmogony rather less than our own roughly spherical ancestors did.

[5] At 41a3–6 the Demiurge's address is jointly to *both* classes of god.

[6] I owe this point to discussion with Robert Wardy.

And resemblance to the divine is a quintessentially Platonic thread running through the story. Partly by means of this inversion of the divine-human hierarchy, the story told by Aristophanes serves as a subtle reminder that Plato's ideal is always subject to a qualification. To "become like god *to the extent that is possible*" (*homoiōsis theōi kata to dunaton*) is how it is most famously put in the *Theaetetus* (176b1). In the *Timaeus*, the same ideal (to which we will be returning) is expressed by the prediction that if one fosters one's intellect one will, "*to the extent that it is possible for human nature to share in immortality*, in no degree fall short of this" (90c). We must always and inevitably fall short of the divine ideal. Our ancestors forgot this vital qualification, and in their ill-fated assault on Olympus seemed to mistake themselves for the real divinities – perhaps a further distorted anticipation of the *Timaeus*, where the spherical gods of cosmology *are*, at least scientifically, superior to the traditional gods.

Finally, the stories told by Timaeus and Aristophanes run parallel when it comes to the remedy for our loss of divine sphericity. The serious philosophical message of the *Timaeus* is that you can regain your divine rotations of thought by making your head alone – rather than, say, your heart or your stomach – the core of your true being. The comic counterpart of this in Aristophanes' story is that we are all seeking to regain some vestige of our former divine sphericity by coupling in love with our missing other half. And what further links the two stories is that both, using the identical phrase, describe this striving as an attempt to return to our "original nature" (*Tim.* 90d5; *Symp.* 191d1–2, 192e9, 193c5, d4) and thereby to attain the highest form of happiness (*Tim.* 90c5–6; *Symp.* 189d2, 193d5). In the light of the Timaean parallels, we can provisionally conclude that Aristophanes' speech, at least for Platonically informed readers, represents love as the human drive towards godlikeness. To a limited extent, if so, Aristophanes is anticipating Diotima's thesis about love's true nature, namely as an expression of the human desire for immortality. How the two explanations of love nevertheless *differ* is a topic to which I shall turn shortly.

4. Why the *Timaeus*?

Before that, I must reply to an obvious objection. On grounds of both style and content, it is almost universally agreed that the *Timaeus* postdated the *Symposium*, probably by decades. Assuming that near-consensus to be correct, can the *Symposium*'s interpretation have relied on its intertextuality with a work not yet in existence?

The first point to make in response is that Timaeus' speech has a very special place in the Platonic corpus, as the only text to set out what looks like a Platonic *system*.[7] In recent years, many scholars have denied, to a greater or lesser degree, that there is any such system in the corpus: Plato's brilliance, it is suggested, lies partly in the fact that he did no more than portray individual thinkers asking investigative questions, without necessarily committing even them, let alone himself, to any of the specific answers they entertain.[8] Attractive as it is, this characterization seems to me to take inadequate account of the *Timaeus*. In Timaeus' speech many if not most of Plato's major philosophical themes recur, but this time woven together into something that looks like a complete philosophical system.

It is not *quite* as simple as that, because those themes are readdressed here not precisely in the terms employed in the earlier dialogues, but from the point of view of physics and cosmology, the formal topic of Timaeus' speech. Nevertheless, numerous earlier[9] Platonic themes feature in the *Timaeus*, unmistakably as components of a system. I have set these out in an appendix. It is clear from this that Plato, whatever formative stages and changes of mind he may have undergone, did develop a global system, many of whose major components were eventually assembled in the speech put into the mouth of Timaeus.

Given such a premise, we should not be surprised if we find a dialogue likely to predate the *Timaeus*, such as the *Symposium*, presupposing in its readers some degree of knowledge of that system, including components that had not had an explicit airing in any preceding dialogue. These previously unwritten doctrines, even if unfamiliar to Plato's public readership, may well have been already known at least to his inner circle. And it is unsurprising if they prominently included his cosmological doctrines, since in dialogues before the *Timaeus* he had not yet, other than tangentially in the *Phaedo* (96a–99c, 108e–109a),[10] put these in writing.[11]

[7] I am discounting the *Seventh Letter*, whose authenticity has been rightly subject to sustained doubt: see now Burnyeat and Frede 2015.

[8] Varieties of this approach are developed by, for example, most of the contributors to Press 2000, and by Peterson 2011.

[9] I am excluding here the two dialogues we can confidently date after the *Timaeus*, namely *Critias* and *Laws*, but provisionally including late dialogues which may predate it: *Sophist*, *Statesman* and *Philebus*.

[10] To which we might add the *Philebus* (28c–31a) and *Statesman* (269c–274e), if it is assumed that these too predated the *Timaeus*.

[11] For example, at *Phd.* 72a11–d5 Socrates argues for the cyclical reincarnation of souls on the ground that, were dying not reciprocated by a return to life, everything would end up dead. He does not say that everything would *already* be dead, so (a) is not assuming that life on earth has existed from infinite time past, and (b) is rejecting as unacceptable the assumption that at some future time it will

I therefore submit that, despite the probable late date of the *Timaeus*, to assume the presence of some of its theological and cosmological ideas in the immediate background to Aristophanes' speech is entirely reasonable. Platonically informed readers at the time of the *Symposium*'s publication, or at least the more attentive of them, would have been equipped to spot these allusions. His broader public readership would not have been, but their comprehension of, and amusement at, Aristophanes' story taken at face value need not have been in any way impaired by this. As for us modern readers, our possession of the *Timaeus* enables us, at least to a moderate extent, to share the privileged glimpse below the surface enjoyed by the former group.

5. Socrates' Speech as an Advance on Aristophanes'

It is now possible to turn to a comparison between the speeches of Aristophanes and Socrates. Elsewhere I have advocated, and defended in part, an interpretative thesis according to which the sequence of speeches in the *Symposium* is contrived to represent a steady progression towards the Platonic truth.[12] The very arbitrariness of the sequence, depending as it does on such dramatic details as Socrates' late arrival and Aristophanes' attack of hiccups, serves to reassure us that it is really the dramatist, Plato himself, who is in control of it.

Thus, for example, Agathon's speech not only improves rather explicitly on the understanding of causality manifested earlier by Phaedrus, but already displays in embryo, albeit with a degree of misunderstanding, some of the key Platonic theses that will be spelt out by Socrates. In the present chapter I wish to advance a similar "crescendo" reading: that the human goal, that of becoming godlike, while absent from the earlier speakers' attempts to capture love's divine nature, is twice presented as the real aim of love: it is first sketched misleadingly by Aristophanes, then correctly by Socrates.[13]

cease. Implicitly then, embodied life has existed for only a finite time past, but will exist for infinite time into the future – thanks, we must assume (cf. 97b8–99c8), to the world's creation by a benevolent intelligence. And that is the asymmetric thesis that Timaeus' narrative will, probably decades later, put in writing for the first time. (I set aside as irrelevant the fact that some Platonist readers of the *Timaeus* denied that he could have meant it.)

[12] Sedley 2006.

[13] Further arguments, on different grounds, for Socrates' speech as in particular correcting that of Aristophanes are developed in Destrée 2015, in Obdrzalek (this volume), and in an unpublished manuscript by Robert Wardy, among others.

In Socrates' speech, the lesson in erotics, which he quotes from the priestess Diotima, culminates in her description of a rare human privilege, the attainment of immortality (211d8–212a7):

> "What," she said, "do we think it would be like if it befell someone to see the Beautiful itself, pure, uncontaminated, unmixed, and not replete with human flesh and colors and much other mortal rubbish, but could gaze upon divine Beauty itself in its uniformity? Do you think," she said, "that the life of someone with his gaze fixed on that, viewing it with the appropriate faculty and enjoying intimacy with it, is an ordinary life? Do you not appreciate," she said, "that here alone, where he sees the Beautiful with the appropriate faculty, will it be his lot to give birth, not to images of virtue, since what he is making contact with is not an image, but to true virtue, since he is getting a grasp on truth; and that, having given birth to true virtue, and nurtured it, it belongs to him to become dear to the gods, and to him too, if to any human being, to become immortal?"

It is made clear that this cryptically described ascent to immortality, whatever it may amount to, outclasses the lesser, surrogate kinds of immortalization to which everyone may aspire by aiming to live on vicariously through their biological progeny (207a–208b) or their creative legacy, the latter being in different cases moral, artistic, or political (208c–209e). What Diotima has in mind is founded instead on an increasingly direct engagement with beauty, one so intense as to culminate in communion – a sort of intellectual intercourse – with the Form of Beauty itself.

There is reason to be confident that this account of the supreme human attainment is meant to be read as contrasting favorably with that of Aristophanes. Consider Diotima's closing prediction that this achiever's immortalization will somehow follow from his becoming "dear to the gods." On the surface, and thus for readers unschooled in Platonic thought, this seems to hint at the rare privilege of apotheosis, literal immortality bestowed by the gods on a favored high-achiever like Heracles. But earlier in her lesson Diotima has assured us that a mortal nature can become immortal *only* by procreation (207c9–d3); and in the lines just quoted she has made it clear that this supreme human achiever is no exception, by emphasizing that his achievement too lies in giving birth to something, namely to "true virtue."

To understand her added reference to his becoming dear to the gods we should, rather, connect it to one of Aristophanes' own closing remarks (193a7–b6):

> This [punitive bisection by the gods] is the reason for encouraging every man to behave towards the gods with total reverence, so that we may avoid the one fate and achieve the other, with *Erōs* as our leader and commander.

> Let no one act against him. Yet anyone who is hated by the gods *is* acting against him. For by becoming dear to this god and achieving reconciliation with him, we will find and meet our own beloveds, which at present very few of us do.

Thus, according to Aristophanes, winning the favor of the gods, in the person of *Erōs*, is the instrumental means to the incomparable happiness that lies in the recreation of our former complete selves. Diotima's implied response to this is to substitute a different significance of divine favor, not as the instrumental means to happiness, but as the hallmark of its attainment. For divine favor amounts to appreciation, by the best beings, that one is living the best life.[14]

It is true that Diotima, who is not personally present, could not have actually heard Aristophanes' speech. But the pretense that she is nevertheless somehow responding to its content has already been emphatically planted by Plato at 205d10–206a1, where she remarks: "And according to one account, those who love are those who are seeking their own other half. But according to my account, love's object is neither a half nor a whole unless, my friend, it is in fact good. . . . For the only object of human love is the good." And to remove any residual doubt that this really was a correction of Aristophanes' thesis, the point is made explicit immediately following Socrates' speech, when we hear that ". . . Aristophanes tried to say something, because Socrates had mentioned his speech" (212c5–6). This highlighted link between the speech of Aristophanes and Diotima's reported lesson in erotics, with the latter correcting the former, is clearly one we are being invited to notice. When we return to Diotima's closing words, in which she responds to Aristophanes' remarks about divine favor, we can now see that they are, in effect, an amplification of that earlier correction. Because Aristophanes overlooked the fact that love is essentially good-focused, he was able to assume that securing divine favor plays a merely instrumental role in realizing love's goal. In reality, she is now adding, the blessing of these supremely good beings *follows from*, and is in a way the hallmark of, one's own hard-won attainment of the best possible mode of life.

6. Intellectual Divinization

Can we make further progress with the understanding of Diotima's closing description of the supreme human life? In particular, is the "true

[14] Cf. Sheffield 2006: 147.

virtue" that such a life offers to be understood as moral virtue, intellectual virtue, or perhaps some sort of synthesis of the two? Taken by itself, her actual wording may be insufficient to put the passage's philosophical meaning beyond doubt.[15] But we now have an additional diagnostic tool at our disposal: the recognition that Aristophanes' recipe for human happiness, of which Diotima's lesson is at least in part a correction, is itself to be understood as a perversion of Plato's true account of divinization spelt out in the later *Timaeus*. If that is so, we may reasonably expect the *Timaeus*, properly understood, to contain the key to the true account. And that expectation gains further strength from another point I argued earlier, that the *Timaeus* is the nearest we have to Plato's own systematic statement of his philosophy. To turn for help to this canonical dialogue in particular is by no means either arbitrary or opportunistic.[16]

According to the *Timaeus*, as mentioned earlier, the human head, housing the rational part of the soul, is approximately spherical because it is modeled on the perfectly spherical heaven. The astronomical rotations of the spherical world-god along its two constituent circles, that of the Same and that of the Different, are quite literally that cosmic god's acts of thinking. And if we ourselves practice mathematical astronomy to a high enough standard and internalize those motions we will, again literally, be replicating the world-god's thoughts in our own souls. Nor is this achievement of expertise in astronomy an end in itself: rather it is the route to philosophy, the greatest of all blessings available to humans (47a–b). The *Timaeus* is Plato's one dialogue devoted to physics and cosmology, and in keeping with that, as noted earlier, it is telling us about the attainment of happiness from a specifically physical point of view.

Now another part of the same dialogue's physics concerns the physiology of the human soul, which, as in the *Republic*, has three parts. The soul's rational part is found in the head, and is immortal. The two irrational parts of the soul have locations below the neck – the spirited or competitive part in the chest, the appetitive part in the midriff – and both, being intimately linked to the body's functioning, share its mortality.

[15] For example, although "the appropriate faculty" used in the ascent is undoubtedly the intellect (*nous*; see Bury 1932: 132), that does not suffice to show that the virtue attained is intellectual virtue, because moral virtue too involves the use of *nous* (*Meno* 88a–c). I am myself persuaded by Sheffield's 2006 defense of an intellectualist reading; but cf., on the other side, Destrée in this volume.

[16] That is not to say that I consider Plato's other two main philosophical "ascents" – *Rep.* V.19d–521b and *Tht.* 172a–177c – to differ essentially from the Timaean account.

It is in the light of this physiology that Timaeus characterizes the choice of lives. First, he emphatically reiterates the location of our divine component in the head (90a–b):

> Concerning the most authoritative kind of soul found in us, we must have the following thought. God has given it to each of us as a divinity (*daimōn*)[17] – this thing which we say dwells in the topmost part of our body and raises us up from the earth towards what is akin to us in the heaven, because we rightly call ourselves a heavenly plant, not an earthly one. For the divinity keeps our body upright by suspending our head and root from the place out of which our soul was first born.

The consequences regarding mortality and immortality then follow (90b–c):

> Hence if someone has devoted all his interest and energy to his appetites or to competition, all his beliefs must necessarily be mortal ones, and altogether, so far as it is possible to become *par excellence* mortal, he will not fall the least bit short of this, because it is the mortal part of himself that he has developed. But if someone has committed himself entirely to learning and to true thoughts, and it is these among the things at his disposal that he has most practiced, he must necessarily think immortal and divine thoughts, provided that he gets a grasp on truth. And so far as it is possible for human nature to have a share in immortality, he will not in any degree lack this. And because he always cultivates that which is divine, and has the divinity (*daimōn*) that lives with him well ordered (*eu kekosmēmenon*), he will be preeminently happy (*eudaimōn*).

This is a vital Platonic passage on the nature of supreme happiness (*eudaimonia*). Every human being, indeed every animal, possesses an immortal component, the divine rational soul, but that is not enough to make every human being immortal. Godlikeness is a goal for a complex being, consisting of a body and three soul parts, to aspire to during an incarnate existence. That is when each of us has to decide which of the soul parts to make the core of our being. Those who pursue self-indulgent bodily pleasures have identified with the appetitive soul; and competitive types have identified with the spirited part of the soul. In doing so, both types are locating their identity in something mortal and transient. In complete contrast, those who have chosen an intellectual path are both fusing their real self with their one divine and

[17] In the Timaean context there is no need to take *daimōn* to refer to one of the intermediary beings distinguished as *daimones* at *Symp.* 202d–204b. At *Tim.* 40d6 (summarized above, p. 93), even Zeus and the other Olympians are *daimones*, and they are certainly gods (41a4). The choice of *daimōn* at 90a3–4 rather than *theos* is preparatory for the etymology of *eudaimonia* at 90c4–6.

immortal component, and sharing the eternal thoughts that god himself thinks, thereby attaining as great a degree of immortality as is available to the human race.

Some scholars[18] have challenged the inference that the godlike life extolled here is purely intellectual, and not also moral. The inference can, however, be amply supported from the text. Moral virtue was analyzed by Plato in *Republic* IV as a harmonious relation among the three soul parts; and in the *Timaeus* virtue thus conceived is revisited from a physical perspective just in passing, at 89e3–90a2:

> Just as we have often said that there are three kinds of soul triply housed in us, and that each has its motions, in the same way now too we must say, in barest outline, that whichever of them spends its time in idleness and with its own motions at rest must become very weak, while whichever of them is exercised must become very strong. *Hence we must take care that they have their motions commensurate with each other.*

The words that I have emphasized are Timaeus' sole reference to the psychology of moral virtue (approached here, as we would expect, from the point of view of physics). He then turns, in a passage already quoted earlier, to the godlikeness and preeminent happiness of the purely intellectual life, treating it at considerably greater length (90a2–d7). Here is his culminating description of such a life (90c6–d7):

> Now for everybody there is one way to cultivate (*therapeia*) every part, and that is to grant to each part its own proper nourishments and motions. For the divine element in us, the motions which are akin to it are the thoughts and revolutions of the whole world. Everyone should take a lead from these. We should correct the corrupted revolutions in our head concerned with becoming (*genesis*), by learning the harmonies and revolutions of the whole world, and so make the thinking subject resemble the object of its thought, in accordance with its ancient nature (*archaia phusis*); and, by creating this resemblance, bring to fulfilment the best life offered by the gods to mankind for present and future time.

The best and happiest human life is here said to be attained by aligning our microcosmic rational rotations, the thoughts inside our heads, with the macrocosmic rotations of the divine world soul, seen in the heavens.

[18] See, e.g., Russell 2004, Armstrong 2004, Mahoney 2008, Silverman 2010. In this context, note that although at 42b those who live justly are said to attain happiness, by contrast, at 90a–d they are not said to be either godlike or to have attained the highest form of happiness.

In other words, as already emphasized, astronomy is a bridge discipline that can make our own thoughts godlike. Similarly in *Republic* VII astronomy was one of the five bridge disciplines that can liberate our souls from their focus on the world of "becoming" (*genesis*) and help replace it with a focus on pure being (*ousia*).[19] Hence it is highly credible that the above translation, "We should correct the corrupted revolutions in our head concerned with becoming (*genesis*)," is correct[20] – meaning that the attainment of intellectual godlikeness involves leaving behind the sensible world of "becoming" and instead focusing our thought on the pure "being" that Plato typically associates with the unchanging world of Forms.[21] There seems no way that a life devoted even in part to the exercise of moral virtue could be said to detach itself from "becoming."[22]

It is time to pull together what I hope have proved to be some substantial threads in Plato's discourse. The final ascent to communion with the Form of Beauty described by Diotima represents the pinnacle of human achievement. In so far as she singles it out as a human being's strongest possible bid for immortality, she portrays it as a kind of godlikeness. What does this amount to?

Across his dialogues Plato may well appear to take up more than one position on the question whether the best and most godlike life is purely intellectual, or moral too. But a brief survey will reveal the dominance of the intellectualist thesis.

Since Plato's god is essentially good, there is no reason in principle why godlikeness should not, in whole or in part, take the form of moral

19 525b5, c5, 526e7; cf. 534a3.

20 Many have preferred to translate "We should correct the revolutions in our head which were corrupted around the time of our birth (*genesis*)." Both readings are linguistically and philosophically acceptable, but the latter contributes nothing relevant to the immediate context, nor is there any apparent reason for Timaeus to emphasize the psychological confusion of infancy rather than that due to e.g. moral misalignment (cf. 90b).

21 Cf. the emphatic statement of this dualism at *Tim.* 27d–28a.

22 For confirmation, compare *Tim.* 34b, on the Demiurge's initial creation of the rotating heaven: "And, a circle turning in a circle, he set it up as one single heaven, able thanks to its virtue to associate with itself and in no need of another, but satisfied with its own acquaintance and friendship. Thanks to all these things, he created it a happy (*eudaimōn*) god." This is the perfect, divine "happiness" –that of the world-god – to which human happiness is at the end of the dialogue called an approximation. The world, an intelligent living being, is the only occupant of the universe (31a–b), and hence has (comic as it may sound) no social or political life: there are no neighboring fellow-beings for it to interact with – despite which, it is a model of *eudaimonia*, enjoying its internal rotations of thought in splendid isolation. This confirms that those who attain happiness by replicating its revolutions inside their own heads will be becoming contemplators, not socially or politically virtuous beings.

virtue, and in at least one passage, from *Republic* X, it clearly does. Socrates remarks there that by being just one will "become as like god as is possible for a human being," and thus secure the gods' protection (613a–c). It is important, however, to take into account that this is said in support of the dialogue's strictly supplementary and secondary aim of showing that justice is desirable for its consequences or "rewards" (612a–b) as well as for its own sake. To explain more fully why being just should represent the height of godlikeness, Plato might well refer us to the celebrated digression in the *Theaetetus* (172a–177c). There the goal of "becoming as like god as possible" again leads, as in *Republic* X, to one's becoming "just" (176b2), but this is attained by a self-distancing from the civic environment so radical that justice seems to have been redefined as amounting to something like detached impartiality. Such a redefinition once again enables the contemplator to possess justice and the other moral virtues, yet still to remain free of actual moral activity.

Such a reading of the Book X passage has in fact already been prepared for earlier in the *Republic*, namely in Book VII. There it is made clear (519d–521b), albeit without any reference to godlikeness or immortality, that the life of pure contemplation is in Plato's eyes a better one than *any* life spent exercising civic virtues like justice. For it is a matter of agreement between Socrates and Glaucon that the philosophers educated by the ideal city will, to the extent that they have to join in governing it, have a worse life than if they could stay permanently outside the cave and simply contemplate. Some of the scholarly discomfort about taking this assertion at face value seems to arise from the assumption that contemplators thus described will not even *be* morally virtuous. Yet the very same passage does attribute to them at least the moral virtue of justice, which is indeed cited as the reason why, when ordered to interrupt their contemplative activity and help in government, they will obey (520e1). And the central books of the *Republic* have already by this point suggested why they will be just. In Book VI we learn (485d6–e5) that philosophers have the moral virtue of moderation (*sōphrosunē*) simply because all their desires are channeled into intellectual goals, with none left over to pursue bodily indulgences. The *Theaetetus* digression suggests that their "justice" is similarly analyzed: their concentration on intellectual activity, and consequent disregard for the civic context, results in a godlike impartiality. The relevant mark of an intellectual life is not the absence of moral virtue, it is the absence or minimization of activity in accordance with moral virtue, thanks to its possessor's total concentration on intellectual activity instead.

Thus, I submit, the overwhelming tendency of Plato's dialogues predating the *Timaeus* is to associate godlikeness with a life of pure intellectual activity. Viewed against this background, it should be no surprise that the *Timaeus* has likewise proved to be rather emphatic that the supremely happy and godlike life is one centered on intellectual activity alone.[23] Hence when Diotima asserts that the highest human achievers will attain immortality by giving birth to true virtue (212a), there is every reason to expect that this "true virtue" is intellectual virtue, and that the way in which its possessors attain immortality is by placing their own immortal part, the intellect,[24] and its activity, at the very core of their being.

This assimilation of the twin climactic passages, those of Timaeus and Diotima, gets strong support from an intertextual detail that binds them together. Timaeus, as we saw (p. 100), predicts of the contemplator that

> . . . he must necessarily think immortal and divine thoughts, provided that he *gets a grasp on truth* (*anper alētheias ephaptētai*, 90c1-2). And so far as it is possible for human nature to have a share in immortality, he will not in any degree lack this. (90c)

Thus in the *Timaeus* the closest human approximation to immortality depends on "getting a grasp on (*ephaptesthai*) truth," in a context that makes it clear that this refers to pure intellectual attainment. In words that closely parallel Timaeus' prediction, Diotima predicts of her own supreme achiever (p. 97) that it will be his lot

> . . . to give birth, not to images of virtue, since what he is getting a grasp on is not an image, but to true virtue, since he *is getting a grasp on truth* (*hate tou alēthous ephaptomenōi*, 212a5); and that, having given birth to true virtue, and nurtured it, it belongs to him to become dear to the gods, and to him too, if to any human being, to become immortal. (212a3–7)

Plainly "getting a grasp on (*ephaptesthai*) truth" has the same function in both passages, namely as a required means to the highest degree of immortalization. It seems to follow that Diotima too, like Timaeus, is using this expression to refer to pure intellectual attainment. The implicit

[23] As also argued in Sedley 1999 and Sedley (forthcoming).

[24] This wording should not be taken to require soul division. The "intellect" could well be, as in the *Phaedo*, the whole soul, provided that it is sufficiently independent of the body to pursue its own natural agenda.

question guiding her remarks is: what is the true virtue to which, at the very pinnacle of human achievement, one may aspire to give birth? And her punning answer is that *true* virtue is the kind of virtue that you attain by mastering *truth*: in other words, as we can now see more clearly, intellectual virtue.

Three reasons have emerged for following the lead of the *Timaeus* and adopting an intellectualist reading of Diotima's speech. One is *Timaeus*' canonical status within the Platonic corpus. A second lies in an intertextual detail, linking the two, which helped us identify Diotima's "true" virtue as intellectual virtue.

The third, from which this study began, depends on clues built into the *Symposium* itself. Diotima's lesson in erotics is pointedly set up as a correction of Aristophanes' speech. And Aristophanes' tale of human origins and his resultant eulogy of love, once one probes far enough below their surface, prove to represent a comic misunderstanding of the real human quest for godlikeness canonically explained in the *Timaeus*.

Aristophanes appreciates, at some level, that love is the desire to return to our semi-divine spherical origins. But, overlooking the constant Platonic qualification that one cannot become completely like god, he mistakes this desire for an ambition to emulate, rival and even outdo the exercise of power traditionally associated with the Olympian gods. This in turn provides the reason why he misconstrues the divinization to which love seeks to restore us: where true happiness, as unveiled in the *Timaeus*, depends on making intellectual activity the very core of one's being, our ancestors' semi-divine state involved their identifying themselves instead with the competitive tendency in their souls.[25]

Diotima, although she has no apparent interest in astronomical or cosmological science, and hence nowhere alludes to sphericity, does appreciate the real significance of a return to our divine origins. The highest attainment that love can bring us is essentially cerebral: to concentrate our very being into pure intellectual activity. Whether or not the intellect is itself immortal (and the default assumption should probably be that for Plato it is), the eternity of the true thoughts, or brainchildren, that the contemplator shares with god is already enough

[25] My thanks to Frisbee Sheffield for helping me grasp this point. (I say "the competitive tendency in their souls" rather than "the competitive part of their souls" because (a) tripartition of the soul is not obviously present in the *Symposium*, and (b) the distinction of intellectual, competitive and appetitive drives or tendencies can be made even without tripartition, as *Phd.* 68c shows.)

to make this rare attainment the closest a human being can ever come to divine immortality.[26] To say it one more time with Timaeus (89b6–c4), "... if someone has committed himself entirely to learning and to true thoughts, and it is these among the things at his disposal that he has most practised, he must necessarily *think immortal and divine thoughts*, provided that he gets a grasp on truth. And so far as it is possible *for human nature to have a share in immortality*, he will not in any degree lack this."

APPENDIX

Plato's System and the *Timaeus*

The following list of correspondences between components of the Timaean system and theses apparently advocated in earlier dialogues is unlikely to be complete, but I think it is more than enough to confirm the claims made in Section 4 of this chapter:

- god as essentially good and the cause only of good (29d–30a; cf. *Rep.* II. 379b–c);
- the existence of Forms as eternal paradigms (28a–b, 28c–29a, 30c–31a, 52a; cf. *Crat.* 389a–390e; *Phd.* 74d–75b; *Rep.* X. 596a–597d; *Parm.* 132c–d);
- the radical separation of two realms – being and becoming – accessible by distinct cognitive powers (27d–28a, 37b–c, 51d–52a; cf. *Rep.* V. 476d–480a);
- the cognitive defects of perception (43a–44b; cf. *Phd.* 65a–d);
- the special role of astronomy and harmonics as a bridge to philosophy (47a–e; cf. *Rep.* VII. 527c–531d);
- the explanation of false belief (43e–44a; cf. *Soph.* 254b–264b);
- the method of collection and division (83b–c; cf. *Phdr.* 265c–266b; *Phil.* 16b–19b; *Soph.*; *Stat.*);
- the tripartition of the soul (69c–72d; cf. *Rep.* IV and VIII-X; *Phdr.* 246a–254e);

[26] The emphasis here should be on "human being." Even if the rational *soul* is already in its own nature immortal, contemplation is the nearest that *flesh-and-blood human beings* can come to immortality. Since that is plainly the doctrine of *Tim.* 90a–d, at *Symp.* 207d we need see no incompatibility between (1) the assertion there that procreation is the only way in which a mortal nature can attain immortality, and (2) the tacit assumption that the soul, or its rational part, is itself immortal. See, further, Sedley 2009: 159–60.

- the (rational) soul's immortality and transmigration (e.g. 42b–43a, 69c, 91d–92c; cf. *Phd.*; *Phdr.* 245c–249d; *Rep.* X. 608c–621d);
- the theory of recollection (implicit at 41e; cf. *Meno* 81a–86b; *Phd.* 72e–77a; *Phdr.* 249b–d);
- the paradox that all wrongdoing is involuntary (86d-e; cf. *Prot.* 352a–358d; *Gorg.* 467a–468e; *Meno* 77b–78b);
- the thesis that justice makes you happier than injustice does (42b–d; cf. *Gorg.*, *Rep.*);
- the superior happiness of the contemplative compared with the civic life (89e–90d; cf. *Rep.* VII. 519d–521b; *Tht.* 172a–177c).[27]

[27] One might add the political programme of the *Republic*, which is elliptically summarized by Socrates at *Tim.* 17c–19a. It differs in not being part of Timaeus' speech, but it still constitutes evidence against the thesis of Peterson (2011) that neither the speaker Socrates nor the author Plato has any commitment to the political programme of the *Republic*.

CHAPTER 6

Why Agathon's Beauty Matters

Francisco J. Gonzalez

There is a tendency to treat Agathon's speech as the most superficial and philosophically vacuous of Plato's *Symposium*. Though acknowledging that "some valuable points are made," Waterfield, for example, characterizes Agathon's speech as "little more than a tour de force" (2009: xxiv) and concludes: "Underneath the pretty exterior lies a conventional encomium and a conventional view of Love, which reflects the god's portraits we can find in paintings and in literature. It is therefore a perfect speech for Agathon the artist" (xxv). Bury a century earlier likewise judged the content of the speech purely conventional and suggested that nothing better describes it than the Pauline phrase: "Though he speaks with the tongues of men and of angels, he is become as sounding brass or a tinkling cymbal." (Bury 1909: xxxvi). To add just one more to the countless examples of such a negative judgment, Brisson describes the speech as "empty but magnificently constructed" (2006: 245). This impression is of course encouraged by Socrates who characterizes the speech as a piece of Gorgianic rhetoric concerned only with impressing through its choice of words and phrases and not at all with telling the truth about its subject. In other words, Socrates suggests that the speech is an attractive or beautiful one (198b3), but not a good one. Indeed, the speech makes love itself something merely attractive, like the author in whose image it is conceived: despite his name, Agathon is more pretty boy than good.

But careful consideration of Agathon's speech and its place in the dialogue shows that this assessment cannot stand. Considering first its place in the dialogue, Agathon's speech immediately precedes that of Socrates and is thus given a prominent, central place in the dialogue. If we see the series of speeches as an ascent of some sort, Agathon's is near the top. One could of course reject the view that the speeches represent an ascent, as many scholars have done precisely in order to avoid giving Agathon's speech too much honor. Dorter's argument that the speeches cannot form an ascent is based on his unquestioned assumption that the speech of Agathon "even allowing for its humorous intent, can hardly be placed above (or even alongside of) the inspired myth of his predecessor Aristophanes" (1992: 253–254). Bury already made the same point in arguing that the thesis of an ascending order is made untenable by "the obvious fact that Agathon's speech is in no real sense the best or most important of the series; rather, from the point of view of Socrates, it is the worst" (1909: liii).[1] But we do not need to assume such an ascent in order to see in the position of Agathon's speech a sign of its importance. The reason is that the *Symposium* explicitly justifies this position by making it clear that Socrates' contest is with Agathon more than with any other participant. Right near the start we have Socrates' ironic comparison of his wisdom to that of Agathon and then Agathon's suggestion that Dionysus will soon decide between their claims to wisdom (175e7–9). We are reminded of this towards the dialogue's end when Alcibiades in the guise of Dionysus first crowns Agathon and then, upon seeing Socrates, crowns him as well (note that *both* are crowned).[2] Furthermore, if Socrates claims expertise in love (177d7–8), Eryximachus suggests that Socrates *and* Agathon are the two experts in love among the party (193e4–5). Now why would Plato set up this contest and this rivalry if he thought that Agathon was a mere airhead with nothing but pretty words to offer on the subject of love? Agathon and Socrates are the last to speak on the topic of *erōs* because *both* are recognized to have the most to say on the topic and therefore to be the real contenders in the contest of praising *erōs*.

It might seem that Agathon, far from being any kind of expert, as a poet only panders to public opinion and therefore is not worthy of having anything he says taken seriously by Socrates. This is why the short

[1] One exception to this tendency is Sedley 2006. Defending what he calls the "crescendo" interpretation of the speeches, Sedley interprets Agathon's speech as being the one closest to Socrates' own, even calling it "sub-Socratic." As will be noted later, some of the observations Sedley makes in support of this reading coincide with the points made here, though some exception will be taken to his overall account of Agathon's role in the dialogue and of his relation to Socrates.

[2] A point rightly emphasized by Robinson 2004: 93. Robinson interprets this double-crowning as an indication of two sides of the worship of Dionysus: the public polis-cult, represented by Agathon with his dramatic victory at a Dionysian festival, and the private mystery-cult, represented by Socrates through his account of *erōs* in the voice of Diotima and in the language of the mystery religions: see especially 87. Agathon and Socrates on this interpretation are both legitimated, the first as representing discourse that "is exoteric and public, and extends to *all* citizens, who *all* partake of it" and the second as representing discourse that "is esoteric and private, and extends only to those few citizens who are capable of meeting its very high demands, and who also participate in the public discourse" (98). But this interpretation appears to eliminate any real *contest* between Agathon and Socrates: if each has his own domain, what is the contest *for*?

conversation in which Socrates engages Agathon prior to Agathon's speech is of much importance. Here, in response to Socrates' suggestion that he cannot possibly be worried about the opinions of the few present at the party after having addressed a vast multitude in the theater, Agathon protests that he is not so "full of the theater" (194b7) as to ignore that we should esteem only the opinions of the wise and not those of the many (194b6–8). His plays may be "crowd-pleasers," but Agathon no less than Socrates values wisdom and expertise above popular opinion. Indeed, two surviving fragments of the work of the historical Agathon appear to express well Agathon's view here and thus his kinship with Socrates: "No envy would there be in the life of men / If we were all constituted equal by nature;" "To envy wisdom more than wealth is noble" (fr. 24 and 25; Nauck 1889: 768).

If we turn to Agathon's speech itself, we see that far from being empty rhetoric and saying nothing true, it is a conceptually coherent and sophisticated speech that makes for the first time a number of important points with which Socrates will himself agree. These contributions can be outlined as follows:

1) Agathon claims that we must distinguish between the nature of Love and what it effects or produces, criticizing previous speakers for neglecting the former (194e5–195a5). This is presumably why Socrates engages only Agathon in discussion: the latter, unlike the others, has something to say about the nature of love. As Sheffield observes, "If one must begin an investigation, as Socrates suggests, with an identification of the subject matter, then examining Agathon's speech will be the best place to start" (2006: 35). Socrates will therefore explicitly praise the soundness of Agathon's methodology and embrace it as his own.
2) This methodological shift brings with it a shift in how the causality of love is understood. While previous speakers treated love as a verb only rather than as a subject, so that it is a property of people or things that "do" the loving, Agathon makes love itself the subject and cause of loving. This shift in perspective is not only adopted by Socrates, but is essential to his entire argument. As David Sedley has shown (2006: 56–57), the argument by which Socrates tries to prove that love lacks beauty and goodness works at all only if the subject is understood to be not people who love but the love itself that causes them to love. Lovers can of course possess good and beautiful things and still be lovers, but the love itself that causes them to love must, as desire for what is good

and beautiful, be utterly lacking in these properties. In other words, in loving I can myself possess good and beautiful things, but the love that causes me to desire good and beautiful things cannot itself in any way be good or beautiful. In this way, the very starting point of Socrates' account of love would be impossible without the shift towards treating love as itself the cause and subject of loving brought about by Agathon.

3) In addressing the nature of love, Agathon argues it to be happy because both beautiful and good. This identification of happiness with the possession of goodness and beauty will of course play a central role in Socrates' speech (204e1–7). But Agathon is as conceptually careful here as he is in his opening distinction between the nature and the works of love: rather than simply conflating the properties of "beautiful" and "good," he argues for love's possession of each in turn by further analyzing each property into a set of characteristics Love can be shown to possess.
4) Love is shown to be beautiful by being shown to be young, delicate, supple and always in bloom. Though these may at first appear to be trivial characteristics that tell us nothing important about the nature of Love, Agathon's argument in fact has him defending some important claims that imply a critical distancing from the poetic tradition. Love cannot be old because the violent deeds the poets attribute to the gods at the beginning could not have been caused by love, but only by necessity. In Agathon's view, poets like Homer and Parmenides have at the very least failed to make the important distinction between love and necessity, a distinction that Agathon will make again later in the speech to connect beauty and the good in their opposition to necessity. But here he suggests that the poets may not even be telling the truth in their attribution of violent deeds to the gods, since after citing their views, he adds: "If they spoke the truth" (195c2–3).[3]
5) In defending the claim that Love is delicate, Agathon cites Homer, but in a strikingly clever and subversive way. Citing a passage in which

[3] Sedley suggests that we understand 195c1–3 as follows: "and the ancient goings-on concerning the gods, of which Homer and Parmenides speak, were due to Necessity, not to Love, *<as they themselves would say> if they were speaking the truth*" (2006: 67–68). On this reading, Agathon is agreeing with Phaedrus that Homer and Parmenides made Love rather than Necessity rule during the time of castrations, etc., and is claiming that the poets were wrong. Agathon is in this case, as Sedley notes, simply "rejecting their authority" (69). Yet Sedley thereby makes Agathon in another respect more conservative as he has him not question the attribution of immoral actions to the gods (only their attribution to Love), whereas on the other reading ("if they spoke the truth," i.e., about the ancient goings-on) Agathon at least doubts this.

Homer describes Delusion (*Atē*) as having delicate feet because she walks on the heads of men (195d4–5), Agathon first substitutes Love for Delusion, as if he were correcting the poet for confusing the two just as he confused love with necessity. In another important correction, he then claims that Love has delicate feet not because it walks on men's heads: after all, heads are not really soft! Instead, love makes its home in what is truly soft: the souls and characters of men and gods (195e4–7). Agathon thus uses a rather trivial anthropomorphism in a rather subversive way in order to locate love in the soul, as Socrates himself will do.

6) Turning to the argument that Love is not only beautiful but good, he analyzes the latter into the virtues of justice, moderation, bravery and wisdom (196b5–197b3), an analysis that can be recognized as distinctly Platonic.[4] In the judgment of Sedley, "Agathon . . . is speaking with a sufficiently Socratic (or Platonic) voice for it to be worth tracking his ideas and seeing what will become of them in the hands of Socrates himself" (2006: 59). Specifically, Sedley sees the serious content running through Agathon's account of the virtues as lying in the notion that virtue is a matter of non-coercive control, a notion that "has obvious enough resonances with the theory of virtue, in both city and soul, developed . . . in Republic 4" (59). Agathon proceeds to discuss each virtue one by one, defending in each case its attribution to Love. There has been much indignation at the weakness of Agathon's arguments. Agathon's claim that love is just because it commits no violence is described by Dover as "a somewhat reckless statement, considering the importance of *erōs* as a motive of violence and fraud in myth, history and everyday life" (1980: 127). But then would Socrates' account of love be any less "reckless"? The important point is that all the speakers are engaged in the explicit project of defending love against its more negative depiction in earlier literature.[5] But what of Agathon's other arguments? Is love really temperate because it is a desire stronger than, and thus able to control, other desires? Is it

[4] See the interpretation of this part of Agathon's speech in Ficino, *In Convivium* V.8. Citing Adam's observation that the identification of good character with just these four virtues appears to be new with Plato, Bury rather absurdly counters that "a peculiarly Platonic tenet would hardly be put into the mouth of Agathon" (1909: 77). See also Rowe 1998: 164, who insists that there is nothing Platonic about the virtues Agathon describes.

[5] One surviving fragment (though of uncertain attribution) might show that Agathon was well aware of the darker side of love: "Should I judge you hubris or Cypris? Desire or distress of the heart?" (fr. 31; Nauck 1889: 769).

courageous because the god of love is stronger than the god of war? But not sufficient importance has been given to the fact that, weak as they are, Agathon still gives *arguments*. Can that be said of any of the preceding speeches? Even Socrates' speech, put into the mouth of a priestess, has been judged, in its more positive part, as rather lacking in the argument department. Furthermore, Agathon acknowledges, as we will see, that there is some playfulness mixed in with seriousness in his speech. Can a Platonist condemn *that*? Most importantly, Agathon's arguments, however playfully presented, are not as absurd as they are often taken to be. When scholars, for example, find ridiculous the argument that *erōs* is temperate because it is a desire stronger than, and therefore capable of controlling, other desires, one must ask why they don't find the same view ridiculous when defended by Socrates. Have they forgotten that the opposition between temperance and erotic desire in Lysias' speech and Socrates' first speech in the *Phaedrus* is explicitly rejected in Socrates' second speech where true temperance (256b1–2, as distinct from the contemptible purely 'mortal' temperance, 256e5) is achieved through erotic desire? Have they forgotten that in the *Symposium* itself Socrates describes true virtue as being the product of the erotic desire for beauty? In arguing that temperance, rather than involving an opposition to all desire, is rather the ruling of lower desires by a higher desire for a higher object, Agathon is defending a sophisticated and distinctly Platonic conception of temperance.

7) Among the virtues, Agathon significantly devotes the greatest amount of space to the *wisdom* of love (196d5–197b9). Surviving fragments show Agathon to have been, as he is here, especially concerned with the notion of *technē* (see frs. 6, 8, and 20; Nauck 1889: 764–765, 767). Socrates' own tendency to compare with *technē* the kind of wisdom that constitutes virtue is notorious. Sedley, noting the importance of Agathon's emphasis on wisdom, comments that nevertheless "Agathon's view of wisdom (*sophia*, the goal of philosophy) is a deeply unphilosophical one, and the same may be said of his treatment of virtue in general" (2006: 62). Agathon of course does not include philosophy in his treatment of wisdom, but to consider this a defect is to assume that Socrates has already won the contest and that the nature of philosophy and its relation to other forms of knowledge is something perfectly clear. Furthermore, while Agathon here characterizes love as being a poet like himself, he does so in the context of describing love as a "poet" in the broadest sense possible that includes

not only all artistic production, but also all natural and technical production. Love's wisdom is an ability to produce or create in general. This is another idea that will be taken up by Socrates with his characterization of love as giving birth and with the suggestion that poetry like love has both a broader and a narrower meaning (205b8–c10).[6]

8) In the context of claiming that the gods associated with different arts discovered these arts through the power of love, Agathon returns to the idea that what reigned at the beginning, if the stories of the poets are to be believed, was not love, but necessity (197b7).[7] But this idea now enables him to connect the notions of beauty and goodness that have until now been kept distinct. Agathon first claims that the love that ended the disputes between the gods and inspired the different arts was the love *of beauty* (197b5). In thus treating beauty as the object of love, Agathon is of course introducing the idea that will prove absolutely central to Socrates' own account; in later critiquing the ambiguity in Agathon's formulation, Socrates is also acknowledging a debt. But Agathon goes even further: he proceeds to conclude that it is the love of *beauty* that brings what is *good* to both men and gods (*ek tou eran tōn kalōn pant'agatha gegonen kai theois kai anthrōpois*, 197b8–9). Beauty, if distinct from the good, is still a cause for good. Again, the anticipation of Socrates is impossible to ignore, especially since for Agathon too it is apparently through providing wisdom that the love of beauty is a cause of good.

9) Finally, the speech concludes with a poetic peroration that is clearly distinguished from the rest of the speech in form, as it exhibits the rhythms and alliteration of verse,[8] and adds nothing to its content, as it only recaps the main conclusions. Poet he may be, but Agathon still knows the difference between argument, however playfully expressed, and poetic flourish.

Agathon's speech is thus rigorously organized according to important conceptual distinctions: between the nature of Love and its effects, between beauty and goodness as the two components of Love's

[6] See Stokes 1986: 156–157. Sedley also stresses the way in which Agathon's connection of love with poeisis and his broadening of the sense of both terms anticipates Diotima (2006: 60–61), even suggesting that "Diotima is formally theorizing what Agathon has already done *de facto*" (61).

[7] Much is made of this distinction by Ficino, *In Convivium* V.11. In a surviving fragment of Agathon we find *technê*, here associated with love, explicitly opposed to both necessity and chance (fr. 8; Nauck 1889: 765).

[8] See Dover 1980: 124.

happiness, between the different characteristics that comprise beauty and the good respectively, between the analysis itself and a poetic peroration that only recaps the conclusions of the analysis in verse. Furthermore, if we consider all of the anticipations of key points in Socrates' own speech outlined here, it seems impossible to deny that the contributions of Agathon's speech far outdo in importance the contributions of all the other speeches.

But why, then, does Socrates dismiss the speech as mere pretty rhetoric with no truth content? One puzzle in Socrates' reaction to the speech is indeed just how unfair it is. While Agathon's speech does contain some pretty Gorgianic rhetoric, especially in its last part, it also contains, as we have seen, much more than that. Most importantly, Agathon is quite aware of the distinction between this kind of rhetoric and the attempt to say the truth about love since he concludes with these words: "Let this, Phaedrus, be my account dedicated to the gods, partaking partly of play (*paidia*), partly of measured seriousness (*spoudē metria*), to the extent of my ability" (197e7–8). Belfiore rightly finds in this statement "a self-awareness shared by none of the other five speakers" (2012: 137) and therefore an indication that Agathon's *amathia* "is less serious than that of the other speakers" (136). Here Agathon acknowledges the playfulness of his speech, playfulness that would presumably include the play with words and sounds, the mischievously subversive use of the poets, the more blatantly sophistical argumentation (e.g. Love is courageous because Aphrodite is stronger than Ares!), and the flights of poetic fancy, especially in the entire concluding section: precisely the kind of playfulness, in other words, that readers of Plato find in his own dialogues! Yet Agathon also claims a measure of seriousness and with ample justification, as we have seen.[9] What, then, is Socrates' reaction? Unbelievably he says: "I didn't find the rest quite so wonderful, but who would not be enchanted in hearing the ending with its beauty of language?" (198b3–5). Socrates thus chooses to ignore the serious content of the speech and focus only on the beautiful language concentrated in its conclusion!

[9] Centrone notes that this mixture of seriousness and play is what characterizes the true art of writing in the *Phaedrus* 276bff. (in Nucci 2009: xxv), a connection also made by Heidegger in a seminar on the *Phaedrus* he gave in the summer of 1932 (2012: 143). Rowe rightly observes that with this comment Agathon distinguishes himself from Gorgias (in a way, I would add, that Socrates deliberately ignores!): while Gorgias characterized his *Encomium of Helen* as mere play (*paignion*, fr. 11. 21), Agathon insists on the partial or moderate seriousness of his own speech (1998: 166). Rowe nevertheless asserts: "It is not clear where exactly the seriousness of Agathon's speech is supposed to lie; but then P. clearly wishes to leave us with a picture of someone who has a distinctly uncertain relationship with anything resembling the truth" (166).

This unfair focus should give us some pause before simply accepting the critique that follows.[10] Indeed, we should remember that Socrates is in a contest with Agathon, which means that he naturally seeks to belittle the contribution of his rival.

The upshot of Socrates' critique is that Agathon's is a beautiful speech, but lacks truth (see 198e2, 199a7, b3). This is indeed a puzzling critique in a number of ways. First, as we have seen, there is much in Agathon's speech that Socrates himself will acknowledge as "true" in his own speech. Therefore, as we have seen, Socrates can make this critique only by initially ignoring the serious content of Agathon's speech and focusing on the poetic peroration. Second, Socrates targets with his critique not Agathon in particular, *but all of the preceding speeches.*[11] He claims that none of them understood an encomium as required to tell the truth, but thought it sufficient to say anything to magnify the subject, whether true or false (198d7–e2) Third, when after this general condemnation he turns to Agathon's speech in particular, the first thing he does is praise as correct the organizing principle of Agathon's speech: i.e. that we need to exhibit the nature of *Erōs* before exhibiting its effects (199c3–5), a principle reiterated at the start of Socrates' own speech (201d8–e2). This is not to deny that the principle undergoes some modification in Socrates' adoption of it. As Sedley has argued (2006: 52–54), Agathon's starting point is an account of what love is like (*hoios estin*, 195a4) that takes the form of a description of the qualities that make love good and beautiful, rather than an account of what love is, i.e. its essential nature, which is Socrates' own starting point. If Sedley, accordingly, concludes that "Agathon's method is not yet fully Socratic" (54), that is not to deny the extent to which it *is* Socratic. Fourth, the question to Agathon with which Socrates begins his elenchus is formulated thus: "Come, since you have so beautifully and magnificently (*kalōs kai megaloprepōs*) expounded in other respects what Love is, tell me this about it: is Love such as to be the love of something or of nothing?" (199c6–d2). Finally, while Socrates indeed goes on to refute a central contention of Agathon's speech, i.e., that Love is itself beautiful and good, he claims at the start of his own speech that he once believed exactly what Agathon believes (201e3–5). There is no reason to dismiss this as mere politeness; Socrates has not

[10] Nucci appears to consider Socrates' response here as justified by the weakness and therefore negligibility of Agathon's arguments (2009: p. 115, n. 189). This is why it is important to show that the "serious" part of Agathon's speech is not so weak and empty as Nucci and others take it to be.

[11] Though Rowe (1998: 167) insists that Agathon is the main target.

shown himself elsewhere in the dialogue to be very concerned with politeness. Rather, if he engages Agathon in discussion, this is because he recognizes in Agathon a serious position that he himself once held. Agathon's view, after all, is not so obviously ridiculous or false. After outlining Socrates' refutation of Agathon, Sheffield rightly notes: "But this is not to say that Agathon's speech is nonsense. Socrates goes on to show that Agathon is right that *Erōs* has some relationship both to beauty and to divinity; he is muddled about the precise nature of those relationships. This is a muddle to which Socrates himself, apparently, was subject, before he met the mysterious Diotima (201e3–7)" (2006: 36). Dover, despite expressing "our" annoyance at Agathon's "verbal sophistries or his apparent inability to draw distinctions which, if drawn, would profoundly affect his generalizations" and claiming that the speech "is appropriate to a man whose business in life is the manipulation of language," must nevertheless concede: "In so far as it subsumes under *erōs* all kinds of desire for *ta kala* (197b8) and seems to attribute to this desire all good in the life of gods and men, it may be regarded as expressing, although in ways which make it immediately vulnerable to systematic criticism, some degree of 'right opinion' . . . on the role of *Erōs* as Diotima sees it" (1980: 123). Given that Diotima assigns "right opinion" to that same intermediate position occupied by *Erōs* and by the philosopher, this is actually high praise.[12] It is hard to avoid the conclusion: if all of the speeches failed to speak the truth about Love, Agathon's speech in Socrates' view came the closest and is the most deserving of serious discussion.[13] Of course, this means that Socrates's judgment disagrees with the prevailing view in scholarship on the dialogue that tends to consider Agathon's speech the most vacuous and least worthy of serious discussion among all the speeches.

Presumably one reason why Agathon's speech has not been taken more seriously is Socrates' repeated description of the speech as "beautiful," reflecting Agathon's own extraordinary beauty,[14] and the assumption that beauty is something superficial having little to do with truth. One of the

[12] See also Allen 1991: 44, n. 69.

[13] As Centrone suggests, "il suo discorso sembra contenere molti spunti accettabili nell'ottica di Platone; ma forse proprio per questo sarà anche quello attaccato piú direttamente nei suoi fondamenti" (in Nucci 2009: xxii). Stokes has sought to show how Socrates' critique of Agathon genuinely engages with the content of Agathon's speech, so that "Agathon sheds the foolish weakness he is often saddled with, just as Socrates sheds his overbearing rhetoric. This passage, at least, can now be read as a *dialogue*" (1986: 145).

[14] Considering all the surviving testimony, Lèvêque concludes: "Éclatante beauté, telle est donc l'impression qu'Agathon produisit sur tous ses contemporains" (1955: 36).

central points of similarity, however, between Socrates and Agathon is to be found in their understandings of the relation between beauty and goodness. Both neither completely identify the two terms nor see them as separable. Central to Socrates' own speech is Diotima's substitution of "good" for "beautiful" in order to arrive at the conclusion that what we seek from the possession of beautiful things is happiness (204d–e). At the same time, this substitution does not appear to presuppose a simple identity given the different roles assigned to the beautiful and the good in the higher mysteries: what the lover pursues, both in its different manifestations and in itself, is beauty and not the good, while the good, in the form of true virtue, is what the lover gives birth to through intercourse with beauty.[15] The relation is thus neither a simple identity nor a sharp distinction. Socrates therefore would hardly be justified in dismissing the beauty of Agathon's speech, and indeed Agathon's own beauty and the beauty of love on his account, as *mere* beauty, as something superficial having no necessary connection to goodness. At the very least, this beauty of Agathon's is something that could lead us to the good.

It is significant that immediately after calling Agathon's speech beautiful, Socrates' asks him if anything good is not also beautiful (201c1–2). Some, such as Waterfield (2009: 84), have taken this to imply that the contrary is not true, i.e. that not everything beautiful is good, and have seen here an implicit critique of Agathon. But since what Socrates seeks to establish here is that to be deprived of beautiful things *is* to be deprived of good things, an opposition of the beautiful to the good (i.e. the suggestion that some beautiful things are bad) is not even implied. Even in his critique of Agathon's rhetoric, Socrates does not oppose beauty and truth, but rather suggests that they go together: a good encomium is one that *chooses the most beautiful truths* (198d3–6).[16] Thus there is nothing to suggest that Socrates sees the relation between beauty and goodness or truth as a discordant one. It is hard to see, then, how Socrates could join so many modern commentators in dismissing Agathon and his speech as "merely" beautiful.

[15] See Stokes 1986: 154–155 and 181. As he notes with regard to Diotima's "higher mysteries," "The functions of the good and of the beautiful in the argument and its exposition are quite different" (181). See also Sedley who denies that the good and the beautiful are ever identical in Plato's dialogues (2006: p. 49, n. 4).

[16] As Nucci notes, commenting on this passage: "La bellezza seque la verità ma le dà anche luce" (2009: 117, n. 194).

As for Agathon himself, he surely is not guilty of simply reducing goodness to beauty. As we have seen, his speech clearly distinguishes between the two: he first sets out to show how *Erōs* is *kallistos* (195a8–196b5) and then how it is *aristos* (196b5–197b10). As Berg notes, "Agathon is thus the first speaker since Phaedrus to distinguish the beautiful and the good and he makes explicit what Phaedrus left implicit" (2010: 77).[17] As we have also seen, however, Agathon relates the two characteristics, seeing the love of beauty as a means to acquiring what is good, as it is in the highest mysteries of Diotima's account.[18] Thus Agathon's understanding of the relation between the good and the beautiful appears no different from Socrates' own. Furthermore, far from sacrificing truth to beauty, Agathon questions the veracity of the poets[19] and carefully distinguishes between the more serious and the more playful aspects of his own speech.

One must therefore suspect that the reason for the contest between Agathon and Socrates and for Socrates' unfair critique of Agathon's speech is that the beauty cultivated and promoted by the poet is not so easy to separate from the goodness pursued by the philosopher. The beautiful Agathon is not so indifferent to goodness and truth as Socrates pretends and Socrates is not so indifferent to beauty as he sometimes pretends. In the words of the *Philebus*, after all, in the nature of beauty lies the power of the good (64e5–6).[20]

One might of course be tempted to identify Agathon with the mere appearance of the good while identifying Socrates with its reality, just as one might be tempted to identify poetry with mere imitation and philosophy with an unmediated grasp of the truth. Thus Allen, though showing the many ways in which Agathon's speech anticipates Socrates',

[17] Yet Berg claims that Agathon goes on to conflate the two in attributing the power of effecting good to *erōs* as a poet, i.e. as a maker of images: "What Agathon shows, then, is that the beautiful is an image in speech of the good that speciously appropriates to itself the being of the good. Agathon's entire speech is just such an image. His claim, then, that wisdom is the good is the beautiful masquerading as the good. His god *Erōs* in the wisdom of his making is the unreal unity of the beautiful and the good" (88). This critique I address later.

[18] See Stokes 1986: 125–126, who claims that Agathon is trying to have things both ways. But isn't Socrates as well?

[19] Rowe simply dismisses this evidence: "whether Agathon has any interest at all in 'truth' must be at best an open question (cf. S. at 198d–e)" (1998: 163).

[20] Commenting on the distinction between beauty and the good in Agathon's speech, Ficino concludes: "bonitatis florem quemdam esse pulchritudinem volumus" (V.1.40). But for Ficino there are two senses to this analogy: beauty is the flower of the good not only in the sense that it is the outward manifestation of inner goodness, but also in the sense that, as the flower carries the seed from which other flowers will grow, beauty leads us to the good (V.1.40).

concludes: "Both speeches are rhetorical. But Agathon's rhetoric deals with appearance, as Socrates' examination of it will show, and Diotima's with reality" (1991: 40). Likewise, Sedley, while emphasizing the Socratic content of Agathon's speech, in the end sees in Agathon nothing but "a pale ghost of the Platonic truth" and "mere 'images' of the philosophical understanding in which real virtue resides" (2006: 65). If Sedley acknowledges that Agathon's speech comes closest to the Platonic position, this "closest" is still in his view immeasurably far. For Berg, Agathon is "a peculiarly Socratic false image of Socrates whose sole expertise is erotics" (2010: 89). There can be no doubt that Agathon's speech shows him to be an imitator par excellence, as it literally depicts love *in his own image*. Furthermore, this is the characteristic of Agathon that is emphasized in his portrayal by Aristophanes in the *Thesmophoriazusae*. There, in the context of explaining why he is dressed as a woman, Agathon argues that the poet must himself be beautiful in order to compose beautiful plays, since "one necessarily composes things like one's nature" (l. 167). This is a principle both explicitly articulated in Agathon's speech in the *Symposium* when he cites with approval the old saying that like is drawn to like (195b5) and put to work there, since both the beauty of the speech itself and the beauty it attributes to love are only reflections of Agathon's own beauty. But if we return to Aristophanes' play, Agathon there is made to express the view that imitation is not simply the result of being good or beautiful, but can itself be that by which we become good and beautiful. In claiming that the poet must become like his characters, Agathon explains that "*mimēsis* can provide us with the things we do not possess" (l. 155–156).[21] It is thus possible that in imitating the beauty and goodness of love Agathon seeks not only to reflect what he takes to be his own nature, but also further to become himself good and beautiful. Here it is worth noting that Socrates describes the young Agathon in the *Protagoras* as being not only very beautiful in appearance, but as having a beautiful and good nature (315d7–e1). Furthermore, it would be wrong to identify Agathon with the poetic tradition Plato otherwise criticizes. For one thing, as we have already noted, Agathon, unlike the other speakers, treats his poetic sources critically.[22] This should not surprise us since Agathon's distinctive

[21] Lèvêque sees here "une évolution dans la conception de l'artiste: il n'est plus le créateur d'une oeuvre qui exprime avec une nécessité intime sa nature profonde; il devient un acteur qui veut produire une impression et se prête, pour atteindre son but, à toutes les transformations de son être. A la place de la *phusis* nait la *technē*, à la place de l'inspiration qui contraint, la rhétorique préméditée" (1955: 125).

[22] See Belfiore 2012: 136.

trait as a tragedian was to invent his own plots rather than imitate the traditional stories told by the poets.[23] And Agathon's theatre, from what we know of it, could be considered to be especially philosophical in character.[24]

If we are tempted to think that Socrates has nothing to do with the imitation practiced by Agathon, we should first recall that Socrates goes to Agathon's party all dressed up because, he explains, Agathon is beautiful and he must go to him looking beautiful (*houtō kalos gegenēmenos*, 174a5). But then just a few lines later he alters a proverb to describe himself and Aristodemus as good men going unbidden to the feast of the good (174b4–5). So it is Socrates himself who is here not distinguishing between beauty and goodness, is ascribing both to Agathon, and is understanding our relation to both as one of imitation. Furthermore, if we are inclined to criticize Agathon for describing love in his own image, asserting that he thereby misses the truth about love, we should recall that Socrates does the same thing in describing love as ugly, barefoot and poor! Socrates is even like the Agathon of the *Thesmophoriazusae* in giving his speech in the guise of a woman! Finally, Agathon's claim in Aristophanes' play could be made Socrates' own: we become what we imitate and therefore the solution to not possessing goodness and beauty is to imitate them. In short, while there can be no doubt that what Agathon provides is in some sense an image, to assume that such an image is to be disparaged and rejected by the philosopher is to assume that the philosopher is capable of an unmediated access to the truth. Diotima of course describes such an ideal, but to believe that Socrates or any other philosopher could fully attain it, as

[23] "Nevertheless even in tragedy there are some plays with but one or two known names in them, the rest being inventions; and there are some without a single known name, e. g. Agathon's *Antheus*, in which both incidents and names are of the poet's invention, and it is no less delightful on that account" (Aristotle, *Poetics* 6, 1451b19–24). Lèvêque argues that this was the play with which Agathon achieved the victory celebrated in the *Symposium* (1955: 55). One piece of evidence he offers is the use of forms of the word for "flower" (*anthos*) at 196a8–b2, which can be plausibly taken as an allusion to the title of the tragedy (56; see also 111). Apart from its being original, nothing is known about the play's plot; even the title *Flower* has been disputed (see Lèvêque 1955: 105–114). From the other titles that have been preserved, it is clear that Agathon was often faithful to the old classical subjects. But he was also an innovator with regard to the musical dimension of tragedy and in two respects: he reduced the choruses to mere intermezzi with no necessary connection to the plot and he introduced a chromaticism that enabled him to express all the nuances of the sentiments and passions (151). As Lèvêque concludes, "C'est donc avant tout comme un novateur que se présente Agathon . . ." (153).

[24] As Lèvêque notes, "nous retrouvons dans la tragédie d'Agathon cette même attitude réflexive, ce même besoin de connaître l'homme et le monde, cette même curiosité inlassable de l'esprit, ce même effort d'analyse s'appliquant à la totalité du réel. Son théâtre est un théâtre raisonneur, et même philosophique et, comme tel, rapelle de près celui d'Euripide" (1955: 116–117).

Sedley apparently does (see: 65), is to ignore the context of Diotima's teaching and thus to misread the dialogue as a whole.[25]

It is here, however, that we can begin to perceive where the real difference between Socrates and Agathon lies. If Agathon tends to think that he is what he imitates, that he possesses what he loves, Socrates interprets all imitation as desire and all desire as lack. Agathon the poet is satisfied with images because he fails to see the great gulf that separates the image from the original. This is why Agathon's wisdom is manifest and bright (*lampra*), while that of Socrates is "ambiguous like a dream" (*amphisbētēsimos hōs onar*, 175e3–4). Because he in contrast recognizes this gulf, Socrates can at least envisage, through the eyes of the priestess Diotima, a beauty that is no longer an image and the contact with which will give birth to goodness that is no longer an image (212a4–6). But if Socratic *erōs* recognizes the deficiency of images and is directed beyond them, that need not make it any less enamored of images. On Socrates' account, it is only through beautiful images – and this includes *beautiful bodies* – that we can access, if at all, the good. That Socrates critiques Agathon and the beautiful images he represents, that he wishes to go beyond him, in no way shows that he does not remain attracted to him.

Agathon, we must note, is indeed attractive for more than his physical beauty. Not only does the serious content of his speech show him to possess at least an approximation of the wisdom Socrates himself seeks, but he also recognizes that he can at best offer a "measure" of the truth according to the limits of his abilities. This is reflected in the perfect graciousness with which he endures what can only be described as extremely rude behavior on the part of Socrates and in his acceptance of his refutation with an open acknowledgement of his ignorance rather than with anger or evasion.[26] Agathon is indeed one of the very few good interlocutors in Plato's dialogues and we should not forget that he is in the current dialogue the only person Socrates chooses to engage in conversation. If in comparison to Alcibiades he lacks a sufficiently passionate nature and does not experience fully the pain of shame regarding his deficiencies, this makes him less of a lover but not less of a beloved.[27]

[25] See Gonzalez 2012.

[26] Lèvêque does not neglect to emphasize the goodness of Agathon: his graciousness, hospitality, solicitude towards his many friends, but also his courage in publicly defending the politician Antiphon at a very sensitive and dangerous time (for details, see 1955: 46–47).

[27] Lèvêque in stressing the similarities between Agathon and Alcibiades (1955: 78–79) ignores the important differences in character.

This is made clear at the dialogue's end when Socrates expresses his desire that Agathon sit next to him so that he can praise him as Alcibiades praised Socrates: Socrates even claims that "I'm really desirous of praising him" (223a2). While on the usual assessment of Agathon and his speech, Socrates' desire here must come as a surprise (though not for long, as commentators always have ready to hand the convenient device of dismissing surprising claims as being only "ironic"), there is nothing surprising about it on the current reading. After having critiqued Agathon and his earlier self for not conceiving of love as a lover (204c1–3), Socrates is eager to praise Agathon as the embodiment of the good and beautiful qualities that belong to the *beloved.* Socrates indeed twice in the dialogue addresses Agathon as "beloved" (201c9, 222d5). After Alcibiades' speech praising Socrates the lover as if he were the beloved and as if he possessed a wisdom he disavows, Socrates is eager to counter by assuming the role of lover again in praising someone who, having misunderstood what it means to be a lover, can still be an object of love.

The dramatic action is significant here. At first Alcibiades tries to come between Socrates and Agathon, but only to witness what he describes as Socrates' resourcefulness in getting Agathon to sit next to him (223a8–9): a description that clearly echoes Diotima's description of love's resourcefulness as explained by its mother Poverty lying down with its father Resource (203b7–c1). But in the end it is the sudden arrival of drunken revelers that comes between Socrates and Agathon (223b2–6). Is it too much to hear the suggestion here that Alcibiades and the drunken revelers come between Socrates and *the good* he desires, or at least its beautiful image?[28] We can assume, of course, that Socrates' praise of Agathon, like Alcibiades' praise of Socrates, would have been mixed with critique, and this for the simple reason that it would have been a praise of *the good* and therefore implicitly a critique of the eponymous person who is only a deficient if beautiful appearance of the good. Yet Socrates knows perfectly well that the pursuit of the good cannot dispense with beautiful images, however deficient.

Even the disorder that puts an end to the speeches and prevents Socrates from praising Agathon cannot stand in the way of Socrates's passion for dialogue. And who is the last person to stay awake in discussion with

[28] Belfiore finds this play already in Socrates' refutation of Agathon: ". . . when Socrates says that *Erōs* is deficient in (or needs) good things (*tōn agathōn endeēs*; 201c5), he is simultaneously refuting Agathon and paying him a compliment, by stating that *Erōs* is in need of Agathon. This pun also helps explain why Socrates addresses Agathon as "beloved." In identifying him with the things *Erōs* needs, Socrates casts Agathon in the role of beloved, a role that Agathon's speech already gave to his soft and delicate *Erōs* (see 204c1–5)" (2012: 176).

Socrates but Agathon? Even if Socrates is trying to persuade both Agathon and Aristophanes that their respective arts should form one expertise, Aristophanes nods off well before Agathon, the latter not falling asleep until it was already daylight (223d8), leaving us to wonder if in the end it is only Agathon who can follow Socrates' point and perhaps even be persuaded by it. Even Rowe must grudgingly admit that "Agathon has shown at least some ability to follow an argument, and certainly more than Aristophanes (But perhaps this is to press the text too hard?)" (1998: 215). Furthermore, if Rowe can see a critique of Agathon in the final argument only by assuming that Agathon "was exclusively a tragic poet" (214), there is evidence of the historical Agathon bringing the forms of tragedy and comedy closer together in key respects and even, if one scholion is to be believed, writing comedies himself. One scholiast of Aristophanes' *Frogs* describes Agathon as *kōmōidopoios* (Lévêque 1955: 84). Lévêque dismisses this as an error perhaps having its origin in Socrates' argument at the end of the *Symposium* (87). But why not instead take this as some evidence that Agathon was persuaded by Socrates to the extent of going on to write comedies? Lévêque himself sees an anticipation of the New Comedy in Agathon's innovation of an original plot (113) as well as his innovative reduction of the choruses to simple intermezzi (141). In this case Agathon would have much in common with that tragedian-turned-writer-of-tragicomic-dialogues named Plato. But at the very least the concluding conversation between Socrates and Agathon as all others have fallen asleep or passed out confirms the kinship between the two suggested by the nature and central importance of their rivalry in the dialogue.[29] While most commentators do not consider Agathon worthy even of speaking before Socrates, Dionysus crowns both. And Socrates, far from begrudging the poet his laurels, does not allow the destructive infatuation of Alcibiades or the indiscriminate noise of the multitude to keep him from giving Agathon what is surely the highest possible praise: engaging him in serious conversation. It is for this purpose, after all, that Socrates made himself beautiful.

[29] At the very least, there is between Socrates and Agathon, as Lévêque has concluded, "une solide amitié" (1955: 44). Completely groundless is Rowe's claim that "Certainly, by the end of the dialogue it will have become perfectly clear that Socrates has no high opinion of Agathon's qualities, either as intellectual or as poet" (1998: 161). Edmonds (1931: 2.1.2., note 10) suggests that the following verse that has come down to us under Plato's name (see Diogenes Laertius 3, 23, 3) was written by Plato impersonating Socrates: "When I kiss Agathon my soul is on my lips, whither it comes, poor thing, hoping to cross over" (trans. Edmonds). Lévêque, not considering the possibility suggested by Edmonds, just dismisses the verse as a fabrication by someone who forgot the respective ages of Agathon and Plato (1955: 53).

CHAPTER 7

Erōs *and the Pursuit of Form*

F.C.C. Sheffield

It has become relatively commonplace to refer to Plato's erotic philosophy.[1] It is often unclear what Plato's erotic philosophy refers to, however, though it usually involves claims about the importance of Plato's characterization of philosophy as a form of *erōs*, and of Socrates' claim to have an "erotic art" (e.g. *Phdr.* 257a3–b6). Nor is it clear where the significance of *erōs* resides exactly. First, the characterization of the philosopher in terms of *erōs* seems important to some dialogues (e.g. *Symposium*, *Republic*, and *Phaedrus*), but drops from view entirely in others (e.g. *Apology*, *Crito*, *Theaetetus*). Second, *erōs* is prominent in those dialogues in which there is a focus on the moral education of the young. Since *erōs* played a role in the educational conventions of the day, the pederastic-cum-educational context can carry much explanatory weight and might eclipse anything of deeper philosophical importance. Third, a lack of philosophical significance might be seen in the fact that *erōs* appears to receive little attention from Aristotle, who was otherwise a keen commentator on many aspects of Plato's thought. As one scholar has put it: "Aristotle tacitly disowns Plato's divine *erōs*."[2] Such considerations might be taken to show that *erōs* was not, after all, a theme of enduring significance for Plato.

The *Symposium* is uniquely placed to shed light on these issues, since there is an explicit argument for the claim that *erōs* is a philosopher (204b–c), and Socrates' account claims that the proper object of *erōs* is an intelligible object, the Form of beauty (211d). One might think that *erōs* is not a natural candidate for an orientation towards the supreme intelligibility and divinity of the Forms, since it was a phenomenon often associated, though by no means exclusively, with passionate sexual desire. This chapter argues that attending to the characteristic features of *erōs* in

[1] There have been numerous studies recently, e.g. Rhodes 2003, Alan-Scott and Welton 2008, Gordon 2012, Belfiore 2012.

[2] Walzer 1962: 241, quoted by Price 1989: 236.

the *Symposium* can clarify precisely the sense in which *erōs* is, in fact, a uniquely appropriate orientation to have towards intelligible and divine Forms, given the kind of value wisdom is, for Plato, and the role he wants it to play in our lives. With this in place, we will be able to appreciate better the significance of *erōs* for Plato and to address Aristotle's limited, though arguably significant, engagement with Platonic *erōs*. Or so I shall argue.

1. *Erōs* and the *Kalon*

To unpack the relationship between *erōs* and philosophy, one must begin, as Plato does, by considering a basic feature of *erōs*: its relationship to beauty. The relationship between *erōs* and the *kalon* was axiomatic for the Greeks, and a repeated feature of Plato's accounts of *erōs*; the claim that what is most beautiful is most lovable occurs in three dialogues (*Rep.* 402d: *kalliston erasmiōtaton*, and *Tim.* 87d7–8: *kalliston kai erasmiōtaton*; cf. *Phdr.* 250e1), and it is implied in a fourth argument in our text (*Symp.* 204b2–3).[3] In these contexts embodied beauty is to the fore, the perception of which seems to be a fundamental experience of what is beautiful for embodied human souls.[4] Though the *kalon* is a difficult term to translate, both "the beautiful," and "the fine," or "praiseworthy," capture much of its sense, whose range is broader than the superficial, or cosmetic, appearance of a thing.[5] To call something *kalon* was to appraise the object, and to suggest that it has a relationship with the good (*to agathon*). Since the *kalon* has a connection with the appearance of a thing, and the good of a thing, one way to capture this connection is to say, with Kosman (2005), that "it is the mode of the good that shows forth; it is the splendor of the appearance of the good."[6] The *kalon* is how the goodness of a thing – a body, a soul, a poem or law – appears to us.[7]

[3] See also *Charm.* 167e where *epithumia* has pleasure as its proper object, whilst *erōs* is directed towards the *kalon*. Konstan 2014: 62 has argued that "the classical Greek notion of beauty is closely related to *erōs*, that is, passionate desire. Indeed, I would say that the fundamental response that was excited by beauty in ancient Greece was understood to be precisely desire."

[4] See Lear 2006: 116 and Prauscello 2014 who argues that it is because *erōs* is associated with beauty, particularly visual beauty, that it is available to children and cultivated as an important part of the educational program of the *Laws*.

[5] The *kalon* is difficult to capture with our narrow notion of beauty. For rich discussions, see Kosman 2010 and Barney 2010.

[6] See Kosman 2010: 355 and Lear 2006: 107 who talks about "the excellence that beautiful things manifest."

[7] In the *Republic*, goodness is the standard for beauty (452e; cf. 457b). Compare the discussion of artistic imitation, where Socrates speaks of the "virtue, beauty, and correctness" (*aretē kai kallos kai orthotēs*) of a utensil, animal, or action (601d), where these terms seem synonymous. The definition

Since our attendance to beauty is revealing of a conception of value, even visual perceptions of beauty can indicate where we see value to reside in the world. As such, visual beauty can provide initial conceptions of what is fine, or praiseworthy, and reflection on our notions of beauty can contribute to the formation of something like an embryonic moral sense.[8] The axiomatic role of the *kalon* in Plato's scheme of values, shown by the central role given to the *kalon* in the attainment of virtue and happiness in the *Symposium*, the *Phaedrus*, and the educational program of the *Republic*, goes some way towards explaining the use to which Plato puts *erōs* in a number of works. One reason why *erōs* matters is because the *kalon* matters to Plato, and our natural responsiveness to beauty – *erōs* – can be used as a way into the good life. This begins to explain the use to which *erōs* is put in the *Laws*, for example, where it is deliberately and actively cultivated by the lawgiver as part of the education of children, and also the *Republic's* claim that the end of the young guardian's education is love of the beautiful (403c).[9]

This relationship between *erōs* and beauty explains the precise sense in which philosophy itself is, for Plato, a form of *erōs*. In one of the very few explicit arguments in the *Symposium* Socrates argues that *Erōs* must, in fact, be a philosopher on the grounds that *erōs* is concerned with beauty, and wisdom is one of the most beautiful things (204b2–3). So, one important object of *erōs*' pursuit must be wisdom. This argument does not commit Socrates to the view that wisdom is the only object of *erōs;* just as there may be other beautiful objects besides wisdom (it is said that wisdom is *amongst* the most beautiful things), so there may be – and clearly are – forms of *erōs* other than philosophical *erōs*. The argument does rely on a particularly strong construal of the relationship between beauty and *erōs*, though. For if the claim were only that if something is beautiful then it is desired, it would not necessarily follow that *erōs* pursues wisdom. The claim is also needed that if something is perceived to be beautiful then it is desired (where the perception of beauty is sufficient and not just necessary for *erōs*). The argument runs as follows: if something is perceived to be beautiful *erōs* desires it; wisdom is perceived to be beautiful, therefore *erōs* desires wisdom. It also seems to be the case that wisdom is desired not

of virtue as a kind of (*tis*) health or beauty of the soul (444d–e) also shows the connection between beauty and excellence, or goodness.

[8] So Lear 2006: 112 on the importance of beauty in the education of the *Republic* writes that: "Where the love of beautiful art develops before the advent of rational understanding, one's sense of beauty or the fine will provide presuppositions for later deliberation."

[9] See Prauscello 2014 who has done so much to shed light on the role of *erōs* in the *Laws*.

because it is just an instance of beauty, but because it is *one of the most beautiful things* (204b3). The superlative suggests a correlation between the degree of perceived beauty in the object and the *erōs* experienced for that object. With this in place, the argument is that *erōs* is concerned with the beautiful (204b3); the more beautiful the object the more *erōs* desires that object; wisdom is one of the most beautiful things (b2-3); therefore *Erōs* is, in the highest degree, a lover of wisdom.

The notion that wisdom is an object of erotic attraction is not mere metaphor.[10] Though philosophical *erōs* is not sexual in any sense, it is nevertheless truly *erotikos*, properly speaking, and not in some transferred sense; for all *erōs* is concerned with beauty (e.g. *Symp.* 206e). It is first and foremost the notion of an attachment to beauty that clings fast to *erōs*. The fundamental experience of *erōs* is a desire for beauty, the most basic expression of which is sexual, where this is simply one of its common forms. There are other forms of *erōs* that have nothing at all to do with sexual experience, other than sharing with it an orientation towards beauty.[11] Given the range of phenomena designated *kalon* – bodies, souls, forms – there will be a range of objects to which *erōs* is responsive. Many passages in Plato associate a Form with beauty, this is not just a property had by the Form of beauty: *Crat.* 439c; *Euthd.* 301a; *Laws* 655c; *Phd.* 65d, 75d, 100b; *Phdr.* 254b; *Parm.* 130b; *Phil.* 15a; *Rep.* 476b, 493e, 507b. Given that *erōs* is, for Plato, the name of that specific desire *for beauty*, and the notion that wisdom is one of the most beautiful things, and its objects, the Forms, are supremely beautiful, we can appreciate why one could have *erōs*, properly speaking, and not in any "transferred sense" for the forms.[12] Philosophical *erōs* would not emerge were one to consider wisdom simply, though perhaps rightly, to be the highest good; it emerges specifically and properly when one comes to desire wisdom *as one of the most beautiful things*. Socrates' "erotic art" consists in his ability to make people see the beauty of wisdom – not just its goodness, or its centrality in the good life – but its *beauty*; for all *erōs* is concerned with beauty (*Symp.* 206e). Socrates' art would not be *erōtikos* were it to argue us into

[10] Nor is philosophy a form of *erōs* only in some "transferred sense," as Belfiore 2012: 9 claims. For arguments against a metaphorical sense, see Halperin 1985: 188.

[11] See Ludwig 2002: 121 for evidence of a long poetic tradition of non-sexual *erōs*.

[12] There is an issue here about how one could have *erōs* for an intelligible object, if beauty has a connection to the manifest *appearance* of a thing. In the *Philebus, nous* is said to have a greater share in beauty than pleasure (65e). The appearance must be an intelligible one and the agent of perception must be the eye of the soul, rather than the eyes of the body (to which Plato refers to in a number of works: *Symp.* 219a, *tēs dianoias opsis*; *Rep.* 533d, *to tēs psukhēs omma; Soph.* 254a, *tēs psukhēs ommata*).

the pursuit of philosophy by reasoned argument about its goodness; it is *erōtikos* insofar as it encourages a desire for wisdom by making apparent, in a variety of ways, its *beauty*.

2. The Hallmarks of *erōs*

One would still like to know what it is about the nature of this desire that makes it suitable to characterize the philosopher's orientation towards wisdom. Plato might have stuck with arguments for the claim that wisdom is the highest good, and bypassed *erōs* and beauty altogether, or given these phenomena a more marginal role, perhaps. Though *erōs* is not used exclusively to characterize the pursuit of Forms, it is used consistently enough to think that there is a commitment beyond the context of the *Symposium*. In the *Phaedo*, *erōs* is also used to characterize the orientation towards forms (66e2–4, 67e5–68a2, 68a7–b6 and 73d where it is an analogy for recollecting Forms), as it is in the *Republic* (485b, 490b, 501d2) and the *Phaedrus* (252c–253b).[13] In the *Timaeus*, *erōs* is connected to *nous* and the search for primary causes (46d7–e2), though this clearly differs from the "all venturing *erōs*" that appears in the mortal soul as part of its disturbances (69c). And it is cultivated as the appropriate response to the ideal of perfect citizenship in the *Laws*, as Prauscello (2014) has shown. The lawgiver should nurture a particular kind of *erōs* through a variety of communal social practices (688a5f). Children will be led in play *to desire passionately* what they are to become when they grow up: to "fall in love with" the idea of perfect citizenship (643c8–d3). An education that aims at virtue from youth will cause the soul of the young *to have erōs* for the idea of becoming a perfectly good citizen (643e4–5). The impression one has from the *Laws* is that *erōs* is deliberatively and actively cultivated as the appropriate response to the ideals required for the state, much as the *Symposium*, the *Phaedrus*, and, arguably, the *Republic* and the *Phaedo*, suggest that *erōs* characterizes the philosopher's relationship to the Forms. The question is why that is.

This question intersects with a larger one about the role and relevance of desire as such, though I am concerned here with the role and relevance of *erōs*, as opposed to any other kind of desire. Why reflection on desire as such plays a role in the characterization of the virtuous agent (viz. the philosopher) highlights a strand of Plato's thinking in which, like other ancient ethical theorists, he does not focus solely on rules for good action, but on

[13] There is also *erōs* terminology use to characterize the pursuit of wisdom in a number of other dialogues that do not mention Forms. See, for example, *Lys.* (204b1–2); *Euthd.* (282).

the virtuous agent's character and life (Annas 1993). Since what we care about and love passionately shapes the course and nature of our lives and in that way determines our chances of happiness, Plato has much to say about desire and its proper regulation. Nowhere is this clearer than in the *Symposium*, where we see how the lives of prominent Athenians have been shaped by their loves, and how each fares accordingly. And if desire does play such a role in Plato's articulation of the good life, then it becomes important to specify those desires that play a role in our ethical lives precisely. For if the relevant desires arise *spontaneously*, for example, their role in the life of the ethical agent might inhibit our ability to administer praise and blame. If the relevant desires do not involve any *appraisal* of the object, they might have a tenuous relationship to intelligibility, and it would be difficult to appreciate how they could play a role in the philosophical life. So, if we are to appreciate how *erōs* plays a role in the good philosophical life, as it surely does in the *Symposium*, *Republic*, and *Phaedrus*, and how it can be deliberately and actively employed in the pursuit of forms, this requires careful attention to its characteristic features. To those I shall now turn.

Erōs is a desire of a specific kind. When someone is in the grip of *erōs* there is something the agent wants, and this is something he lacks (either now or in the future: 200e3–5). But *erōs* is more than a lack and longing; it involves cognitive components, specifically an evaluative judgment of its object as *kalon* or *agathon* in some respect, and the object in question is desired under that description (201a8–10, b6–7, c4–5, 202d1–3, 203d4).[14] The object of *erōs* is not just desirable, but also intelligible, insofar as it is thought of some kind that presents to the soul some good or beautiful object deemed worthy of *erōs*. This is significant when we come to account for how such a desire could fall under the scope of philosophical interest and education at all. If this desire had no relationship to intelligibility then it would not be a resource capable of being deliberately and actively employed by philosophical practice, as it is in the "ascent" passage (210–212). *Erōs* involves cognitive components. Indeed, the myth of *Erōs*' birth, which is supposed to illuminate the nature of *erōs*, makes it plain that *erōs* is not just a blind drive, or passionate yearning: it is a cognitively informed state of desire, or motivation, that combines an awareness of lack and a longing (*pothos*) for some object perceived to be *kalon*, with some kind of deliberation about how to remedy that lack and take steps towards

[14] This is given more precise formulation later on: note the guarded expression at 204d3, "as you say," and the more careful "concerning the beautiful" at 204b3. As we learn later, the ultimate goal of *erōs* is not beauty, but *eudaimonia*, and beauty plays a role in its acquisition.

realizing the desired goal (203d5–7). In virtue of his father, *Erōs* is a schemer (203d4) and inherits *epiboulia*. This is what is indicated in the aetiological myth of *erōs* by the description of *Erōs' dual* parentage. An experience of *erōs* is complex and cognition-involving, then, which makes it appropriate, though perhaps not yet uniquely so, to characterize the range of objects to which *erōs* is receptive and the diverse pursuits and actions that fall under its domain.

To explain our persistent attraction to beauty, Socrates considers its aim. Significantly, given what our ultimate aim will turn out to be, he begins by substituting "good" for "beauty" to clarify the aim of *erōs*, before he is able to explain the attraction to beauty. It seems obvious to Socrates that when we desire some *good* thing we do so because we think it will make us happy. This is the ultimate aim of desire because:

> One no longer needs to go on to ask "And what reason does the person who wishes to be happy have for wishing it?" Your answer seems complete. (*Symp*. 205a2–3; trans. Rowe)

Erōs is a specific kind of desire concerned with good things and happiness (205d). The fulfilment of this desire is reached only when we find something that makes life "worth living" (211d), that for the sake of which every action is pursued (210e5–6). *Erōs* refers specifically to desires for objects considered to be central to our happiness (204e–205a, 205d). Though some scholars have argued for a Socratic conception of desire in this work, according to which all desire, not just *erōs*, shares this characteristic, this is not obvious from the claims stated here.[15] Though it is compatible with the claim that *erōs* is that area of desire concerned with good things and happiness that *all* desire is so orientated, this need not be the case. Any other desires to which we might be subject are not on the agenda in this work.[16] There is some terminological slippage in the initial characterization of *erōs* here: *boulesthai* and *epithumein* are used interchangeably at numerous points (e.g 205a5–b1), but this need indicate only that *erōs* is a specific kind of desire (*epithumia*), namely, a kind of desire that is concerned specifically with good things and happiness, and not that all desire is so concerned.[17] What is clear is that when something is pursued *with erōs* it is thought to be capable of satisfying the desire for *eudaimonia* and

[15] On this issue, see Irwin 1995: 303, Price 1997: 254–5, and Rowe 2006; for a more restricted scope to Socrates' claims here, see Sheffield 2006: 214–5.

[16] As Kahn 1996: 264 also argues.

[17] Distinctions among desire terms are operative in the *Charm*. (167e14–15) where *epithumia* is related to a desire for pleasure and *boulēsis* for the good.

sought as a way in which to attain that end. A beautiful person, or thing, may be misleading in this role, but the point is that when that person or thing is pursued with *erōs*, it is valued as supremely beautiful (204c4) and capable of delivering *eudaimonia* (in some way that remains to be clarified).

This *erōs* for good and beautiful things is characterized as a movement towards the divine in the *Symposium*: *erōs* operates between the mortal and the immortal (202d–203a), and the desire for good and beautiful things is a desire for the happiness that characterizes the divine state (202c10–d5). When something is desired with *erōs*, when the object is thought to be something that makes life worth living, the object of desire is *idealized*, so much so that we view them as coming as close to the divine as we imagine possible: they are *teleon kai makariston* (204c4). Though the divine may not play such a role in our thought today, for the Greeks the gods would be the very yardstick of idealization:[18] to say something is supremely beautiful and perfect and blessed, just is to understand that object as sharing in the divine. So, *erōs* is a specific mode of valuation, one in which we see the object as that which, more than anything else, makes life "worth living," as holding out the promise of divine *eudaimonia*.[19]

The dispositional features that characterize *erōs* can be explained in light of this aim. The intensity and enthusiasm that characterize this desire are due to the fact that the objects it pursues as valuable are desired as goods that matter to us in this particular kind of way, as things whose pursuit we consider, more than anything else, to make our lives worth living.[20] The reason why someone in the grip of *erōs* does not give up, and seeks

[18] Though one might not think that *erōs* is an appropriate orientation to have towards the divine, *erōs*' relationship to the divine has been on the agenda from the start, and is clear in the characterization of *erōs* as a *daimōn* whose proper function is to mediate with the divine (202e–203a).

[19] To say it is "that which, more than anything else, makes life worth living" is a way of capturing the central role the object of *erōs* plays in the attainment of *eudaimonia*. These are goods ranked highest in value in a life worth living. Plato describes bodily health as something without which life is not worth living at the end of *Rep.* IV, while holding that mental health is higher in value. I am trying to capture the way in which the objects of *erōs* are central to *eudaimonia*. I thank David Sedley for prompting me to clarify this point. Another way to consider the issue is to say that the desired object is seen as an end and valued non-instrumentally, though this, again, requires careful formulation. When something is pursued with *erōs* the agent in question does see a potential gain in his *eudaimonia*. The beautiful object is pursued for the sake of an ultimate aim, which is the agent's own happiness. So it might be that the object is seen as good just in itself, by which is meant, as in the division of goods in *Rep.* II, all by itself conducive to *eudaimonia*, whereas good for its effects means that the effects are what is conducive to *eudaimonia*. An experience of *erōs* might value its objects in both ways. For example, the form of beauty is that for the sake of which all *erōs* strives (210e6) and also valued for the sake of the virtue and happiness that results (212a2–6). I thank Nicholas Smith for pressing me on this point.

[20] See Ludwig 2002: 13 on erotic obsession: "*Erōs* occurs in cases in which the desire, whether sexual or not, becomes obsessional and the subject of desire becomes willing to devote nearly all his or her

(*zētein*, 205e1, 203d4) possession of the object with much enthusiasm (*spoudē*, 208b6), and cherishes it (*aspazesthai*, e6), is *because* these are objects seen as those which, above all else, make life worth living. The distinctive aim of *erōs* also explains its characteristic activity, or *ergon*: reproductive, or creative, activity in the beautiful (206c1f.). For since the object is valued in this way, one does not just want to gaze at its value, nor possess it in the sense in which one wants to get a bit of cake. For the activity of *erōs* to meet the demands of its aim – *eudaimonia* for the agent – a particular kind of change needs to be effected, which is significant, lasting, and transformative for the agent's life. Nor does one desire to care for the object in such a way that the beloved thing is benefitted; for the objects of *erōs* are seen as beautiful, perfect, and blessed (*teleon kai makariston*: 204c4–5), and are viewed as having some relationship to the divine. The desiring agent does not desire primarily to effect a change in the beloved object, to love and care for it in such a way that it will be benefitted and changed. Rather, he desires to change *himself*, particularly, to obtain a measure of divine happiness, by coming to possess some good that the valuable object manifests for him, and in which he perceives himself to be in need. This explains the characteristically productive mode of activity. This is the way in which mortal creatures like ourselves try "to have a share in" the divine *eudaimonic* life (208b5).[21]

To have *erōs* for something, then, is to desire to achieve a share of divine happiness by coming to possess whatever we perceive to be of value in the object in a particular way. And whatever change we effect in ourselves to secure its possession must be an enduring and lasting change if it is to satisfy the desire for something that makes *a life* worthwhile; for the goal is *eudaimonia* (205d). Different kinds of beauty are pursued by different kinds of desiring agents because they are seen to be appropriate to

life, time, or resources to achieving the goal. *Erōs* tends to engage the whole self or to throw every other concern into the shade." Cf. Scott 2007 on the "tunnel vision" that accompanies *erōs*.

21 One might wonder how this conception of *erōs* fits the *Phaedrus*. At 253a7–b1 the lover tried to make his beloved as much like the god he resembles as possible, so he is trying to change his beloved in some way, as well as himself. Both parties are drawn into greater resemblance with the god in whose train they followed in the celestial circuit. I thank Nancy Worman for raising this objection. The thought here need not rule out change in another. If we return to the *Symposium*, law-givers such as Solon and Lycurgus are clearly trying to make a change in the cities for which they legislate (209d–e); this is how such desiring agents try to achieve *eudaimonia*, given their specification of that aim and the importance of honour to its acquisition. The point is just that insofar as this is an expression of *erōs*, the primary purpose of that activity is to effect a change in the desiring agent himself, namely to secure a name for himself and win renown and satisfy his desire for *eudaimonia*. So, though *erōs* does not rule out a change in the relevant object, this is not the central purpose of its activity.

the acquisition of the desired good in each case; they exhibit something of value that the agent wants to reproduce himself – a fine city might facilitate the production of fine laws, a beautiful soul might inspire an attempt to capture that beauty in speeches that make decent souls into beautiful souls and so on, and cognitive engagement with beautiful bodies and souls will facilitate the production of wisdom. *Erōs* for bodily beauty manifests itself in the attempt to capture that value by the production of physical offspring, thought to provide "memory and happiness for all time to come" (208e4–5); *erōs* for a beautiful city or soul might issue in an attempt to capture that value by the production of fine poems or speeches, thereby securing an honourable life as a poet or educator for their producers (208c3, 209b). *Erōs* is a fundamental urge to self-creation and our relentless pursuit of beauty a drive to reproduce the value we see in the world and capture it in a life of our own, as parents, poets, legislators, or philosophers.[22]

The following features explored in the *Symposium* can be identified as the hallmarks, specifically, of *erōs*:

(i) It is a *specific mode of valuation* (involving cognitive components), in which the object is seen to be beautiful in some respect (201a8–10, b6–7, c4–5, 202d1–3, 203d4);
(ii) The object is *idealized* as "perfect and blessed" (204c4);
(iii) And it is held to be something whose possession by the agent is thought, more than anything else, to make *life worth living* (205d);
(iv) It has accompanying dispositional features, such as longing, intensity enthusiasm, a strength of focus,[23] and a restless search for possession of the object (208b6, e6);

[22] See Halperin 1985:182: *erōs* is "the desire to realize an objective potential in the self." One might be concerned that there is a lack of fit between this account of *erōs* and the examples of erotic attachment given in the characters of Apollodorus, Aristodemus and Alcibiades. To what extent are they pregnant in soul and desire to reproduce in beauty? To what extent is their desire non-reciprocal? As Alcibiades' criticism of Socrates shows, he longs for Socrates to "reciprocate" and to "impregnate" him. I thank Nicholas Smith for putting this objection to me. Apollodorus sees Socrates as an embodiment of *eudaimonia* and his constant "practice" of the speeches at Agathon's symposium (however misguided as a way in which to partake of the philosophical life) seems to be the way in which he tries to capture something of that value in a life of his own and to distinguish it from "rich businessmen's talk" (173c–d). In the case of Alcibiades, he evidently sees great value in Socrates (216a), but given what capturing that value requires of him – arduous philosophical practice – he fails to engage in a creative life of his own and in that sense fails to allow his *erōs* for Socrates to reach its proper expression. It is more attractive for him to be productive in the political arena and secure honour; his *erōs* for Socrates loses out to a competing *erōs* for honour (216b).

[23] This can be seen in the ascent where the focus on *erōs* for the form of beauty leads the desiring agent to disdain the body. Compare *Phdr.* 252a1–6 on how *erōs* marginalizes other desires and concerns.

(v) There is a structural *asymmetry* between the desiring agent and the object of his pursuit: he lacks something of value possessed by the desired object (200e3–5);

(vi) The desire is *nonreciprocal*;

(vii) It manifests itself in *creative activity* (206cf.) in which the agent tries "to reproduce" the value manifested by the desired person or thing in his own character and life, "to have a share of the divine" (*athanasias metechei*) (208b5).

Attending to these features, and thinking about the kind of value wisdom is for Plato, allows us to appreciate why *erōs* might be a good "fit" for that orientation. The objects of wisdom are not just *beautiful*, but also *intelligible*, and so require a mode of orientation that is cognition-involving (i). The idealization involved in *erōs* is also relevant (ii).[24] The specific mode of valuing involved in *erōs* is one in which one attends to the object in its ideal state – as *teleion kai makariston* (204c4), detached from, say, the snub-nose, or lack of punctuality. This way of attending to the object can be preparatory for the more sophisticated kind of abstraction deployed in the ascent, in which it is precisely this tendency to attend to the object in its perfection that enables someone in the grip of *erōs* to explore beauty in a more abstract way. It need not lead there, of course; but to see the object in its perfection is to see it, albeit dimly, in its intelligible aspect, and this allows the agent in question to move beyond the immediate object of its attention, which it has already, in its idealization, to some extent, abstracted from its immediate appearance.

Further, there are many arguments in the dialogues, including the *Symposium*, designed to show that wisdom is that which, above all else, makes life worth living (*Ap.* 29d–e, 38e; *Euthd.* 281e2–282a6; *Symp.* 211d1–2; cf. *Rep.* 445a). If this is the kind of value that wisdom is, for Plato, then it will not be enough to have just *any* desire for wisdom; that would not indicate that one values the object in question in the proper way. Any other desiring relation to the object will expose one as having the wrong view about the value of wisdom, namely that it is lower in value than its true ranking. Someone with *erōs* does not pursue wisdom for instrumental purposes, such as impressing beautiful youths, or for the sake of honour; rather, someone with *erōs* for wisdom recognizes the supreme value of wisdom, as something that, more than anything else, makes life worth living (iii). Its employment by Plato, then, highlights the kind of

[24] See Halperin 1985: 174.

value wisdom is, for him, the role he thinks it should play in our lives, and the manner in which we should pursue it (iv).

3. Acting for a Divine End

The explanation given so far is not sufficient to explain the use Plato makes of *erōs*, however. One might consider desire to be an important part of the characterization of the virtuous agent, and argue that wisdom is the highest good towards which desire should aim, without characterizing that orientation in terms of *erōs* (compare Aristotle). Here is where hallmarks (v)–(vii) take centre stage. The asymmetry, lack of reciprocity, and characteristically "reproductive" action of this desire, are features that make *erōs* a particularly appropriate term in which to characterize action for the sake of an end perceived to be of supreme value and divine. As such, it is a particularly appropriate term in which to characterize the pursuit of divine ends, such as Plato's Forms.[25]

The proper end of all *erōs* is the Form of Beauty, that for the sake of which (*hou heneka*) all *erōs* strives (210e6). This is an end of a specific kind: it is supremely beautiful, divine, and does not suffer change in any way (210e–211a). Though divinity is not always a feature of the Forms to the fore, it is in the *Symposium* and the *Phaedrus,* those dialogues in which *erōs* is central as the response to the Forms in question (211e3).[26] Forms are perfect, changeless, self-sufficient, and divine (211a1, 211b3–5, 211e1), and as such any desiring relationship we have towards the Forms must be one that honours not only the *asymmetry* and lack of reciprocity between the desiring agent and these objects (as *erōs* does), but it must also be one that highlights the specific nature of how one acts for the sake of such an end (as *erōs* also does). When we act "for the sake of" the Form (210e6, 211c2) with *erōs*, we act for its sake in the sense that it is the ultimate object to be attained (210e6), but we act ultimately for *our* sake in the sense that the goal is

[25] *Erōs'* relationship to the divine has been on the agenda from the start. *Erōs* is defined as an intermediate *daimon*, whose power (*dunamis*) is to mediate with the gods. The work of *erōs* as a *daimonic* mediator is manifested in our attempts to secure *eudaimonia*, that state that characterizes the blessed gods (202c7, 205d1), and whose best expression is contemplation of a divine Form (211d). The etymology of *eudaimonia* cannot fail to be significant here. Our happiness is to be understood as the proper functioning, the being well, of the *daimōn erōs* in us. As Long 2004: 126 has argued, "In order to understand ancient philosophical usage of *eudaimonia* we need to attend to the word's etymology and its implicit reference to goodness conjoined with divinity or *daimon*." Nowhere is this clearer than in the *Symposium's* characterization of *erōs* as a *daimōn*, the best "co-worker" with human nature (212b; cf. *Tim.* 90b–c with Sedley 1999: 320).

[26] For Forms as divine see also *Phd.* 80b1, 84a9; *Rep.* 517d4–5, 500c9–d1; *Phdr.* 246d8–e1.

to change ourselves in accordance with it (the purpose of its characteristic reproductive activity: 212a5–7). We do not act "for the sake of" the Form in the sense that we desire to benefit the Forms, any more than we desire to benefit the gods when we attend to them in the *Euthyphro*; *erōs* is a different kind of affective relationship to cattle-rearing in this respect (13b–c).[27] So with our orientation towards the Forms: what is under consideration are desires of this particular kind, namely those in which an agent responds to something he perceives to be of supreme value (the telic component), and desires not to possess, but to *produce*, something *for himself* in relation to the desired object, whilst the object remains unchanged (its "reproductive" activity). *Erōs* is uniquely suited to capture that.

It may not be accidental, then, that *erōs* emerges most strongly in those dialogues in which the theory of Forms plays a central role: the *Phaedo*, the *Symposium*, the *Phaedrus*, and the *Republic*.[28] Attending to the structural features of this desire shows why it is well suited to meet the requirements of an orientation towards divine Forms. The *Philebus* suggests that such considerations are indeed part of Plato's conception of *erōs*. In that work a distinction is drawn between *genesis* and *ousia* with the example of lover and beloved (53cff.). This serves as an illustrative example of this phenomenon because one kind is "sufficient to itself, the other in need of something else ... the one kind possesses supreme dignity, the other is inferior to it." Further, the one exists "for the sake of something" and the other is "that for the sake of which the former is always coming into being." This is used to clarify the way in which *genesis* changes in accordance with being, just as a lover changes in accordance with his beloved; for the other (the beloved/being) is in need of nothing, since it is already in possession of supreme "dignity." The use of *erōs* in this context highlights the *asymmetry* of the relationship, the *non-reciprocal* nature of the relationship, and how *one changes in accordance with the other*. All three features help to articulate the specific orientation towards Forms.

[27] At *Euth.* 13b–e Socrates distinguishes between two ways of acting for the sake of an end: hunting and cattle raising are ways of acting for the sake of an object of care where one aims at the benefit of the object cared for, and Socrates is moving to distinguish this case from that of acting for the gods, who do not need to be benefitted. Euthyphro is confused because piety does not aim to benefit the gods and make them better in the manner of Socrates' earlier examples of care. The implication is that there is an alternative construal of acting for the sake of an object of care (*therapeuein*). This is a distinction that becomes more explicit in Aristotle (*DA* II.4 415b2–3, b20–1; *Phys.* II.2 194a35–6) with Lear 2004: 75 n.9.

[28] There is also *erōs* terminology use to characterize the pursuit of wisdom in a number of other dialogues, which do not mention forms. See, for example, *Lys.* (204b1–2); *Euthd.* (282); and *Gorg.* (cf. *Prt.* 309a1–2 with c2). See also *Tht.* 66d.

One might argue that acting "for the sake of the good" is surely not problematic under ordinary circumstances, i.e. when there's no danger of anyone's supposing that anyone else's benefit is involved.[29] But one might think that an issue does arise over how we act for the sake of a specifically *divine* end; this was highlighted as problematic in the *Euthyphro* (13b–e). Even if it is clear that one is not acting in a way that benefits *the object*, one needs to clarify how one does act exactly. Not to possess the object in any straightforward way, in the way that an object of appetite might be had. Nor just to gaze at its value; that would do nothing to make it our own as part of a life worth living. If the pursuit of wisdom it to become that transformative enterprise Plato saw it to be, then our relationship to that end must be able to carry the weight of its transformative potential for our lives. Here the language of *erōs* is particularly helpful. The characteristic action of *erōs* is to want "to have a share in," to change in accordance with the perceived value in the object, to "approximate" the object of its attention, and so to capture that value for the agent himself.[30] This feature of *erōs* was also appreciated by Neo-Platonists; Plotinus and Proclus made *erōs* central to their accounts of the movement of all things towards the One, where each entity becomes the best image of its progenitor. They saw that the hallmarks of *erōs* are uniquely suited to action for a divine end.[31]

4. From Ethics to Metaphysics: *Erōs* and Aristotle

The significance of this structure of *erōs* when characterizing a relationship to a divine end was, arguably, not lost on Aristotle. And here I am deeply indebted to Lear (2004) who has argued that Aristotle uses *erōs* in a context that employs features highlighted in Plato's *Symposium*.[32] A sketch of the

[29] I thank Christopher Rowe for prompting me to clarify the argument here.

[30] One might be concerned that embodying the value of the desired object, or "having a share of" (208b3), is not a form of *productive* activity, which is *erōs'* characteristic work (206cf.). In the *Sophist*, imitation belongs to the art of making (219b1). There are various kinds of production: farming, or any caring for mortal bodies, and caring for fabricated things, and imitation.

[31] Plotinus associates *erōs* with the notion of *homoiōsis*, "becoming like" (VI 7, 31, 10). He compares the erotic movement towards intellect and the One with the experience of lovers who wish to see their beloved, to become like him, and to become one with him. See Armstrong 1979 and Beierwaltes 1986: 304. Cf. Proclus (*In Alc.* 61. 3–5): all that exists is moved towards the One by *erōs*. He also discusses "assimilation to the origin." Note also *erōs* as "the binding guide of all things" (64). On Proclus' use of *erōs*, see Quispel 1979.

[32] Lear (2004: 209) argues that the *Symposium* supports a traditional reading of Aristotle "according to which the first heaven expresses its love for the Prime Mover by approximating it." Chang (2002) highlights parallels between Plato's *Symposium* and Aristotle's *Metaphysics Lamda*, though he is more concerned with parallels between Plato's treatment of the Beautiful and "Aristotle's understanding of the Unmoved Mover in its nature and function."

evidence should highlight further the significance of these features of Platonic *erōs*. The distinction between two ways of acting for the sake of an end, one where the agent seeks to benefit the object, and the other where the goal is to be attained or realized by the agent, is explicit in Aristotle, who employed it in at least three works (*De An.* II.4 415b2-3, b20–1; *Phys.* II.2 194a35–6; *Metaph.* 1072b1–3). Two of these are deeply resonant of the *Symposium*. For example, in *Lambda*, Aristotle confronts a puzzle about how unmoved movers move. For Aristotle, what has the power to move things without itself being moved is an object of desire or thought – *to orekton kai to noēton* (1072a26–7). When we desire something, the *kalon* object moves our faculty of desire, which then moves us to action without itself changing in any way (1072a27–8 with Lear [2004: 74]). So, if there is some supremely beautiful object that the first heaven desires this could be an unchanging cause of the motion of the heavens.[33] Aristotle goes on to make a distinction between two kinds of "for the sake of which" relations.

> And that the "for the sake of which" is present among the group of unmovable things is made clear by the distinction: For there is the "for the sake of which" as an object of benefit and the "for the sake of which" as an object to be attained or realized, and of these the one is [moveable] and the other is not (*Metaph.* 1072b1–3).

Since it is central to some ends "for the sake of which" we act that they are changeable (e.g. when they are benefitted), Aristotle needs to rule out such cases; it is to do so that he employs this distinction between two ways of acting for the sake of an end. Objects of desire are among ends to be attained, and which we pursue to improve our own condition, not theirs. After Aristotle has made this specific distinction he goes on to claim that the Prime Mover moves the heavenly bodies as something loved (*hōs erōmenon*, 1072b3). Though Aristotle had previously talked about unmoved movers in general as objects of desire with terms such as *epithumia*, *boulēsis* and *orexis* (1072a26–29), he shifts specifically to the use of *erōs*: the Prime Mover *kinei hōs erōmenon* (*Metaph.* 1072b3).[34] It is not obvious how to read this line. It could be read as "in the way a beloved boy moves," or "as an object of *erōs*." On either view, one need not suppose that the Prime Mover actually is itself

[33] There is some controversy here about whether the Prime Mover is a final cause (Elders 1972, Ross 1924, and Lear 2004), or an efficient cause (Berti 2000). I am following the interpretation of Judson 1994 and Lear 2004 where the final cause is also an origin of motion.

[34] As Sedley (2000: 334) argues: "The language of desiring and imitating is too prominent . . . to be ignored."

an object of *erōs*; the claim is that the Prime Mover moves as an object of *erōs* moves (without itself being literally an object of *erōs*). The point is simply that *erōs* demarcates a particular way of acting for the sake of an end, which is uniquely suited to capture the relationship Aristotle envisages here.[35] Merlan (1946: 1–30, esp. 3), Elders (1972: 35–6 and p174) and Lear (2004: 79, 209) connect this with the *Symposium* to articulate a notion of final causality as imitation. Lear argues that "Perhaps Aristotle wants to indicate with his use of the word *erōmenon* that the first heavenly bodies are related to the unmoved mover as lovers are related to the Forms of the Good and Beautiful in Plato's *Symposium* and *Phaedrus*" (2004: 79); "Plato called the urge to approximate a superior mode of being love" (2004: 72, citing *Symp.* 206e2–207a4). This is a plausible suggestion given the features of *erōs* explored earlier. For *erōs* is an asymmetrical relationship, one in which the object is seen as supremely beautiful and in need of nothing and, as a result, a relationship in which one seeks to effect a change in oneself and not in the objects for whose sake one acts. I am here in agreement that Aristotle is drawing on Platonic *erōs*, and the features that make this, rather than any other desire-term, appropriate for action in relation to the divine. For both thinkers, given the ends in question, the structure of *erōs* is uniquely appropriate.

It might also be tempting to suppose that the features Aristotle's use of *erōs* highlights in the *Metaphysics* explain the comparative neglect of *erōs* in his ethics.[36] The reasons may expose differences in the ethical approaches of Plato and Aristotle. There is a degree of pluralism and, arguably, particularism in Aristotle's ethics that might sit uncomfortably with the monolithic demands of *erōs*. What must be done on any particular occasion depends on the circumstances, which are many and various. Though in all virtuous action one aims for the *kalon*, the virtuous agent is not aiming at some relevant Form; there is no one object that is a clear candidate for myopic focus, obsessive devotion, and imitative action.

[35] I thank Terence Irwin and Pierre Destrée for pressing me on this point.

[36] Though Aristotle discusses *erōs* in the context of friendship (*NE* VIII.4, IX.1), it plays a marginal role in his account of interpersonal relationships, as it does for Plato. Aristotle rightly saw that *philia* was of greater significance to Plato's account of interpersonal relationships and he appropriated Plato's threefold classification of *philia* relationships from the *Phaedrus* and the *Laws* (*NE* XIII & IX), on which see Sheffield 2011 and El Murr 2014. The lack of attention to the paideutic function of *erōs* in Aristotle's ethics, which was important to Plato in some dialogues (on which, see Belfiore 2012), can be explained by thinking about the kind of audience Aristotle has in mind in the *Ethics*. For Plato, one of the ways in which *erōs* is employed is in converting young men to philosophy, particularly via an attachment to Socrates, but Aristotle's ethics is designed to engage those who already aspire to the good life, not those who need seducing into it.

If what Aristotle appreciated in Platonic *erōs* was its ability to capture action in relation to a divine end – for Plato, the intelligible Forms, for Aristotle, movement in relation to the Prime Mover – then what role would it have in the practically orientated *Ethics*? This is an area in which immaterial, divine, entities are not center stage, and so perhaps *erōs* is as redundant to Aristotle in his ethics as Plato's Forms.[37] This neglect, then, need not be an indication that we have over-estimated its significance for Plato; rather, it is an indication that we have neglected to attend to the metaphysical significance of *erōs* for Plato, one whose significance was appreciated by Aristotle.[38]

[37] In the call "to immortalize" to the extent that one can (*NE* X, 1177b33), there are intimations of the idea that we are imitating Aristotle's contemplative god (on which see Sedley 1999: 325), but Aristotle provides little detail about the nature of contemplation and its objects here. This seems to reflect the practical orientation of the *Ethics* as a whole. I thank Iakovos Vasiliou for prompting me to think further about this passage.

[38] My thanks to participants at the Cambridge B Club (2013), the Toronto ancient philosophy workshop (2014), particularly Jennifer Whiting, Iakovos Vasiliou and Suzanne Obdrzalek, and the Louvain workshop (2015) for much helpful discussion. I would also like to thank James Lesher, Christopher Rowe, David Sedley and Andrea Sangiovanni for helpful comments.

CHAPTER 8

The Mortal Soul and Immortal Happiness

Andrea Nightingale

In an article written in 1950, "Immortality in the *Symposium*," Hackforth argued that Plato had deliberately eliminated the immortal soul from Socrates' speech in this text. Plato made this move, he claimed, because he had grown skeptical about his proofs for the immortality of the soul in the *Phaedo*. As Hackforth argued, previous scholars had simply assumed that the soul is immortal in Socrates' speech in the *Symposium*, even though there is no solid evidence for this claim. These scholars made this assumption because they took it for granted that the claims in the *Phaedo* about the immortal soul had to be valid in the *Symposium* as well.[1] After Hackforth's article, other scholars weighed in. In a direct response to Hackforth, Luce attacked his view, arguing that "the relation of the two doctrines [the immortal soul and the Forms] is one of logical entailment. If the Ideas exist, it can be deduced that the soul is immortal."[2] These scholars were working on the question of Plato's development as a philosopher and the relation between different dialogues. In this chapter, I accept Hackforth's claim that there is no immortal soul in the *Symposium*, but I do not discuss the development (or unity) of Plato's doctrines.[3] Rather, I examine Diotima's conception of the soul as something that ages and dies alongside the body. I also investigate her claim that the soul gains immortality by way of its discursive offspring.

To understand these issues, I analyze Diotima's assertion that every soul longs to possess goodness forever (205a). Since possessing goodness in this life makes us happy, possessing goodness forever would give us everlasting happiness (which I call "immortal happiness").[4] Diotima's notion of a

[1] Hackforth 1950. [2] Luce 1952: 140.

[3] I do not accept Hackforth's claim that Plato deliberately eliminated the immortal soul in the *Symposium* because he felt that the proof for the immortality of the soul in the *Phaedo* was unsuccessful. I am generally against discussing Plato's "intentions."

[4] Diotima's discourse on immortal happiness differs from the eudaimonist position adopted by Socrates and Plato, which focuses on achieving happiness in this life (which I call "mortal happiness") by

mortal soul achieving immortal happiness may seem paradoxical: to have immortal happiness, the soul should be immortal; yet Diotima insists that the soul is mortal. Indeed, Diotima's emphasis on the desire for immortality brings human mortality and finitude into bolder relief. But Diotima introduces the notion of "possessing goodness forever" in order to claim that one can gain a kind of immortal happiness by giving birth to bodily and psychic offspring. One "partakes in" (*metechei*) immortality by the ongoing goodness of one's offspring and descendants (208b). And, insofar as one partakes of immortality, one also partakes of immortal happiness: for Diotima, the two go together. To be sure, one does not experience everlasting happiness personally, while one is alive: we are mortals, not gods. Still, Diotima claims that the man who gives birth to virtues and great discourses (*logoi*) will have the highest form of immortality that is available to humans. Producing excellent and virtuous offspring that live on everlastingly through generations confers on its creator a kind of immortal happiness.

What, then, is the nature of the soul's offspring and how do these "children" endure over time? To address this question, I examine two models of psychic pregnancy set forth by Diotima – models that differ in crucial ways. In the first model, great poets and lawgivers gain immortal happiness by way of posthumous fame. They have given birth to poems and lawcodes that confer immortality on them by their lasting glory. In the second model, a philosophic lover gives birth to ideas and discourses on virtue in the presence of his beloved. In the ideal scenario, this lover engages in philosophic dialogues that enable him to ascend the ladder of love and contemplate the Form of Beauty. However, even after he grasps the Form and gives birth, he still needs to "nurture" his offspring by ongoing philosophizing (211b). Clearly, his offspring are not fixed texts (like a poem or a lawcode); rather, they take the form of an ongoing dialogue that is not finalized. This ongoing dialogue nonetheless gives the philosophic lover immortal happiness. But the philosopher gains immortal happiness in a way that differs from that of the great poets and lawgivers. Men like Homer and Solon got lasting fame, as Diotima claims. But the philosophers do not achieve happiness through fame.[5] How, then, do the philosopher's ideas and arguments – his "offspring" – give him immortal happiness? Diotima does not answer this question. She does indicate that the philosophic lover lives the happiest form of life because he engages in

becoming wise and virtuous. The basic Socratic/Platonic eudaimonistic claim is that virtue and wisdom alone lead to happiness (see, e.g., *Apol.* 30b, *Euthd.* 280d–282d, *Meno* 87d–89a).

[5] Plato regularly asserts that the philosopher does not seek fame but rather truth and goodness.

ongoing dialogues and contemplates the Forms (211d).[6] However, to offer a satisfying account of the philosopher's immortal happiness, Diotima would have to discuss the long-term future of the philosopher's discursive children (as she does with the poets and lawgivers). As I will argue, we can best understand Diotima's notion of the philosopher's immortal happiness by recourse to Socrates' discourse on the philosopher's "immortal seed" in the *Phaedrus*.

1. The Mortal Soul

Let us begin by examining Diotima's conception of the human soul. As she claims:

> In one way only can the soul succeed [in achieving immortality], and that is by generation, since it can always leave behind it a new thing in place of the old. It is only for a while that each living thing can be said to be alive and the same, as a person is considered the same person from childhood until he is an old man: however, though he may be called the same, he does not possess the same properties within him; he always becomes a new person, since he is losing things, such as his hair, his flesh, his bones, and his blood and body altogether. And this is not only true with respect to his body but also with his soul (*kata tēn psuchēn*): we find that none of his customs, habits, opinions, desires, pleasures, pains or fears, ever stay the same in him; some of these come to being (*gignetai*) in him, while others perish (*apollutai*). And here is a yet stranger fact: with regard to our possessions of knowledge (*epistēmai*), some of them come to being (*gignontai*) in us and others perish (*apolluntai*). We are never the same person in regard to these possessions of knowledge, and each individual piece of knowledge suffers the same fate. That which we refer to as "practicing" (*meletan*) exists because our knowledge (*epistēmē*) is always departing. Forgetfulness is a departure (*exodos*) of knowledge while practicing implants again a new memory (*kainēn ... mnēmēn*) in place of the memory that has departed, and so preserves our knowledge (*epistēmēn*) enough to make it seem (*dokein*) the same. Every mortal thing is preserved in this way; not by being exactly the same forever, like the divine, but because that which gets old (*palaioumenon*) leaves behind another new thing that is similar to the original. Through this device, Socrates, a mortal thing partakes of immortality, both in its body and in all other respects. (207c–208b)

Here, Diotima asserts that the soul ages and changes ongoingly. Indeed, the mortal soul has to create some "new" idea in the face of the "exodus"

[6] Diotima mentions only one Form, Beauty. But we can safely assume that there were other Forms. Her claim that the philosopher achieves the best (and, we infer, happiest) life is at 211d.

of one that has perished. Indeed, her repeated use of *gignomai* and *apollumai* for the soul's knowledge (*epistēmē*) conjures up the world of becoming. Like the body, the soul ages and loses things – its ideas and thoughts are forgotten and must be replaced with new ones once these have died away. To be sure, Diotima does seem to hint at some sort of higher mind when she says that the philosopher contemplates the Form of Beauty "by that which it is right for him [to behold Beauty]" (*hōi dei*) and that he "looks at Beauty with that by which beauty can be seen" (*hōi horaton to kalon*) (212a). But these vague phrases do not offer any robust evidence that the rational part of the soul is immortal. Certainly Diotima does not suggest that the soul is "akin" to the Forms: on the contrary, she sets the finite and changing soul in stark opposition to the eternal, changeless Forms. If we accept Diotima's claim that the soul is mortal, then we must consider its relation to the unchanging and eternal Form of Beauty.

Diotima says that the Form of Beauty "always exists and does not come to be or pass away, wax or wane" (*aei on kai oute gignomenon oute apollumenon, oute auxanomenon oute pthinon,* 211a). This language of "coming to be and passing away" is identical to Diotima's earlier claim that the soul's desires, passions, and opinions "come to be and pass away" and that its *epistēmai* also "come to be" and "pass away" (207e–208b). The eternal being of the Form thus stands in stark contrast to the soul, which ages, changes, and dies. It may seem that, during the time in which the philosopher is contemplating the Form, his soul has temporarily escaped from the world of change. Yet, given that he has a mortal soul, the philosopher's mind beholds Beauty even as his soul changes and ages in time.[7]

Note that Diotima's notion of a mortal and aging soul stands in contrast to Plato's conception of the soul in the *Meno*, *Phaedo*, *Republic*, *Phaedrus*, *Timaeus*, and *Laws*. In these dialogues, Plato sets forth the idea that the soul is immortal and ageless. To cite but a few examples, consider Socrates' claim in the *Republic* that no bodily ailment (including death) can destroy the soul, nor can the soul be destroyed by its own badness: "For when its own vice and the evil appropriate to the soul cannot kill and destroy it, the evil appointed for the destruction of another thing [the body] can hardly destroy the soul or anything else, except that for which it is appointed.... Then,

[7] It is not clear that Socrates sees one or another Form when he is standing on someone's porch or standing all night long thinking while he is on a military campaign; still, we can see that his philosophical thought takes place in time. See Blondell 2006, who tries to figure out what rung of the ladder of love Socrates has reached.

since the soul is not destroyed by any evil –either its own or that of another – it must necessarily exist always and if it always exists it is immortal" (610e–611a). In the *Republic*, the soul does not age or die as the body does; the soul can become ethically worse or better, but these conditions do not lead it to die. Note also Socrates' claim in the *Phaedo* that the soul is akin to the Forms: "but when the soul investigates by itself alone, it goes to the realm of the pure, the everlasting, the immortal and the changeless and, being akin (*suggenēs*) to these [the Forms], it is with them always (*aei*) whenever, itself by itself, it is not hindered, and it ceases from its wanderings and is always the same and unchanging (*aei kata tauta hōsautōs echei*) with the changeless, inasmuch as it lays hold on these things" (79c–d). In the *Phaedo*, Socrates contrasts the soul with the body and likens it to the Forms. Thus, when the soul separates itself from the body using reason, it finds itself to be "immortal and changeless." Of course, the immortal soul does not have the ability to be unchanging like the Forms: it can become better or worse, wiser or more ignorant. But the soul does not age or decay – it is everlasting and ageless.

2. Immortality and Happiness

It is in the context of the mortal and aging soul that we must examine Diotima's discussion of the human desire for immortality and happiness. Diotima begins this discourse by asking Socrates what one gains by loving beautiful things (204d). Since Socrates is unable to answer this question, she explicitly substitutes the love of goodness for the love of beauty: "what is the object of loving goodness?"[8] As Socrates responds, the lover "wants goodness to be his own" (204e). "And what is the point of having this goodness?" she asks. "To be happy," Socrates states (204e). Diotima proceeds to sum this up: "the happy (*eudaimones*) are happy by the acquisition of good things, and there is no need to ask why men wish to be happy. The answer you give has its *telos*" (205a). Here, Diotima sets forth the basic eudaimonist axiom: everyone wants to be happy and they gain happiness by possessing good things.[9]

However, Diotima now adds a new and quite different idea: all people want the good to be theirs "forever" (*aei*) (205a, 206a). In short, they long to have immortal goodness. Note that they do not simply desire

[8] Lear 2007 offers an excellent interpretation of the move from beauty to goodness in this passage.

[9] Note that Diotima does not explain what she means by "possessing good things." By "good things," we infer, she is referring to virtue and wisdom (which one develops by practicing philosophy).

immortality in itself – this immortality must include everlasting goodness. The person who wants to possess goodness forever is, we can infer, aiming to be happy forever, that is, to be immortally happy. Diotima thus moves from the desire for mortal happiness to the desire for immortal happiness. As she explains, humans can only achieve immortal happiness indirectly, by producing good offspring by way of reproduction.[10] Indeed, reproduction in the presence of the beautiful is the only way that a mortal can partake of immortality:

> Why reproduction (*gennēsis*)? Because this is the ever-existent and immortal for the mortal. A lover must desire immortality along with the good (*meta agathou*) if what we agreed on earlier was right, that love wants the good to be one's own forever. It follows from our argument that love must desire immortality (*athanasias*). (206e)

As Diotima emphasizes, one needs to achieve immortality "with goodness" – without this, one would not gain immortal happiness.

There is a vast difference between wanting mortal happiness – to be happy in one's own life – and wanting immortal happiness. Plato tends to focus on mortal happiness in the dialogues that discuss the happy life.[11] Why, then, does Diotima focus on the desire for immortal happiness? We must note, first, that death and immortal glory are prominent in this dialogue. Indeed, the topic of death and eternal fame were brought up in the very first speech in the dialogue. There, Phaedrus says that lovers (and even beloveds) are willing to die noble deaths on behalf of their partners. He cites the examples of Alcestis, who dies in the place of her husband Admetus, and Achilles, who chooses death in order to get revenge for the slaying of his lover Patroclus. As Phaedrus claims, these deaths brought Alcestis and Achilles great and lasting honor (180a–b). He even says that Love has "the greatest power in regard to the acquisition of virtue and

[10] The notion of "immortal happiness" may seem bizarre: even if a man produces excellent offspring, he will not be around to enjoy this. Note that Diotima says that the individual "partakes in" immortality and happiness – he gets an everlasting life by way of his offspring.

[11] This is true whether the soul is mortal or immortal. Thus, in the *Apology*, Socrates says that he is not sure what will happen after he dies: he may go to sleep forever or there may be an afterlife. Whether or not there is an afterlife, however, he believes that being a virtuous soul is necessary and sufficient for having a happy life here on earth. In the *Republic*, which contains the view that the soul is immortal, Plato suggests that being wise and virtuous makes one happy during one's own life; a good afterlife is an additional reward that must only be considered after one has fully understood that living wisely and virtuously is its own reward (614a). As Socrates says in *Republic* II, he needs to show that being just in this life makes a person happy even without any external rewards (358b). To be sure, the philosopher who achieves virtue and wisdom may believe that he will be rewarded in the afterlife, but he aims for happiness in this life. He is certainly not deferring gratification in the hope of a later reward.

happiness (*aretēs kai eudaimonias*) to men, *whether they are alive or have passed away*" (180b, my italics). How, we must ask, can Love make one virtuous and happy after one dies? Phaedrus speaks of lasting glory and honor, but does not explain the rather bizarre notion of being good and happy after one dies. As we will see, Diotima will discuss this notion in detail.

Aristophanes also addresses death and the longing for immortality in his speech. He deals with this less directly than Phaedrus, but he sets forth key ideas that will be addressed in Socrates' speech. As Aristophanes claims, the "original humans" were round and whole beings who did not experience *erōs*. They did have offspring, but they produced these by laying eggs in the earth, like cicadas. These powerful creatures were nonetheless mortal. And, as mortals, they attacked the gods. However – and this is a crucial point – they had the will to power even if they did not have *erōs*.[12] As I suggest, this attempt to overcome the gods is rooted in their desire to be gods. That is, they had a desire for immortality. Aristophanes does not spell this out, but we can infer that they attacked the gods in order to become gods themselves. Of course, these hubristic humans were promptly cut in half by the gods. At that point, they were so traumatized and full of longing that they started to die away. The gods decided to move the genitals to the front so that humans could enjoy the pleasures of sex. This was not meant to provide a full union between the two halves, but it did allow people to live and go about their business. Still, the humans groped to understand the intense desire that they felt for their other halves: "there are people who live their entire lives together and still cannot say what it is that they want from each other. No one thinks that sexual intercourse is the reason why each lover takes so much joy in being with the other. Clearly, the soul of each lover longs for something else. But he cannot state what this is, but he only divines what he wants and guesses at it in riddles." (192c–d). In Aristophanes' view, present-day humans most of all desire to be fused with their other halves and to become whole again (the longing for immortality is no doubt present as well, though Aristophanes does not mention this).

In Aristophanes' myth, Hephaistos, coming upon two lovers, asks them the question that is at the core of the entire dialogue: "What is it that you really desire?" In posing this question, Aristophanes points to a basic fact about the human condition: we ongoingly feel desire that is never satisfied, and we strive to find the object of desire that will finally offer us complete

[12] As Aristophanes puts it (190b) "they had great ambitions" (*ta phronēmata megala eichon*).

fulfillment. In the myth, Hephaistos offers to weld the lovers back together to make them whole again. But he makes it clear to them that they will still have to die: "as long as you live, the pair of you, being as one, can share a single life; and, when you die, in Hades you will be one instead of two, having shared a single death" (192e). Thus, the original human longing to become immortal (and escape death) will not be satisfied.

Nonetheless, Aristophanes claims that Love offers humans true happiness. As he says, "there is just one way for the human race to be happy (*eudaimon*)," that is, for each person to find his or her other half. The ongoing relationship between true lovers thus brings about "happiness" (*eudaimonia*). But he complicates this claim in his comments at the end of the speech:

> For not only does Love bestow this great benefit on us *in the present* (*en tōi paronti*) by leading us to that which is ours, but he also furnishes great hopes *in the future* (*eis to epeita*): if we treat the god piously, he will restore us to our primal nature and, by healing us, make us blessed and happy" (*makarious kai eudaimonas*, 193d; my italics)

Aristophanes first says that Love makes us happy "in the present" if we find our other half. But, as we can see, this is a relatively limited form of happiness. For Love will make us "blessed and happy" (*makarious kai eudaimonas*) "in the future" when he restores us to our original nature. In that future – whenever it may come – we would gain not only happiness but "blessedness" because we have been restored to wholeness and unity. Clearly, this is a higher form of happiness. Yet, as Aristophanes showed earlier, the original humans were not "blessed" in the sense of being immortals. For, as he had stated, if the lovers were welded together, they would "die together" (*tethneōte*) and go to Hades "as a united and whole being" (192e). While this is, evidently, a happier scenario than the present one, it is clear that the original humans will die all the same.

As we have seen, the original humans longed for divine powers and attempted to take immortality away from the gods. If we were restored to our original nature, then, we would be back at square one: we would no longer have *erōs* but we would still desire an immortally happy life. We would long to be godlike.[13] In short, Aristophanes' speech does not offer a solution to our longing for immortality. He does, however, address the topic of happiness. Indeed, he sets up two levels of happiness – the one

[13] Cf. Nussbaum 1979: 133–4, who says we should not long for Aristophanes' "whole" original form; in her view, these "self-sufficient" beings had no desires at all. I do not see the primitive humans as self-sufficient (since they are mortal and desire immortality).

that humans have in the present life when they find their other half, and the one in a future time in which, restored to wholeness, humans transcend *erōs* and no longer feel erotic desire. In his mythic portrayal of the human desire for immortality and happiness, Aristophanes sets up Diotima's discussion of mortal and immortal happiness.

3. The Soul's Offspring

Let us turn now to Diotima's discussion of the desire for immortal happiness. As she says to Socrates, "if you are willing to look at the ambition (*philotimian*) of men, you would marvel at their irrationality (*alogias*) if you did not think about the things I have spoken of and if you did not consider the terrible state they are in through their desire to become famous and have immortal glory laid up for them forever" (208c). Diotima cites the examples of Alcestis, Achilles, and Codrus, all of whom struggled and died for the sake of fame. These claims echo the speech of Phaedrus, who said that Alcestis and Achilles died for their partners and ended up gaining great glory (180b).[14] Indeed, Diotima states that these people died because they expected "the immortal memory of their virtue" (*athanaton mnēmēn aretēs*) to last and give them ongoing fame. Here, Diotima explicates a very traditional Greek idea: that one can achieve lasting glory by dying in some glorious way. But Diotima's claims are much more complicated than this. As we will see, she proceeds to set forth two different models of psychic reproduction that confer immortal happiness on the procreating soul: (1) that of a poet or lawgiver who gives birth to a glorious poem or lawcode and thus gains everlasting fame, and (2) that of a philosophic lover who gives birth to and "rears up" his discursive children with his beloved partner through ongoing dialogue.

As Diotima argues, some people who are pregnant in soul give birth to "intelligence and virtue" (*phronēsin te kai aretēn*). She states that "all poets" (*hoi poiētai pantes*) beget these virtues and also "those craftsmen who are known as inventors" (*dēmiourgōn … heuretikoi*; 209a).[15] As we will see, Diotima will return to the poets later on, specifically mentioning Homer

[14] Clearly, Diotima herself had not heard Phaedrus' speech; my point is that her ideas align themselves with those of Phaedrus.

[15] One is struck by her claim that poets and craftsmen bring about intelligence and virtue: this flies in the face of Plato's demotion of these putatively wise men in the early and middle dialogues. But she clearly believes that poets and inventors have created glorious things that rightly gave them immortal fame. Referring to Homer, Hesiod, and lawgivers like Solon and Lycurgus, Diotima notes that "many shrines" have been set up for these men on account of their immortal children (209e).

and Hesiod (209d). There, she groups together poets and lawgivers, adding Solon and Lycurgus to the mix. Given that Diotima links poets and lawgivers, I will take it as an assumption that these men are pregnant with traditional forms of *phronēsis* and *aretē* but do not have the highest forms of virtue. Poets and lawgivers give birth to virtues that are embodied in poems and lawcodes; they do not achieve the "true virtue" that the philosopher gives birth to when he sees the Form of Beauty. Indeed, as Diotima indicates at the end of her discourse on the ladder of love, only philosophers give birth to true virtue; non-philosophers who give birth to virtues without contemplating Beauty only have images (*eidōla*) of the true virtues (212a).

Before she turns to the poets and lawgivers, however, Diotima proceeds to discuss a lover who has the greatest kind of *phronēsis*: "the ordering (*diakosmēsis*) of cities and households is the greatest and most beautiful aspect of wisdom, which we call moderation and justice" (*sōphrosunē te kai dikaiosunē,* 209a). As she says, the lover must first find a beloved whose soul is "beautiful, noble, and well formed" (209b). In the presence of this beloved's beauty, the lover gives birth to discourses about virtue: "straightway toward such a man [the beloved], the lover is resourceful in discoursing about virtue and about what a good man is and what he should pursue (*euporei logōn peri aretēs kai peri hoiōn chrē einai ton andra ton agathon kai ha epitēdeuein*), and he attempts to educate him (*paideuein*)" (209b–c). Here, the lover "gives birth to and begets those things that he was pregnant with long ago" (209c). Note, however, that the lover gives birth to *logoi*, which he uses to educate his beloved, though he himself is pregnant with the virtues of justice and moderation. Indeed, Diotima focuses on his discursive offspring (*logoi*), which need to be reared up with the beloved, but does not tell us how this makes the lover develop his own virtues. We may infer that the lover develops the virtues in himself even as he educates the beloved by way of discourse and dialogue. As I see it, in order to accomplish this, the lover must rear his discursive offspring through philosophical investigation. By ongoingly examining the virtues with his beloved, he becomes virtuous over time and also educates his beloved so that he, too, becomes more virtuous. In this passage, then, Diotima begins her discussion of the philosophic lover – the man who will later ascend the ladder of love (model #2 above[16]).

[16] I discuss model #2 first because it is articulated at the beginning and at the end of this part of Diotima's discourse. Since model #2 is not completed until the end of Diotima's speech, I marked it as "model #2."

It is important to note that, after the lover gives birth, he and his beloved collectively raise his psychic "children":

> When he lays hold of that beautiful person and associates with him, he gives birth to and begets those things that he was pregnant with long ago.... And, together with him, he shares the nurturing (*sunektrephei*) of the newborn (*to gennēthen*), so that men of this kind have a much greater partnership with one another (*koinōnian . . . pros allēlous*) than do parents of children, since they have shared in common (*kekoinōnēkotes*) more beautiful and immortal children (*paidōn*).[17] (209b–c)

Here, Diotima places great emphasis on the fact that the couple "collectively raise" (*sunektrephei*) the offspring and thus have a "partnership" that involves "sharing in common" the psychic children. This partnership focuses on rearing up "*logoi*" that the lover has given birth to – discursive babies that need a great deal of support if they are going to grow and mature.[18] As I have suggested, these two are engaging in philosophic dialogues.

Diotima makes a similar point in her discourse on the ladder of love. When the lover ascending the ladder moves from loving bodies to loving a beautiful soul, he enters into a serious relationship with the beloved:[19] "it shall suffice for the lover to love and to care for [his beloved] and to give birth to and to search (*zētein*) for discourses (*logous*) which will make young men better" (*hoitines poiēsousi beltious tous neous*" (210c). Note that the lover who falls in love with a young man who has a beautiful soul engages in a "search" (*zētein*) that takes place *after* he has given birth to a psychic child in the presence of his beloved. Here, the philosopher's search specifically focuses on virtue and on the right education for young men. Thus, Diotima picks up on her earlier discussion of the lover and beloved who collectively "rear" the lover's *logoi* – *logoi* that dealt with virtue and education (209b–c).[20] Finally, at the very end of her discussion of the

[17] Note that Diotima refers to "children" in the plural; for this reason, we may infer that the lover gives birth to many ideas and discourses when he is with his beloved.

[18] One could imagine that the beloved would have some of his own ideas to give birth to as he encounters beautiful things himself (though Diotima does not make this explicit).

[19] Given that the beloved has a beautiful soul, we can infer that the lover has to get to know this person well enough to grasp that he has a beautiful soul. To be sure, as many scholars have noted, the lover on the ladder seems to have little association with his beloved on the upper rungs: Diotima does not mention the beloved again, and this suggests that the lover may have left the beloved behind when he further ascends the ladder. I do not want to enter into this debate – my focus here is on the lover-beloved relationship. Diotima does say that the philosophic lover engages in "unstinting philosophy": this implies that he is engaging in philosophic dialogue (he is not doing philosophy simply on his own).

[20] Note that the lover described in the earlier passage (209c) and the philosopher ascending the ladder in this passage both give birth to *logoi* that specifically deal with educating the young: this forges a direct link between the lover in 209b–c and the lover on the ladder of love.

ladder of love, Diotima brings up the philosopher "nurturing" and rearing his offspring once again: "to that man begetting true virtue and rearing it up (*threpsamenōi*), it comes to be that he is loved by the gods and, if any human could become immortal, it would be him" (212a). Even after he contemplates the Form of Beauty, he must rear up his children – his virtues – with ongoing investigation.

Let us return to the earlier passage about the lover giving birth to *logoi* about virtue in the presence of his beloved (209b–c). As we have seen, the lover's "offspring" comes out as an infant that needs to be reared over a period of time. The lover and his beloved engage in ongoing discussions and dialogues about virtue and goodness. This indicates that the lover is a philosopher (and, if he has chosen his beloved well, this young man also has a philosophic soul). After discussing the collective "rearing" of the lover's offspring, Diotima makes an important claim: the lover and beloved "have a share in children that are nobler and more immortal (*kallionōn kai athanatōterōn paidōn*) than ordinary children (209c). But what makes these discursive children "more immortal"? As we have seen, the lover gives birth to discursive offspring that must be reared up and tended to over time: his *logoi* do not add up to a final product. In these dialogues, the lovers work on ideas that are tested under examination and revised again and again. There is no final end to this project – no "last word" or argument on the topic. Even if the philosopher reaches the point of contemplating the Form of Beauty and giving birth to "true virtue" ("because he has grasped true Beauty"), he still has to rear this offspring up by setting forth yet more arguments (212a). It is therefore hard to understand how these unfinished dialogues are "more immortal" than all other human creations (209c).

Diotima does not clarify her claim that the lover's philosophic *logoi* are "more immortal" than all others. Rather, she promptly moves to poets and lawgivers who gave birth to glorious artifacts (model #1 above). She explicitly mentions Homer, Hesiod, Lycurgus, and Solon – famous procreators of glorious and lasting poems and lawcodes (209b). However, in the case of these men, she focuses only on their "offspring" (*ekgona*, 209d). She refers to the creation of finalized *logoi* (poems, lawcodes) that have lasted for centuries and made their creators everlastingly famous. Indeed, these men created fixed and finalized texts that do not need to be "reared up" the way that philosophical *logoi* do. Poems and lawcodes are vastly different from the unfinalizable arguments that are ongoingly examined through dialogue.

As I have argued, Diotima sets forth two models of psychic reproduction: (1) that of a poet or lawgiver giving birth to a finished product, and (2) that of a philosophic lover giving birth to and raising his own *logoi* through dialogues with his beloved. She claims that all of these men achieved immortal happiness by way of their psychic offspring. It is worth noting that Diotima offers no evidence that the successful poets and lawgivers who gave birth to glorious artifacts achieved happiness while they were alive: she focuses only on their famous offspring. As she claims, these men gained immortal happiness posthumously, by way of the everlasting fame of poems and lawcodes. When we turn to the happiness of the philosophic lover, however, we run into the opposite problem: Diotima explicitly says that this man gains mortal happiness if he ascends the ladder of love – he has a "life most of all worth living" (211d) – but she does not explain how he achieves immortal happiness. She focuses on the philosophic lover while he is alive, but does not make any reference to the afterlife of his discursive children. We are thus left trying to figure out how the philosopher's offspring are in fact everlasting and how the philosopher gains immortal happiness.

4. Finished and Unfinished Discourses

As Diotima claims, the Form of Beauty serves as a midwife that enables the philosophic lover to give birth to "true virtue." Still, the lover must articulate his knowledge and virtue by way of arguments. Indeed, as she says, when the philosopher has contemplated the Form of Beauty and given birth, he then "rears up" (*threpsamenōi*) this newborn offspring (212a). The philosophic activity does not end when one has grasped the Form: contemplation brings about new ideas – ideas that need to be developed by way of philosophic dialogue. And, through dialogue, the philosopher will give birth to more ideas, and this means yet more nurturing. In short, the philosopher does not create a single *logos* that takes the form of a finished product. The philosopher must engage in a lifelong inquiry, introducing new ideas that require examination, testing, and revision. Certain ideas die away and others come into being as the conversation moves forward: there is no single, finished discursive "child."[21]

[21] I agree with White 2004 that we should not take the philosopher's contemplation of the Form of Beauty as the final end of his desire; rather, his goal is to give birth to *logoi* that will survive him after he dies (and thus confer a sort of immortality on him). I differ from White, however, in the nature of these *logoi*. As White claims: "the immortality attained by the philosopher *qua* mortal consists in his living on in the philosophical works that he leaves behind him" (2004: 366). In short, the philosopher gives birth to "discourses" that survive him in the form of fixed "works." As I argue, the philosopher's discourses are not fixed (yet they still have a way of conferring a posthumous immortality).

Poems and lawcodes, by contrast, are fixed and finalized discourses.[22] Indeed, in the *Phaedrus*, Plato identifies the lawcodes of Solon and Lycurgus as written texts. There, Socrates claims that anyone who authorizes a law and has it written down is a "logographer" (258b). Speaking about written laws and those who authorized them in Athens and other city-states, Socrates says: "The writer [who claims authorship for a law] says, 'It was voted by the council' or 'by the demos' (or both) and 'so-and-so stated', naming and praising himself with great solemnity, and then states even more things after that, displaying his own wisdom to those who approve and sometimes even creating a long document. Does this seem to you to be anything other than a written speech (*logos suggegrammenos*)?" (258b).[23] While Socrates is, in part, poking fun of the self-aggrandizement of contemporary politicians, he nonetheless argues that, in writing laws, they create texts like those of Solon and Lycurgus: "When he [the man enacting a law] becomes a good enough politician or king so as to gain the power of Lycurgus, Solon, or Darius, and becomes an immortal speechwriter (*athanatos ... logographos*) in his city, doesn't he think of himself as equal to the gods while he is still alive and don't later generations believe this about him as they look at his writings" (*theōmenoi autou ta suggrammata*)?" In this last passage, Plato suggests that the man who enacts and inscribes laws gains immortal fame by way of his writings. This man is identified as an author of a fixed text that can be read by people in later generations. In the *Phaedrus*, Plato places the written text (including legal and poetic texts) in contrast with spoken philosophical dialogue: while the text says the same thing again and again, the philosopher can answer questions, offer arguments, pose new questions, and come up with new ideas. As we have seen, in Diotima's discussions of the

[22] Some may reject the notion that the lawcode of Lycurgus was a fixed text. While many modern scholars see Lycurgus as a merely mythical figure, the ancients believed that Lycurgus had authored the "Great Rhetra," which was most certainly a written text (though it did not contain a full set of laws). On the legends dealing with Lycurgus, see Tigerstedt 1965: 70–8 and passim; on the written/unwritten laws in Sparta, see MacDowell 1986: 5.

[23] Note that Plato offers a long analysis of written vs. unwritten laws in the *Statesman*. There, Plato says that the good statesman using unwritten laws is preferable to rulers and cities that are bound by written laws. In the absence of a good statesman, however, the second best thing is for a city to follow a written lawcode unwaveringly. Plato uses this latter model in the *Laws*. We also find Megillus giving a short account of Lycurgus' laws in the *Laws*. However, Megillus' account is cut short by the Athenian, who swiftly claims that Lycurgus had a very different objective than instituting laws that were aimed primarily at military valor and warfare (*Laws* 630d). Here, the Athenian conjures up an ideal lawgiver whose overall aims are identified with those of a newly interpreted Lycurgus. On Plato's treatment of the ideal lawgiver (and Lycurgus and Minos) see Nightingale 1993. On Plato's discussion of written vs. unwritten laws in the *Statesman* and *Laws* see Nightingale 1999.

discursive children of the poets and lawgivers (model #1) and of the philosophic lover (model #2), she effectively contrasts a finalized discourse to an ongoing and changing philosophic discourse. We find this same contrast in the *Phaedrus*, though it is set up in different terms: finalized written texts vs. open-ended philosophical dialogue.[24]

5. The Immortal "Seed" of the Philosopher in the *Phaedrus*

Although the *Phaedrus* offers a very different conception of the soul than we find in *Symposium*, these two dialogues do share some key ideas. In particular, in the *Phaedrus*, Socrates explicitly draws a key distinction between finalized written discourses and ongoing philosophical dialogue. Also, Socrates uses this distinction to explicate the way in which the philosopher gains both mortal and immortal happiness by way of ongoing dialogue. In contrast to the *Symposium*, however, the *Phaedrus* describes the "parenting" of discourse in terms of fathering rather than mothering. A philosopher's spoken discourse is his "legitimate" (*gnēsios*) child: because is it "ensouled" (*empsuchos*), the philosopher's speech can respond to questions and defend his ideas. His written texts, by contrast, are bastard children because they cannot defend their father's discourses by answering questions and setting forth new arguments (278a).[25]

To clarify his valorization of spoken philosophical dialogue over written texts, Socrates sets forth the distinction between a gardener planting seeds in a garden of Adonis and a farmer planting his seeds in a fertile field (276d). What is a garden of Adonis? These gardens were created by women celebrating the Adonia festival. As Xenobius explains, the plants in these gardens "... are sown in small clay vessels and grow only to the point of becoming green; then they are carried away along with the dying god and are thrown into springs."[26] Because Adonis died young, the women threw the potted gardens away as soon as the first green shoots appeared in the soil. Thus, the plants did not grow to the point of bearing fruits and seeds. Socrates compares the plants in these gardens to written texts: discourses

[24] Note that Plato does not suggest that all spoken discourse is better than written discourse. Thus, at *Phdr.* 277e, Socrates places oral rhapsodic performances in the same category as written speeches; see also *Prot.* 328e–329b for the claim that rhetoricians, "like books," do not answer questions but just carry on with the speech without variation or interruption.

[25] Note that Socrates says that it is fine for the philosopher to write things down "as old age advances," but he makes it clear that this is not a "serious" mode of discourse (276d).

[26] Zenobius 1.49. For a discussions of the Adonia festival, see Detienne 1977: 64–6, 78–80, and Winkler 1990: 189–93.

that are written down do not grow and take on life; they are not "ensouled" (*empsuchos*, 276a). They are words without seeds.

Socrates now introduces a farmer who sows his seeds "in the place that is fitting" and tends them until they reach maturity (276b). His crop, growing over eight months, contains plants that have fruits and seeds. These seeds carry on the life of the plant after it dies. Socrates associates the farmer with the philosopher. Like the farmer, the philosopher "plants" his discourses in the proper place – the minds of other philosophical souls. Only a philosopher engaging in dialogues with students can transmit discourses that have a lasting seed: "when a [philosophical] man, using the art of dialectic, taking hold of a fitting soul, plants and sows discourses there that are accompanied by knowledge, which are able to defend themselves and the man who planted them, and are not fruitless but contain a seed (*ouk akarpoi alla exontes sperma*), from which other discourses (*logoi*) growing in other minds are able to make [the seed] immortal forever; and these [discourses] make the man who possesses them happy (*eudaimonein*) to the greatest extent possible for humans" (276e–277a).[27] Here, the philosopher plants discourses in the student's mind that enables him to develop good philosophical arguments – the student can defend his own claims with arguments and can also defend the philosopher who sowed them to begin with. The student thus develops arguments that will reach philosophical maturity – arguments that are fruitful and full of seeds. From these seeds yet other discourses grow up in other people's minds. As Socrates emphasizes, the seed finds its way into more and more minds and thus becomes "immortal." As Socrates says at the end of this quote, the philosopher himself lives the happiest possible life – he has mortal happiness while he lives– and, we can infer, he gains immortal happiness because his seed is immortal.

We must note that the philosopher does not plant a fixed and finalized discourse into another person's mind. Each person has to develop his own arguments that keep the seed alive – arguments that continue to build upon the original philosopher's questions and ideas. As Socrates claims, the philosopher's dialectical discourses are his legitimate sons (*huieis gnēsious,* 278a). From these "sons" of the philosopher, "children and brothers grow up (*ekgonoi te kai adelphoi … enephusan*) in the souls of other men" (278a–b). The seed of the philosopher is therefore "immortal," since it produces words and seeds that grow in other souls, from one

[27] Note that the philosopher must first understand ideas about justice, beauty, etc. (278a) before he plants his discourses in others.

generation to another. One could argue, as Berger does, that seeds planted in the fields by farmers grow into the exact same plant again and again: thus, by analogy, the philosopher plants a discourse in other souls that is replicated again and again in an identical formulation.[28] But Socrates is clearly using the word "*sperma*" both as the seed of a plant and as a man's semen. Since Socrates emphasizes the philosopher's discursive "brothers and sons," we should conceive of the seed as a discursive sperm that creates new and different arguments (just as a father's physical children are not identical to himself). Socrates does not claim that the same argument is rehearsed again and again by different speakers.

The philosopher's ideas take on immortality – and give the philosopher immortal happiness – because generations of philosophical souls carry on the dialogue. The seed gives life, again and again. Paradoxically, the philosopher's initial ideas become immortal because they are changed and altered as the dialogue moves forward through generations. This model stands in stark contrast to the model of creating a finalized discourse like a poem or lawcode. Immortal happiness, for the philosopher, is not a matter of fame. Rather, the point is that philosophical ideas are kept alive forever *through new and different arguments.*

To be sure, this model of the father implanting fruitful discourses in a philosophical soul is totally alien to Diotima's model of a pregnant philosopher giving birth to discourses. Plato uses these different models because he is focusing on different aspects of philosophical dialogues in these texts. In the *Symposium*, he places almost all the emphasis on the philosophical lover, who "gives birth" to ideas in the presence of his beloved. Diotima does mention that the beloved shares in the rearing of the discursive children, but she does not discuss how the philosopher's ideas enter into the beloved's mind and develop there. Nor does she discuss how the beloved matures into a philosopher and gives birth himself in the presence of a younger man. Diotima focuses only on one couple and not on generations of philosophers. For this reason, she is not able to explain how the philosopher can be immortally happy. To do this, she would have to talk about the generations of the philosopher's offspring. Still, she does indicate that the lovers who give birth to virtuous and glorious offspring gain immortal happiness. She explains how this works when poets and lawgivers give birth to glorious artifacts that confer on them everlasting fame. But she ranks the philosophic lover above the poets and lawgivers because he gives birth to the best virtues and discourses.

[28] Berger 1990.

Oddly, she does not explain how the philosopher achieves immortal happiness through his offspring. It is in the *Phaedrus* that Plato brings in generations of philosophers. In this dialogue, he focuses on the transmission of ideas through the ages. He claims that this transmission takes place through ongoing dialogue, not by a fixed and finalized discourse. Using the metaphor of the plant, fruit, and seed, he shows us how the philosopher's ideas germinate in many souls, through generations. In my view, the only way that Diotima could come up with a satisfying account of the philosopher's immortal happiness would be by focusing on the philosopher's offspring and showing how the beloved (and, in turn, his beloved, and so on) produced new life. If she had extended her model of discursive reproduction over generations, she could have shown how philosophic "birth-giving" kept the philosopher's original discourses immortal.

Clearly, the metaphor of the philosopher's "fathering" of a discourse that carries his seed in the *Phaedrus* differs from the metaphor of the philosopher giving birth to discursive offspring in the *Symposium.* But Socrates' claim in the *Phaedrus* that generations of philosophers preserve the "seed" of the *logos* – keeping philosophy alive over long periods of time – could, with some modification, work with the model of birth-giving in the *Symposium.* Thus, the philosophic lover could give birth to offspring that takes life in his beloved: after all, the beloved is helping to "rear up" these offspring. And the beloved is no doubt pregnant with discourses and virtues himself. The lover is educating his beloved and, we can infer, training him to engage in philosophic dialogues. Indeed, since the philosophic lover gives birth to "beautiful and magnificent discourses" (*kalous logous kai megaloprepeis*, 210d), the very beauty of his *logoi* can function as a midwife to younger philosophic souls. These souls, in turn, develop their own arguments and give birth to these in the presence of a younger man with a beautiful soul. Thus, the philosophic lover's offspring stays alive by way of the ongoing dialogue of generations of philosophers. In short, it does not matter whether a philosopher fathers or mothers a discourse: the key point is that his *logoi* are transmitted to the souls of younger men and these men, in turn, hand new discourses down to the younger generation, and so on. Thus, the *logoi* are kept alive by way on ongoing dialogue: they are preserved not as a fixed text but by open-ended discussions of core philosophical questions.

CHAPTER 9

A Fetish for Fixity?

Christopher Shields

1. Looking at Last to Beauty

Extravagant even among Plato's language of Forms, Plato's expression for his ultimate object of love in the *Symposium* is Beauty "itself, taken by itself, within itself, uniform, and existing always" (211b1). He sets as ideal for humans "to see Beauty absolute, pure, unmixed" (211e), a final vision that associates the mortal viewer with the divine so as to become god-beloved and indeed, to the degree that it may belong to our mortal lot, to become ourselves immortal (212a5–7).

One may well wonder why gazing upon an abstract object, however unalloyed and permanent, should be described in such rapturous terms; one may even recoil in the face of such description. After all, we live and love in a world of change and impermanence, of development and decline, of ever-shifting context and unending variegation. Those we actually know and love do not exist always, are complex rather than uniform, and are embraced by us in their impurity as imperfect admixtures of the moral and the immoral, as aspiring, sometimes succeeding and sometimes failing – as indeed we hope that we may ourselves be accepted, aware as we are that we are not ourselves impervious gods but mortals, human and frail. From this perspective, Plato's conception of the culmination of human life may seem to us to be not its apotheosis but rather its abnegation. If so much actually captures his attitude, then his account of the ideal of beauty cognized might give us pause; indeed, one might think, if so, such an ideal *should* give us pause.

We might, then, reasonably step back to take the measure of Plato's motivations in promoting the permanence of beauty, and to determine the degree to which he in fact regards its contemplation and the subsequent generation to which that contemplation gives rise as a goal of human existence.[1]

[1] Some scholars seem to understand this to be beyond dispute. So, e.g., Bury 1932: xliii: "Thus, the whole process is, in a word, a system of intellectual training in the art of dialectic, in so far as it concerns *to kalon*. And the end to which it leads is the vision of and converse with Ideal Beauty,

To many scholars, at any rate, these theses seem asserted or implied in the ascent towards Beauty depicted in Diotima's speech in the *Symposium* (esp. 204d–212a). She evidently sketches a kind of hierarchy of value, one beginning in the common love of a beautiful boy, moving then through various levels of abstraction, to the point where the Form of Beauty is itself cognized directly. One would like to know, in the first instance, the source and character of the comparative value. What qualifies the vision of the Form of Beauty as the pinnacle of human existence? This question in turn breaks down into more basic questions, one general and several specific to the Form of Beauty. First, in general, why should a vision of a Form – any Form – qualify as valuable? Is the value, for instance, more than merely epistemic? Second, having sorted that, we may wonder what qualifies the Form of Beauty, uniquely among all Forms, for this office. Why should the Form of Beauty be, as a relative matter, more worthy of being valued than more prosaic objects of love, which are themselves beautiful only imperfectly by participation? What, in short, is the character and source of this particular valuation? Again, merely epistemic? Aesthetic? Moral? Prudential? Some admixture of these? Some other value altogether?

If we focus on the Form of Beauty in the *Symposium*, we should note straightaway in precisely this connection that we will need to confront its relation to the Form of the Good, which is exalted above other Forms in a work written in the same general period of Plato's philosophical career, namely *Republic* V.[2] In that work, Plato states flatly that the Form of the Good "surpasses in dignity and power" even Being itself, offering it as the last and greatest thing to be learnt (504e4–5, 505a2), as something responsible for all knowledge and truth (508e3). If we assume that the Form of the Good and the Form of Beauty are discrete Forms,[3] then we may seem to have competing pinnacles, two fulfillments, two coping stones of human existence.

Even waiving that, whatever its relation to the Good, there remains a pressing question about the Form of Beauty internal to the *Symposium* itself: why should we think that catching a vision of this Form is to be

followed by the procreation of veritable virtue. It is to be observed that this is expressly stated to be not only the final stage in the progress of *Erōs* but the most perfect state attainable on earth by man."

[2] In terms of the stylometric data and philosophical temperament, the *Symposium* seems close to the *Phaedo*, a fully Platonic dialogue in the sense of adumbrating a full theory of Forms, one of a piece with the theory of the *Republic* V, which seems to contain a back-reference to the *Phaedo*. There are, to be sure, other ways to understand the relations between these dialogues, both thematically and chronologically; nothing in the argument of the present paper requires this dating.

[3] Not everyone does so assume. I take up this question in Section 2.

privileged to such a degree that other, highly valuable human activities are shunted aside in its favor? This, in effect, is the question Vlastos posed so pointedly when he wished to know why Plato should think himself justified in advancing the view that as one climbs the ladder to the vision of the Beautiful itself one should come to despise those whom one has loved as inferior, even to the point of casting them aside once their usefulness has been depleted.[4] It seems brutal and callously inhuman to suggest that it is good and proper first to love someone for their physical beauty and then their beauty of soul only to cast them aside when other, more abstract and encompassing ideals come into view (210b–d).

One may have the sense that such allegations are in their turn too harsh, that, when given the opportunity, one can and should – and in any case *will* – gravitate towards beauty of ever greater value over beauty of ever diminishing lesser value. Perhaps, but that primarily serves to redirect attention back to our first question: why should the cognitive grasp of a Form, however beautiful it is understood to be, be regarded as something so exceedingly valuable? What, precisely, is the value that Plato understands to be invested in this activity? In the *Symposium*, as in other dialogues of its period, Plato plainly regards the grasping of Forms as intrinsically valuable, as something for the sake of which other things are done but whose own surpassing value neither needs nor admits of any further defense or justification.

Among the various things one might mean by regarding it as intrinsically valuable – as something most finally good, as unimprovably, incorruptibly, autonomously good, as non-derivatively good in its own right – the Form of Beauty seems, at the very least, highly prized amongst Forms, and certainly always to be preferred relative to sensible instances of Beauty at any level of generality. Why?

[4] Vlastos 1981: 31: "We are to love the person so far, and only insofar, as they are good and beautiful. Now since all too few human beings are masterworks of excellence, and not even the best of those we have the chance to love are wholly free of streaks of the ugly, the mean, the commonplace, the ridiculous, if our love for them is to be only for their virtue and beauty, the individual in the uniqueness and integrity of his or her individuality, will never be the object of our love. This seems to me the cardinal flaw in Plato's theory." I should stress that the purpose of this paper is not to respond directly to Vlastos' complaint, except incidentally insofar as we can come to see that the tendency in Plato's thought he decries is actually a consequence of a deeper, more pervasive pattern in Plato's philosophical orientation. For discussions of Vlastos' contention see Nussbaum 1986, Kosman 1976, Gill 1990, Price 1989, Rowe 1998, Kraut 2008. For an intelligent attempt to show that this entire discussion is "misguided" see Sheffield 2012. While I doubt Sheffield's contention, I think, and show indirectly, that the entire discussion is miscast, or at least incompletely engaged until such time as the appropriate hierarchy of value in the ascent is explicated.

It is easy to imagine various justifications for these sorts of contentions, some more and some less attractive. One plausible and comprehensive, but relatively neglected motivation derives from Plato's overarching drive towards *homoiōsis theōi* – a coming to be like unto god. Although others have rightly observed the role of this motivation in a general way,[5] citing this principle in general by itself does not go far enough towards explaining Plato's commitment to pursuing Beauty itself, alone and by itself. For the drive to become like god underspecifies or indeed can misspecify Plato's motivation. The correct specification – or specifications – at once permit us to make sense of Plato's florid characterizations in the *Symposium*: the correct specification equally shows why Plato's zeal for Beauty amounts to far more than a fetish for fixity. As a welcome consequence, once we have suitably contextualized Plato's more comprehensive motivation for turning his gaze to the Form of Beauty, the discomfiting censure given voice by Vlastos dissolves, or at least dissipates by being redirected. If we strive to assimilate ourselves to the ideal of Beauty in keeping with the directions of a Diotima, so that we may become godlike, and we thereby, in consequence, lose some measure of our enmeshment in the perceptible world of transient variegation, then to the degree that there is a fault in our conduct, the source of the difficulty resides in Plato's overarching doctrine of *homoiōsis theōi*.

In fact, Plato's dominant contrast is not one between an unstable, jealous love of a morally mottled human individual and a serenely pure but sterile contemplative love of an immutable Form, but rather one between the striving impermanence of the ever attenuating mortal and the unsurpassably flawless beauty of the perfectly divine. The divine in the *Symposium* has, so to speak, nowhere to go and so no reason to strive; the mortal by contrast, has only to strive and never to arrive. Her approach to Beauty is unavoidably asymptotic; still, Plato implies, being closer to the divine is always preferable to being further from it. So, a rational eudaemonist will on this basis already rightly gravitate towards Beauty, leaving behind the receding inferior as she does. One may, of course, find a form of censure for this impulse as well, but to the degree that this may be so,

[5] Sedley 1999 first called attention this matter to English speakers in a landmark article; Merki 1952 had offered an earlier, more comprehensive study, beginning with Plato and extending to Gregory of Nyssa, though had not sought to sketch its philosophical ramifications as Sedley did. The phrase *homoiōsis theōi* is evidently first introduced by Plato in the *Theaetetus* (see n. 22), only to be repeated several dozens of times in the Neoplatonists and Church Fathers, most often in quotations and direct ascriptions to Plato. Typical is David, *Prol. Phil.* 26.15: "he [Plato] says that philosophy is a process of becoming like god so far as is possible for a human being."

any criticism of Plato takes on a new and different hue. To understand that someone has abjured the pedestrian in favor of assimilating himself to god is, in all moral respects, relevantly unlike criticizing someone for using a human instrumentally as a conduit to Beauty, casting aside all concern for him once his usefulness has been exhausted.

We move to this conclusion in four stages. First, we must address two preliminary matters about the presupposition undergirding the presentation of the issues as we have presented them so far, concerning first the supposition that the Form of Beauty *is* in fact offered as a kind of final culmination in Plato's *Symposium* (§2). We then look to a critical assessment of Plato's ideal of Beauty, given in primarily epistemic and eudaimonistic terms, neither of which lend an entirely attractive understanding to his reasons for disregarding the transient in favor of the permanent (§3). We counter this criticism by situating Plato's drive towards Beauty in his broader ideal of *homoiōsis theōi* – but this too is unhelpfully vague, since we may, in seeking to be godlike, in fact seek many different things. It matters which dimension of this impulse we foreground (§4). Finally, we turn to the more general question of the degree to which our initial ill-ease at Plato's assent towards Beauty may reassert itself in another guise, even in the broader context of a *homoiōsis theōi.*

2. Preliminary Concerns

So far we have been speaking freely of the drive towards a vision of Beauty as a drive towards a final or ultimate good. This has inclined many simply to identify Beauty with the Good, treating the Form of Beauty as identical to the Form of the Good under another guise. The Good is equally, of course, regarded as a final or ultimate end (*Rep.* 504e4–5, 505a2, 508b5–8). More fundamentally, should we, even in the first instance, represent the Form of Beauty as a final end at all? For this widespread contention can be, and has been, responsibly challenged.[6]

In the character of Diotima, Plato offers the following characterization of an ascent towards Beauty, as a hierarchy of love-worthy objects, beginning in the love of a single boy, but growing ever more general and abstract:

1. We begin in homoerotic terms: first a man falls in love with a beautiful boy, which inspires him to give birth to beautiful ideas. Already at this first phase, then, the fecundity of Love is in view.

[6] See especially White 2004.

2. This very fecundity, however, induces the lover to recognize that the beauty in all bodies is the same. This assertion is made without argument, but seems a near consequence of Plato's habitual univocity assumption, namely that φ-things admit of a single, non-disjunctive account displaying the essence or nature of φ-ness (see, e.g. *Meno* 70a–71d, 72a–b, 72c–e, 74b–76b; *Rep.* 475e–480a, 507a–b, 596a4–8).[7]
3. Having moved, though, to this level of abstraction, the lover now values the individual boy less and focuses on the soul, which is, by contrast, itself invariant and permanent, in comparison with the flowing river of matter which constitutes our bodies through time.
4. In its turn, this focus on the soul gives rise to thoughts of discourses (*logoi*) used in instruction, which themselves have their finest expressions in laws, permanent and fixed. Here too, then, Plato emphasizes the comparative value of the permanent over transient. Indeed, he comes to say, rather starkly, that the lover who has advanced so far will come to despise (*kataphronei*; *Symp.* 210b5, 216d8) those formerly serving as the locus of love.[8]
5. With the fixity of beauty now in sight, the lover comes to love knowledge itself, which is still more fixed as it is expressed in universal laws, in virtue of their being necessary. The lover's gaze is thus fixed on "the great sea of beauty, and, gazing on this, he gives birth to many gloriously beautiful ideas and theories, in unstinting love of wisdom (*philosophia*)" (210d).
6. Finally, though, summit day approaches and this visage of Beauty overtakes us suddenly (*exaiphnēs*): we at last love Beauty Itself. Long left behind, then, is the solitary, shifting beautiful boy, who seems simply no longer in view.

Several themes emerge in this ascent. First, Diotima envisages a general drive from particular to general or universal. She then also, second, understands this drive as a movement from the contingent and variable to the necessary and fixed. Finally, third, she associates a hierarchical value ranking with the assent: each ascending level offers a successively more valuable object of love.

[7] "As you know, we habitually hypothesize a single form in connection with each of the many things to which we apply the same predicate" (*Rep.* 596a4–8).

[8] Some would like to soften this contention by noting, correctly, that *kataphronein* can mean, more mildly, "look down upon" or "think slightly of." However it is rendered, however, the word indicates a comparative disvaluation.

This last theme has occasioned the most concern. If the highest level offers the greatest value, then one succeeding in its attainment will naturally look down – will naturally and rightly disvalue – the objects at the lowest level. What precisely is, though, the attainment at the top? Plato describes, or seems to describe, the attainment purely in cognitive terms, as a kind of intellectual vision: one led to the top of the ascent comes to "see beauty itself, unalloyed, pure, unmixed" (211d9–e1). Immediately upon this attainment, the lover will be released from concern with the vagaries of mottled human beauty and all such inanity (*phluaria*, 211e2). This very mental vision (*idein*), then, seems the culmination. Thus, scholars have so characterized it, variously describing it as the "final object" or "final goal," as its "primary object" or "primary goal," or even simply as the "ultimate object" or "ultimate objective" of the lover.[9]

Even so, Diotima does not characterize the Form of Beauty (*to kalon auto*) as the ultimate *goal*; and she does not characterize its contemplation as the final end of the lover's life. She maintains, rather, in keeping with Plato's more normal practice, that the lover, in common with all other humans, seeks *the good*, the lasting possession of the good (*to agathon*), as the final human end (205e7–206a1, 207a, 207c; cf. *Rep*, 504d, 586e; *Lys*. 222a–d; *Gorg*. 467–8; *Meno* 77b–78c). One might reasonably conclude, then, that the final goal of love is not the serene contemplation of Beauty itself, but rather the secure possession of the Form of the Good.

To many that may, however, seem little more than a postponement strategy: many scholars take it as given that the Form of Beauty simply *is* the Form of the Good under another name. Some, indeed, will take this as axiomatic (relying, evidently, on such passages as 187c, 201c, 203d, 204e; cf. *Prot*. 360b; *Hip. Maj*. 297b–c; *Phil*. 64e).[10] In fact, however, the *Symposium* contains a much weaker doctrine, namely that good and beautiful things are co-extensive,[11] which would no more license the identity of the Good and the Beautiful than the co-extensivity of the -god-beloved and the pious would license the identity of the pious with being god-beloved in the *Euthyphro*. Far from being axiomatic, then, the proposed identity seems to rely on an insufficient and so incorrect inference. We have, then, not a postponement but rather a distinction, one which plainly permits Diotima to treat the vision of the Form

[9] White 2004: 151 n. 7 helpfully compiles references of this sort.

[10] So, e.g., Dover 1980: n. to 204d3.

[11] So, e.g., at 201c, where we have *tagatha kai kala*, inquiring, then, only whether good things are beautiful and beautiful things good. This general point is appreciated by Price 1989: 16 and suitably deployed in Wedgwood 2009.

of Beauty as a culmination of an attraction consistent with a larger, overarching ultimate end.[12]

3. Epistemic and Eudaimonistic Motivations

Even granting that much, one might nonetheless be inclined to treat the lover's disregard for the objects on the lower end of the assent, whether or not this disregard is contemptuous, as problematic. What might be Plato's motivation?

Two very different motivations suggest themselves in Plato's language, both corresponding to the broader and narrower questions posed above, namely the questions of why we should care so stridently about knowledge of Forms at all, and then why, in a more focused way, we should focus on the Form of Beauty so fiercely. The first motivation is purely epistemic; the second, which may overlap with the first, is more broadly eudaimonistic.

Plato describes the lover at the moment of apprehension as being suddenly overtaken, as if by a vision. He then, however, characterizes the features of the object seen in some detail, suggesting that the vision is neither blinding nor non-discursive. He says:

> One who has been schooled in matters of love to this extent, viewing beautiful things (*ta kala*) rightly and in an orderly fashion, as he approaches the end of his erotic affairs, will have something wonderful, beautiful in its nature revealed to him; and this, Socrates, is that for the sake of which all his earlier labors were undertaken. First of all, it is always (*aei on*) and neither comes to be nor perishes (*oute gignomenon oute apollumenon*), neither grows nor decays; it is not beautiful in one respect and in another ugly, nor now but not then, nor beautiful in relation to one and ugly in relation to another, nor in one place beautiful and in another place ugly, nor will it be beautiful to some and ugly to others. Nor again will it be presented to him as something beautiful, for instance some face or hands, or of anything else of which the body partakes; nor will it be some particular claim or some particular knowledge, nor as somehow being in some other thing, as in some animal or in the earth or the sky or any other thing at all. Rather, it will be itself, taken by itself, within itself, uniform, and existing always (*auto kath' hauto meth' hautou monoeides on*). (210e2–211b1)

[12] This remains consistent with the contention at 210e4–6 that as he approaches the end (*telos*) he is overtaken, grasping the beautiful as that for the sake of which (*hou heneken*) the lover has labored. The notion of the end (*telos*) here seems primarily non-technical (as in "reaching the end of our journey"); and that for the sake of which (*hou heneken*) is consistent with the end of one series being subordinate to another, as when we exercise for the sake of health.

Beautiful things, by contrast, will change and vary, will come into being and perish. Their vicissitudes will however, do nothing to perturb or in any way malign the Form of Beauty, and this despite the fact that they qualify as the beautiful things they are *only* by participating in the Form of Beauty and indeed only to the extent that they may be said so to participate.

This description of the Form of Beauty is entirely in keeping with Plato's characterization of the Forms as objects of knowledge (*epistēta*): Forms are Forms precisely because they escape the context-sensitivity of sensibles (*Phd.* 78d10–e3; *Rep.* 485a10–b4, 508d4–9, 521d3–4, 534d2–3; *Tht.* 181b8–182a8; *Soph.* 242e2–3; *Crat.* 411a1–c6; *Tim.* 51d). Forms are suited as objects of knowledge, then, in virtue of their shiftlessness: they do not vary from context to context, from time to time, from relation to relation, from knower to knower. Forms are suitable objects of knowledge, that is, in view of their purity and permanence. Beyond being purely and precisely what they are and nothing else, they will not, like the statues of Daedalus, arise in the night when out of view and scamper away (*Meno* 97d; cf. *Hip. Maj.* 282a). It seems inescapable that Plato is here trumpeting precisely these epistemic features of Forms in describing the Form of Beauty: as unshifting, it, like all other Forms, is ideally suited to serve as an object of knowledge.[13] The suggestion thus lies near that the superiority envisaged for the Form of Beauty is entirely generic, in keeping with that of all other Forms, and thus that the source of its surpassing value in relation to items on the lower rungs of Beauty is primarily epistemic rather than moral or aesthetic. They provide stability and fixity for knowledge, in place of the variegated and fractured images of sense perception.

This, then, will be the source of their value: by moving from the particular to the general, from the beautiful boy to Beauty itself, alone

[13] Here compares especially *Tim.* 51d: "If understanding and true opinion are distinct, then these things existing by themselves definitely exist—these Forms, the objects not of our sense perception but of our understanding only. But if—as some people think—true opinion does not differ in any way from understanding, then all the things we perceive through our bodily senses must be assumed to be the most stable things there are. But we do have to speak of understanding and true opinion as distinct, of course, because we can come to have one without the other, and the one is not like the other . . . Since these things are so we must agree that (i) that which keeps its own form unchangingly, which has not been brought into being and is not destroyed, which neither receives into itself anything else from anywhere else, nor itself enters into anything else anywhere, is one thing. It is invisible—it cannot be perceived by the senses at all, and it is the role of understanding to study it. (ii) The second thing is that which shares the other's name and resembles it. This thing can be perceived by the senses, and it has been begotten. It is constantly borne along, now coming into being in a certain place and perishing out of it. It is apprehended by opinion, which involves sense perception."

and by itself, we acquire something of immeasurable *epistemic* worth.[14] So prized is knowledge by Plato, on this approach, that the possibility of cognitive achievement will dwarf other, lower, non-cognitive types of love. The value of this hierarchy is thus purely object-driven: the more elevated the object, the more elevated our relation to it; higher relations supplant lower relations because lower objects are inferior to higher objects. The value scale is, on this approach, simply and unapologetically cognitive.

So much, though, seems wholly unsatisfactory. It first of all does not address our original second question, concerning why the Form of Beauty *in particular* should be described in such rapturous terms. So far, as a purely epistemic matter, the points about context-insensitivity are perfectly general, pertaining to all Forms as objects of *epistēmē*. Moreover, even bracketing that, the undoubted epistemic superiority of Forms, including the Form of Beauty, does little to explain – and still less to justify – the sort of hierarchical value reflected in the ascent to Beauty. It is true that one cannot know or understand a sense particular in anything like the sense required for *epistēmē*. This hardly, however, gives reason to release all focus on sense particulars. More to the point, it gives us no reason not to *love* them; but the ascent does proceed by supplanting object of love for object love, until such time as the lover's attention is focused exclusively on the Form of Beauty.

One may doubt this. Perhaps, one may say, this is simply the single-minded zealousness of Plato's rational eudaimonism (*Prot.* 358c–d; *Gorg.* 468b; *Meno* 78b). According to a standard understanding of this commitment, Plato holds that all rational motivation depends on the desire for happiness, where this desire is in one way or another egoistic. In effect, "it is rational for one to desire a state of affairs if and only if one rationally believes that that state of affairs will contribute to one's own happiness."[15] If happiness in fact consists in the contemplation of Forms, then it will simply be a consequence of Plato's rational eudaimonism that in pursuing my own happiness, I will come to set aside as valueless, or at least as of inferior value, objects whose contemplation does not provide the happiness afforded by Forms. Lesser objects seem to have at best instrumental value;

[14] This comparative value is succinctly characterized by Fine 2003, 4–5: "Indeed, one of [Plato's] main projects is to distinguish knowledge from both belief as such (whether true or false) and from true belief in particular, and to explain why knowledge is both more valuable and more difficult to achieve."

[15] Wedgwood 2009: 308. To be clear, however, Wedgwood proceeds to develop a novel and distinctive understanding of this commitment (319–24) – one taking us away from the topic currently under consideration.

and once their instrumentality is exhausted, they seem to have no independent value at all. So, perhaps Plato's purely epistemic motivations, when understood against the backdrop of his rational eudaimonism will after all suffice to explain his predilection for fixity.

This seems unlikely. First, there is a sense in which the epistemic justification is unsuitably arid. We are on this understanding asked to contemplate the contextless immutable Form of Beauty in preference of any sort of ordinary human love. Surely this only returns us to our original question, the question of why we should value epistemic fixity so strongly over doxastic variability. It seems simply to supplant the *interpersonal* connection given in the love of a human with the *impersonal* connection given in an intentional relation to an abstract object. If that were Plato's final word on the matter, then he really would be guilty of a sort of fetish for fixity.

More importantly, second, there seems to be a general question about whether Plato in fact endorses the form of rational eudaimonism here ascribed to him. Indeed, there is a question as to whether he is best understood as a rational eudaemonist in the *Symposium* at all. Kraut, for one, doubts this.[16] He contends, with some plausibility, that as commonly understood, rational eudaimonism "conflicts with the deepest idea that guides Plato's ethical thought, which is that one should live one's life in response to something superior to oneself." This insight, however developed, has a good deal to be said for it. Indeed, it points, if only obliquely, to the deeper and more comprehensive orientation motivating Plato's attraction to the Form of Beauty, namely his doctrine of *homoiōsis theōi*, that is, our drive to become like god. It might, in a certain way – in the way of the *Symposium* – point to a way in which Plato's rational eudaimonism *is* a way of living in response to something superior to oneself. Such rational eudaimonism would, however, be a far cry from the most narrowly egoistic understandings of that view.

We in fact already have some indication of Plato's deeper orientation in what we have already seen – and this provides our third and final reason for setting aside the epistemic justification, even as it is articulated within the context of any rational eudaimonism which Plato might nonetheless be thought to espouse. This is that we have not been given any direct reason to conclude that contemplation of the Form of Beauty *is* after all the end of human life. On the contrary, in addition to the points already mooted to the effect that Plato does not state or imply this in the

[16] See Kraut, Chapter 13 in this volume.

Symposium, we should note that he in fact states unequivocally that our final object of love is *not* Beauty, but the Good: "there is nothing else that human beings love other than the Good" (206a). At a bare minimum, then, we should not suppose that according to the presentation of the *Symposium* the pinnacle of human existence is the serene contemplation of the Form of Beauty. We are guided rather everywhere and always, in a manner fully in keeping with the doctrine of *Republic* V, by a desire for the Good (cf. also *Phil.* 20b; *Gorg.* 467d; *Charm.* 163d–e).

4. Striving to Be Like God

If we are seeking the source and character to the ever-increasing value of the ascent in the *Symposium*, the safest answer seems be this: higher levels are more godlike and lower levels are less godlike. Diotima says that "every mortal nature forever seeks to be deathless so far as this is possible" (207d2–3). As Sedley aptly observes, in the *Symposium* this drive involves "casting our relationship to god in terms of striving towards a divine paradigm,"[17] a kind of striving that Diotima immediately characterizes as eventuating in an impulse to participate in deathlessness by reproduction. More godlike is more valuable than less godlike: as we approach the divine, we move into a more valuable version of ourselves.

Still, there is something terribly peculiar in Diotima's understanding the property of being godlike merely in terms of being deathless (*athanaton*, 206e8). First is the observation that this impulse, however vivid and gripping, is essentially negative in character.[18] To escape death is to strive not to die. This is odd, however, to say the least, since by the time of the *Phaedo*, Plato is fully committed to the immortality of the soul. So, on the assumption that the *Symposium* is at least of the same general period of the *Phaedo*, literal reproduction is neither necessary nor sufficient for immortality: it is not sufficient, since being a member of an deathless species is not itself deathlessness for the individual who so participates (hence, on this approach, the qualification "as far as possible," *kata to dunaton* at 207d2), and it is not necessary, since the soul is already, in view of its own simple nature, independently immortal in any case. Finally, third, it is hard to connect a drive towards immortality, understood as

17 Sedley 1999: 310–11.

18 This is a point astutely made by Sedley 1999: 310: "This profound analysis of living creatures' aspirations picks out what might seem an essentially negative drive, the animal kingdom's ubiquitous fear of death, and reinterprets it as a positive ideal towards a higher ideal." To this one might only add that it might seem that way because it *is* that way.

species-dependent deathlessness, with the richly epistemic character of the ascent. For though we have said that the epistemic superiority was not the sole value ground in the *Symposium*, we have not said that Plato's characterization of the value of the Form of Beauty was bereft of epistemic or cognitive dimensions. On the contrary, as we have seen, it is plainly characterized in richly epistemic terms, fully in keeping with the descriptions of Forms as suitably stable objects of knowledge elsewhere in the corpus. Merely reproducing, which we (most of us) do anyhow, seems not to implicate us in the sort of cognitive or broader psychological development Plato envisages as a source of value. In this sense, reproduction is both irrelevant and unsuitably monodimensional.

Godlikeness is, in any case, much more multifaceted. Accordingly, to say that we have an impulse towards becoming like god underspecifies our locus of motivational value in this domain. After all, one can easily imagine many routes in addition to immortality in terms of which one might seek godlikeness. Already amongst the Church Fathers of late antiquity, for instance, we observe a full range of alternatives beyond mere immortality. Thus, for example, Clement of Alexandria speaks simply in contrastive terms of seeking to move away from the created image, to become less derivative, more authentic, and generally complete and perfected.[19] Eusebius of Caesaraea speaks as if the process of *homoiōsis theōi* were primarily the process of winnowing away the body to become more purely psychological beings, from being ensouled to *being* souls.[20] Gregory of Nyssa stresses the dimension of freedom: free will, he contends, is what puts humans on a path towards godlikeness.[21]

In their different ways, all these traits are prefigured in Plato, along with deathlessness, as we have already seen; but we also, significantly, find Plato himself indisputably highlighting still other dimensions along which it behooves humans to strive for godlikeness. In the clearest statement of Plato's conviction in the entire corpus,[22] the digression of the *Theaetetus* (172b–177c), where Socrates breaks the ongoing narrative with a striking paean to the philosophical life, we encounter a clear verbal parallel to the language of the *Symposium* regarding the philosophical impulse towards godlikeness. We are best served, Socrates intones, if we escape the unavoidable evils of mortal life by fleeing towards the divine: "And that is why we

[19] *Excerpta ex Theodoto* 54 (PG 9.685 A) and *Stromateis* 2.22 (PG 8.1080 C).

[20] *Praeparatio Evangelica* 7.4 (PG 21.513 B).

[21] *Catechetical Oration* 21 (PG 45.57 D).

[22] This is also the only place where Plato uses the exact phrase *homoiōsis theōi*, which occurs only once in Plato (*Tht.* 176b1). This seems also to be its first occurrence in the extant canon.

should escape from here as quickly as we can. To escape is to become like god as far as possible (*homoiōsis theōi kata dunaton*)" (176b1).

So far, this advice, however salutary, is none too directive until it is specified *how* we are to become like god, until, that is, the dimension, or dimensions, of godlikeness to be sought are specified. For example, if we seek deathlessness single-mindedly, then, as we have seen, we court an unattractive egoism, rooted in an essentially negative impulse. Helpfully, though, in the *Theaetetus* Plato is immediately forthcoming about the axes of assimilation. Just specifies the character of *homoiōsis theōi*: "becoming like god is to become just and holy, together with wisdom" (*Tht.* 1762–3). The list is noteworthy both for its exclusions and inclusions. Not mentioned is deathlessness (*athanaton*), though its omission does not constitute any form of denial. Instead, both moral and cognitive virtues are highlighted: the philosopher strives to become just and holy (or pious, *hosion*), but not merely so, but to do so together with wisdom (*meta phronēseōs*, *Tht.* 176b2). Here the cognitive dimensions evidently function as a kind of constraining specification, so that one exemplifies these virtues as tinctured by reason. Reason (*phronēsis*) is not, that is, listed as a further virtue alongside justice and holiness; instead, the directive is that one should realize these virtues minimally *in a rational manner* or, more likely, *as informed by* or *with the oversight and assistance* of reason. (Here, as at *Apol.* 32b, the preposition "with" functions rather like the English "She walks with God" or "He proceeds in all his dealings with a keen sense of fairness.") In the *Theaetetus*, then, the process of *homoiōsis theōi* is a complex, rationally virtuous affair, and not merely a negative impulse to avoid death. Here, at least, one might think that the process is consuming and transformative: to become like god is to change one's deportment, one's dispositions, one's dealings with others (cf. *Phdr.* 249e4–250b1).

Is this richer notion of *homoiōsis theōi* relevant to the hierarchical valuations of the *Symposium*? Some scholars have thought not,[23] but this gives short shrift to the characterization of love's ascent depicted there. Even within the ascent proper, we encounter the action-governing consequences derived from the drive towards becoming like god. The suggestion that we do so "so far as possible" (*kata to dunaton*) is not restricted in the dialogue to becoming as "immortal" as possible by participating in biological generation. While generation is here indeed so understood

[23] So Sedley 1999: 310 ff. In parting company with Sedley on this matter, I should make clear that in my estimation his article on this general question remains the best piece written in English on the topic.

(206a–c), Diotima expressly extends the notion to encompass being "pregnant in the soul" (209a2), a kind of pregnancy issuing in offspring more beautiful and more deathless (*kallionōn kai athanatōterōn*) than the biological variety (209c8–10). The issue here includes poems and constitutions, and even discourses about virtue (*logoi peri aretēs*; 209b–c), extending so far as general education (in the ways of endeavoring to be a good man (208c1–2; cf. *Phdr.* 252d5–e1). Finally, and most generally, one initiated into the ways of Beauty will, by contemplating this Form, turn outward and extend his generative activity, bringing forth many beautiful and magnificent words and thoughts in a fecund form of philosophy (209c–e).

Given these sorts of extensions, we would be unjustified in restricting the drive for *homoiōsis theōi* in the *Symposium* to mere biological reproduction. It embraces, instead, the sort of rich, multifaceted conception of the *Theaetetus*. In so striving, we do not wish to become merely deathless, participating in immortality in the contribution we make to our eternal species. Rather, we are to become as immortal as possible in our own expression and expansion of rationally virtuous life: prolific in the propagation of beauty, engendering magnificent words and thoughts, discoursing about virtue, endeavoring to help others to do the same, who may then, in their turn, engage in the same exalted form of life. This, then, will be Beauty's iteration, which encompasses the epistemic values with which we began, to be sure, but embraces as well the virtues, both moral and intellectual, pursued always under the auspices of reason.

5. Conclusions

If we have come this far, then we have in clear view the source and character of the hierarchy of value in the ascent of the *Symposium*: it is indeed epistemic, though not merely or austerely so; it is after all self-involving, as rooted in a generous form of rational eudaimonism, and not in a narrow or non-altruistic manner; it is a value of immortality, but not as a frightened, essentially negative flight from death in the biological domain. Instead, the value of the ascent is a campaign of *homoiōsis theōi*: becoming closer to god. It is better to be closer to than further from the divine, but to be closer to the divine requires first the inculcation of a panoply of reason-structured virtues, followed by the iteration of the same in others, in an endless procession of beauty.

Still, even now one may wonder: what has happened to the beautiful boy who, as an object of love, has been despised and left behind?

The answer now seems twofold, in a way providing little cause for castigation or rebuke. First, he has not been left behind altogether, but rather elevated so that he may himself participate in Beauty itself, not merely as a pretty shape, bound to atrophy and fade, but as a beautiful soul which in its turn becomes a novel agent of Beauty's demands. The boy in turn, when schooled in rationally structured virtue, will become engaged in his own right in seeking to elevate yet another along the path of *homoiōsis theōi.*

Yet even at this remove one may feel some disquiet in the face of Plato's injunction to turn away from the passionate contingencies of our quotidian days, engrossing though they may be as we encounter and engage them, in favor of the intransience of the divine, serene and imperturbable in its perfection. Perhaps, but to the extent that the immortal does reign supreme over the mortal, one may – indeed, Plato proposes, one *ought to* – disdain the lesser in favor of the greater. So, finally, a process of *homoiōsis theōi* does after all commend turning one's love from a lesser to a greater beauty, and so does then enjoin a lover to disdain what has been left behind. Plato does indeed have, in this way at any rate, a fetish for fixity; but the fixation of this fetish, what is at last loved by the lover schooled in the way of philosophy, is the ceaseless value the vision of Beauty begets.[24]

[24] I am grateful to the editors for their welcome interventions. I thank also Brian Daley, S. J. for instructive discussions regarding what it might mean to undergo a process of *homoiôsis theôi.*

CHAPTER 10

Generating in Beauty for the Sake of Immortality: Personal Love and the Goals of the Lover

Anthony W. Price

1. Preface

It is characteristic of Platonic dialogues to lack any clearly demarcated topic, certainly as a whole, and often even within the parts of a whole. Eryximachus' proposal, prompted by Phaedrus, is that each symposiast give a speech in praise of *Erōs* (*Symp.* 177d2–5). Socrates' response is at once compliant and subversive: "It's not likely that I would say no, seeing that I claim not to understand anything but erotics" (*ta erōtika*, d7–8, tr. after Rowe). This at once intimates that he will be presenting nothing less than his own philosophy. When it comes fully to his turn, he cites a supposed "woman of Mantinea" (201d2), Diotima, as his teacher in "erotics" (d5), again, it will turn out, in a wide sense. Of course, the occasion imposes a focus that will fit what Eryximachus and Phaedrus had in mind; and yet within his own philosophy everything connects.

It should not surprise us, therefore, when Socrates has Diotima begin to explain what utility *erōs* has for human beings (204c8) by a lucid statement of the core of Socratic moral psychology:

> "Come on, Socrates: the person who loves, loves good things; why does he love them?"
> "To have them for himself," I said.
> "And what will the person who has good things get by having them?"
> "That," I said, "I'm better placed to answer: he'll be happy (*eudaimōn*)."
> "Yes," she said, "because those who are happy are happy by the possession of good things, and one no longer needs to go on to ask 'And what reason does the person who wishes to be happy have for wishing it?' Your answer seems to be final." (204e2–205a3)

The methodology is typically Socratic: to identify the benefits that *erōs* brings, one needs first to define the good that human beings ultimately desire. Only by reference to that can a common opinion about the utility of *erōs* be tied down by an account of the reason (*aitias logismos*), and so become knowledge (*Men.* 98a3–4); the rest – which is the remainder of the *Symposium* – is rhetoric.

As the discussion proceeds, a further twist derives a specification of the utility of *erōs* from a refinement of the teleology. It is said to be common to all human beings that they always (*aei*) want to possess good things (205a6–8); this most likely conveys that in every action a human being aims at his own good (which is a familiar tenet of Socratic psychology). However, that thesis gradually makes way for a different one: human beings desire to possess the good always, that is, forever (206a11–12). The transition is verbally deft (being marked by a simple shift in the position of *aei*), but not disguised: it is with an equal necessity (note the gerundive *prostheteon*, 206a6, a10) that we are to spell out a love of the good as a love *to have* the good (a6–7), and to have it *always* (a9). Of course, there is no logical inference from desiring to have the good to desiring to have it always; yet it may suit Plato's present purposes to impose both supplements. Doing so is debatable, and yet, in the present context, fruitful.[1]

There follows an ambiguity that at once complicates the task of exposition, and confirms how closely Socrates' moral psychology connects with his erotics:

> *erōs* is for one's having the good forever . . . Given, then, that *erōs* is always of this,[2] in what manner will those pursuing it do so, and through what activity, if their intense zeal would be called *erōs*? What really is its function? . . . I'll tell you: it is generating in beauty, whether in respect of the body or of the soul. (206a11–b8)

What does *erōs* mean here, and does it have one meaning, or two? The commonest reading is stated succinctly by Christopher Gill: "Here Diotima uses the general motive identified as 'love' in 205a–206a to explain the subdivision of this motive (marked by a special 'enthusiasm and intensity') that is normally called 'love'" (1999: 78, n. 112).[3] However, others suppose that *erōs* retains a single sense and reference throughout these lines.[4] Is the way of loving now indicated by the phrase "generating in beauty" *the* mode by which generic love operates, or *a* mode by which it operates, viz. when it takes the form of what is idiomatically called *erōs*, where this is conceived as a species within the genus?

[1] For and against the second supplement, contrast Wedgwood 2009: 36–7 with Santas 1998: 55, n. 39.

[2] I read *toutou* for the mss. *touto*; see Vlastos 1973: 21, n. 57. However, it is possible to pursue (*diōkein*) an occupation as well as its object; so Sier 1997: 222.

[3] So Gilbert 1909: 54, Bury 1932, 1st edn 1909: xxxvii n., et al.

[4] So Sier 1997: 99 ff., 220–2, Rowe 1998a, 1998b: 181–2, et al.

An answer to this question may help or hinder an understanding of the two notions "having the good forever" and "generating in beauty." The former can be paraphrased as "immortality together with good" (206e8–207a1); when it is then said that *erōs* is of "immortality" (207a3–4), this confirms that desire aims at *both*, though together and not separately, since nothing is desired but the good (205e1–206a1). Now it was a previous thesis that desire presupposes lack (200a9), so that its objects are neither present (*parōn*) nor reliably available (*hetoimos*, 200e2–3); it follows that the immortality in question cannot be identified with that which is argued in the *Phaedo* to be an essential and secure aspect of soul as such. Two alternatives remain. There is the vicarious immortality that Diotima will relate to the procreating of offspring, physical or mental, and identify as the one way in which the mortal can partake of immortality (208b2–4). And there is the proprietary immortality that may be achieved by a human soul that achieves assimilation to the divine; this is not explicated in the *Symposium*, but may well be indicated at the climax of the ascent passage (212a5–7). "Generation in beauty" is again variably interpretable, in part depending on whether we interpret the *erōs* that motivates it as specific or generic. Paradigmatic is intercourse, physical or mental, either of a man with a woman whom he impregnates with a new human being, or of a lover with a boy whom he inspires with a new mental life. However, the notion becomes extended, both in its occasion and in its upshot. Poets, inventors, and legislators may count as generating in the beautiful though there is no mention of a loved one; and what they generate may ultimately be a reputation. Philosophers generate in a beauty that becomes depersonalized, and what they generate remains only debatably interpersonal.

While there is much here to be fruitfully debated, I doubt whether we can resolve the ambiguity of 206a11–b8 with any confidence. It may be indeterminate whether talk of "generation in beauty" locates *erōs* as a species of desire, or reconceives desire in a manner that illuminates the goals of *erōs*. Different difficulties arise in either case; yet these are independent of the answers to what we may think the most interesting questions.

2. Generation in Beauty

The object of *erōs* is to possess the good forever (206a11–2, 207a2). Nothing is presumed about life after death, perhaps because Diotima is describing universal aspirations that cannot depend upon distinctive Platonic views at variance with traditional Greek religion (which bleakly envisaged immortality without the good). What nature already provides, as a rescue from mortality, is sexual reproduction. Both in procreating and nurturing offspring, all animals display an intense commitment that Diotima interprets as an aspiration towards the eternal possession of the good; hence we may impute not just to human beings, but to "mortal nature" in general, an innate if mostly inarticulate orientation towards immortality (207a6–d3).

What indicates that procreation offers more than a simulacrum of survival over time is that it re-enacts the pattern of an automatic loss and replacement of bodily parts that alone enables an animal to live through a lifetime (207d4–e1). If living bodies persist through time, it is only through processes analogous to those active in sexual reproduction. Hence, if we count renewal through a lifetime's sequence of physical changes as a form of persistence that satisfies a desire for survival, we should count renewal through a sequence of descendants as also satisfying that desire. If we can only conceive the second as *vicarious* survival, this may be because of a crucial difference: as boy grows into a man, the boy disappears as the man appears, whereas, when a man begets a boy, the man remains *in* existence as the boy comes *into* existence.[5] And yet, as I have heard Derek Parfit ask of cases of fission in which a person seems to split into two persons, why should a double success thereby count as a failure? Logic may forbid a father to say, pointing to his son, "I am *there*, and also *here*"; and yet physical continuities link his past self to *both* present places.

Diotima speaks analogously of the persistence through a lifetime of a mind or mentality, with two salient differences. First, the rehearsing or conning or going over (*meletan*, 208a4) that replaces one memory with a new one is most naturally interpreted as a conscious activity that is under the control of a subject. Second, whereas the processes of disappearance and reappearance are applied to "the whole body" (207e1), they are never ascribed to the soul *itself* as well as to its contents. These points are doubtless linked: it is the soul as a continuing subject that renews its own states. (This is how, though Diotima is silent about the Platonic doctrine of the essential immortality of the soul, she does not exclude it. This will matter later.) Now, just as I replace one memory by another just like it by *reminding myself of it*, I may pass on an idea to another person by *informing him of it*.[6] This is where Diotima locates the Greek tradition of

[5] Thus Wordsworth's analogy, "The Child is father of the Man," is inexact.

[6] As David Mabberley pointed out to me, this anticipates Richard Dawkins's notion of the meme (analogous to the physical gene), defined in the Merriam-Webster Dictionary as "an idea, behavior

pedagogic pederasty: "It's by contact with what is beautiful [viz., a boy], and associating with it, that he [the lover] begets and procreates the things with which he was so long pregnant" (209c2–3). This actually resembles mental continuity within a life more than sexual reproduction resembles physical continuity; for rehearsing a thought by oneself and communicating it to another are both intentional activities, whereas the self-renewal of a body is an automatic and unconscious process.[7]

In both cases, what is first prolonged, and then propagated, is a *life*, physical or mental. The existence of a living body over time reduces to the continuation of a series of bodily changes; the soul that animates the body becomes the source of a life that flows, after the body has procreated or given birth, through later branches of the same series. The existence of a soul over time is not so reducible; and yet a soul that directs a stream of mental life naturally *identifies with* it, so that it continues to value the stream even after this has flowed into a tributary directed by another soul.[8]

Thus erotic love evidences the fundamental teleology of desire for "immortality together with the good" (206e8–207a1). This deep diagnosis of the springs of sexuality has implications for Plato's sexual morality. Pausanias' moralizing pederast was set on sexual pleasure, but willing to accompany it with philosophy and the rest of virtue (184d1). Diotima's lover pregnant in soul may or may not make love to the boy, but must view this as at worst a perversion, and at best a diversion; for it fails to connect – even if it does not conflict – with his fundamental orientation towards immortality.[9]

or style that spreads from person to person within a culture." In Dawkins's terminology, it is a transmission of memes that Diotima here has in mind. Patrick Wagner points out to me that it is anticipated in the framing dialogue that opens the *Symposium* (172a1–174a2): an account of the speeches has passed from Aristodemus to Phoenix, to anon, and so to Apollodorus, and now passes (more reliably, since Socrates has vetted its fidelity, 173b4–6) from Aristodemus to Apollodorus, and so to the reader.

[7] According to *Phd.* 87d9–e1, this process too is the work of the soul. As "mortal nature" (*Symp.* 207d1) evidently signifies the nature of a *living* thing, and the soul brings life to a body (*Phd.* 105d3-4), this is not inconsistent. The *Phaedo* shares the *Symposium* view of a human body not as a substance parallel to the soul, and clearly distinct from all other bodies, but as a location of *processes* of decay and renewal.

[8] It is doubtless only in a derivative and diluted sense that a soul remains alive within some stretch of life, physical or mental, that owes its nature and existence to that soul, but is actually directed by another soul; from which it does not follow that nothing desirable is achieved (cf. Price 1997: 34). A different complaint, ethical rather than metaphysical, might be that the lover is making use of another's life for the sake of his own vicarious survival (love as colonialism?); for a reply to that, see Price 1997: 98.

[9] Still less is there any room for human love-making, animalistic or acratic, that lacks any orientation towards *eudaimonia*; for Socratic desire, and emotion in general, is a child of overall judgement. See Price 1997: 254–5; 2011: 95–8, 254–5.

Other aspects of Diotima's account may be troublesome. She further relates human quasi-immortality, as vulgarly conceived, to a lasting memory that is passed on either to one's descendants, or to future generations steeped in one's poems or drilled in one's laws (208e3–5, 209d3–4, e3–4). Within pederasty, this was a commonplace dear to love-poets (cf. what Ibycus promised to Polycrates, and Theognis to Cyrnos). Heterosexually, it complicates the initial contrast (cf. 206c1–3) between physical and mental procreation (or between genes and memes); but that is no objection. Since the goal is a *good* reputation, this does not earn any complaint (*pace* Obdrzalek 2010: 422–3) that here, in contrast to 206e8–207a1, immortality is being pursued *without* the good.[10] And yet it seems out of place. It is true that first-person memory may be added to the continuities that she has described as making a unity of a single life: if I remember doing something, this may count as a continuation of my doing it that helps to hold my life together.[11] However, it is only in a very loose sense that surviving in human memory after one's death is a way of surviving: you and I can remember *that* Odysseus outwitted the Cyclops (at least in Homer's story), but we can't, ourselves, remember *outwitting* him. If Odysseus' life has had an impact upon ours it is through our reading the *Odyssey*, and not through any transmission that could make our lives a partial prolongation of his.[12]

What, anyway, of generation in beauty? It is a familiar point that Plato plays with the ambiguity of *tokos* and *tiktein* between begetting, and giving birth.[13] Even sexually, male procreation is described in the language of pregnancy and birth-pangs (206d7–e1). Mentally, the lover welcomes the boy both as a mother of their future children, and as a midwife who may relieve him of his own pregnancy (209a8–c7). Talk of "generation in beauty" fits a man's being inspired by the beauty of a woman or boy to impregnate a body or mind with a continuation of his own life, biological or mental. A branch of his physical life develops

[10] Contrast the "Herostratic fame" (as it came to be called) of the man who burnt down the temple of Diana of the Ephesians in order to be remembered forever.

[11] Yet this is a different kind of continuation from a constancy of "traits" and "habits" (*tropoi* and *ēthē*, 207e2): I may now remember doing things that I can, or would, never do again; and I may act in character without recalling how I acted in the past.

[12] As Obdrzalek (2010: 421) notes, leaving behind a reputation is not leaving behind something *like oneself*, which was a requirement of vicarious immortality at 208b1–2. Against that, one might cite Socrates' anxiety in the *Rep.* that the stories one hears, especially in one's childhood, must strongly affect one's character (III, 386a1–392c6). Yet that point is not made here. When propagating virtue is linked to winning a reputation, it is the former that is presented as a means to the latter (209e2–4); that, if little more, I concede to Scott (2007: 150).

[13] See Dover 1980: 147.

within the woman's body before achieving independence at birth; a branch of his mental life is established within the boy's mind. What is the initial role of beauty? Physically, Diotima supposes, here in obvious faithfulness to experience, sexual attraction is a condition of a man's actualizing his reproductive potency (206d3–e1). Assimilating begetting and giving birth, she makes beauty a condition of both, so that both take over the latter's dependence on Fate and *Eileithyia* (d2–3). What of mental procreation? Diotima pursues analogies: the lover fertile in soul "goes around looking for the beautiful object in which he might procreate; for he will never do so in what is ugly" (209b2–4); at the same time, "he warms to beautiful bodies rather than ugly ones because he is pregnant" (b4–5). She presents her thoughts with a seductive facility that should not silence doubt. Even within personal relationships, why should physical beauty be requisite to the transmission of a mental life? Mental fertility seems well exemplified in Socrates' narrative of his relations with Diotima, which surely does not presuppose that he was good-looking when young.[14] And why should we not find a paradigm of fertile psychic love not in a lover, however platonic, but in a father and mentor? George Devereux once wrote, I don't know how truly, "The Greek father usually failed to counsel his son; instead, he counseled another man's son, in whom he was erotically interested" (1967: 78). And yet a paternal union of generation, nurture, and education may seem to us to provide by far the fullest paradigm, *both* physical *and* mental, of the transmission first of life and then of a way of life.

Such queries arise with renewed force when we turn out attention to a wider social context. In invoking the impact of poetry and legislation, she applies the language of generation freely: all poets are "procreators" of wisdom and the rest of virtue, things "that it is fitting for the soul to conceive and bring to birth" (209a2–4); legislators such as Lycurgus and Solon "procreated" laws and virtue of all sorts, which have since counted as their "children" (d4–e4). Yet in this context she makes no mention of personal beauty as a partner or midwife. Are we to suppose that *this* generation is *not* in beauty?[15]

[14] Gill (1999: xxxiv) also well asks how we are to understand the lightly sketched role of the anonymous guide (210a6–7, c6–7, e2–3, 211c1).

[15] According to Rowe (1998a: 255), Diotima is imputing the backroom presence of a *bel ami* – but with evident irony. Apparently serious is Spenser, *The Faerie Queene*, preface to Book IV: "Which so who list looke backe to former ages,/And call to count the things that then were donne,/Shall find, that all the works of those wise sages,/And brave exploits which great Heroes wonne,/In love were either ended or begunne." Which one may doubt.

How do these problems bear on the rival readings of 206b1–3? Should they incline us to interpret the *erōs* that is exercised in generation in beauty as specific, or as generic? One might take the difficulties I have identified to arise precisely out of a reading of the *erōs* of 206b3 as specific and idiomatic; for it falls outside such *erōs* that a mentality can equally be propagated within a personal relationship without sexual attraction, and that it can also be propagated, and more widely, outside any personal relationship. However, it is worth noting what is said, and what is *not* said, about the function of poetry and legislation. As I cited, Diotima is happy here to apply the metaphor of *procreating* (209a4, d7, e2) *children* or *offspring* (d2, e4). Yet she does not speak in this context explicitly of generation *in beauty*. All that mention of Homer, Hesiod, Lycurgus and Solon is asserted to confirm is the superiority of children of the mind to children of the body (209c7–e4). So it may be that she has to be willing to concede that, while generation in beauty, understood as a function of personal *erōs*, is indeed important as a mode of propagating ways of thinking and acting and thereby achieving a kind of immortality, it enjoys no monopoly in this role.

Thus a specific reading of the *erōs* of 206b3 is possible; is a generic one impossible? If the phrase "generation in beauty" is to apply to the operation of generic *erōs*, we cannot think of this beauty as restrictedly erotic. Yet Codrus may have been inspired by the charms of his sons to lay down his life in order to preserve his kingship for their sake (208d4–5); most parents find their children prepossessing. What of poets and legislators? Dover speculates as follows: "Diotima does not explain the beautiful medium 'in' which Homer 'generated' poems or Solon laws, but it can only be the virtuous character of the societies for which Homer sang and Solon legislated" (1980: 151–2). That is certainly one possibility; it does not tell against it that Plato may himself have taken a dim view of that character – for we know from the *Republic* that he also took a dimmer view of Greek poets and legislators than he puts into the mouth of Diotima. However, we do not have to suppose that the beauty was actual and external; we might rather envisage that the beauty that inspired them, real or meretricious, characterized their own dreams of a legendary past or a reformed future.

If this speculation is permitted, it can defend the most generic reading against what may have seemed a fatal objection; for if *erōs* is to be identified with desire in general, as Socrates conceived that, and generation in beauty is its one mode of operation, *every* human action, however mundane, must be ascribable to the inspiration of beauty. This was already not easily applicable to gymnasts and money-makers (mentioned alongside more idiomatic "lovers," and philosophers, at 205d4–5). However, once we allow the beauty to be prospective, we can suppose that gymnasts look forward to the glory an Olympic crown, and money-makers to the glory of funding a tragic chorus or a chariot team.[16] And the idea can be extended indefinitely: *any* action aims at the good, and is therefore inspired by the prospect of a beautiful goal.

How, therefore, are we to interpret the *erōs* exercised in "generation in beauty"? So far in the *Symposium*, we are left with at least two options, generic and specific. Either of them can be seen to fit what follows. Here *erōs* will be reconceived afresh as generating in a beauty that is increasingly intense, but decreasingly erotic (in any familiar sense). We may read it either as starting with a narrow conception of *erōs* that is gradually extended, or as advancing through a genus subsuming all forms of *erōs*; we do not have to decide. In either case, Diotima carries us along by a continuity that accommodates new conceptions both of beauty and of immortality.

3. The Ascent

There has been, and will always be, debate about how closely to connect the ascent passage (201a–212a) to what has preceded it. It is here at last that *erōs* is linked to philosophy, and more particularly Platonic philosophy. I have argued in the past (Price 1997: 38–54, 257–60) that Diotima must still have in mind generation in beauty as it has been expounded since 206b7–8 if her line of thought is not to be broken-backed. Taking this to involve a personal relationship (much as Socrates will spell out in the second speech of the *Phaedrus*), I particularly appealed for textual support to her talk of "correctly loving a boy" (or "boys," 211b5–6), *through* (or *thanks to*) which – and not *long after* which – the lover approaches his final destination. It is now time for a reconsideration, one that will not exclude what I proposed, but set it besides other possibilities.

This passage merits the closest of readings. Though there is not time for that here, it may help to focus on some points of significant detail if I start by taking a structured translation of a single lengthy and long-breathed sentence, lightly revised, from Price (1997: 39):

A1 (210a7) First, if the guide guides him rightly, he must love one body,
A2 (a7–8) and generate there beautiful discourse,

[16] I owe this point to Suzanne Obdrzalek.

A3 (a8–b3) and then himself realize that the beauty of any one body is closely akin to that of any other, and that, if one must pursue beauty of appearance, it is great folly not to consider the beauty of all bodies one and the same;

A4 (b4–6) having realized this he must become a lover of all beautiful bodies, and slacken his intense love of the one, disdaining it and thinking little of it;

B1 (b6–c1) after this he must think beauty in souls more valuable than that in the body, with the result that, if anyone was sound of soul and had even a little bloom, this would suffice for his loving and caring for him,

B2 (c2–3) and bring forth and search for such discourse as will improve the young,

B3 (c3–5) in order that he may now be forced to look upon the beauty in practices and laws and see that it is all akin itself to itself,

B4 (c5–6) in order that he may think the surface beauty of the body a little thing;

C1 (c6–7) after practices he must be led to branches of knowledge, so that he may now see the beauty of these,

C2 (c7–d4) and looking towards beauty already in its width he may no longer be base and pettifogging in his slavery to the beauty of one, but having turned to the wide sea of beauty and contemplating it,

C3 (d4–6) he may bring forth much beautiful and fine discourse and thoughts in ungrudging philosophy,

D (d6–e1) until, strengthened and nourished there, he catches sight of a certain branch of knowledge that is single, and such as to be of the following beauty.[17]

I shall now annotate each step in turn.

At A1, the object of love is "the boy who represents beauty itself to the lover" (Reeve 2011). This is an individualized version of Hippias' naïve answer to the question "What is beauty?": "A beautiful girl is beauty" (*Hip. Maj.* 287e2–4.) It is an unreflective and indeed inarticulate state that fails to identify qualities that make the boy beautiful. The lover already advances beyond that when, at A2, the guide encourages him to put his love into words descriptive of the boy's physical beauty, most aptly (no doubt) in poetry. While the verb gennan can mean "beget" as well as "bear," the adverb "there" (*entautha,* 210a7) rather indicates the presence of an addressee than a

[17] I follow Reeve (1971: 326) in deleting a clause that runs from 210d1 to d3; see also n. 24.

joint role in generation (unless the loved one is a Narcissus). John Ferrari (1992: 256) is not quite right to say that the mode of discourse (or of *logoi*) already has beauty as its topic; yet it will have to apply general terms, and so introduce what he calls a "comparison class." Which leads into the generalizing A3: that "the beauty of all bodies is one and the same" (210b3) is the ontological equivalent of a linguistic thesis that "—is beautiful" has the same criteria whenever it is predicated of a body (or such a body). Which in turn leads into A4: as beauty is the ground of love, the lover finds himself loving all beautiful bodies.[18] All this implicitly limits the range of relevant bodies to those that are proper objects of love, and indeed of this kind of love, viz. boys' bodies.

It is most likely not the one body that the lover comes to "disdain and think little of," but his initial "intense love" of it (so Nehamas 2007: 112). On the other side, one might (with Sier 1997: 275) cite B4, to this effect: perhaps the lover thinks little (not nothing) of *any particular body* after A3, just as he will think little (again not nothing) of *beautiful bodies in general* after B3. However, to love *all* beautiful bodies is rather to love *each* than to love either the property or the set. Any instance is only one instance, and so no great matter in itself; but to disdain each is to disdain all, which cannot be the attitude of the lover of all beautiful bodies. So we may follow Nehamas.

The upshot is a promiscuity rather poeticizing than sexual (Price 1997: 47; Nehamas 2007: 114–16). Nehamas questions whether the lover now loves all beautiful bodies equally, citing Socrates himself, widely susceptible, and yet always loyal to Alcibiades.[19] About Plato's general view, he may well be right (if we may cite the reciprocal fidelity celebrated at *Phdr.* 256a7–e2); but what is implicit in our present text? It is a general theme within the ascent passage that *erōs* is a conative response to a cognitive input: one loves what one finds beautiful. Moreover, if the cognitive ascent is bound to weaken one's commitment to lesser beauties, one must love things to the extent that one finds them beautiful. Hence Diotima cannot permit the lover both to find two boys equally beautiful, and to love one more than the other; nor can she permit the lover of one boy who meets another who appears more beautiful not to love the second more than the first. Which, if true, goes to show that there is no perfect match between what Socrates will say Diotima has persuaded him of (212b1–2), and his own way of life (if Nehamas identifies this rightly).

[18] Cf. the general impressionability that Socrates ascribes to Glaucon at *Rep.* V. 474d1–4.

[19] For the love (as Marlowe's *Edward II* puts it) of "grave Socrates' for "wild Alcibiades," Nehamas refers to *Prot.* 309ab, *Gorg.* 481d, *Symp.* 213b–d; one may add *Symp.* 216d2–3. However, Suzanne Obdrzalek points out to me that the *Symp.* passages testify much less clearly to this than the other two.

While the transition from A1 and A2 to A3 and A4 was generalizing, that from A to B is ascending. The lover next comes (we are not told how) to value "beauty in souls" (210b6-7) above physical beauty. The generality of this (note "souls," plural) helps disambiguate the ambiguity of the "if"-clause that follows: is it "if *someone* was sound of soul and had even a little bloom," or "if *anyone*" was so, that "this would suffice for his loving and caring for him?" The former (which I had wrongly assumed) returns from the generality of A4 to a single object of love as at A1; the latter (preferred by Nehamas 2007: 115) remains with a plurality, and so avoids a discontinuity with A4. And yet the new mode of loving, which involves not only admiring but finding the time to be caring (*kēdesthai*, c1), will have to be selective, even arbitrarily, of one or a few.

The lover himself may seem undemanding: he is satisfied by a *sound* soul with a *little* physical bloom. Yet while this is sober in tone, it is not so very new in content: the pederast of the lesser mysteries *had* to prefer beautiful bodies to ugly ones, and selected a soul "beautiful and well-born and of a good natural disposition" (if those are fair renderings of *kalos*, *gennaios*, and *euphyēs*, 209b6); one may compare the "fitting soul" at *Phdr.* 276e6, which (in the language of Mark iv 3–9) is good and not stony ground for yielding fruit out of seed. There must be some presence of physical, and more promise of mental, beauty.

The upshot is again a kind of discourse: the lover is motivated to "bring forth and seek out such discourse as will improve the young" (210c1–3). Unfortunately, this is a crux: Bury (1932), Dover (1980), and Vicaire (Robin/Vicaire 1989) all delete "and seek out" (*kai zētein*), which, put *after* "bring forth," is at best an instance of *hysteron proteron.* Bury (1932: 126) is splendidly dismissive of attempts to ascribe a point (with the put-down "But this is futile"). Yet Sier (1997: 276) aptly contrasts a previous passage (209b7–c2). How, we may ask, can the lover at this stage of the ascent, who has yet to attend to good practices and laws, make a better job of ethical education than the lover of the lesser mysteries who, once he has selected a recipient, is *immediately fluent* (*euthys euporei*, b8) in words of edification? Well, being a seeker, he lacks the complacency that reduces the fluent to the facile.[20] We might still prefer him to hold back for a time. Yet he will look around, and take advice; he should do little harm, even if

[20] In a phrase let drop in another context by David Wiggins, the *logoi* of 209b8 are "low-octane, readily available." As Ferrari (1992: 256) observes relevantly, "The mark of the individual suitable for the ascent is that he does not take the nature of the beautiful for granted." He alone "approaches these things correctly" (210a2), and so is led from and by the Lesser to the Greater Mysteries.

he is not yet ready to do much good. To the extent that his project succeeds, any selected beneficiary will *become* deserving of his predilection.

At least *he* benefits: it is because he is trying to do better that he is *compelled* (210c3) to advance towards an appreciation of the beauty of practices and laws. This compulsion comes from what the guide already knows, and he is coming to know, to be necessary for cognitive progress.[21] It is a compulsion to *look* (c3, c7, d4, e3), and so to *see* what is there to be seen (c4, c7, d7, e4). These are both things that the lover has to do *for himself*, even under guidance.[22] He will now (where the "now," *au*, marks a parallel with the generalizing move within A3) look at the beauty in practices and laws (which direct the soul in decision and action), and see that it is all akin. "Akin" (*syngenēs*, c5) is weaker than "closely akin" (*adelphos*, b1), most likely for a conceptual reason: while boys' bodies are all of a kind, practices and laws are of different categories (though they connect, for laws prescribe practices). The upshot may puzzle us: B4 chimes neatly with A4 ("thinking little of," c5–6, echoes "thinking . . . a little thing," b6), thus confirming A and B as just *two* levels; and yet what does B4 add to the starting-point of B1 in ranking beauty of soul above beauty of body? However, it is an easy suggestion that what is added is *consolidation*: what was in B1 a presumption necessary for further progress has by B4 become an inference from a clear grasp of the unity within variety of the ethical world.[23]

Ascent to the next level is instigated by the guide, who persuades the lover that good practices, though directed by the laws of society, need to be grounded in an understanding that both confirms and enhances their value. On the Platonic principle that if one thing lends beauty to another, it is itself beautiful (indeed, more so), the beauty of branches of knowledge becomes apparent as progress is made. The lover now has a view of beauty in its full extent, and can escape any limited preoccupation with just one locus of value.[24] Turning his eyes to the wide sea of beauty and

[21] Sier (1997: 277) cites parallels that are recurrent in *Rep.* VII. 515c6, d9, 524c7, e4, 526b1–2, e3, e7, 529a1.

[22] This was already emphasized at 210a8: the lover must *himself* grasp the close kinship of physical beauty, where the *auton*, though grammatically "rather otiose" (Bury 1932: 125), is well explained by Rowe (1998: 194–5).

[23] Nehamas complicates the relation to A to B by supposing that beauty of character is manifest in the body (2007: 122). Which is attractive, but dubiously Platonic; cf. Price 2002: 178–81.

[24] Once we follow Reeve's deletion (n. 17), we can take the "one thing," which the subject now appreciates within a wider perspective as not particularly an individual (man or boy) or practice, but any isolated object of enthusiasm. If Reeve is right, it was doubtless the unclarity of this which gave rise to an inept gloss.

contemplating it, he can "bring forth much beautiful and fine discourse and thoughts in ungrudging philosophy."

Especially worthy of attention here is the term "ungrudging" (*aphthonos*, 210d6). It doubtless applies to the guide, who is already a philosopher; yet in fact it is applied to the lover. "In relation to whom?", we have surely to ask. Most pertinent may be a passage in the *7th Letter*, whether it be authentic Plato or not (though of course it is less significant as *evidence* if it is not):

> Only when all of these things – names, definitions, and visual and other perceptions – have been rubbed against one another and tested, pupil and teacher asking and answering questions in good will and ungrudgingly (*aneu phthonōn*) – only then, when reason and knowledge are at the very extremity of human effort, can they illuminate the nature of any object. (344b3–c1, tr. Morrow)[25]

Of course, *logoi* have many purposes. As the ascent has proceeded, they were first expressive of an emotion (a7–8), but preparatory of a shift into generality (a8–b3); then they were ethically edifying (c1–3), but preparatory of a wider view of the ethical world (c3–5); finally, here (d4–6), they are preparatory of the climactic vision that will come of the final ascent to a vision of the Form (d6–e1). Within A, they were addressed, and doubtless communicated, to the boy who inspired them, but not as a mode of education. Within B, they were communicated to anyone with both a native ability to benefit, and the opportunity to enter into a significant relationship with their author. Within C, if they are to count as constituting *ungrudging* philosophy (d6), the philosophy must be imparted to one recipient or more. Here, in inviting German (Schirlitz 1890: 30–2, Gilbert 1909: 58), a learning (*Lernen*) by the lover is also, and even (if we trust the *7th Letter*) at the same time, a teaching (*Lehren*) of one disciple or several.

Finally, at level D, the lover's view of *all* beauty becomes a vision of a *single* thing, Beauty itself. Ferrari expresses this with great felicity (1992: 258–9): at C2, "he is looking back from the height he has scaled, and sees beauty as a whole, but a whole of great multiplicity;" now, within D, "he turns his face to the peak, and comes to see beauty as a unity," viz. as a Form. Here there is no further talk of *logoi*. This need not mean that the achievement is his alone. Beauty itself is "beyond words" (Ferrari 1992:

[25] Other exclusions of *phthonos*, all in interpersonal contexts, include *Prot.* 327a7–8, b5, *Phd.* 61d10, *Rep.* V., 476e6, *Phdr.* 253b7, and especially, since they apply to the gods (which will be crucial to my conclusion), *Phdr.* 247a7, *Tim.* 29e2, *Ep.* 988b7. As is clear in these passages, a lack of *phthonos* is displayed in a willingness to pass on a privilege – whether virtue, knowledge, or skill – to another.

259): it can be adumbrated apophatically (211ab), but not articulated in a *logos* (211a7). If an understanding of it can be shared, this must be not through verbal communication by one person to another, but within participation in a vision, or joint achievement of insight. The ascent is complete, though the lover's labors and rewards are not yet exhausted.

4. Becoming as Immortal as a Man May

A significant sentence, looking both behind and ahead, is this:

> When someone goes up by these stages, through loving boys in the correct way (*dia to orthōs paiderastein*), and begins to catch sight of that beauty, he has come close to reaching the goal. (211b5–7, tr. Gill)

Sier (1997: 150 n.) objects that *dia* with the accusative indicates a cause, and not a continuing role. The English "through" may signify either, but is his term "Ausgangspunkt" ("starting-point") adequate to the case? Discarding boys at an early stage hardly counts as loving them rightly, which rather demands educating them as best one can (Price 1997: 259).

There has indeed been a change in the lover's direction of attention. It is not that he is now described as "loving" impersonal objects; for talk of "loving" (*eran*) falls away after its personal applications at 210a7 and c1 (Ferrari 1992: 258). Instead, the lover is related to them by a language of "seeing" (*horan*), "looking" (*blepein*), "looking at" (*theasthai*), and "contemplating" (*theōrein*). There now applies a well-known saying by Saint-Exupéry: "Aimer ce n'est point nous regarder l'un l'autre mais regarder ensemble dans la même direction" ("To love is not for us to look at each other but to look together in the same direction," 1939: 203). Even where just a pair of lover and loved one remains (which is one possibility), neither monopolizes, or even particularly occupies, the attention of the other. As I have put it before, "The person one loves becomes a drop in the ocean *qua* object of contemplation, but a major investment *qua* recipient of a mentality" (1997: 208, n. 5).[26] Love has been transformed; personal love may not have been discarded.

It is striking that the lover's goal is not quite yet reached (211b6–7) when he catches sight of Beauty itself. Reeve (2012: 183) identifies it

[26] It is thus that I would apply a remark of Richard Kraut's (2008: 298): "A beautiful *soul* cannot be loved to excess – so long as one goes about loving that person in the right way." As he also notes (2008: 299), we can re-apply here what was said before: a "firmer friendship" should ensue on sharing in "more beautiful and immortal children" (209c6–7).

with generating true virtue (212a3–5), and it must be that, or what comes of that.

So how does the ascent culminate?

> Do you think, she said, that it will be a poor life that a man leads who looks thither and views that (sc. Beauty itself] with that by which it has to be viewed, and consorts with it? Or do you not reflect that there alone he will succeed, seeing Beauty with that to which it is visible, in generating not images of virtue but true virtue, inasmuch as he is laying hold not of an image but of the truth? And that, generating and nurturing true virtue, he will have the privilege of becoming dear to the gods and, if any man can, immortal himself also? (211e4–212a7)

This links viewing Beauty (which may have seemed to *constitute* a liveable life, 211d1–3) to consorting with it in a fertile way. It identifies a *means*, generating true virtue, and an *end*, achieving immortality of a kind. How is either to be interpreted?

"True virtue" clearly contrasts with the unphilosophical virtue of 209b7–c2 (and of *Phd.* 82a11–b3, *Rep.* VI. 500d1–9). About whether it is generated *in anyone else* the text is silent. In this respect, and in several details, one may compare *Rep.* VI. 490a8–b7: there, if one "lays hold" of the nature of each thing "with the appropriate part of the soul" (b3–4), and "mingles" with reality (b5), one may "bring forth intelligence and truth" (b5–6). (The last is not distinct from true virtue as conceived by Socrates.) However, how one interprets the silence here may depend on how one reads what follows. There would seem to be just two alternatives that at least fit *either* what we have read in the *Symposium*, *or* what is well evidenced elsewhere. I believe (cf. Price 1997: 259–60) that these can be reconciled, and even connected.

If we wish to rest 212a5–7 solely on what has come before, we have to read it as an intensified, if inexplicit, offer of vicarious immortality. Comparable then must be a passage in the *Phaedrus:* in contrast to "the man who is able to amuse himself with words, telling stories about justice and the other subjects you speak of" (which applies to the poets of the *Symposium*),

> It is far finer if one is in earnest about them; when a man make use of the science of dialectic, and taking a fitting soul plants and sows in it words accompanied by knowledge, which are able to help themselves and the man who planted them, and are not without fruit but contain a seed, from which others grow in other soils, capable of rendering it forever immortal, and making the one who has it as happy as it is possible for a man to be. (276e2–277a3)

Here, "the one who has it" applies not just to the present possessor, but to any man, within a would-be never-ending sequence of recipients, who is thereby made happy in his turn. The conclusion is parallel to *Symp.* 212a5–7, though that offers as much not of *happiness*, but of *immortality*, as is possible *for a man* (emphatic in both passages).[27]

Yet I doubt whether this captures the sense of 212a5–7, not so much because of the silence as for this reason: to create her climax, and justify its tone of triumphalism, Diotima needs to hold out the promise of a kind of immortality that is no longer subject to contingency; but vicarious immortality must depend upon the chances of transmission and survival. Even if she wishes the lover to generate true virtue in another, she cannot allow his own immortality to *depend* upon that. Otherwise, a Socrates whose chosen disciple turns out like Alcibiades must fail of his goal through bad luck. (Here a later speech clarifies an earlier one.)

What sort of immortality, then, does 212a5–7 promise? It is one that comes as the reward for an assimilation to the divine: "The way to escape [from earth to heaven] is assimilation to a god so far as is possible; and assimilation is becoming just and pious together with wisdom" (*Tht.* 176a8–b2; cf. *Rep.* VI, 500d1–2, X, 613a7–b1). This is achieved by becoming oneself perfectly virtuous, and thus similar (*Tht.* 176b8–c2), and therefore dear (*Laws* IV. 716d1–2), to the gods. The immortality that follows cannot be reduced to the essential and inescapable quality assigned to the soul in the *Phaedo*, though it is consistent with it, and makes the best of it. It is one that the soul *comes* to enjoy (note *genesthai*, 212a6), most likely as a "grant" from the gods (O'Brien 1984: 201) that they "confer" or "bestow" upon him (Sedley 2009). It may rescue the soul from any risk of perishing (if the human soul is not everlasting by nature); it must preserve it against any danger of lapsing. Guaranteed become both the *quantity* and the *quality* (in Bury's terms, 1932: xlv, n. 2) of its ensuing life.[28]

Where does this leave the recipient (or recipients) of "ungrudging philosophy" (210d6)? The demiurge of the *Timaeus*, who, being himself good, was free of *phthonos*, wanted "all things to become like himself,"

[27] "If any man can" (212a6–7) does not suggest that perhaps no man can, but rather signifies "more than any other man"; see Bury 1932: xliv, O'Brien 1984: 197–8. Rowe (1998b: 200) compares a similar "if" at 211d2.

[28] For a close linkage between immortality, divinity, and *eudaimonia*, cf. *Tim.* 90b6–c6. That then prescribes conforming the motions of one's understanding to the harmonies of the universe (d1–5), which is itself a purely intellectual achievement. Given the theoretical concerns of the *Tim.*, this should not surprise us. For a succinct statement of a multi-faceted conception of assimilation to the divine, see Obdrzalek 2011: 10–13.

so far as is possible, and "everything to be good and nothing to be bad" (29e1–30a3). It holds generally that, if acquiring true virtue is to render a man dear to the gods, he must *practice it for others.*[29] In the present context, he must take advantage of any opportunity to imitate their generosity and *transmit virtue to others*; this has been for Diotima a recurrent theme. Thus vicarious immortality is not set aside; for achieving it can be contributory, though it is not essential, to the best of immortalities. What this last demands is a willingness that it be shared; men must wish the best for one another if they are to become themselves like gods.

[29] This is indicated at *Rep.* X. 612e2–6, 621c4–7, *Phil.* 39e10–11, *Laws* XI. 931e4–5, *Alc.* 134d1–2.

CHAPTER 11

Alcibiades the Profane: Images of the Mysteries

Radcliffe G. Edmonds III

1. The Vision of the Beautiful and the Problem of Alcibiades

> *Suddenly* he will see something beautiful in its nature, this is that thing, Socrates, on account of which all his previous toils have been. . . .
>
> And *suddenly* a banging on the courtyard door presented a huge noise as of revelers, and they heard the sound of a flutegirl. . . . and not long after they heard the sound of Alcibiades in the courtyard, very drunk and bellowing loudly, asking where Agathon was and demanding that they take him to Agathon.
>
> (*Symp.* 210e 4–6; 212c5–7, d3–5)

Just as the vision of the Beautiful itself *suddenly* flashes in upon the philosophical lover after long explorations of *Erōs*, so too another vision *suddenly* appears to the symposiasts after a long evening's worth of explorations into *Erōs*. Right after Socrates' speech, where the prophetess Diotima describes the mysteries of *Erōs*, comes the speech of a man notorious for the profanation of mysteries. Alcibiades also makes use of references to sacred mystery rites in his drunken, rambling, and passionate speech about the love of Socrates. Plato uses this juxtaposition of mystery ritual imagery to elucidate not only the philosophical nature of the encounter with the Beautiful itself, but also the problem of Alcibiades.

The spectacular disaster of the life of Alcibiades was a problem to which Plato, and many other Socratic thinkers, returned repeatedly. Why should this brilliant aristocrat, possessed of every excellence from courage to intellect, the ward of Pericles and follower of Socrates, the bold and cunning general who transformed the course of the Peloponnesian War so many times, why should he have gone so wrong, dying at the hands of assassins after betraying every side on the war multiple times, cuckolding the king of Sparta, and profaning the most sacred rites of Athens?

The association with Alcibiades was assuredly a factor in the trial and execution of Socrates after the war; he was perhaps the most outstanding example of a youth whom Socrates was accused of corrupting.

The problem remains in modern scholarship. Why did Alcibiades' famous relationship with Socrates not produce the ideal philosophic leader? Was Alcibiades simply unfit for philosophy, too obsessed with pleasure and honor to comprehend the lessons of philosophy? Or is Socrates' inhuman indifference to this appealing figure to blame, a "failure of love," as Vlastos has notoriously labeled it?

In the *Symposium*, Plato deploys the imagery of mystery rituals and the idea of Alcibiades as a profaner of mysteries to provide at least a partial answer to this vital question. Far from being fundamentally unfit for philosophy, Alcibiades engaged in his weird relation with Socrates precisely because he was, as a brilliant youth full of potential, able to perceive the beauty in Socrates. But because he failed to understand that the beauty he perceived was not a possession of Socrates (or even something that could be possessed), he tried to take possession of that beauty for himself, just as he tried to appropriate the Mysteries of Eleusis for himself. His *pleonexia*, his overreaching to take possession of the divine beauty he sees in Socrates, is echoed in the dialogue by the reminders of Alcibiades' future as a profaner of mysteries.

In this chapter, I argue that misunderstandings of the nature of ancient Greek mystery rituals and the Eleusinian Mysteries in particular have obscured the resonance these images would have had for Plato's audience. Modern scholars frequently imagine that mystery rituals involve the transmission of secret teachings, often as part of a tripartite structure of purification, instruction, and revelation, rather than an experience that brings the worshipper into an encounter and continuing relationship with the divinity. So too, modern scholars mistakenly assume that Alcibiades' profanation of the mysteries involves a comic parody of the rites, a mocking display of contempt for Athenian traditional beliefs, rather than an arrogant appropriation for himself of one of the most authoritative religious symbols of the Athenian community. These misunderstandings occlude the serious work that Plato is doing with the imagery of the mysteries in the *Symposium*.

2. The Mystery of the Mysteries

It is worth beginning by reconsidering the nature of the mystery rituals themselves, since misconceptions about these rituals have obscured the way Plato employs the imagery. First, the imagery of mystery rituals in the *Symposium* is not limited to the Mysteria of Eleusis, but includes other rites, such as those of the Corybantes, the Orphica, and Dionysos, all of which, like the Eleusinian rites, could be called *telea* or *teletai*. Second, the Eleusinian Mysteries did not consist of a neat sequence of preliminary purification, followed by the Lesser Mysteries, and culminating in the Great Mysteries, but the Mysteria at Eleusis could be experienced either as an ordinary mystes or as an epoptes. Most importantly, the impact of such rites does not come from the imparting of some mystic doctrine but rather from the extraordinary experience itself.

The words for such rituals, *telea* or *teletai*, are often misleadingly translated as "initiations" but "perfections" would be more accurate, since such rites serve not to introduce the worshipper into a group of other worshippers but rather to improve or perfect the worshipper's relationship to the god.[1] Mysteries may be considered a special class of such rituals that are performed, not in public view, but with an audience limited only to the performers.[2] The term "mysteries" may derive originally from the name of the festival at Eleusis for the goddesses Demeter and Kore, but such was the prestige of these rites that "mysteries" becomes a general term in ancient (and especially modern) sources for all rites of this kind.[3] In the *Symposium*, the scene with Alcibiades abounds with allusions, not just to the Eleusinian Mysteries but to a number of others. As many commentators have noted, Alcibiades' appearance, drunk with wine and wreathed in ivy, in company with flutegirls and revelers, evokes the epiphany of the god Dionysos, and he refers to the Bacchic frenzies, which he and others of the company have undergone in the presence of Socrates:[4]

> And then again I see the Phaedruses, Agathons, Eryximachuses, Pausaniases, Aristodemuses, and Aristophaneses – and why is it necessary even to mention Socrates himself? – and all the others. For you all have shared in the madness and bacchic rites of philosophy.[5] (218b)

He then proceeds to quote the familiar opening tag of the Orphic poems, bidding the profane to "close the doors of your ears" (218b). He describes his own reactions to Socrates as being those of someone undergoing the

[1] On these terms, see Dowden 1980, as well as Edmonds 2013: 211–7.

[2] Cf. Strabo 10.3.9 on the types of rites, where the difference between mystic, secret rites and public ones is only one of a number of distinctions.

[3] As Graf 2008 suggests.

[4] Cf. Agathon claiming that Dionysos will judge between him and Socrates before the night is out. *Symp.* 175e.

[5] The explanation of these plurals in Gallop 2004 is not convincing, but the puzzle remains.

Corybantic rites, stirred up to leaping frenzy. The images of the *teletai* pervade the scene, reinforcing the connection, so natural to any fourth-century reader of Plato, between Alcibiades and these rites.[6]

2.1. *The Mystery of Eleusinian Mysteries*

It is the Mysteries at Eleusis, however, that loom largest in the background of Alcibiades' entrance, since his conviction for profaning these mysteries occurs little more than a year after the date in which the dialogue is set. The resonances of the allusions to the Eleusinian Mysteries have been misunderstood by scholars, however, because of misconceptions about what actually went on in these rites. The ancient sources respect the idea that the Mysteries are to be kept secret, so no description of the rituals survives, except for those of the early Christian apologists, whose confused and contradictory polemical accounts do not inspire confidence in their accuracy. Various attempts have been made to reconstruct the rituals, but the tripartite schema most recently expounded by Riedweg seems to be most influential in the interpretations of the *Symposium*.[7]

Riedweg, in his study of mystery terminology in Plato, sees the references in the *Symposium* to the Greater and Lesser Mysteries as reflecting an actual sequence of initiations focused on imparting secret doctrines to the initiates. Plato, in his view, constructs Diotima's account of *erōs* along the model of the Eleusinian Mysteries, following a tripartite pattern that would have been familiar to the Athenians of Plato's day as the sequence of the Mysteries. Riedweg's pattern has been influential in recent discussions of the passage, but it unfortunately misrepresents the Mysteries, providing an overly simplified schema based on the systematizations of later Christian and Neoplatonic writers. The tripartite schema is simple and appealing to use, but, as H. L. Mencken famously said, for every complicated problem, there is always an easy solution – "neat, plausible, and wrong."[8]

[6] Not only was Alcibiades infamous for his profanation of the Eleusinian Mysteries, but he is associated with the rites of Kotytto in testimonies to Eupolis' *Baptai*, see Furley 1996: 131–133 on Kassel-Austin PCG V: 331–42. The contention of Hatzfeld 1951: 178–181 that his indictment for profanation involves these mysteries instead of Eleusis has not convinced many.

[7] Cf. the attempts in Mylonas 1961, with the more recent "thin description" in Bremmer 2014. Sattler 2013 provides an overview of the pre-Platonic evidence for the elements of the rituals. Clinton 2003 attempts to rework the evidence discussed in Dowden 1980, but he still tries to stick with a tripartite scheme set up by Clement and Theon. Better reconstructions may be found in Sourvinou-Inwood 2003 and Bowden 2010: 26–48.

[8] H. L. Mencken, "The Divine Afflatus," New York Evening Mail, 16 November 1917.

Riedweg divides up the schema into three stages: a preliminary purification, a teaching of the mystery, and a final revelation, and he argues that these three stages reflect the stages of the Eleusinian Mysteries, the preliminary rites of purification, the Lesser Mysteries, and the Greater Mysteries. The basis for this neat tripartite schema is in fact the Christian author, Clement of Alexandria, who creates it as part of his project of bashing the Greek mysteries as a whole:

> It is not then implausibly done that purifications start off the mysteries among the Greeks, just as also among the barbarians the washing. After these are the small mysteries, which have some foundation of instruction and of preliminary preparation for what is to come after; and the great mysteries, in which nothing remains to be learned of the universe, but only to contemplate and comprehend nature and things. (*Stromata* 5.11.71.1–2)

This neat progression of a mystic curriculum is reinforced by other late evidence, primarily from systematizing Neoplatonists who are taking the prestigious ancient Mysteries, no longer performed in Eleusis, as authorization for their own Academic curricula.[9]

As Dowden has shown, however, these three stages do not in fact reflect the practice of the rituals at Eleusis. Rather, the ancient evidence consistently makes a distinction between the *muēsis* and the *epopteia* as two kinds of experience of the Eleusinian Mysteries; the performance of the former ritual makes one a *mustēs*, while the latter is a further experience open only to those who have already undergone *muēsis*. While the precise nature of the *epopteia* remains a mystery, the evidence suggests the revelation of some kind of image that has a profound impact on the *epoptēs*, the one who "looks upon" it.[10]

A passage from Plutarch that describes the way Demetrius sought to undergo the whole experience of the Eleusinian Mysteries during his brief stay in Athens lists the Lesser Mysteries, the Greater Mysteries, and the *Epopteia* as the rites involved, but the Lesser Mysteries at Agra appear to have been a different ritual than the Great Mysteries at Eleusis, while the *epopteia* takes place as a higher level of participation in the Greater Mysteries (*Demetrius* 26.1–2). Dowden points out how the pair of the Lesser Mysteries at Agra and the Greater Mysteries at Eleusis, two different

[9] As Dowden 1980: 419 wryly remarks, "Scholarly tidying up of the untidy historical facts has occasionally been assisted on the path to perdition by a curious passage of Theon of Smyrna" (*De Util. Math.*,14–15 Hiller).

[10] Dowden 1980: 425 suggests that only the *epoptai* entered the *Telesterion* for this final revelation, given the size of the building at Eleusis and the number of participants each year. Other scholars suggest that the *mustai* were blindfolded; see, e.g. Clinton 2003.

festivals, become conflated with the *muēsis* and *epopteia* in the (Greater) Eleusinian Mysteries, leading scholars ancient and modern to see the Lesser Mysteries as standing in the same relation to the Greater as the *muēsis* to the *epopteia*.[11] As a result, Diotima's reference to the *epopteia* has been construed as an allusion to the Greater Mysteries, while the erotic interactions she has described previously are imagined as Lesser Mysteries:

> With respect to these erotic matters, Socrates, you might perhaps be made a *mustēs*, but with respect to the rites and *epoptika*, on account of which these matters also are, I don't know if you would be capable. (201a)

This confusion has led scholars to map the elements of Diotima's speech onto Clement's tripartite schema. The *elenchos* becomes seen as the preliminary purifications, while the Lesser Mysteries are seen as the occasion for the transmission of the teachings, the secret doctrines of the Mysteries.[12]

This schema helps perpetuate one of the most serious misconceptions in modern scholarship about the nature of the mystery rites, the assumption that the "mystery" is a secret doctrine imparted to the initiates in the ceremony, and that this knowledge is the key benefit the initiate derives from the rite. On the contrary, the key aim of all the *teletai*, including the Eleusinian Mysteries, was to improve the worshipper's relation with the god through a closer contact and experience of the deity. Aristotle famously says that "for those undergoing the *teletai* it is not necessary that they learn anything, but rather that they experience something and transform their disposition, becoming clearly accustomed" (fr. 15 Ross = Synesios, *Dion* 8.43). The "something (*ti*)" that is experienced is understood as a kind of contact with the divine, perhaps even, as in Euripides' *Bacchae*, a face-to-face encounter with the deity (470–474). Lucius, in Apuleius' *Golden Ass*, likewise describes his initiation into the mysteries of Isis as culminating in an act of worshipping the gods face to face (*Met.* 11.23). Lucius' description of the process, like that of Plutarch (fgt.178 Sandbach), is full of imagery of light and darkness in bewildering succession, fear and confusion before the final revelation.

[11] The reference in Plato's *Gorgias* 497c further complicates matters, since Socrates seems to suggest that one cannot do the Greater Mysteries before the Lesser. "You are fortunate, Callicles, in that you have become a *mustēs* in the greater things before the lesser. I didn't think that was permitted." However, this passage may not be referring to the Lesser Musteria at Agra and the Greater Musteria at Eleusis but more generally to mysteries, since it is unclear when the rites at Agra became associated with the Eleusinian ones.

[12] Riedweg 1987: 21 sets out a sequence of *elenchos, didachē +muthos*, and *epoptika*, which he finds parallel to *Symposium* 199c3–201c9, 201e8–209e4, and 209e5–212a7, respectively. This division has been picked up by other commentators, for example, Belfiore 2012: 141.

The *teletai* in the mysteries provide the ultimate kind of contact with the deity, a step beyond the kind of interactions involved in normal religious ritual such as prayer and sacrifice. Such interactions are perhaps most concisely described in the *Symposium* itself, in Diotima's description of the work of the daimonic in connecting mortals and gods:

> Interpreting and transporting human things to the gods and divine things to men; entreaties and sacrifices from below, and ordinances and requitals from above: being midway between, it makes each to supplement the other, so that the whole is combined in one. Through it are conveyed all divination and priestcraft concerning sacrifice and ritual. (202e)

All ritual works to bring together gods and mortals; the mortals provide sacrifices and honors for the gods, while the gods provide, through their superior power, things that mortals cannot obtain without their help. Diotima tendentiously proclaims that a daimonic intermediary is necessary, since gods and mortals cannot mix, but even still the connection between the two can be more or less close, and much of the practice of Greek religion is involved in building closer and more positive relations with the gods. Historians of religion have analyzed the reciprocal pattern of relationships between gods and mortals in Greek practice, comparing the Greek hospitality code (*xeneia*) and its reciprocal (though not always equal) gift exchanges.[13] The bonds of obligation between gods and mortals resemble those of host and guest, and they can be built up more closely through the exchange of favors over time as well as by special occasions in which particularly significant favors are exchanged.

The performance of a mystery ritual is one such special occasion, differing not so much in kind from the normal practices of religion (prayer and sacrifice, etc.) as in intensity. By performing the special rituals of the *teletē*, the worshipper does special honor to the deity and thus brings himself into a special relationship with the deity where the deity will respond with special favors. As the Homeric *Hymn to Demeter* proclaims:

> Blessed is he among men upon earth who has seen these things; but he who is uninitiate and who has no part in the rites, never has a share of such things when indeed he is perished in the shadowy gloom. (480–482)

The blessings for mortals in the Mysteries are contingent on the proper payment of honors to the goddess, since, as Hades tells Persephone, "there will be a recompense for all time for those doing you wrong, whoever does

[13] See especially Parker 1998, as well as Pulleyn 1997 on prayer and Naiden 2013 on sacrifice.

not sacrifice and appease your wrath, reverently performing rites and paying fit gifts" (367–369). Those who do offer the special honors receive special blessings, both in life and after death when they are in the special care of Persephone; the happy afterlife of the Eleusinian initiates is not a special secret revelation but a benefit resulting from their special relationship with the Queen of the Dead.[14]

Such rituals bringing the worshipper into closer contact with the god could be repeated, by some perhaps once or twice in a lifetime, by others on a frequent basis. The sacrifices and rituals involved in such experiences require a certain investment of time and energy, not to mention expense, but not every person would choose to devote such attention to improving his relations with the deity. The Eleusinian Mysteries involved the daylong procession along the Sacred Road, a hike of twenty kilometers or so, not to mention other expenditures of time and money in the preparations.

Making use of more familiar Christian parallels is always dangerous, but undergoing such *teletai* was more analogous to performing a pilgrimage than receiving baptism. As with pilgrimage, some people might choose to do it more often, like the superstitious man caricatured by Theophrastus, who goes to the Orpheotelest for a *teletē* once a month, bringing his kids along with him (*Characters* 16). Likewise, performing a *teletē* for one deity by no means precluded doing so for another, any more than taking a pilgrimage to Canterbury precluded going to Compostela or Jerusalem. Each performance of the ritual was a service to the deity, and earning the favor of multiple deities through multiple *teletai* was a sign of a pious disposition (as well as an indicator of sufficient wealth and leisure to indulge in the practice).[15]

2.2. *The Extraordinary Experience*

One consequence of understanding mystery rituals as repeatable occasions for coming closer to the deity is that it becomes easier to understand that they did not hinge upon the imparting of special knowledge, which would make multiple repetitions pointless, but upon the experience itself, the

[14] Cf. Crinagoras, *Greek Anthology* 11.42. Bowden 2010: 23 notes that the descriptions of the happy afterlife, while different from the traditional gloomy Hades of *Odyssey* 11, nevertheless resemble the fate promised Menelaus as a benefit of having Zeus as his father-in-law: "The afterlife promised to initiates looks very similar to that of Menelaus, and the explanation of it is the same: like Menelaus, initiates have been in close contact with a god." For further on the lively afterlife, see Edmonds 2014.

[15] Apuleius *Apologia* 55 boasts of having performed the rites of many Greek mysteries and of preserving the tokens in his house.

encounter with the divine. Such an understanding helps to clarify how Plato uses the imagery of the mysteries to describe the experience of philosophy, not as the one time imparting of secret knowledge but as an ongoing lived experience.[16] The culminating experience of Diotima's ascent to the Beautiful itself is not an explanation of the Theory of Forms or even the secret knowledge that the phenomenal world is a reflection of the true world of the Forms; rather it is an encounter with the Beautiful itself, where the philosopher contemplates the Beautiful itself, face-to-face as it were:

> She said, "What do we think, if for someone it should be possible to see the Beautiful itself, simple, pure, and unmixed, and not filled up with human flesh and colors and all that other mortal rubbish, but if it were possible to behold in single form the divine Beauty itself? Do you think," she said, "that a man there would have a worthless life, while he is looking at it, by that which it is necessary for him to behold it, and while he is together with it?" (211e–212a)

Historians of religion, drawing on the work of the anthropologist Whitehouse, have recently started to employ a distinction between two modes of religious experience to help make sense of the patterns of Greek religion and the mystery cults in particular.[17] Whitehouse, drawing on his work in Melanesia, distinguishes between doctrinal religion, where worshippers engage in the frequent repetition of texts or rituals that impresses the central ideas and practices upon their memory, and imagistic religion, where particular intense experiences impress themselves on the worshippers' memories. In imagistic religious contexts, Whitehouse argues, "virtually no attempt was made to communicate religious ideas as bodies of doctrine. Revelations were codified in iconic imagery, transmitted primarily through the choreography of collective ritual performances. Religious representations were structured as sets of revelatory images connected by loose (and somewhat fluid) thematic associations, rather than as cohering strings of logically connected dogma" (Whitehouse 2000: 14).

Such experience of revelatory images matches the testimonies for the mystery cults quite well, and the category of imagistic religion helps us understand the kind of experience Plato's audience would have thought of when faced with Plato's imagery of mystery rituals as a metaphor for philosophy.

[16] Cf. *Epist.* 7, 341c5–d2.

[17] Bowden 2010 provides a good overview of the Mystery Cults engaging with this idea. See further the studies in Martin and Pachis 2009 and Whitehouse and Martin 2004.

Accustomed as modern scholars are to doctrinal forms of religion, with complex theologies, orthodoxies, and catechisms, we expect doctrinal accounts rather than revelatory imagery, but Plato provides his readers, not with a Theory of Forms (ever), but rather with references to divine visions, experiences that can never be adequately described, like the Beautiful itself which can only be indicated by a series of negatives:[18]

> It neither comes to be nor perishes, neither waxes nor wanes; next, it is not beautiful in part and in part ugly, nor is it such at such a time and other at another, nor in one respect beautiful and in another ugly, nor so affected by position as to seem beautiful to some and ugly to others. Nor again will the beautiful appear to him like a face or of hands or any other portion of the body, nor as a particular description or piece of knowledge, nor as existing somewhere in another substance, such as an animal or the earth or sky or any other thing, but itself by itself with itself existing forever in singularity of form. (*Symp.* 211ab)

Such an experience is *arrhēton*, not to be spoken of or ineffable, not because it is a secret that must be kept, but because no account of the experience can capture the experience itself.[19]

So too, such an experience is repeatable; the revelation of the beautiful itself is not a one-time disclosure of the hidden nature of the cosmos, but rather a special perception of existing reality. Much ink has been spilled in scholarly debates as to where Socrates stands on Diotima's ladder – has he attained the final vision or is he merely working his way up the ladder, enjoying the beauties of laws and customs now that he has moved beyond bodies and souls? While various scholars have argued for particular stages of development, Blondell suggests that Plato depicts Socrates simultaneously at various stages, while Lowenstam argues that Socrates oscillates, like *Erōs*, between the bottom and the top.[20] Such explanations become even more convincing if the progression described in Diotima's speech is not thought of as a once-and-for-all climb up the ladder analogous to passing through the curriculum of the mysteries imagined in a three-part sequence, but rather as the renewed participation in a rite involving different levels of engagement with the deity. Like an *epoptēs* who has gone through the Eleusinian Mysteries before and performs the rite again with the experience of the *epopteia* in his mind, Socrates can experience once again the beauty of bodies or souls or even laws, recalling his

[18] Cf. *Phdr.* 247c, as well as *Epist.* 7 341c5–d2.

[19] Cf. Bremmer 2014: 18; Bowden 2010: 22.

[20] Blondell 2006: 177: "Socrates is everywhere, and therefore nowhere. We cannot pin him down or plug him into an orderly sequence." Cf. Lowenstam 1985: 94–98.

experience of the Beautiful itself as he does so. Perhaps at moments he can again experience the sublime revelation of the Beautiful itself, but, like the climax of the Mysteries at Eleusis, such an experience is momentary, even if the recollection of that experience affects his understanding of the rest of his life.[21]

It is worth noting that later Platonists understood the ascent up Diotima's ladder in precisely this way. Porphyry tells us that his master Plotinus, following the methods described in the *Symposium*, ascended to union with the divine four times, while Porphyry himself achieved this feat only once, in his sixty-eighth year (*Vit. Plot.* 23). The idea in modern scholarship of a single ascent and revelation would have been nonsensical to these Platonists, just as the idea that a mystery rite could only be experienced once would have seemed nonsense to Plato's audience. The mystery of the mystery rite lay not in some secret revealed but in the extraordinary experience of that special ceremony, which could not be spoken of without failing to do it justice, without reducing the honor due to it.

2.3. *The Nature of Profanation*

If we need to adjust our understanding of what a mystery rite is and how Plato and his audience would have understood it, what impact might that have upon the way we understand the profanation of the Mysteries of which Alcibiades was accused? If there is no secret to reveal, why should the Athenians become so overwrought about Alcibiades' behavior? Modern accounts of the profanation scandal struggle with the problem of what seems the disproportionate response of the Athenian people to Alcibiades' profanations of the Mysteries, but a better understanding of the nature of the profanation can not only help explain their reaction but also help illuminate the effect of Plato's use of mystery imagery in the *Symposium*. Alcibiades' profanation was so disturbing, not because he offended the simple piety of the Athenians by revealing the secrets of the Mysteries to the uninitiate or because he showed his rationalistic contempt of that simple piety by making a mockery of the rites, but precisely because Alcibiades performed the rituals *pro-fanum*, outside their proper place in the Eleusinian sanctuary, appropriating the rites properly performed by the whole city for himself in a private home.

[21] Ionescu 2007 makes some good suggestions about the ways in which ideas of recollection that make a greater appearance in the *Phaedrus* appear within the *Symposium*, although her account is troubled by reliance on the model of the Lesser and Greater Mysteries.

Many modern accounts of the profanation are inclined, following Dover, to regard Alcibiades' performance of the rituals as a parody or mockery: "Athenian society in the late fifth century embraced a wide variety of opinions on the existence and nature of the gods, on the value and efficacy of ritual, and on the extent to which supernatural beings could take a joke. Alkibiades and his friends are not likely to have cherished simple piety; parody of the mysteries at a private entertainment could no doubt be exceedingly funny; and no more need be said on the question of whether, or why, the mysteries were parodied" (Dover 1970: 283).[22]

Alcibiades and his set, on this account, are dissolute, immoral aristocrats, products of the sophists' rationalist teachings, making fun of the simple piety of their less sophisticated fellow Athenians.[23] The party atmosphere, enlivened by wine, causes them to forget the discretion that intellectual elites must employ to conceal their true contempt of the ordinary folk of the city, and, as a result, they suffer from the backlash.[24] The common folk resent doubts being cast upon their cherished beliefs and overreact with tragic results in the time of crisis on the eve of the Sicilian Expedition. "The cause of both calamities," claims Nails, "was the ignorance – superstition and religious hysteria – of the Athenians" (2006: 180).[25]

While the mistreatment of intellectuals by the ignorant masses is a perennially favorite idea among scholars, such a reading fails to explain the situation in many respects. All the sources, starting with Thucydides, who of all ancient authors would be most likely to condemn the thoughtless superstitions of the masses, treat the profanations as an indicator of political conflict; Alcibiades was suspected of aiming at a tyranny. "It is not at first easy to see," comments Dover, "why such impieties should have been taken as evidence of a political conspiracy" (1970: 284). Yet Thucydides brings a long digression on the story of the tyrannicides, and Plutarch is clear that the Athenians immediately thought that the mutilation of the Herms and profanations of the Mysteries were both signs of a conspiracy to overthrow the democracy.

[22] MacDowell 1962: 211 points to the presence of comic poets among the group.

[23] Cf. Murray 1990: 158–159. Murray draws parallels with the groups of young aristocrats mentioned in the Demosthenic speech against Konon (54), the *Ithyphalloi* (the Erections) and *Autolekythoi* (the Wankers), as well as the *Kakodaimonistai*, in Lysias fr. 5 = Athen. 12. 551d–552b, who deliberately meet on ill-omened days in defiance of popular beliefs.

[24] Cf. Aurenche 1974: 165.

[25] Cf. "Thoughtless religious fervor is dangerous, a persistent and insidious kind of ignorance that leads to errors and that can be perpetuated by priests and priestesses" (Nails 2006: 201).

So too, all of the evidence points not to a comic mockery of the rituals but rather to a comprehensive performance of the Mysteries, not once for a laugh, but repeatedly with different groups of participants under the direction of Alcibiades in the role of Hierophant.[26] Hence the formal indictment preserved in Plutarch,

> Thessalus, son of Cimon, of the deme Laciadae, impeaches Alcibiades, son of Cleinias, of the deme Scambonidae, for wronging the goddesses of Eleusis, Demeter and Kore, by performing the mysteries and showing them forth to his companions in his own house, wearing a robe such as the Hierophant wears when he shows forth the sacred secrets to the initiates, and calling himself Hierophant, Poulytion Dadouchos (Torch-Bearer), and Theodorus, of the deme Phegaea, Keryx (Herald), and hailing the rest of his companions as Mystae and Epoptae, contrary to the laws and institutions of the Eumolpidae, Kerykes, and Priests of Eleusis. (*Alcibiades* 22.3–4)[27]

As Graf argues, the problem is not that they are being parodied, but that the rites are being performed by the wrong people in the wrong place at the wrong time (2000: 124).

Herein lies the key to understanding the political panic that the scandal generated. The performance of the Eleusinian Mystery ritual by Alcibiades in a private home was understood, not as the frivolity of a drunken aristocrat, but as a symbolic appropriation of the rites of the whole community for his own private use, just the sort of appropriation of public things for private use that marked the tyrant. In the same vein, Plutarch relates an accusation that Alcibiades used the gold and silver ceremonial utensils that belonged to the city for his daily meals, another tyrannical appropriation of the ritual things of the city for his own private ends (*Alc.* 13.2).[28] The Eleusinian Mysteries were one of the most potent symbols of Athenian identity, cited in Athenian imperialist propaganda as one of the great benefits that Athens brought to the world.

[26] Murray 1990: 155: "There is no evidence whatsoever that the Mysteries were parodied: all our evidence shows that they were performed, that the ritual was followed accurately. Nowhere is there any suggestion, as a possible defence, that the occasions were jokes or ritually unreal in any way, that the Mysteries were not actually divulged – the performances were illegal, sacrilegious, and immoral, but not unreal." Pace Hunter 2004: 14, n.15, who adduces Plut. *QC* 1.4 621c and Heraclitus *QH* 76.7 to claim that the performances were sympotic entertainment. The Heraclitus passage does use *paizonta* for the performance of the rites, but in parallel with playing the role of rebel and founder, so not in a frivolous sense, while the Plutarch passage actually critiques Alcibiades for turning a symposium into a telesterion.

[27] Cf. [Lysias] 6. 51.

[28] There is, perhaps, less reason to believe this charge than the accusation that he performed the Mysteries, but it nevertheless indicates the way in which Alcibiades' contemporaries imagined him as a potential tyrant.

In Herodotus' tale of the phantom Eleusinian procession that betokened the defeat of Xerxes at Salamis, the mysteries represent the continuing existence of the Athenian community despite the sacking of the city itself by the Persians, so their appropriation by an individual would be a shocking seizure of authority over the whole polis (Herodotus 8.65). By taking the role of the Hierophant for himself and performing the rituals, not in the sacred space hallowed by the tradition of the community but in a private house, Alcibiades lays claim to authority over the whole community, acting like a tyrant.

Indeed, subsequent events reinforce this association. When Alcibiades returns from exile and is welcomed in triumph back to Athens, one of his first acts is to lead the mystery procession from Athens to Eleusis, part of the ritual that the Athenians had been unable to do for years because of the Spartan occupation of Decelea. This act has been seen as his repudiation of the charge of blasphemy, of not taking the Mysteries seriously, but the reactions of his contemporaries shows how it was understood. Plutarch writes:

> When he had determined upon this course and made known his design to the Eumolpidae and Heralds, he stationed sentries on the heights, sent out an advance-guard at break of day, and then took the priests, *mustae*, and mustagogues, encompassed them with his men-at-arms, and led them over the road to Eleusis in decorous and silent array. So august and devout was the spectacle which, as general, he thus displayed, that he was hailed by those who were not unfriendly to him as Hierophant and Mustagogue. No enemy dared to attack him, and he conducted the procession safely back to the city. At this he was exalted in spirit himself, and exalted his army with the feeling that it was irresistible and invincible under his command. People of the humbler and poorer sort he so captivated by his leadership that they were filled with an amazing passion to have him for their tyrant, and some proposed it, and actually came to him in solicitation of it. (*Alc.* 34.5–6)[29]

The clamor by the people to have Alcibiades as tyrant after this public performance in which he is acclaimed as Hierophant is of course precisely what his aristocratic enemies feared when rumors of the profanations first circulated; Alcibiades' attempt to appropriate the position of leader of the Eleusinian Mysteries indicates his potential to become tyrant.

[29] As Wohl 1999: 372 comments, "The demos' response to his charisma – a charisma that is always implicitly or explicitly sexual – is the desire to be ruled by him; they long to be ruled by him as a tyrant."

The contrast between the celebration at his return and the outrage at his earlier profanations points to Alcibiades' fundamental problem – something like the Eleusinian Mysteries cannot really be appropriated privately; attempting to take them for himself is a failure. The rites only have their full impact and meaning when performed by the right people in the right place at the right time, so any private appropriation is doomed to failure. Alcibiades can only take for himself the trappings of the Hierophant, only take over the words and actions of the rite; he cannot actually exclusively possess the Eleusinian Mysteries. His error is to think that by appropriating the symbols and trappings, he can possess what they indicate, the Mysteries themselves. In the *Symposium*, Plato exploits this gap between symbol and reality to explain Alcibiades' problematic relation with Socrates and his ultimate failure to live philosophically, depicting Alcibiades as someone who continually seeks to inappropriately appropriate, to possess things that cannot be possessed.

3. The Profanity of Alcibiades

Right from his entrance, Alcibiades appropriates authority in the gathering, naming himself the Master of the Revels and changing the rules of the game the symposiasts have been playing all evening. In place of the sober encomia to *Erōs*, he puts forth a revelation of the mystery of Socrates. He frames his revelation with the tag from the Orphic poems, "close the doors of your ears, ye profane," a line that signals that the following discourse is marked with special authority (*Symp.* 218b).[30] Like Orpheus, Alcibiades will sing for those of understanding, revealing the sacred mysteries of his erotic relations with Socrates. Alcibiades' arrogant assumption of this hierophantic role contrasts sharply with Socrates, who has presented himself as being warned by Diotima that he may not be capable of handling *ta telea kai epoptika* of *erōs* (210a).

Alcibiades claims that he alone has seen the divine images concealed within Socrates, pierced the veil of his irony and opened him up like one of the Silenus statues.

> I'd say that he is most like the *silenoi* sitting in the herm-makers' shops, which they've made holding a syrinx or a flute, the ones that, when you open them up, have statues of gods within. . . . When he is being serious

[30] This text is the earliest attestation of the line that becomes almost a regular *sphragis* to mark Orphic poetry (as the address to Kyrnos marks Theognidea). See Bernabé for the attestations. Cf. Edmonds 2013: 75.

> and opened up, I don't know if you have ever seen the statues within him. But I saw them once, and they seemed to me so divine and golden and totally beautiful and amazing, so that, in a word, whatever Socrates wished must be done. (215a–b, 216e–217a)

Alcibiades' experience of this encounter with the divine is, like the experience of the mysteries, a powerful imagistic experience that he cannot adequately frame in words, one that kindles his desire for the beauty that he has seen and impels him to action.

Alcibiades, however, reacts in a characteristically wrong fashion to this experience, attempting to appropriate rather than to adore. Amazed by the beauty he perceives, he tries to take it for his own, offering his own golden bloom of youth in exchange for those golden divine statues. Socrates warns him of his error, pointing out two problems. First, if youthful beauty could be exchanged for wisdom it would be as bad a bargain as the famous Iliadic exchange of bronze armor for gold. Second, however, Alcibiades is mistaken in thinking that the beauty he sees *in* Socrates is actually the beauty *of* Socrates, a possession of Socrates' that he can hand over:

> My dear Alcibiades, you are perhaps in truth a man of no mean ambition, if indeed it turns out to be true, the things you are saying about me, and there is some power in me through which you might become better. You would be seeing an incomparable beauty in me and one wholly different from your own fair form. However, if having discerned this you are trying to share it with me and to exchange beauty for beauty, you are intending to overreach not a little, it seems to me, but rather you are trying to possess the truth of beauty instead of the appearance and, in truth, you think to exchange gold for bronze. But, blessed boy, examine this better, lest it escape your notice that I am nothing of the sort. (*Symp.* 218e–219a)[31]

Socrates rebukes Alcibiades' characteristic overreaching (*pleonexia*), but more importantly he reaffirms the point he made earlier to Agathon that wisdom is not the sort of thing that can be passed from one person to another and that any wisdom he might appear to have is as evanescent as a dream, a version of his characteristic claim to know nothing (175d–e).[32]

The divine golden statues that Alcibiades sees in Socrates are thus not really *in* Socrates, but, like the images in a dream, signs that point to something else. They are, in fact, like other *agalmata*, statues of gods set up

[31] The reference is to the scene in *Iliad* 6.232–6.

[32] Agathon claims of the wisdom Socrates found while meditating on the porch, "it is clear that you found it and have it," but Socrates denies that he has anything that can be possessed and exchanged in the way that, e.g., Pausanias suggests in erotic relations.

for worship in the temples, representations of the divine, not the divine thing itself. Alcibiades can no more take possession of Socrates' wisdom by sleeping with Socrates than he can take possession of the gods by appropriating their statues from the temples. Nevertheless, just as Alcibiades tries to appropriate the divine favor of the Eleusinian goddesses by taking possession of the trappings and symbols of the Mysteries, so too Alcibiades tries to appropriate the wisdom of Socrates, trying to snatch the golden statues within the man whom he imagines as a statue himself.[33]

3.1. The Potential of Alcibiades

As Nails notes, "often enough even now, the love of wisdom begins with a crush on Socrates," but Alcibiades spectacularly fails to move beyond this beginning (2006: 196). Various scholars have rightly pointed out Alcibiades' error in directing his attention to Socrates rather than the wisdom, but without a clearer understanding of the way Plato uses the imagery of the profanation of the mysteries it becomes harder to explain how Plato can be placing the blame for the failure on Alcibiades and not, at least to some extent, on Socrates' idea of love.[34] Plato uses the imagery of the Corybantic rites to indicate that Alcibiades is fit for, and indeed in great need of, philosophy, while he manipulates his audience's ideas of Alcibiades' profanations, the mutilation of the Herms and the appropriation of the Mysteries, to show that the problem lies in Alcibiades' overreaching appetite, not in Socrates' indifference to him.

Some commentators have dismissed Alcibiades as a drunken fool, so corrupted by pleasures as to be unfit for philosophy.[35] The reason, however, that the failure of Alcibiades to live philosophically is such a problem for Plato is that Alcibiades in fact was so well qualified to excel in philosophy and yet still failed so spectacularly.[36] The ancient biographical tradition emphasizes Alcibiades' intelligence and capacity, and Plutarch

[33] Cf. Nussbaum 1986: 196: "There is a strong possibility that Alcibiades wants Socrates to be a statue – a thing that can be held, carried, or, when necessary, smashed."

[34] Reeve 2006: 98, "It follows that Socrates' apparently virtuous failure to succumb to his seduction is also a less virtuous failure to make him virtuous." Cf. Rosen 1987: 279: "The unsatisfactory character of the love affair between Socrates and Alcibiades is a necessary consequence of the peculiarity of Socrates' *Erōs*, which can only desire divine things or beings." The debate ultimately goes back to Vlastos' critique of Platonic *erōs* in Vlastos 1973.

[35] Cf. Rosen 1987: 281–2.

[36] Sheffield 2006: 202: "Alcibiades was a particularly promising associate, a talented man of the city who was clearly attracted by what Socrates had to offer. Why did philosophical *erōs* fail to get a firm hold on Alcibiades?" Cf. Destrée 2011: 194; Dover 1980: 164.

explicitly claims that he took up with Socrates because he recognized, through his own innate talents, the value of Socrates (*Alc.* 4.2.).[37] In the *Symposium*, Plato has Alcibiades himself indicate his readiness for the mysteries of philosophy through the image of the Corybantic frenzies. Alcibiades claims that the words of Socrates are like the tunes of Marsyas, the tunes attributed to Olympos that are used in the Corybantic rites:

> They alone possess the soul and reveal those who have need of the gods and mysteries, because they are divine. . . . For my heart leaps within me more than that of any Corybantic reveler, and my eyes rain tears when I hear them. (215c, e)[38]

Commentators have puzzled over how such tunes might reveal those in need of *teletai*, since the limited evidence for the Corybantic rites (much of which is indeed from Plato) suggests frenzied dancing spurred on by music in the Phrygian mode.[39] A passage from the *Phaedrus* suggests that such frenzy (*mania*) may serve to indicate those who need to engage in special ritual connections with the gods, either to appease their wrath for some wrongdoing committed by themselves or their ancestors or for some other reason:

> Moreover, when diseases and the greatest troubles have been visited upon certain families through some ancient guilt, madness has entered in and by oracular power has found a way of release for those in need, taking refuge in prayers and the service of the gods, and so, by purifications and sacred rites, he who has this madness is made safe for the present and the after time, and for him who is rightly possessed of madness a release from present ills is found. (244d–e)

The mad frenzy of Corybantic possession thus signals an individual who should perform *teletai* to gain a better relationship with the divine. By using this Corybantic imagery, Alcibiades describes himself as one of those people whose need for the mystery rites of philosophy is signalled by his response to the words of Socrates.[40]

[37] Cf. 6.1. The Platonic *First Alcibiades* 104ac likewise makes the point that Alcibiades has every advantage, not just of family and position, but of natural talents as well.

[38] The parallel passage in the Platonic *Minos* 318b–c is clearly derivative of this one and offers no further insights.

[39] The fundamental study remains Linforth 1946, who is, however, too apt to compare the rites to a psychological treatment. See further Edmonds 2006.

[40] As Destrée suggests, "these *logoi* that make Alcibiades feel like a corybant may be understood as another image for the cathartic refutation Alcibiades has just alluded to" (2011: 196). Such a reading, however, depends too heavily on the imagined tripartite schema and misses the resonances of the Corybantic rituals for Plato's audience.

Alcibiades, then, is not one of the completely ignorant described by Diotima, who do not even know that they are in need (204a).[41] As Destrée points out, Alcibiades not only responds passionately to the divine golden images in Socrates, he sees those same *agalmata* in the words of Socrates as well (221e–222a).[42] He responds with desire to the allure of wisdom that he sees in Socrates and his words, but he ultimately fails to live philosophically, as a true lover of wisdom, not because he is immune to the siren call of the siren Socrates but because he fails to understand how to love properly. Rather than adoring the wisdom he sees in Socrates, he tries to possess Socrates, seeking to appropriate the mystery for his own instead of joining in the celebration.

3.2. The Problem of Alcibiades

Other scholars have connected Alcibiades' failure with the imagery of the profanation so abundant in this section of the dialogue, but inaccurate understandings of the ancient Greek *teletai* in general and the Eleusinian Mysteries in particular undermine their arguments. Reeves suggests that Alcibiades' focus on physical sexual relationships amounts to a perversion or profanation of the mysteries of *erōs* (2006: 140). More insightfully, Sheffield identifies Alcibiades' "idolatrous attachment" to Socrates with his profanation of the mysteries, "Socrates' reaction here suggests that Alcibiades' profanation of the Mysteries of philosophy was to misidentify its real object" (2006: 204). However, the imagery of profanation goes beyond the intellectual error of misidentifying the object; it involves the kind of action Alcibiades engages in while trying to satisfy his desires.

In her analysis, Sheffield follows the problematic division of the Eleusinian Mysteries into Greater and Lesser, arguing that the distinction in the philosophic mysteries of *erōs* depends on the object, "those in the lower mysteries desire honor (208c3), whilst those in the higher mysteries make virtue their goal" (2006: 95). This model of a sequential set of mysteries, however, distorts Plato's imagery in the dialogue and provides a confused picture of how Alcibiades might profane the mysteries. Alcibiades does not profane the great mysteries of philosophy simply by remaining stuck in the lesser rites, nor does his speech profane the

[41] Again, the Platonic *Alcibiades* 1 develops this idea (starting with 118b). Cf. Belfiore 2012: 181.

[42] "Even if Alcibiades is talking about Socrates' speeches, as we are used to them from the early dialogues, and not about Diotima's teaching, he seems to have really seen the importance of their 'inner' message, and he seems to have understood them" (Destrée 2011: 202).

mysteries by providing a comic (or even satyric) representation of them.[43] As the analysis of the ancient evidence for the scandal of Alcibiades' profanation of the Eleusinian Mysteries shows, comic parody is not at issue here, but rather arrogant appropriation.

Like Sheffield, Steiner sees Alcibiades' problem as an excessive idolatry of Socrates, but she links it with the other profanation scandal in which Alcibiades is reputed to be involved, the mutilation of the Herms. Even if this outrage was more likely the work of a different oligarchic faction, Plato's fourth-century audience would have lumped the mutilation of the Herms together with the profanation of the Eleusinian Mysteries as crimes of which Alcibiades was guilty.[44] The violent image in the allusion to the flaying of Marsyas evokes the violence done to the Herms, and Steiner compares Alcibiades' relationship with the Socrates whom he describes as a silenus statue to other stories of individuals who attempt sexual relationships with statues, always an unfortunate affair (Steiner 1996: 92).[45] Such relations mistake an image for the reality, the sign for the signified, just as Alcibiades mistakes the golden images within Socrates (and his words) for the divine beauty to which they point.[46] Alcibiades tries to satisfy his desire for wisdom as though it were an appetite that could be terminally gratified, like thirst with a drink of water or lust with sexual intercourse, but since wisdom, like the Good and the Beautiful or any divine thing, cannot be possessed by a mortal, his desire must remain an ever-renewing longing.[47] His attempts to appropriate the golden images of wisdom through sex with Socrates are just as fruitless and perverse as

[43] As Sheffield 2001: 201 suggests. The reading of Alcibiades' speech as a satyr play version of the serious speech of Diotima nevertheless provides many insights into the relation between the speeches. See Sheffield 2001 and Usher 2002 for such readings, which do not, however, help us understand the imagery of profanation as much as the theme of comic, tragic, and satyric poetry. Plato, as usual, plays with multiple levels of imagery simultaneously.

[44] As Steiner writes: "Had Alcibiades only followed Aristodemus' example, and left the image standing on the neighbouring porch (*prothurōi*, 175a) unmoved, he might never have been implicated in the episode which contributed to the blackening of his reputation" (1996: 100).

[45] Kindt 2012 examines a number of stories about interactions with religious statues, including the problem with *agalmatophilia*; see also Edmonds (forthcoming) for Plato's use of sexual assault upon an image in the *Phaedrus*.

[46] Reeve 2006: 128 (likewise Reeve 2004: 97) mistakes the nature of the *agalmata* as signs when he imagines them as the embryos with which Socrates is pregnant. Like statues in temples, the golden *agalmata* that Alcibiades sees as representations of the divine beauty he longs for. He does not imagine that he himself can be made pregnant with them through some process of sexual transmission; he wants to take them for himself.

[47] In Halperin's terms, Alcibiades acts as if his desire for Socrates were appetitive, rather than a truly erotic desire (1985: 176).

any assault upon a statue or any attempt to take over the Athenian community's Mysteries of Eleusis by means of private celebrations.

Scholars who see Socrates as indifferent or even hubristically contemptuous of Alcibiades make the same error as Alcibiades in imagining that the wisdom Alcibiades desires is something Socrates has and can transmit. Gagarin, for example, sees the episode as indicative of Socrates' failure as a teacher, while Lear goes so far as to blame Socrates' indifference for the collapse of one of the world's great civilizations.[48] Plato, however, does not bring in the famous figure of Alcibiades the profane to critique Socrates as a callously cold and indifferent teacher.[49] The imagery of the mysteries – ignored, belittled, or misunderstood by these modern commentators – provides for Plato's readers, more familiar than modern readers with the phenomenon of such rites, an understanding of how Alcibiades goes wrong. The point of the metaphor is that the philosophy Alcibiades desires is not some piece of information that he can learn (*mathein*) and keep for himself, but rather an experience he must undergo (*pathein*), like a ritual of the mysteries. Alcibiades' speech recounts his own profanation of the mysteries of the love of wisdom, his attempt to appropriate the divine for himself by taking possession of the sacred things and using them for his own benefit, and Plato's ancient audience would see the parallels, not just between the mysteries of *Erōs* and of Eleusis, but between Alcibiades' profane attempts to appropriate them both. Alcibiades thus becomes a figure for all the promising young aristocrats who attempt to appropriate the power of philosophical reasoning to serve their own appetite for power – Callicles, Critias, Charmides, perhaps even Glaucon and Adeimantus, or Phaedrus and Eryximachus. They all see in Socrates something valuable, something desirable, something beautiful, but they all fail to comprehend it.

The close encounter with the divine in the Mysteries is a powerful affective experience that can be repeated, just like erotic encounters with beauty in its various manifestations, but the revelation of the Beautiful

[48] Gagarin 1977: 37: "As a teacher of others, Alcibiades reveals, Socrates is a failure, in Vlastos' words, 'a failure of love.'" Lear 1998: 164: "Insofar as Alcibiades is trapped in the human-erotic, he can, from Socrates' perspective, go fuck himself. It does not matter to Socrates what the consequences are. From the vantage of Athenian culture, this encounter between Alcibiades and Socrates must be judged a failure of inestimable cost. Nothing less is at stake than the future of one of the world's great civilizations." Likewise Blanckenhagen 1992: 67: "Had Socrates slept with Alcibiades not 'like a father or older brother; but as a true erastes, he might well have channeled the manifold gifts of this most gifted of all Athenians in a classical, a 'Periclean', direction and would have made him the best statesman Athens ever had."

[49] Nails 2006: 196 rightly defends Socrates' choice not to go along with Alcibiades' plan.

itself, like the *epopteia* in the Mysteries, is a profound experience which alters the way one understands, not just future encounters with the beautiful but past ones as well. Alcibiades' scandalous failure in philosophy is illuminated by the parallel with the Mysteries he scandalously fails to treat with proper respect. The beauty, power, and magnificence of the most holy of Athenian rituals do not transform Alcibiades the profane into a pious person; they cause him to desire to appropriate them, and he reacts in the same way to the beauty, power, and magnificence of Socrates' philosophy. In the *Symposium*, Plato uses the imagery of the Mysteries to elucidate the nature of philosophy, both in the metaphor of the *epopteia* of Diotima the prophetess and in the profanations of Alcibiades the profane.

CHAPTER 12

How Does Contemplation Make You Happy? An Ethical Reading of Diotima's Speech

Pierre Destrée

1. Contemplation and Happiness: The Problem

> That is here, if anywhere, my dear Socrates, said the visitor from Mantinea, that life is worth living for a human being, in the contemplation of Beauty itself (211d1–3).[1]

This powerful sentence could be taken, and has actually been taken by some interpreters, notably Frisbee Sheffield,[2] as a sort of motto of the message Plato wants to convey to his readers through Diotima's mouth. But what does it mean exactly? This moment in life, when the philosopher has reached the peak in his ascent and contemplates the Form of the Beautiful, is what should bring him *eudaimonia*, happiness. Happiness is for humans the ultimate object of their desire insofar as they desire some goods, the possession of which makes you happy. In the context of pederastic love, the mature lover (*erastēs*) desires the beautiful young boy (*erōmenos*), and it is the eventual sexual "possession" of the latter that makes the former happy. In the context of the ascent, Diotima states that, similarly, it is through *sunousia* – a word meaning, depending on the context, either meeting, or sexual intercourse – that the philosopher, once he gets to the top of the ladder of love, meets the Form of the Beautiful, or "possesses" it. Yet possessing a good must be concretized as an activity or production. Exactly as in the case of pederastic love, where *sunousia* with a beautiful boy must eventually lead to the lover's ejaculation, the *sunousia* with the Form of the Beautiful must lead to a certain "giving birth" (which is of course the female – here metaphorical – counterpart of male ejaculation):[3] the man who is contemplating the Form of the Beautiful

[1] Except for this first quotation, for which I have used Rowe's translation, I use Howatson's version of the *Symposium* (Howatson and Sheffield 2008) throughout my chapter (sometimes with slight modifications).

[2] Sheffield cites it a dozen times through her monograph (Sheffield 2006).

[3] On this see now Leitao 2012: chap. 6.

"will give birth not to mere images of virtue but to true virtue, because it is not an image that he is grasping but the truth. And when he has given birth to and nurtured true virtue it is possible for him to be loved by the gods and to become, if any human can, immortal himself" (212a). These are the last words of Diotima's speech, and the conclusion of her whole speech: it is thanks to the contemplation of Beauty itself that the philosopher is able to produce true virtue, i.e. to practice some truly virtuous activity which in turn allows him to be loved by the gods and become immortal. And since desire for happiness actually amounts to desire for immortality, as Diotima has stressed (207a), obtaining immortality through this contemplation and subsequent truly virtuous activity, should constitute perfect happiness.

Such a broad understanding only gives you the logical frame of Diotima's argument, not its content. As Plato himself seems to have warned his readers, the first sentence I quoted comes from "a visitor from Mantinea," or more literally, "a stranger (*xenē*) from Mantinea." This rather emphatic phrase may perhaps convey the connotation that her sentence should be regarded as something unexpected, "strange," to the Athenian symposiasts gathered at Agathon's house (and for Plato's immediate readership), and indeed uttered by a seer ("from Mantinea" is an obvious pun on the word *mantis*, "seer"), that is, something rather obscure which needs to be interpreted.[4] For how exactly should this contemplation of Beauty itself make your life worth living, that is, happy? What does that production of "true virtue" which is generated by that contemplation of Beauty amount to? What does this "virtue" precisely refer to?

According to Sheffield, the virtue at stake here must be the excellence of one's *nous*, the intellect; giving birth to true virtue should therefore be read as activating the exercise of one's intellect. And what Diotima adds in the same breath seems indeed to support that reading: when the philosopher has activated his *nous*, and "nurtures it," that is exercises it in contemplating the immortal Form of the Beautiful, he obtains immortality indeed, which is the real object of his desire; and that makes him someone

[4] It should be noted that the term "stranger" is used no less than three times to characterize Diotima (201e3, 204c7, 211d2), which is quite unusual in Plato (one other example is the repeated address, "dear visitors" (*ô xenoi*), in the *Laws* where indeed Plato stresses the fact that the interlocutors are from different places and live under different laws); for the meaning of "strange," see *eg* Aeschylus *PB* 688–9: "strange words" (*xenous logous*). As to Diotima's demotic, Socrates himself refers to this pun in saying: "One would need the art of divination (*manteia*) to interpret what you say. I don't understand that" (206b9–10).

loved by the gods who love their kin, and who, as Aristotle will explicitly say, are such contemplators indeed. As to the "mere images of virtue," they refer to the moral and political virtues, with honour as the good they procure, which were described earlier, in the so-called "lower mysteries." Or to say all of this under the description of finality, when she presents that religious analogy, Diotima makes explicit that the ascent that constitutes the "higher mysteries" is the end, the *telos* (like the latter that are called *telea*, i.e. "final initiation"), of the whole initiation, and correlates the end of our desire, while honour can hardly be the final, and truly immortal, object of our desire. In brief, and to put this in quasi Aristotelian terms, according to Sheffield, Plato would be defending the idea that a philosophical, or contemplative, life (*bios theōrētikos*) constitutes our final, or perfect happiness, while the political life (*bios politikos*) whose central good is honour is only an "apparently" (Aristotle says more positively, "secondary" – *NE* 10.8.1178a8) happy life.

This interpretation, of which I have given a very rough summary, gives us a coherent and forceful defence of the reading which could arguably have been made by Aristotle (at least if one takes his famous defence of the contemplative life in *NE* 10.7–8) as a sort of explicit development of what Plato only adumbrated. But is it the reading Plato wanted his readers to make of his Diotima speech? Does contemplation itself constitute what gives human life its worth – or in other (Aristotelian) words, does contemplation constitute happiness?

As readers familiar with Plato's so-called early dialogues cannot have missed,[5] that crucial sentence repeats a motive we found in the no-less famous sentence Socrates pronounces at the end of his second speech in the *Apology*: "But if I say it's the greatest good for a man to discuss virtue every day, and the other things you've heard me discussing and examining myself and others about, on the ground that *the unexamined life isn't worth living for a human being*, you'll believe me even less when I say that" (38a).[6] But of course, the context of this sentence, in the *Apology*, is ethical and political (and there is absolutely no hint at anything like contemplation in that dialogue). For such daily examination, Socrates explains proudly, the Athenians have him to thank, who, as a sort of "missionary" sent to Athens by the god, has spent his whole life trying to help people practice such examination: "I tried to persuade each of you to care not about any of his possessions, but about himself and how he'll become best and wisest;

[5] Oddly enough, Sheffield does not refer to this passage.
[6] For the *Apology*, I use C.D.C. Reeve's translation (Reeve 2002).

and not primarily about the city's possessions, but about the city itself" (36c). To "care about oneself" means to improve oneself in order to become virtuous, and therefore happy. Logically speaking, it should then have come as no surprise that Socrates, when found guilty and asked to suggest his own sentence, proposes being accommodated in the Prytaneum, he who makes the Athenians "really happy" while athletes who have won at Olympia only experience a "seeming happiness," that is the contentment that honours bring (36d).

I imagine one could argue that in the *Symposium* Plato simply re-used the catchword he used in the *Apology* in a totally different context; now that he is defending his own theory of the Forms (which admittedly does not appear – or has not yet appeared? – in the *Apology*), Plato might even be seen as in fact advertising a very different conception of virtue, knowledge and happiness from the conception Socrates (or at least, Plato's Socrates) had defended so far. But this sounds implausible to me. As I will show in the following pages, there are in the speech of Alcibiades quite a few passages that obviously echo crucial passages from the *Apology*, and which are at odds with a "theoretical" understanding of happiness.[7] And since that last speech is, I take it after many other interpreters (including Sheffield), to be read as a diptych to Diotima's, it must be the case, I contend, that the two must be consonant on that key issue.

2. Intelligence and Virtues in Alcibiades' Speech

Admittedly, the last speech of the *Symposium* must be read as a crucial part of the whole dialogue. This is what Plato announces quite clearly at the very beginning of the *Symposium* when he has the unnamed character ask Apollodorus to tell him about "the meeting between Agathon, Socrates and Alcibiades" (172a); in other words, the core of that meeting – Plato here uses the word *sunousia* for the first time in the *Symposium* – must be located in the second part of the dialogue, which includes Socrates' speech, which begins with a refutation of Agathon, and Alcibiades'.

To be sure, Alcibiades is very drunk, and his speech is meant to be funny, and very much in the mood of a real symposium with the flute girl coming back and the liberal wine consumption that indeed gives a

[7] Christopher Rowe recently tried to defend the idea according to which even in the *Apology*, "Socrates saw his life as one of the intellect" (Rowe 2013: 321). I don't see any evidence for this in the *Apology* (or in any so-called Socratic dialogues) – unless one adds (which Rowe does not) that the object of that "intellect" is moral virtue.

symposium its very name. But Plato makes Alcibiades repeat again and again that he will tell us the truth (214e, 215a, 216b, 219c): at a first level, this may simply mean that he is going to tell one true version of his love story with Socrates and the way he didn't manage to seduce him (and indeed the symposiasts will laugh about his frankness in all of this: 222c); but it must also warn us readers that all this is going to involve serious matters despite the humorous tone. And more precisely, his speech is, as Socrates will characterize it afterwards, a "satyr-play, or silenus-play (*saturikon drama kai silēnikon*)" (222d3–4): by this, Socrates refers to Alcibiades' characterization of him as a Satyr and a Silenus (two words taken as synonymous), but he also characterizes Alcibiades' speech as being an instance of the genre satyr-play, where some tragic story or features are parodied and which were staged after a set of three tragedies.[8] And indeed, many parts of the speech are to be read as a parody of Diotima's speech (which might be considered "tragic" at least in the sense that it is written in an elevated and serious-minded style); in particular, the so-called seduction scene is an obvious parody of the highest mysteries Diotima has just described. Since, then, this speech must contain some "truths," and must be seen as a sort of parodic diptych to Diotima's speech, it must also tell us something important in regard to this speech, offering as Sheffield has called it, a "revisitation" of it (Sheffield: 186). But a revisitation of what?

I contend that Alcibiades' speech should be taken as neither a critical undermining of Diotima's approach, nor as offering another point of view on her speech, but as providing the conclusion Plato's readers should now draw from Diotima's message.[9] Since Alcibiades, Plato implicitly argues, became a wretched person and a failed politician because he didn't (or couldn't) receive Socrates' education, it in turn implies that had he got that education right, he would have become a morally good person,

[8] On this, see esp. Sheffield 2001; and Belfiore 2012: chap. 4.

[9] According to the first, critical approach, following Vlastos' famous study (Vlastos 1973), Michael Gagarin argues that Plato meant to accuse Socrates of *hubris,* which is to be seen as a consequence of his philosophical ascent; Socrates would paradoxically be credited for having become the perfect philosopher, but as having been incapable of educating the youth properly (Gagarin 1997). According to Martha Nussbaum who replies against Vlastos, through this last, very poignant speech, Plato would have been advocating another, more humane and down-to-earth view of *erōs* (Nussbaum 1986). Among those who also favour a more positive approach, Dominic Scott argues that Plato's main point was to picture the point of view of the beloved instead of the point of view of the lover – as is the case in Diotima's presentation (Scott 2000). Alternatively, focussing on Alcibiades' description of Socrates, Frisbee Sheffield argues that Plato's aim was to underline, through humour and parody, the "complex nature" of the philosopher that Diotima's speech presented (Sheffield 2001 and 2006).

and an outstanding politician. The philosophical education that Diotima teaches Socrates must therefore at least include some features that should lead to such a hoped-for result. It is certainly true that Diotima's last words are ambiguous: in saying that contemplation of the Form of the Beautiful is what gives human life its worth, "it is unclear," John Ferrari writes, "whether that vision is the cause of virtue or its occasion" (Ferrari 1992: 260), that is whether the activity of exercising true virtue is caused by that contemplation, or constitutes its implementation. But if Alcibiades' speech is to be seriously meant as the diptych to Diotima's, which implies that the former is also supposed to shed some light on the latter, it seems to me that Plato wanted his audience to draw the conclusion that contemplation is what makes human life worth living insofar as only this allows one to become truly virtuous, and therefore happy – where virtue must mean moral or political virtue.[10]

By the time Plato wrote this dialogue, Alcibiades had been assassinated, and his direct readers would still have in mind the embarrassing, undeniable fact that he had been one of the most (in)famous "disciples" of Socrates. So what Plato wants to show these readers, through Alcibiades' own mouth, is that Alcibiades totally failed to be properly educated, and not only wasn't Socrates responsible for that but also that he had had some good reasons for accepting him as a "disciple": Alcibiades was not only a brilliant, intelligent, promising young man, but he was – Plato emphasises this if only for the sake of his defence – also genuinely willing to become a morally good person, and that's the reason why he came to Socrates. This is what is alluded to when Apollodorus describes Alcibiades' entrance: "The voice of Alcibiades was heard in the courtyard; he was very drunk and shouting loudly, asking where Agathon was and demanding to be taken to Agathon" (212d4–5). The repetition of the name of Agathon draws the readers' attention to the pun on the adjective *agathos*, "good" – a pun that was apparently common.[11] This could hardly be just

[10] F. Sheffield has suggested to me that contemplation could be an end in itself, and moral virtue a consequence of such activity. But if contemplation would be such an end and therefore constitute happiness, moral virtue would be considered an appendage of happiness rather than a constitutive part – something (I believe) Plato opposes. Nevertheless, I don't take contemplation to be a pure means towards becoming virtuous; I rather take the *mathēma* of the Beautiful that contemplation provides you with to be intrinsically moral, and the moral virtues to be the implementation, so to speak, of that knowledge.

[11] See also 174b, and *Prot.* 315d8–e2. In Aristophanes' *Frogs*, Agathon is (ironically?) called an *agathos poiētēs* (83–85). This pun should recall Socrates' own entry into the party (which had already begun when he finally arrives): when Aristodemus meets Socrates, Socrates invites him to join even if he hasn't been invited, adding as a means of justification: "Come with me, so we can prove the proverb

an innocent joke: if it humorously reminds Plato's audience how morally wretched Alcibiades ended up, it also highlights the very fact that, contrary perhaps to what this audience may have felt, Alcibiades was at first seriously in search of moral education or improvement. And indeed, what we find in the first part of his speech is a genuine, almost moving, recognition on his part that he failed to be educated despite every effort by Socrates:

> When I used to listen to Pericles and other great orators I naturally thought they spoke well, but I was never affected to anything like the same extent. My soul wasn't in turmoil, and I wasn't disturbed by the thought that I was a slave to my way of living. But after listening to this Marsyas here I was very often reduced to thinking that being as I was, *my kind of life was not worth living*. And this, Socrates, you will not deny. I am still very well aware that if I allowed myself to listen to him I would not be able to hold out and I would be affected in exactly the same way. For he compels me to admit that even with all my deficiencies *I nevertheless take no care for myself*, but instead *I involve myself in the concerns of the Athenians*. So I stop my ears to *his Siren song* and force myself to run away so as not to spend the rest of my life sitting here at his side. What I have felt in the presence of this one man is what no one would think I had it in me to feel in front of anyone, and that is *shame*. And it is only in front of him that I feel it, because I am well aware that I cannot argue against him or deny that I ought to do as he says. Yet when I leave him I am equally aware that I am giving in to *my desire for honour from the public*. So I skulk out of his sight like a runaway slave, and whenever I do see him I am *ashamed* of the admissions I have made to him. (215e–216c)

This extraordinary passage can, and I think should, be read as an echo of some key passages from the *Apology*. The insistence here on the "care" of the self is one evident feature, but perhaps the closest echo we have here is from this passage:

> . . . as long as I draw breath and am able, I won't give up practising philosophy, exhorting you and also showing the way to any of you I ever happen to meet, saying just the sorts of things I'm accustomed to say: "My excellent man, you are an Athenian, you belong to the greatest city, renowned for its wisdom and strength; are you not *ashamed* that you take care to acquire as much wealth as possible and *reputation and honor*, but what about *wisdom and truth*, about how your soul may be in the best possible condition, *you take neither care nor thought*?" Then, if one of you disagrees and says that he does care, I won't let him go away immediately,

wrong, and make it say: 'To good men's (*agathōn*) banquets too go good men uninvited'" (174b), where the name Agathon is here clearly alluded to.

> but I'll question, examine, and test him. And if he doesn't seem to me to possess *virtue,* though he claims he does, I'll reproach him, saying that he treats the most important things as having the least value. (29d–30a)

The tone and mood of the two passages are quite different. But one can hardly miss seeing the *Symposium* passage as a sort of instantiation, from the perspective of the "disciple," of what Socrates presents in the *Apology*: with his practice of the *elenchos*, Socrates aims at making one ashamed of the things one values, such as money or honour, which shame should lead to care of the soul, i.e. the search for true moral knowledge. In a way, Alcibiades succeeded at that: at the time he met with Socrates regularly, he genuinely felt ashamed in front of him. It is that he also felt deeply attracted by honours, and that is what prevented him from pursuing his education. Plato actually accuses the Athenians themselves of corrupting Alcibiades who had every wish to become a morally good person; if one may use the language of the *Republic* here, it is by offering him overwhelming honours that the Athenians fuelled his *thumos* in the wrong direction, preventing him from achieving his Socratic education.[12] But contrary to what might appear, if *philotimia*, craving after honours, is what prevented Alcibiades from pursuing his sessions with Socrates, and listening to his "Siren song" (that is, one may suppose his *sophia*, as the Sirens in the episode related in the Odyssey promise to deliver a certain knowledge: *Od.* 12.188), it cannot mean that Alcibiades should leave the political arena and dedicate himself to contemplative philosophy. He should certainly not "involve [himself] in the concerns of the Athenians": but this only means being involved in the *bad* concerns the Athenians have, i.e. their quest for power and prestige. As Socrates clearly tells the Athenian citizens in the *Apology* passage, taking care "to acquire as much wealth as possible and reputation and honor" and no "wisdom and truth" while their city is "renowned for its wisdom and strength" is shameful. But that certainly does not imply that the Athenians should abandon their political concerns: what they should do is first "take care of their soul," that is acquire moral knowledge, and then, through that moral knowledge, reflect on political matters in the appropriate way. What Socrates says a little further on states this very powerfully: "I say: It's not from wealth that virtue comes, but from virtue comes money, and all the other things that are good for human beings, both in private and in public life" (30b). This means that it is through virtue that good things, such as money, can be really good

[12] On this, see the interesting remarks by Wilburn 2015: 20–4.

things – and this is true both in the private and in the public sphere. Read from that perspective – which Plato seems to suggest by using the same vocabulary and images – our passage from Alcibiades' speech must therefore not be taken as if Socrates would have been advising Alcibiades to withdraw from politics, but to give up on the honours one usually seeks when doing politics, and to care for himself, which would enable him to become, as he will say later on, a *kalokagathos* (222a6), i.e. a perfect man and citizen who takes care of the city itself.

The seduction scene is another story of a missed opportunity to be properly educated, and again it is Alcibiades himself who does not hesitate to reveal his failure – except that here, he doesn't seem to understand why he failed to be properly educated. And here again, Plato, it seems to me, turns this into an accusation against Athens. The reason why Alcibiades failed in this is, first of all, because of the conception of pederastic love that all the symposiasts present share: the idea that the lover (*erastēs)* must aim at transmitting his knowledge to his beloved *(erōmenos)*. This is something Plato makes his readers laugh at (and we may suppose that through laughter those readers will view all of this with a critical eye), as the joke with the wool thread testifies right at the beginning (175d–e), as if such transmission could be done via sexual contact from one person to another![13] We find the same sexual innuendo in the ascent, where Plato emphasizes the idea of a *sunousia* and contact with the Form of Beauty that should replace the *sunousia* between the lover and his beloved. To be sure, the way Alcibiades behaves is laughable – his insistence on having sex with Socrates is not appropriate for a beloved – but the reason why he is doing it, and why he is bound to fail to be philosophically educated by Socrates is due to a shared misconception among the symposiasts of how to educate the youth. But what is the most interesting for my purposes is the reason why Alcibiades, here again, wants to be educated by Socrates: "For me, nothing is more important than to become as good a person as possible (*beltistos genesthai*), and I think no one would be better fitted to assist me in this aim than you" (218d). Here again, Alcibiades insists that he is genuinely committed to becoming a morally good person, and that this is the very reason why he comes to Socrates, and is eager to get his share of his "amazing beauty (*amēchanon kallos*)" (218e2). Of course this is a parody of the ascent Diotima has just described, with Socrates being taken by Alcibiades as if he were a sort of instantiation of the Form of the Beautiful, which was also described by Diotima as "a marvellous beauty (*thaumaston*

[13] On this joke, and Plato's criticism of pederasty, see esp. Brisson 2006.

kalon)" (210d4–5).[14] But what the parody reveals is that what one seeks after is happiness, which amounts to the search for practical wisdom that makes one virtuous, and which Alcibiades believes Socrates must be able to transmit to him.

This reading is confirmed by the way Alcibiades presents the golden statues Socrates is supposed to have inside himself. Socrates, Alcibiades famously says at the beginning of his speech, is like a statue of (or perhaps a statue moulder of) a Silenus which contains "statues of gods (*agalmata theōn*)" inside it (215a–b). But it is only at the end of his speech that he explains what these "statues" must be thought to amount to:

> This is a point I did not mention at the beginning of my speech, it is also Socrates' discourses that are very like those images of Silenus which open up. If you let yourself listen to them they all seem utterly ridiculous at first hearing, because he wraps everything up in words and phrases which are indeed like the hide of some rude satyr. His talk is all about pack-animals and blacksmiths and cobblers and tanners, and he always seems to be saying the same things in the same words, so that any simple-minded bystander unused to this kind of thing might simply laugh at what he was saying. But if ever you see his discourses opening up and you get inside them, first you will find that his are the only discourses that have intelligence within them (*noun echontas endon*), and then that it is also most divine and contains the greatest number of statues of virtue (*agalmata aretēs*). Moreover, they range over most, or rather all, of the subjects one should consider if one intends to become fine and good (*kalokagathos*). (221d–222a)

Bury rightly comments: "The whole of this account of Socrates' *logoi* is virtually an encomium of his *sophia*" (1909: 166). True, Alcibiades only explicitly mentions the sort of discourses Plato's readers find in his so-called Socratic dialogues, with these rather vulgar and common (the contrary of divine!) examples of craftworkers which were, most probably, a sort of landmark of the historical Socrates that Plato's audience was accustomed to.[15] But these discourses are in fact full of "statues of virtue" – statues that were presented in the middle of Alcibiades' speech as "divine and golden, so utterly beautiful and wonderful" (216e7–217a1), that is, one may suppose, statues similar to, or reflecting as it were, the Form of the Beautiful. The term "statue" Alcibiades repeatedly uses is a little strange (as is the fact that we don't know of any other reference to these statues of Sileni Plato seems to present as being something familiar), and one may be

[14] On this, see esp. Steiner 1996.

[15] This is also a feature we find in Xenophon: *Mem.* I 2, 37; IV 2, 22; IV 4, 5.

tempted to refer it to the very negative expression of "images of virtues" by which Diotima describes the virtue of honour. But one (perhaps main) reason for this usage is the (very likely) fact that these higher mysteries had their peak in the revelation of the statue of the god, or goddess, that was worshipped – a revelation that is analogous to the revelation of the Form of the Beautiful. And since Alcibiades takes Socrates to be so to speak an instantiation of that Form, it is not surprising that he seems to revere him as if he were a statue, himself full of statues of virtue which he claims he once saw; so this repeated usage of the term "statue" may be part of Alcibiades' misunderstanding as to Socrates' role. But, whatever the case may be, the most important, and positive, feature for my present purposes is the very fact that those statues, or discourses, are, as Plato forcefully says, "the only discourses that have intelligence within them." Since the contemplation of the Form of the Beautiful, Diotima clearly said, provides its contemplator with a *mathēma* – a science which consists in knowledge "of the Beautiful itself" (211c8–d1) – one can hardly avoid the conclusion that Socrates' discourses come in the aftermath of his contemplation of that Form. Thus, Plato seems to want his readers to conclude, just as Socrates came to the priestess Diotima to learn a special knowledge she possessed, so here you have Alcibiades coming to Socrates the Silenus in order to share his knowledge – a Silenus is generally thought to possess a special knowledge too, if only, as Socrates repeats, the knowledge of *ta erōtika*, that is, one may suppose, knowledge as to how to deal with one's own *erōs*, or one's desire for happiness. Thus, Socrates is the knowledgeable man who should best serve as the appropriate *erastēs* and teacher for the promising young Alcibiades.[16] But what does this knowledge Alcibiades is looking for amount to? Or rather, what is it for? Plato has Alcibiades state it quite clearly: Socrates' discourses "range over most, or rather all, of the subjects one should consider if one intends to become fine and good (*kalokagathos*)," that is, as I already pointed out, a fine and good man in the ethical-*cum*-political realm – with the consequence, Plato's readers would have drawn: had Alcibiades succeeded in being properly educated by Socrates, he would have become the virtuous citizen and outstanding general he might have been expected to become given his talents.

Now of course such a conclusion is Alcibiades'. So perhaps, one might argue, this is what Alcibiades wrongly concluded or hoped for himself, but there seems to be no strong reason why one should take this as the conclusion Plato's readers must have drawn from Diotima's speech or,

[16] On this see esp. Prior 2006: 146–47, and 153.

more generally, from the dialogue as a whole. But it would be strange if Plato had given such a rather clear conclusion to the last speech of his dialogue if it was a conclusion his readers were expected *not* to draw. As one interpreter has astutely noticed, "The fact that Alcibiades' speech ends with the same kind of long dative-and-infinitive construction that also marks the end of Diotima's speech invites us to compare them" (Leitao 2012: 214). And since the exact meaning of Diotima's last sentence was left pending – in the air as it were – it seems rather more plausible to read Alcibiades' concluding sentence as providing the clue as to how interpret Diotima's. But not only that. There is also another, more explicit, argument for my proposal. In fact, it is Diotima herself who used that term, *kalokagathos*, which expressed the typical Athenian ideal of what a citizen should look like: "No god pursues wisdom (*philosophei*) or desires to be wise (*sophos*) because gods are wise already, and no one who is wise already pursues wisdom. But neither do ignorant (*amatheis*) people pursue wisdom or desire to be wise, for the problem of ignorance (*amathia*) is this, that someone who is neither fine and good (*kalon kagathon*) nor wise (*phronimon*) is still quite satisfied with himself" (204a). Admittedly, the knowledge that is at stake in philosophy, or quest for wisdom, remains undefined; but it is striking that the term *kalokagathos* is used in this context, which seems to make us readers conclude that the wisdom people pursue is what should allow them to become citizens who are expected to display perfect virtue in both the private and political domains.

3. The Praise of Socrates' Virtues

Let's now have a look at the third, and longest, part of Alcibiades' speech, the very vivid eulogy of Socrates' virtues.

In a thought-provoking article, Melissa Lane has argued that in fact this eulogy should best be referred to the natural virtues a future philosopher needs to have in order to be able to concentrate on his philosophical quest, and not as a consequence of Socrates' having reached the peak of the ascent (Lane 2007). As Plato says more explicitly in *Rep* VI, future philosopher-kings must be chosen among those who have proved to have a "philosophical nature," i.e. those who are naturally inclined to, among other things, temperance and courage. Temperance is especially important in the framework of a hydraulic understanding of desire: the *epithumia* is rechannelled towards the desire for *sophia*. And this is best seen, Lane argues, in the story Alcibiades tells Agathon's guests, of Socrates spending all night long in meditation, indeed in "seeking (*zētōn*)" (220c5) after what one may suppose must be *sophia*. And Lane consequently concludes that Socrates has not (yet) accomplished the ascent, and that therefore Alcibiades must be wrong in claiming that Socrates is concealing his knowledge from him.

Admittedly, Socrates' resistance to alcohol cannot be explained by any intellectual understanding; but I very much doubt that this could be extended to the other aspects of his temperance, and even less to his courage.

In the seduction scene, there is no explicit explanation given as to why Socrates does not physically react to Alcibiades' sexual advances, but there are, I believe, two reasons that Socrates could have given if asked. The first is evident given the context: if he has made the ascent and contemplated "the Beautiful itself, separate, clear and pure, unsullied by human flesh or colour or by the rest of our mortal nonsense" – that is (I propose) the *erōmenos'* flesh and skin colour as well as the sweet words the *erastēs* addresses to him – there is no reason why he would be attracted to having sex: the *sunousia* with the Form of the Beautiful (212a2) is what they must seek, not sexual *sunousia* if Socrates is to be a teacher according to "true pederastic education (*orthōs paiderastein*)" (211b5–6). But there is also another reason: since knowledge cannot be transmitted through sexual contact, indeed there is no reason why Socrates should indulge in sex; doing so would be in this case immoral in the sense that he would be lying to Alcibiades.

As for Socrates' courage, two features also show his intellectual commitment. Just before citing Aristophanes' witty description of Socrates as "swaggering and casting sidelong glances," Alcibiades says – and this is, we must suppose, the serious part of the description – that he first noticed "how much better he was than Laches at keeping a cool head (*emphrōn*)" (221b). "Keeping a cool head" is exactly the right translation of *emphrōn*, and in Greek, as well as in English, the word has quite strong intellectual connotations, especially if one remembers that Laches, in Plato's eponymous dialogue, is ridiculed precisely because he, a general famous for his courage, cannot define what courage is. Socrates is more *emphrōn* than even Laches because, first of all, he knows full well what he is doing, and why he should behave the way he does: he is well aware that by showing the enemy that he is going to defend himself fiercely while retreating, he won't be attacked. His courage is thus much more than just a "natural," purely instinctive reaction towards the object that causes fear; it is a highly calculated way of behaving according to the circumstances. Now it might be replied that this knowledge is not exactly of the sort that philosophers are supposed to acquire; obviously, no one needs to have reached the peak in the ascent towards the Form of the Beautiful, or the Good, in order to understand how to behave rationally towards enemies on a battlefield!

But there is another example of Socrates' courage Alcibiades relates, which is much more revealing:

> During that battle which resulted in the generals awarding me the prize for valour, it was Socrates and no other who saved my life. He was not prepared to abandon me when I was wounded, and he saved both me and my weapons. In fact, Socrates, I told the generals at the time to give the prize to you, and you cannot fault me for saying this or deny that I am telling the truth. However, the generals had regard to my social standing and wanted to give the prize to me, and you yourself were even keener than they were that I and not you should receive it. (220d–e)

Plato tells us through Alcibiades *why* Socrates is brave: he wants to save his friend's life and also save him from the dishonour of returning home without his arms (a most dishonourable thing for a Greek soldier as it would show that he threw away the arms weighing him down to flee the battlefield more quickly). And even more importantly, Alcibiades emphatically adds that Socrates refused to be honoured for that brave action, which means that he knew fully well that honour is no real good, and that a truly courageous man should not seek honours. But how could he know that, if he had not accomplished the ascent Diotima has described, that which makes you understand that only the Form of the Beautiful can make you able to "give birth not to mere images of virtue but to true virtue," where mere images of virtue must include those that are for the sake of honour? Thus, Socrates has some very good reasons explaining why he should be temperate and courageous; and the fact that he does not act the way he does for honour since (we must suppose) he knows that honour is not a real good, adds to the likelihood that Socrates has actually completed the ascent.

One might reply to this that had Socrates acquired any knowledge, he would no longer be the typical philosopher who, like the god *Erōs*, is always seeking after *sophia*; and he would not be described, as Plato does twice, as trying to make such an ascent, "seeking" indeed as Alcibiades explicitly says, *sophia*. But why must we think that that ascent should be made once and for all? Why think that such contemplation must provide you with definitive knowledge? On the contrary, if the analogy with religious mysteries holds, and since they must be conceived rather as pilgrimages which one may undertake several times in a lifetime than as a one once and for all initiation, it would be odd in fact if Plato had thought that only one ascent should do for an entire human life.[17] After all,

[17] On the mysteries as a pilgrimage, see Edmonds in this volume (Chapter 11).

only the gods, Plato never tires of repeating, are fully *sophos*, and therefore fully happy– human beings can only hope to become "philo-sophers," endlessly seeking knowledge. Like any other human being, Socrates' knowledge must be non-definitive, and that's the very reason why he remains, like *Erōs*, a searcher, and he needs to repeat the ascent time and again; but unlike other men, he is unique in having acquired an outstanding amount of that *sophia*, and therefore, of the virtues of courage and moderation.

4. Back to Diotima: Virtue, Divine Favour, Immortality

I have argued so far that Alcibiades' speech can hardly be read without a strong ethical resonance. Thus, if one agrees that this last speech should be read as the diptych to Diotima's speech, it must also be the case that her speech should best be read in that perspective. But do Diotima's own words allow for such a reading? I contend that it does.

As Sheffield claims, the moral or political happiness that is provided in the lesser mysteries is constituted by honour, which is the highest good sought; but honour is not the perfect good that can produce true happiness; hence, the true happiness that the highest mysteries promise must be of an other sort: its central good must be beyond anything like the moral or political realm. But nothing really indicates that the lesser mysteries are to be left behind once one has reached the highest mysteries. Exactly as we may suppose the lesser mysteries in the religious realm consisted of relating some myths about the god, or goddess to be worshipped, which prepared the worshipper to the revelation of some sacred objects related to, or the statue of, the god or goddess, one should, I propose, read the lesser mysteries as providing an explanation of the realm of activities leading to immortality, while the highest mysteries should be taken as providing the very reason why such and such activity is indeed the one that should give you real immortality. According to Sheffield, that activity should be another activity than the moral-*cum*-political one described in the lesser mysteries. But nothing indicates that this should be the case; on the contrary, as Diotima forcefully says in her presentation of the lesser mysteries, "the most important and beautiful expression of wisdom (*phronēsis*) is the good ordering of cities and households; and the names for this kind of wisdom are moderation (*sōphrosunē*) and justice (*dikaiosunē*)" (209a). Again, one might read this from the Aristotelian perspective where *phronēsis* bears on human affairs while the highest part of thinking, *noēsis*, is beyond the human realm. But I don't see any explicit statement here that would go this (Aristotelian) way. To be sure, as long as the lover is in the lesser mysteries, he thinks the aim, or the central good, of such activity is honour; or put in the terms of the search for immortality, the immortality you think you can bring about through moral or political activity is the honour which a temple may materialize.[18] And of course that good is not the real, or ultimate good one should seek after; and being courageous or building a city for the sake of honour is no "true virtue," either. It is only after one has "seen" the form of the beautiful, or acquired the "science of the beautiful" that one is able to produce "true virtue," because one is now "in contact with the truth," or in *sunousia* with the Form of the Beautiful. Now if we read this from what Alcibiades will be saying, as I have suggested one should if this speech is to play a "revisitation" role, one must conclude that the "true virtue" must refer to moral or political virtues once they have been enlightened by the knowledge, or "science of the beautiful" the philosopher has now acquired (even if imperfectly).

One confirmation of this comes from a famous, and famously long and convoluted, sentence of the *Phaedo* (69a6–c3), where Plato distinguishes true from apparent virtues of "courage, temperance and justice": these remain "an illusory appearance" (*skiagraphia*) of virtue when they are separated from wisdom; it is only, Plato forcefully says there, once these virtues are "accompanied by wisdom (*meta phronēseōs*)" that they become "true virtues." As David Gallop says, "this eloquent but difficult sentence forms the climax of Plato's defence of a philosophical life" (1975: 102). But this (in fact, Aristotelian) expression, "philosophical life," should not be taken in its Aristotelian sense. In this passage, as Plato says at the end of that long sentence, wisdom should work as a purificatory rite, a *katharmos*, which transforms "unpure" virtues into "pure" ones – and not, as an Aristotelian reading would have it, as the intellectual faculty one would aim at cultivating, or "nurturing" for itself. Obviously, the context here is quite different from the context of the *Symposium,* but here too Plato makes an analogy with some religious rites: "So it actually seems that those people who established the rites for us are no ordinary people, but in reality have long been setting a riddle when they say that whoever comes to Hades without initiation and the rites will lie in filth, whereas someone

[18] See 209 e: one example of this is the temple built in honour of Lycurgus in Sparta which is mentioned by Herodotus (I.66) and Plutarch (*Lyc.* 31). As Bury notes, this interestingly echoes what Aristophanes said: "It is my belief that people have entirely failed to understand the power of Love, for if they had understood they would have erected the greatest temples and altars to him and would offer up the largest sacrifices" (189c).

who arrives there purified and initiated (*tetelesmenos*) will dwell with gods" (69e). Here the initiation consists in a purification, not in a "revelation," but the highest degree of initiation (the *telea*, 210a1), or the *telos*, the end of the whole process, is the same in both cases: it consists in obtaining true virtue or happiness, thanks to a certain knowledge or wisdom which finally allows the initiate, or the philosopher, to be hosted, or rewarded, by the gods.

Now any interpretation of the ascent must also explain Diotima's last, rather opaque, words: "When he has given birth to and nurtured true virtue it is possible for him to be loved by the gods and to become, if any human can, immortal himself" (212a). How can my interpretation possibly fit with this?

Let's begin with the love of the gods. What seems to be evident is the fact that the gods love he who is akin to them, i.e. human beings who share a certain property with them. But what property? According to Sheffield, this must be the contemplative faculty, the *nous*, and its activity, the *noēsis*. And indeed, as Aristotle will say explicitly, the man who is loved by the gods is the philosopher who contemplates in a way similar to how they do (*NE* 10.9.1179a22–30). According to Stephen White, this property should rather refer to concern for others: since the gods are crucially the causes of all goods we may possess, it must be the case that they love the philosopher who is the cause of their disciples' good, or happiness (White 2004: 377–78). But, as far as I know, there is no passage in the dialogues where Plato actually uses the adjective, "loved by the gods (*theophilēs*)," in either such context. In fact, when Plato uses this adjective, it is always for marking the idea that the loved person is a morally good and virtuous person; the gods love her because she is a morally good human being in the same way (Plato thinks) the gods are.[19] With my reading of the *aretē* as referring to ethical virtue, the passage is perfectly in line with Plato's other usages of that adjective: since the gods are morally good beings, and they love human beings insofar as they are similar to them, producing true ethical virtue, and "nurturing" it, is the way "to become people that are loved by the gods."

Now what about immortality? Again, Sheffield's strategy is to read this from an Aristotelian perspective: when Aristotle says that contemplation allows you to *athanatizein* (*NE* 10. 8. 1178a33), to *immortalize*, one quite natural reading of this is to say that it is the contemplation of something eternal (for Aristotle, the prime mover, and other such entities) that makes

[19] The three clearest passages are *Rep.* 612e, *Phil.* 39e, *Alc. I* 134d. See also *Laws* 716c.

you immortal; or according to another reading, it is by activating your *nous*, which is immortal, that you live like an immortal god who is eternally contemplating (in this case, *athanatizein* would amount to "living like an immortal being"). But again, there is no clear case where Plato says something like that. According to White (following Hackworth's famous suggestion), the immortality is not personal, but refers to the immortality that the discourses produced in *sunousia* with the Form of the Beautiful conferred on philosophers (White 2004: 377–78). But this would sound rather strange in the present context: as Diotima has stressed, the proposition "we desire immortality" is hardly to be taken in any impersonal way; and indeed when talking about the philosopher's immortality, she expressly says that begetting true virtue permits the philosopher "to become, if any human can, immortal himself."[20]

So what is the good that philosophers desire as being theirs forever? According to my reading, this must be "true moral virtue" that is the central good that constitutes true happiness. But how should this provide philosophers with immortality? I tentatively suggest that we read this from what Plato says at the very end of the *Republic* where the same ideas of virtue, happiness, being loved by the gods, and immortality come together and wrap up the whole argument of why we should be just. There Plato concludes that once we have become true philosophers, we will "always hold to the upward path, practicing justice with wisdom every way we can, so that we will be friends to ourselves and to the gods, both while we remain here on Earth and when we receive the rewards of justice, and go around like victors in the games collecting prizes, and so both in this life and on the thousand year journey we have described, we will be happy" (621c–d).

True, the conception of immortality of the soul seems to be quite different here, since Plato admits, and even wants to prove, that the soul is by nature immortal, if only for the reason that the myth of Er requires it. But despite this difference, it does seem to me that this grand finale can illuminate the rather brief allusion to the philosophers' earned immortality in Diotima's last word. In the *Republic*, too, it is only the philosophers, i.e. those who have made the ascent out of the cave, who are able to obtain true moral knowledge and thus practice true virtue, which allows them to obtain true happiness; and it is only philosophers who are supposed to have that knowledge on display "for ever" – whatever the one thousand year, i.e. eternal, journey they may have to face after death. For only

[20] The Greek wording for this, *genesthai* [. . .] *athanatōi* <u>*kai ekeinōi*</u>, is very emphatic.

philosophers will be able to make the right decisions when facing the choice of a new life and won't be seduced by a life that looks appealing, such as the seemingly brilliant and happiest life of a tyrant; thus, only philosophers will be always virtuous and happy, whatever choices of life they might have to face. Earned immortality is not explicitly evoked in this context; but the same idea is there: thanks to their education, and their contemplation of the Form of the Good, philosophers will remain for ever loved by the gods because of their true virtues, and they will remain truly virtuous and happy in the eternal journey they may have to make after death. And they will go around and enjoy their rewards of virtue on that journey, that is actually (here Plato employs the common language of reward, too, which is not to be taken literally) enjoy their being truly virtuous forever.

Now, as many interpreters have rightly stressed, the way Plato has the soldier Er tell what happens in Hades is very much like describing the spectacle of our own world where people, non-philosophers that is, make their choices.[21] So the whole tale may very well depict, first of all, not any future life, but the actual earthy life. And thus, the "eternal" virtuous life philosophers have gained through their ascent towards the Form of the Beautiful, or the Good, is perhaps nothing else, really, than the firm, secure, and definitive virtuous life that should prevent them from any wrongdoing in the future.[22]

[21] See esp. Halliwell 2007. It is quite noteworthy that in the choice of life scene, the first one who chooses the life of a tyrant "was one of those who had come down from heaven, having lived his previous life in an orderly constitution, sharing in virtue through habit but without philosophy" (619c).

[22] I presented an ancestor of this chapter at the University of Paris IV-Sorbonne and at the University of Cambridge. I am very grateful to Anca Vasiliu and Frisbee Sheffield for their invitation. Thanks to them as well as to Cristina Viano, Jean-Baptiste Gourinat, David Sedley, Nick Denyer and Gábor Betegh for their oral comments and critical remarks. I am also particularily grateful to Radcliffe Edmonds and Frisbee Sheffield for their written comments and suggestions on a penultimate version of it.

CHAPTER 13

Eudaimonism and Platonic erōs

Richard Kraut

1. Eudaimonism Defined

My goal here is to propose an alternative to a widely accepted way of understanding Plato's moral philosophy in general and the *Symposium* in particular. According to the orthodox interpretation that I wish to challenge, Plato is a "eudaimonist." That label is used in different ways by different authors, but what I shall mean by it – and what I take to be its most common meaning among scholars of Greek and Roman ethics – is that one ought to have a single ultimate goal that guides one throughout one's life, namely one's own *eudaimonia* (and no one else's). The word "ultimate" is used here to convey the idea that goods can be arranged in a hierarchy of value: lower goods (purely instrumental goods, for example) are desirable for the sake of higher goods, and the highest or ultimate good is *eudaimonia*.[1] That leaves open the question of what *eudaimonia* consists in, and whether it is to be identified with a single good or several. That is a matter about which scholars who attribute eudaimonism to Plato disagree. But all of them hold that in certain dialogues – the *Symposium* among them – the contemplation of the forms (and especially the form of beauty) is at least one part of what *eudaimonia* is.

Eudaimonism, so understood, is a form of "rational egoism." That term can also be understood in several different ways, but its core meaning is that one's own good, properly understood, should be of *direct* concern to oneself, and that if one should have any concern for the good of others, it is mediated by its relation to one's own good. Rational egoism, so construed, does not hold that self-interest is the only practical reason there is. But it does say that one has reason to benefit others only if it can be shown that one benefits from doing so. The rationality of self-interest is not something that can be or need be justified; but concern for others *does* stand in need

[1] See Irwin 1995: 53. The agent's happiness is "the only ultimate justifying reason."

of justification, which it can receive only by showing how altruism is in one's own interest. One's *ultimate* goal, in other words, should be one's own good and that of no one else; if one also ought to aim at the good of others, that will be a subsidiary or derivative goal, justified by its relation to one's own good. To me, my good is supreme; to you, your good; and so on. At the center of one's practical reasoning, there is just this one thing: oneself.

The eudaimonist reading would not have become so widely accepted were it totally without textual support. In the *Symposium*, for example, Diotima and Socrates agree that every desire is a desire to have something good for oneself, and that the ultimate reason for wanting anything is to be happy (204e–205a). The vision of the Form of Beauty is described as the proper *telos* of a lover's education (210e). Actions that might appear to involve self-sacrifice –the acceptance of death by Alcestis, Achilles, and Codrus on behalf of others – are explained as attempts to achieve immortal fame, and it is thus implied that those noble deeds admit of no justification other than their promotion of the agent's good (208d). Other dialogues – the *Gorgias*, *Meno*, *Euthydemus*, *Lysis*, *Republic* – similarly appear to give the eudaimonist reading solid support.

But there is a fatal flaw in this interpretation: it conflicts with the deepest idea that guides Plato's ethical thought, which is that one should live one's life in response to something superior to oneself. Eudaimonism says: nothing should be of more importance to you than your own good. But Plato thinks each of us of little importance when we are compared with what is outside us – the polis, the cosmos, the gods, the Forms. What misleads scholars who adopt the eudaimonist reading is Plato's conviction that if we respond as we should to what is superior to ourselves, we will achieve *eudaimonia*, and so our response requires no self-sacrifice. The policy of always acting for the sake of one's happiness will never lead one astray – that is the grain of truth in eudaimonism. But that does not make one's happiness the most valuable object there is; it is not the *ultimate* standard of good practical reasoning.

2. Why Does Socrates Remain in Jail?

> "One should live one's life in response to something superior to oneself."

Spelled out more fully, this principle (I will call it the principle of superiority) holds that there are things or individuals of greater importance than oneself, and that one ought to recognize in them the proper standard for how one should act, feel, and think. My next task is to expand on what this means and to say where I find it in Plato's writings.

My first passage is an argument in the *Crito* for the conclusion that Socrates ought not to escape from jail. Such an act would be an attempt to destroy the city of Athens and its laws (50b), which are superior to Socrates (or any other individual citizen) because of the role they played in his birth, nurture, and education (50e). A child is less than an equal of his parents, and still less an equal of his fatherland, which is, in comparison with his parents, "more to be revered and more sacred, and . . . counts for more among the gods and sensible men" (51b).[2]

There is a second perspective from which the *Crito* addresses the issue of escape: will Socrates be better off if he flees? The answer is no. In exile he would be miserable; he would be seen as a dishonored, disobedient, and opportunistic person (53b–e). But earlier in the dialogue it had already been agreed that life is not worth living if one's soul has been corrupted, and that injustice has this effect (47d–48a). That by itself settles the matter: even if Socrates were received with honor in some foreign city, even if he could continue cross-examining his fellow human beings in some alien land, escape from jail would make his life not worth living, because, having done wrong, he would be living with a corrupt soul.

So, Socrates' well-being is only one of several factors relevant to his decision. (Yet other factors are the good of his friends and children: 53b, 54a.) What must be emphasized – because it undermines a eudaimonist reading –is that his well-being cannot be the *primary* factor. It is implicit in the dialogue that if there were a conflict between his good and that of his superiors (his parents, his city), their claims would have greater weight than his, for they are his superiors. Furthermore, and still more important, there is an asymmetry between the reason to remain in jail that stems from his well-being and the reason that stems from the good of the city. The first of these is conceptually dependent on the second, whereas the second stands on its own.

According to rational egoism, the force of any reason one has to benefit others or not to harm them is derived from the ultimate source of reasons: self-interest. But this is not the logical structure of the argument against escape. That Socrates ought not to harm Athens and its laws is a point grounded in the great benefits he has received from them. Those benefits

[2] Unless otherwise noted, I use the translations in Cooper 1997 for all dialogues other than the *Symposium*, for which I use Rowe 1998.

stand on their own as the reason why he must not mistreat them. That he would be harming *himself* by treating them unjustly is a *further* consideration – one that depends on his having a duty to the city. Here rational egoism looks at things the wrong way round. In this case, facts about what is good or bad for the self exist only because there are other independent facts about the interests of others and one's obligation not to harm them.

3. Obeying the Gods: Against Suicide

In other passages, Socrates shows his adherence to the principle of superiority by subordinating himself to "the god" or "the gods." One of the leading ideas of his defense against the charge of impiety is that his practice of cross-examining his fellow citizens is a religious duty: by indicating that no one is wiser than Socrates, the god has in effect told him that he ought to examine others to test their wisdom (*Ap.* 21a–23b). "Wherever a man has taken a position that he believes to be best, or has been placed by his commander, there he must I think remain" (28d). He refers as well to the divine sign to which he always adheres (31c–d). And in the *Phaedo*, he holds that no one ought to kill himself, if his motive is to flee from his corporeal prison in the expectation of a better life in a disembodied world. Why not? Because we are the property of the gods and cannot dispose of ourselves as we please (61e–62e).

What Socrates assumes in the *Apology*, *Crito*, and *Phaedo* is a principle of deference to the wishes, advice, or commands of those who are entitled – because of their wisdom, or benefits they have bestowed, or both – to a position of superiority. Such are one's parents, or the laws, or the gods. Their directives constitute sufficient reason for you to defer to them (or at any rate, to persuade them to rescind their commands). That is by itself one self-standing reason why you ought not to commit suicide – and it is a reason that does not advert to your well-being (as eudaimonism insists all reasons must). The *source* of the divine prohibition against suicide plays an essential role in explaining its reason-giving force.

It is reasonable to wonder why the gods do not want us to escape from the prison of the body as soon as possible. After all, embodiment is a hindrance to the acquisition of wisdom (79c–d), and surely they want us to become wise sooner rather than later. So, if they care for us – and of course they do – why should they not allow us to rid ourselves of this hindrance? Here is one possible explanation: if we sever our social bonds – to our city, parents, children, and friends – merely to rid ourselves of the woes of embodiment, we will doing those others an injustice. As a result, we will be punished (and rightly so) in the afterlife. So suicide would harm others and do us no good.

Here we have the same pattern of argument we observed in the *Crito*. In both cases, the fact that one would be mistreating others, either by escaping from jail or from the prison of the body, is a factor that has reason-giving force on its own. Then, on that basis, it is shown that escape is ill advised for a second reason – it is contrary to one's well-being. One's own happiness is of the utmost importance in each case – but only because something else is even more important.

It is only a conjecture to say that the gods prohibit suicide because killing oneself would mistreat other people. Here is a second possible reading: the gods know when a soul is ready to benefit by becoming disembodied, and one is not ready if one's reason for departing to the other world is merely a desire to improve one's lot.

That, I believe, is a less satisfactory hypothesis, for one wants to know *why* such an individual would not be ready to benefit from death. My first conjecture makes the gods less mysterious than does this second. But the more important point is this: even on this second interpretation, our passage does not admit of a eudaimonistic reading. For the principle of deference mentioned earlier, which says that one should abide by the counsel or command of individuals who merit deference, would still govern the prohibition of suicide. That principle is not grounded in self-interest but stands on its own. You are the property of the gods, and so your wish for self-improvement should not be your ultimate reason to remain here.

4. The Good of the Polis: *Republic*

That "one should live one's life in response to something superior to oneself" is very close to the explicit counsel of the *Theaetetus* that we should, by striving for justice, piety, and wisdom, become "as like god as possible" (176b).[3] But as we have seen in our discussion of the *Crito*, the polis too, as imperfect as it is, is superior to the individual citizen, much as parents are superior to their children. A different way in which the city is superior to its components emerges in the *Republic*: Socrates claims that the ideal city must be constructed not with a view to the greatest possible happiness of some one class of citizens but the happiness of the whole (419b–c). Each citizen must of course have some "share of happiness"

[3] See Sedley 1999 on the importance of this idea for Plato and later Platonism.

(421c) if the whole city is to be counted happy. And in fact, Adeimantus's worry (419) that the philosophers will not be very happy because they are deprived of property is misguided, because it is better for them to be relieved of the burdens of ownership (465b–d). It is nonetheless significant that Socrates is willing, if need be, to make some group less well-off than it might be, if doing so is needed for the well-functioning of the city taken as a unified whole (466b).

The founding of the city, in other words, treats all classes impartially. And this way of thinking would have to be present in the city – most of all among its rulers – if it is to succeed and not degenerate into partisanship and class warfare. Those who govern must be as impartial in their day-to-day deliberations as the founders of the city were in constructing it: they cannot count the good of philosophers as having more weight – simply because it is *their* good – than the good of others. The kind of benefits they enjoy (contemplating the forms and using them to model the city) are greater than those possessed by the other classes; but their skill at governing looks to the good of those ruled, not their own (341d–342c). So, they cannot govern others merely as a way of achieving their own good – as though the city existed for their sake alone. The words I used in my characterization of rational egoism do not apply here: "To me, my good is supreme; to you, your good; and so on." Instead, the formula used by rulers and all citizens must be more complex: "I should seek my own good – provided that doing so does not detract from the good of other citizens. For there is no reason why the city's laws should favor me over them, or my class over others."[4]

5. Apparent Evidence for Eudaimonism

We will soon look more closely at the *Symposium* to see whether it contains support for a eudaimonistic reading, but let us first look outside that dialogue.

In the *Euthydemus*, Socrates asserts that all human beings wish to do well (*eu prattein*, 278e), and the term *eudaimonia* is used interchangeably with doing well (282c–d). Each of us, in other words, seeks his own happiness – and there is no hint here, or in any other work of Plato, that this is other than it should be.

Living well or being *eudaimōn*, Socrates assumes, consists in having good things. The difficult question he poses, at this point in the dialogue

[4] For a fuller discussion of impartiality in Plato and others, see Kraut (forthcoming).

is: *which* good things? He succeeds in convincing his interlocutors that although wealth, health, noble birth, power, and honor seem good, they are not good in themselves –that is, good in all circumstances – but only when controlled by wisdom (281d). What is happiness, then? Socrates might be taken to be saying that it consists solely in wisdom; or he instead might mean that when one has wealth, health, and other such goods, and uses them wisely, that composite is what living well consists in.[5]

For current purposes, it does not matter which of these two interpretations is correct. What we should notice is something that is absent from this passage. Socrates does not say: you should not care about the weal or woe of anyone other than yourself. Nor does he say: the only reason to care about others is that such concern is good for you. It is plausible to read into this passage the assumption that one ought to desire one's own happiness, because that thesis, though not made explicit, is so deeply embedded in the common sense of Plato's world that it can be taken for granted by his interlocutors. Not so the idea that no one else's happiness matters, or that one's own happiness is the only ultimate practical reason there is.

The *Lysis* also makes a distinction between two kinds of goods – those we care about for themselves and those we care about only for the sake of something else. Some things are dear to us only for their instrumental value, but it cannot be the case that everything is a mere means (219c–d). What is really dear to us is that to which the other so-called dear things lead, and which is not in turn dear to us for the sake of something else (220b). Socrates calls this terminal point a "first friend" (219d).

His denial that whatever is good is desirable merely as a means does not get him as far as he thinks. It could be that everything that is desirable in itself is also desirable for the sake of something else. There would in that case be no first friend. But for now the important question is whether he thinks that for each of us there is just one first friend. If so, it would be reasonable to conjecture that this first friend is happiness – that is, *one's own* happiness. In that case, the *Lysis* would contain solid evidence for eudaimonism.

It is reasonable to assume that, according to Plato, we do not desire our own happiness for the sake of some other good to which our happiness is a means. But that does not make him a eudaimonist – it does not make one's *eudaimonia* one's sole first friend. For it could be that some people want happiness not only for themselves but for others as well. And this

[5] See Jones 2013 for discussion.

idea appears prominently in the *Lysis*. When Socrates begins to engage the young boy in dialogue, he asks him whether his parents love him, and this quickly leads to the further thought that his parents want him to be as happy as possible (206d). Parental love is mentioned again in the very passage that we have been discussing: a father, we are told, whose son had drunk hemlock would value wine and the cup it is in, if he thought these things necessary to save his son (219d–e). Is Socrates assuming here that the happiness of the son is desired by the father for his son's sake, just as the father desires his own happiness for itself and not as a mere means? He says nothing to suggest otherwise. A parent's love of his child is taken at face value throughout the *Lysis*. Nothing is said to cast doubt on the common assumption that a good parent wants his child to be happy because he loves his child and not because he sees his child as an instrument to be used for the parent's purposes. A parent who sought his child's well-being solely as a means to his own would be regarded, by us and by Plato's readers, as a parent who does not love his child.[6]

It would be a mistake to think that there is some "logic of desire" according to which one can only desire for itself the happiness of one and only one human being. Could it be that Plato had so twisted a conception of human relations that it made him the victim of a conceptual confusion – made him invent an a priori argument, based on such a "logic," for this conclusion? It would be uncharitable to so read him. But we need not rely solely on a principle of charity. Plato's theory of the creation of the world depends on the idea that desire can reach out to the good of others. The maker of the cosmos is described thus: "He was good, and in the good there never occurs any grudgingness about anything whatsoever. Being devoid of this motive, he formed the desire that everything should become as close in nature to himself as possible" (*Tim.* 29e).[7] Human beings too can be good, and therefore ungrudging in wanting others, and not only themselves, to be happy. The ungrudgingness of the divine world creator is what we should aspire to, if we adhere to the dictum that we should imitate god (*Tht.* 176b).

So, we should take Plato to be saying in the *Lysis* that there must be a first friend – but also to be leaving it open that one can have several first friends – one's own happiness, one's son's happiness, and so on.

6 Vlastos 1981: 7–9 holds that the *Lysis* treats desire as necessarily self-directed, and so a parent's love for a child must be purely instrumental. Thus too Penner and Rowe 2005: 224–225, 260. In Section 9, I propose a different way of understanding Plato's theory of desire.

7 Broadie's translation (2012: 13).

How can many things each be first? Easily: this friend is first in relation to these subordinate goals; that friend subordinate in relation to those goals; and so on.

6. Does One Good Make a Life Happy?

In the *Lysis*, Plato does not ask whether happiness consists in one good or several. But at the beginning of Book II of the *Republic*, we are told that the best goods are those we seek both for themselves and for their consequences. Plato's task is to show that justice belongs in this category, but the interlocutors agree from the start that there are many items in it – knowing, seeing, and being healthy (357b–c). Furthermore, we are told that harmless pleasures are desirable for their own sake (357b). If Plato accepts a principle of great plausibility, he would have a reason to infer that happiness is a composite of several goods, each of which is good for itself. According to that principle, for any group of intrinsic goods, it is better to have more of them than fewer. The larger class of goods has every good (and every amount of every good) that the smaller class has, and more. Since a good is something there is reason to desire and choose, the larger class of goods is the one that is more desirable.

If happiness consisted in just one of the intrinsic goods, there would be something better than happiness. But the idea that you could do better for yourself than to live well (as well as possible) makes no sense. For each person, living well, being happy – having the good or goods in which happiness consists – is the best one can do for oneself. So, there is pressure on Plato to come to the conclusion that happiness is a composite, because he holds that many items are good in themselves. And he explicitly recognizes that the best human lives have several kinds of goods. In Book X of the *Republic*, he argues that a just person will, over the long run, be recognized by others as just – if not by other human beings, then by the gods, and as a result he will have other goods besides a just soul (612a–614a). One can do better than be just while being tortured of the rack: one can be just *and* honored *and* enjoy the simple, harmless pleasures of life. The idea that the best human life contains several different kinds of goods is reaffirmed in the *Philebus*: if one had cognitive excellence of every sort but no pleasure, one's life would be less good than it could be. Simple and harmless pleasures must be added to the mix to create a well-lived human life (21d–22a, 62e–63a).

When Plato is read in this way, the goods in which happiness consists are in some cases goods that are desirable for the sake of other goods.

Justice is one such good. There is nothing about the concept of happiness, as Plato uses it, that requires that all or any of its components be desirable only for themselves. Although happiness is the ultimate end – there is nothing for the sake of which one should want to be happy – no constituent of happiness is required, by virtue of being such a constituent, to be an ultimate end.

That is not how Aristotle constructs his theory of happiness: he holds that because happiness is not desirable for the sake of anything else, the best among happy lives must be one lived for the sake of something that is not desirable for the sake of something else. For Plato, by contrast, the most important prudential question is: what should a life contain if it is to be as good as possible? His answer: a variety of things (some of which are far more valuable than others). Unlike Aristotle, he does not ask: which of these intrinsically good things is like happiness in that it is not desirable for the sake of anything else? On this matter, Plato's approach is more sensible. It is not a point in favor of a good that it leads to no other.

7. The Reconciliation Project

It might be asked: if Plato is not a eudaimonist, why does he devote a lengthy and intricate dialogue – the *Republic* – to a defense of justice that is based entirely on self-interest? Why does he not answer the question, "why be just?" by replying: "because it is good – period?" Or by replying: "because it is good for those who are treated justly?" Presumably he does not give these answers because he thinks they would be inadequate. It might be inferred that he thinks self-interest is the only legitimate standard for answering practical questions. If the best explanation of why a philosopher bothers arguing that p is that he is presupposing q, that is a reason for taking him to believe q – even if q is never explicitly asserted.

The best way to diminish or undermine the force of this argument for a eudaimonist reading is to propose a plausible counter-explanation. Why *else* would Plato argue that justice is advantageous? Here is the answer I propose: To begin with, he recognizes (and asserts several times) that every human being wishes to be happy. Furthermore, as we have seen, he holds that this is not simply one desire among others, of no more importance or urgency than they; on the contrary, it plays a central, organizing role in each person's life. Now, suppose happiness were such that the project of securing it for oneself inevitably brought one into deep and ongoing conflict with others. There would, in that case, be no content to the idea of a common good for all members of the political community.

One would have to decide, on many or all occasions: should I choose my good or that of others? Because of our natural tendency to care greatly about our own happiness, nearly everyone faced with that conflict would prefer his own good, and would let or make others suffer. Peace, cooperation, harmony would at best be short-lived and superficial.

Plato thinks that human life is to a large extent in the hands of gods who care about and sometimes provide for our well-being. We are of course responsible for how well or poorly we fare in life, but we are not solely responsible, since our souls, like our bodies, are the work of divinities who aim at our good. It is therefore hard to believe that our psychological capacities and propensities are such that we cannot live in harmony with each other – that deep conflicts of interest are woven into the fabric of human nature and the human good. That is the picture of human life portrayed by Callicles and Thrasymachus (and revived by Glaucon and Adeimantus). It is a picture that cannot be reconciled with Plato's belief that human life has been designed by benevolent and powerful gods. So his project in the *Republic* is to show that social harmony *is* achievable – that the diverse array of human talents and interests can be blended together into a beautifully functioning whole. The gods have constructed us in such a way that, if we understand the nature of reality, we will see that we can live at peace with each other without having to sacrifice our own happiness.

The hard problem for anyone who wants to defend this optimistic portrayal of human sociability is to show that justice is good for the just person. (It does not need to be argued that justice is good for others – everyone already knows that.) If that can be shown, then there will be two perspectives, each consonant with the other, for evaluating our actions. We can ask whether our actions help or harm others; and also whether they are good for us. The answers to these questions will always point in the same direction. Such harmony between human beings is precisely what we would expect to find in a divinely ordered cosmos.

So we have two competing ways of explaining why Plato defends justice by showing that it is good for the just person. Which is the better explanation? Does Plato begin with the first principle that self-interest is the ultimate practical reason, and derive all other reasons from that? Or does he undertake the project of the *Republic* because he has a religious orientation to ethical questions – an orientation that interprets the human situation as one that, thanks to the benevolence and power of the gods, is potentially peaceful, cooperative, and law-governed?

What favors the second explanation is that, as we know, Plato thinks about ethical questions from the perspective of a larger metaphysical and theological framework. We can ask ourselves how a god who cared impartially for the good of human beings might give us motives and powers that allow us to flourish together as a harmonious community. The gods have given us a deep interest in our own well-being, but also the power of reason, and this enables us to see that caring about the good of others is always consonant with caring about our own good.

The gods of course do not create facts about what is good – they see what is good and act accordingly; and they also give us the power to see what is good and act accordingly. They give us a rational faculty that is able to see that justice is always in our interest as well as in the interest of others; and they create in us both a strong desire for our own good and the ability to devote ourselves to the good of others.

"Someone loves something most of all when he believes that the same things are advantageous to it as to himself and supposes that if it does well, he'll do well, and that if it does badly, then he'll do badly too" (*Rep.* 412d). That psychological fact is the work of gods who care about humanity in general – not just this particular person or this clan. They fashion our souls in a way that allows us to love others and not only ourselves – when we see that we do not have to choose between ourselves and others. That we can love others and not only ourselves is taken for granted. These loves are consonant with each other; the love of others is not the subordinate partner.

Many modern philosophers, most notably Kant and Sidgwick, have the same hope as Plato – that self-interest and other-regarding considerations coincide. They of course use different arguments to show that this hope is rational, and they postpone the reconciliation of self and others to an afterlife. Plato seeks to reconcile us more fully to *this* world – to the life we are living now, before we die. But he is no more a eudaimonist than they.

8. Imitation of the Divine in the *Symposium*

The superiority principle – live your life in response to something superior to yourself – can be found at several points in the *Symposium*. In one respect, all human beings (and even all animals) already abide by it: they look for some way to possess what they take to be good *eternally*, because "mortal nature seeks so far as it can to exist forever and be immortal" (207d). Animals and many human beings reproduce in order to leave behind future generations. Something of the same kind remains in existence, and although this is not the same caliber of immortality as that possessed by the gods, it is an approximation of that ideal of unchanging continuity (208a–b).

Plato should not be taken to mean that we seek (and rightly seek) to have what is good forever (206a) *only* because this is the closest we can come to the condition of the immortal gods. There is more to his idea than that. Quite apart from the existence of immortal gods, it is independently true that having a good for a longer time is better than having it for a shorter period. Because that is so, we are right to want a good to continue to be our own for as long as possible –that is, without end. That would be true even if there were no gods. Even so, Plato believes that there *are* immortal gods, and he seeks to incorporate his theory of how we should live into a larger picture of our place in the cosmos – a conception of how our lives can be superior to those of animals, and even resemble the lives of divine beings in important respects. It is fitting that the gods live forever because eternal possession of what is good is what is best for *any* being. A constraint on ethical theory, as Plato sees it, is that it satisfactorily captures the ways in which all other things in the world to some degree or other fall short of the gods.

The idea that what is good and right for human beings should be explicable as part of a larger natural order is already present in the *Gorgias*. Callicles exploits it when he argues that we are right to seek a larger share of goods than others because this is the rule that prevails in the animal kingdom as well (484c–d). Near the end of the dialogue, Socrates proposes an alternative model of our place in the cosmic order: "wise men claim that partnership and friendship, orderliness, self-control and justice hold together heaven and earth. . . . You've failed to notice that proportionate equality has great power among both gods and men. . ." (507e–508a). There ought to be an orderliness in the human soul that approximates the greater orderliness of the cosmos. Here the superior being whose great value we should respond to is the world-order in which we play a small and brief role. Our smallness is emphasized in Book X of the *Laws*: the cosmos does not operate as it does for our sake, but we for its sake (903b–e). Orderliness is something one should seek in one's soul because order is good wherever it exists, but we see all the more reason to have an orderly soul when we realize that this is our portion of a divine world order.

In one of the stranger tributes to *Erōs* in the *Symposium*, that of Eryximachus, love is portrayed as a binding and harmonizing force at work in every part of the universe – in animals and plants, and in the objects studied by medicine, music, and divination (185e–188d). Although Plato himself makes minimal use of *erōs* in the construction and maintenance of the cosmos (*Tim.* 91b–d), he thinks that something roughly like what Eryximachus says is true: a theory of human love must be part of a larger account of the behavior of animals, human beings, and of the world order to which they belong.

There is at least one other way in which the principle of superiority figures in the *Symposium* – namely, in its application to our relationship to the Forms. We are to live our lives in response to something superior to ourselves – and the Forms, or at any rate some of them (beauty and goodness) – fall into this category. They deserve our admiration, wonder, and devotion; we should take them as models of how we might be. Unlike divinities who are living beings, they expect nothing of us and make no demands on us; they do not tell us to cross-examine our fellow citizens or prohibit us from committing suicide. Even so, our conception of what benefits us must be responsive to their value. I will return to this point in the next section.

9. Eudaimonism in the *Symposium*?

One strain of thought in the *Symposium* does seem, on the surface, to make it nearly impossible to resist a eudaimonist reading of this dialogue. Desire, it seems, is by its very nature directed exclusively at the good of the agent (cf. *Men.* 77c). If one cannot desire what is good for anyone else, it would be plausible to hold that there is no one whose well-being one *should* desire but one's own. For it cannot be the case that human beings ought to desire something that it is not possible for them ever to desire.

The material in the *Symposium* that I have in mind begins with Socrates' examination of Agathon, at the point where they agree that whenever someone has a desire, (a) there is an object of that desire, (b) the object is something that the agent does not have (*ouk echon*), (c) the desire is for the agent's having that object, (d) the agent needs or lacks that which he desires (199e–200a). Socrates then rounds out this picture by adding that all desire is directed at the agent's future rather than his present or past state (200b-d). He later adds that all desire is directed at what is good (205e) – so as to have it forever (206a). But the portion of this theory of desire that needs our attention now is the one that is comprised of propositions (a) through (d).

We should take these statements to apply to anything that might be called a motivational state. Plato moves back and forth between the cognates of *epithumia*, *erōs*, and *boulēsis*; he says nothing to indicate that he is seeking to characterize only one kind of motivational force at work in the soul. Whatever internal state of the soul it is that moves us to act voluntarily will be characterized in the same way by clauses (a) through (d).

It seems that, according to this passage, it is the nature of motivation to be directed at some condition of the agent, and at no one else.

The object of all love, we are told, is something that is beautiful (204b–d) – or, more fully, the possession (*genesthai hautōi*) of what is beautiful (204d). "But what will the person who possesses beautiful things get by possessing them?" Diotima asks. Socrates is stumped, so she asks an easier question: "the person who loves, loves good things: why does he love them?" Socrates replies: "to possess them for himself." Diotima now asks: "and what will the person who possesses good things get by possessing them?" Socrates replies: he will be happy (*eudaimōn*, 204e). Diotima accepts that as the correct answer to her question. Putting these ideas together with (a)–(d), it seems that all desire is directed solely at getting some good for oneself, and that the ultimate object of all desire is one's own happiness.

But there is a powerful objection to this way of reading the *Symposium*: the theory of desire it attributes to Plato is obviously mistaken, and it is hard to believe that he blundered so badly. The theory in question cannot account for the fact that people have desires not only about themselves but about others as well. That is a fact that must be recognized even by a eudaimonist. Suppose, for example, that a boy's parents see him as a mere instrument to be used for their own purposes. Even so, it would still be the case that they want *him* to have certain goods, and that they take steps to secure those goods *for him*. Perhaps they want him to acquire skills that will make him useful to them in their old age, and so they hire a tutor. They want a tutor for him – not for themselves – even if what they ultimately want is their own happiness. It is their action of hiring a tutor that must be explained, and it cannot be explained simply by saying that they seek happiness for themselves. They must have some motivation to take a sufficient means to this end. And so they must want their son to have a tutor.

But the theory of desire put forward in the *Symposium* says that whenever someone has a desire, (a) there is an object of that desire, (b) the object is something that the agent does not have (*ouk echon*), (c) the desire is for the agent's having that object, (d) the agent needs or lacks that which he desires. It looks as though this is simply a mistaken way of describing our example. There is an object of the father's desire, so (a) is not the problem. But what the father wants is that *the son* have what he (the son) does not yet have – an education.

We have three options at this point. First, we can admit that Plato has a theory of desire that cannot be applied even to the desires of a self-interested agent who treats all others as means to his ends. Plato is a eudaimonist because he adopts this obviously inadequate theory of desire.

Second, we can say that clauses (a) through (d) are put forward with a certain kind of case in mind, and that the theory can be modified to cover other kinds. In addition to (b) through (d), that extended theory would say that when A desires something for B, (b') the object of that desire is something that B does not have; (c') the desire is for B to have that object; (d') and B needs or lacks that object.

Third, we can say that the theory does not need to be supplemented by additional clauses; it only has to be interpreted in a way that allows it to apply to desires about other people. Return to the purely self-interested father who wants to hire a tutor for his son. The object of his desire is something that he (the father) does not have: he has not yet hired a tutor for his son. That is what he wants and lacks. Of course, it is a tutor for his son that the father is missing –not a tutor for the father. But in addition to the son's presently lacking a tutor, there is something else that someone in this example needs and does not have: the father's doing what will lead to his son's having a tutor. That is why he undertakes that act: he needs to do so to satisfy his desire.

I believe this third option is best.[8] It allows us to read Plato's theory of desire in a way that saves it from an obvious and fatal flaw. It does so in a way that takes his theory to cover all kinds of desires; we need not add to what he already says, but merely to understand what he says in the right way. In any case, the first option is the worst. We should not read Plato in a way that commits him to an obviously flawed theory when we can read him differently.

Whether we choose option two or three, Plato's theory fits equally well within a eudaimonist or a non-eudaimonist framework. It tells us – not that the *ultimate* object of desire can only be one's own good – but that in all motivation there is something that the agent is missing. Properly understood, that is true.

But what of the passage, cited earlier (204e), in which Diotima asks Socrates: "the person who loves, loves good things: why does he love them?" He replies: "to possess them for himself." Diotima: "and what will the person who possesses good things get by possessing them?" Socrates: he

[8] Here the approach I take differs from the one I proposed in Kraut 2008: 289, 292. Yet another interpretation holds that the dialogue is a critique of "possessive desire"; clause (c), in other words, is eventually rejected. Thus Obdrzalek 2010.

will be happy (*eudaimōn*). Does this not show that the ultimate object of all desire is one's own happiness and nothing but one's own happiness?

It does not. On the reading I propose, Plato believes that we should aim at our own happiness in all that we do. That does not make him a eudaimonist because this is not the only proper perspective for evaluating our lives. He is engaged in a project of reconciliation: it is correct to act always for the sake of one's own good, but one's actions can also be properly evaluated from an impartial perspective. Parents should not and need never sacrifice their good for that of their children, but that does not mean that they should treat their children as mere means. Their ultimate goal should be both their own happiness and that of their children – and there is no reason ever to give up one for the sake of the other. So it is perfectly understandable that Socrates should say that whoever loves does so for the sake of his own happiness. Similarly, when he claims that the noble acts of Alcestis, Achilles, and Codrus were motivated by their desire for immortal fame (208d), we can read this as a way of advancing his reconciliation project. These people responded to the legitimate needs of others, but their actions can also be justified in terms of self-interest.

It is not just the *ethics* of the *Symposium* that presupposes that we respond directly to facts outside ourselves that give us reasons. Its *metaphysics* makes the same assumption. Plato does not portray self-interest as the only motive that is in operation when we respond as we should to the realm of the forms. The object of love is the Form of Beauty or the Form of Goodness. Our admiration and wonder are directed at these objects not because we calculate that it is in our self-interest to have these attitudes; rather, those attitudes are immediate and appropriate responses to the great value of these objects. We love them because they are such as to merit our love. And then a further psychological event takes place: we want to have these objects for ourselves – that is, we want to draw close to them and develop an intimate relationship with them, so that we know them. And when we succeed, we have one of the goods in which happiness consists – we have developed the right relationship with what is most worthy of our admiration. Self-interest is served, but only because we love something other than ourselves – something that is divine, orderly, and eternal, and therefore more worthy of love than ourselves.

On one reading of the *Symposium*, its principal question is: what should be the ultimate object of all human desire?[9] Its answer to that question is simple: contemplating the Forms. But if this reading is correct,

[9] This is the reading defended by Sheffield 2006. See esp. 79, 137–153.

it is surprising that plural characterizations of happiness are never questioned. It is "those who possess good and beautiful things that you call happy" (202c). "Those who are happy are happy by possessing good things" (205a).

We must be on guard not to impose on our reading of Plato a common (and correct) way of understanding Aristotle, which takes him to organize his ethical theory around an ultimate end – the ultimate end in which happiness consists – that is not desirable for the sake of anything else (that is, contemplation). When Diotima portrays the goal of loving as the contemplation of the Form of Beauty (210e), she is best taken to mean not that this alone is happiness but that this activity is the best of the goods that comprise happiness. When we are embodied and embedded in a rich web of social relations with other people whom we ought not neglect or harm, when we interact with the "great sea of beauty" (210d) filled with beautiful souls and laws, we must acknowledge that these people and things are also worthy of our admiration, deference, and concern – not mere stepping stones. The best kind of embodied existence is one lived not in service ultimately to oneself alone or one activity alone, but in the right relationship to *all* these beautiful things.

Bibliography

Alan-Scott, G. and Welton, W.A. (2008), *Erotic Wisdom: Philosophy and Intermediacy in Plato's Symposium*. New York: State of New York University Press.

Allen, R.E. (1991), *The Dialogues of Plato,* Vol. II: *The Symposium*. New Haven: Yale University Press.

Annas, J. (1993), *The Morality of Happiness*. Oxford: Oxford University Press.

(2010), "Virtue and Law in Plato," in C. Bobonich (ed.), *Plato's Laws: A Critical Guide*. Cambridge: Cambridge University Press, 71–91.

(2013), "Virtue and Law in the *Republic*," in R. Patterson, V. Karasmanis, and A. Hermann (eds.), *Presocratics and Plato: Festschrift at Delphi in Honor of Charles Kahn*. Las Vegas: Parmenides Publishing, 199–216.

(forthcoming), *Virtue and Law in Plato and Beyond*.

Armstrong, A.H. (1961), "Platonic *Eros* and Christian *Agape*" *Downside Review* 3, 105–121.

Armstrong, J. (2004), "After the Ascent: Plato on Becoming Like God," *Oxford Studies in Ancient Philosophy* 26, 171–183.

Aurenche, O. (1974), *Les groupes d'Alcibiade, de Léogoras, et de Teucros: Remarques sur la vie politique athénienne en 415 avant J.-C.* Paris: Les Belles Lettres.

Bacon, H. (1959), "Socrates Crowned," *Virginia Quarterly Review* 35, 415–430.

Barney, R. (2010), "Note on Plato on the *Kalon* and the Good," *Classical Philology* 105/4, 363–377.

Beirwaltes, W. (1986), "The Love of Beauty and the Love of God," in A. Armstrong (ed.), *Classical Mediterranean Spirituality: Egyptian, Greek, Roman*. London: Herder & Herder, 189–205.

Belfiore, E. (2012), *Socrates' Daimonic Art: Love for Wisdom in Four Platonic Dialogues*. Cambridge: Cambridge University Press.

Benardete, S. (1993), *On Plato's Symposium*. Munich: Carl Friedrich von Siemens Stiftung.

Berg, S. (2010), *Eros and the Intoxications of Enlightenment: On Plato's Symposium*. Albany: SUNY Press.

Berger, H. (1990), "The Politics of Inscription," in B. Dauenhauer (ed.), *Textual Fidelity and Textual Disregard*. New York: Peter Lang, 81–103.

Berti, E. (2000), "*Metaphysics Lambda* 6," in M. Frede and D. Charles (eds.), *Aristotle's Metaphysics Lambda*. Oxford: Oxford University Press, 181–206.

Blanckenhagen, P. von (1992), "Stage and Actors in Plato's *Symposium*," *Greek, Roman, and Byzantine Studies* 33/1, 51–68.

Blondell, R. (2002), *The Play of Character in Plato's Dialogues*. Cambridge: Cambridge University Press.

(2006), "Where is Socrates on the 'Ladder of Love?'" in J. Lesher, D. Nails, and F. Sheffield (eds.), *Plato's Symposium: Issues in Interpretation and Reception*. Cambridge (Mass.): Harvard University Press, 147–178.

Bowden, H. (2010), *Mystery Cults of the Ancient World*. Princeton: Princeton University Press.

Bremmer, J.N. (2014), *Initiation into the Mysteries of the Ancient World*. Berlin: de Gruyter.

Brennan, T. (2012), "The Nature of the Spirited Part of the Soul and its Object," in R. Barney, T. Brennan, and Ch. Brittain (eds.), *Plato and the Divided Self*. Cambridge: Cambridge University Press, 102–127.

Brickhouse, T. and Smith, N. (2012), *Socratic Moral Psychology*. Cambridge: Cambridge University Press.

Brisson, L. (2006), "Agathon, Pausanias, and Diotima in Plato's *Symposium*: *Paiderastia* and *Philosophia*," in J. Lesher, D. Nails, and F. Sheffield (eds.), *Plato's Symposium: Issues in Interpretation and Reception*. Cambridge (Mass.): Harvard University Press, 229–251.

Broadie, S. (2012), *Nature and Divinity in Plato's Timaeus*. Cambridge: Cambridge University Press.

Burnyeat, M. (1998), "First Words: A Valedictory Lecture," *Proceedings of the Cambridge Philological Society* 43, 1–20.

Burnyeat, M. and Frede, M. (2015), *The Pseudo-Platonic Seventh Letter*. Oxford: Oxford University Press.

Bury, R.G. (1909/1932, 2d revised ed.), *The Symposium of Plato*. Cambridge: Cambridge University Press.

Carone, G. (2001), "*Akrasia* in the *Republic*: Does Plato Change His Mind?" *Oxford Studies in Ancient Philosophy* 20, 107–148.

Chang, K.Ch. (2002), "Plato's Form of the Beautiful in the *Symposium* versus Aristotle's Unmoved Mover," *Classical Quarterly* 52, 431–446.

Clay, D. (1992), "Plato's First Words," *Yale Classical Studies* 29, 113–129.

(2000), *Platonic Questions: Dialogues with the Silent Philosopher*. University Park, PA: Pennsylvania State University Press.

Clinton, K. (2003), "Stages of initiation in the Eleusinian and Samothracian Mysteries," in M. Cosmopoulos (ed.), *Greek Mysteries: The Archaeology of Ancient Greek Secret Cults*. London: Routledge, 50–78.

Cooper, J. and Hutchinson, D. (eds.) (1997), *The Complete Works of Plato*. Indianapolis: Hackett.

Cornford, F.M. (1961), *The Origin of Attic Comedy*. New York: Anchor Books.

Corrigan, K. and Glazov-Corrigan, E. (2004), *Plato's Dialectic at Play: Argument, Structure, and Myth in the Symposium*. University Park, PA: Pennsylvania State University Press.

Craik, E. (2001), "Plato and Medical Texts: *Symposium* 185c–193d," *The Classical Quarterly* 51, 109–114.

Destrée, P. (2011), "The Speech of Alcibiades," in Ch. Horn (ed.), *Platon, Symposion*. Berlin: Akademie Verlag, 191–205.

(2015), "'The Allegedly Best Speaker': A Note on Plato on Aristophanes (*Symp.* 189a7)," *Classical Philology* 110/4, 360–366.

Detienne, M. (1977), *The Gardens of Adonis. Spices in Greek Mythology* (trans. J. Lloyd). Princeton: Princeton University Press.

Devereux, G. (1967), "Greek Pseudo-Homosexuality and the 'Greek Miracle,'" *Symbolae Osloenses* 52, 69–92.

Diggle, J. (ed., transl. and comm.) (2004), *Theophrastus: Characters*. Cambridge: Cambridge University Press.

Dorter, K. (1992), "A Dual Dialectic in the *Symposium*," *Philosophy and Rhetoric* 25/3, 253–270.

Dover, K. (1966), "Aristophanes' Speech in Plato's *Symposium*," *The Journal of Hellenic Studies* 86, 41–50.

(1970), "Excursus: The Herms and the Mysteries," in A.W. Gomme, A. Andrewes, and K.J. Dover (eds.), *A Historical Commentary on Thucydides*, Vol. IV. Oxford: Clarendon Press, 264–288.

(1980), *Plato: Symposium*. Cambridge: Cambridge University Press.

(1989), *Greek Homosexuality*, Cambridge (Mass.): Harvard University Press.

Dowden, K. (1980), "Grades in the Eleusinian Mysteries," *Revue de l'histoire des religions*. 197/4, 409–427.

Edelstein, L. (1945), "The Role of Eryximachus in Plato's *Symposium*," *Transactions and Proceedings of the American Philological Association* 76, 85–103.

Edmonds, R. (2000), "Socrates the Beautiful: Role Reversal and Midwifery in Plato's *Symposium*," *Transactions of the American Philological Association* 130, 261–285.

(2006), "To Sit in Solemn Silence? *Thronosis* in Ritual, Myth, and Iconography," *American Journal of Philology* 127/3, 347–366.

(2013), *Redefining Ancient Orphism: A Study in Greek Religion*. Cambridge: Cambridge University Press.

(2014), "A Lively Afterlife and Beyond: The Soul in Plato, Homer, and the *Orphica*," *Études platoniciennes* 11.

(forthcoming), "Putting Him on a Pedestal: (Re)collection and the Use of Images in Plato's *Phaedrus*," in P. Destrée and R. Edmonds (eds.), *Plato and the Power of Images*. Leiden: Brill.

Edmunds, J.M. (1931), *Elegy and Iambus*. Cambridge (Mass.): Harvard University Press.

El Murr, D. (2014), "*Philia* in Plato," in S. Stern-Gillet and G.M. Gurtler (eds.), *Ancient and Modern Concepts of Friendship*. Albany: SUNY Press, 3–34.

Elders, L. (1972), *Aristotle's Theology: A Commentary on Book Lambda of the Metaphysics*. Assen: Van Gorcum.

Ferrari, G.R.F. (1992), "Platonic Love," in R. Kraut (ed.), *The Cambridge Companion to Plato*. Cambridge: Cambridge University Press, 248–277.

Ficino, M. (1544), *Commentarius in Convivium Platonis*.

Friedlander, P. (1930), *Platon 2*. Berlin/Leipzig: De Gruyter.

Furley, W.D. (1996), *Andokides and the Herms: A Study of Crisis in Fifth-Century Athenian Religion*. London: Bulletin of the Institute of Classical Studies (Suppl. 65).

Gagarin, M. (1977), "Socrates' *Hybris* and Alcibiades' Failure," *Phoenix* 31, 22–37.

Gallop, D. (1975), *Plato: Phaedo*. Oxford: Clarendon.

(2004). "*In Vino Veritas?* Love, Truth, and Socrates in Plato's *Symposium*," in V. Karasmanis (ed.), *Socrates: 2400 Years Since His Death (399 B.C.–2001 A.D.)*. European Cultural Centre of Delphi Publications, 225–232.

Ganson, T.G. (2009), "The Rational/Non-Rational Distinction in Plato's *Republic*," *Oxford Studies in Ancient Philosophy* 36, 179–197.

Gilbert, W. (1909), "Der zweite Teil des *Logos* der Diotima in Platons *Gastmahl* (cap. 24–29)," *Philologus* 68, 52–70.

Gildersleeve, B.L. (1887), "Studies in the *Symposium* of Plato," *Johns Hopkins University Circulars* 6/55, 49–50.

(1909), "Brief Mention" [W. Osler, 1905, *Counsels and Ideals*] *American Journal of Philology* 30, 108–110.

Gill, C. (1990), "Platonic Love and Individuality," in A. Loizou and H. Lesser (eds.), *Polis and Politics: Essays in Greek Moral and Political Philosophy*. Aldershot: Gower Press, 69–88.

(transl.) (1999), *Plato: The Symposium*. London: Penguin.

Gonzalez, F.J. (2012), "Il bello nel *Simposio*: sogno o visione?" *Méthexis* 25, 51–70.

Gordon, J. (2012), *Plato's Erotic World: From Cosmic Origins to Human Death*. Cambridge: Cambridge University Press.

Graf, F. (2000), "Der Mysterienprozeß," in L. Burckhardt and J. von Ungern-Sternberg (eds.), *Große Prozesse im antiken Athen*. Munich: C.H. Beck, 114–127.

(2008), "Mysteries," in *Brill's New Pauly* (Antiquity Volumes edited by H. Cancik and H. Schneider).

Grube, G.M.A. (1927), "Plato's Theory of Beauty," *The Monist* 37, 269–288.

Guthrie, W.K.C. (1975), *A History of Greek Philosophy*, Vol. IV. Cambridge: Cambridge University Press.

Hackforth, R (1950), "Immortality in Plato's *Symposium*," *The Classical Review* 64, 43–45.

Halliwell, S. (1996), "Plato's Repudiation of the Tragic," in M.S. Silk (ed.), *Tragedy and the Tragic*. Oxford: Oxford University Press, 332–349.

(2007), "The Life-and-Death Journey of the Soul: Interpreting the Myth of Er," in G.R.F. Ferrari (ed.), *The Cambridge Companion to Plato's Republic*. Cambridge: Cambridge University Press, 445–473

Halperin, D. (1985), "Platonic *Erōs* and What Men Call Love," *Ancient Philosophy* 5/2, 161–204.
(1986), "Plato and Erotic Reciprocity," *Classical Antiquity* 5, 60–80.
(1992), "Plato and the Erotics of Narrativity," *Oxford Studies in Ancient Philosophy*, suppl. vol., 93–129. [Reprinted in R. Hexter and D. Selden (eds.), *Innovations of Antiquity*, New York: Routledge, 95–125.]
Hatzfeld, J. (1951), *Alcibiade: Étude sur l'histoire d'Athènes à la fin du Ve siècle*. Paris: Presses Universitaires de France.
Heidegger, M (2012), *Seminare: Platon – Aristoteles – Augustinus (Gesamtausgabe 83)*. Frankfurt am Main: Vittorio Klostermann.
Henderson, J. (1991), *The Maculate Muse: Obscene Language in Attic Comedy*. Oxford: Oxford University Press.
(2000), "The Life and Soul of the Party: Plato, *Symposium*," in A. Sharrock and H. Morales (eds.), *Intratextuality: Greek and Roman Textual Relations*. Oxford: Oxford University Press, 287–325.
Hobbs, A. (2000), *Plato and the Hero*. Cambridge: Cambridge University Press.
Hooper, A. (2013), "The Greatest Hope of All," *Classical Quarterly* 63/2, 567–579.
Howatson, M.C. and Sheffield, F.C.C. (transl.) (2008), *Plato. The Symposium*. Cambridge: Cambridge University Press.
Hunter, R. (2004), *Plato's Symposium*. Oxford: Oxford University Press.
Ionescu, C. (2007), "The Transition from the Lower to the Higher Mysteries of Love in Plato's *Symposium*," *Dialogue* 46, 27–42.
Irwin, T. (1995), *Plato's Ethics*. Oxford: Oxford University Press.
Johnson, W.A. (1998), "Dramatic Frame and Philosophic Idea in Plato," *American Journal of Philology* 119/4, 577–598.
Jones, R. (2013), "Wisdom and Happiness in *Euthydemus* 278–282," *Philosopher's Imprint* 13/14, 1–21.
Jones, W.H.S. (transl.) (1923), *Hippocrates*, Vol. 1. Harvard: Loeb Classical Library.
(transl.) (1931), *Hippocrates*, Vol. 4. Harvard: Loeb Classical Library.
Jouanna, J. (1984), "Rhétorique et Médecine dans la *Collection Hippocratique*," *Revue des Études Grecques* 97, 26–44.
Judson, L. (1994), "Heavenly Motion and the Unmoved Mover," in M.L. Gill and J. Lennox (eds.), *Self-Motion: From Aristotle to Newton*. Princeton, Princeton University Press, 155–171.
Kahn, C. (1996), *Plato and the Socratic Dialogue: the Philosophical Use of a Literary Form*. Cambridge: Cambridge University Press.
Kindt, J. (2012), *Rethinking Greek Religion*. Cambridge: Cambridge University Press.
Konstan, D. (2014), *Beauty: The Fortunes of an Ancient Greek Idea*. Oxford: Oxford University Press.
Konstan, D. and E. Young-Bruehl (1982), "Eryximachus' Speech in the *Symposium*," *Apeiron: A Journal for Ancient Philosophy and Science* 16, 40–46.
Kosman, A. (1976), "Platonic Love," in W. Werkmeister (ed.), *Facets of Plato's Philosophy*. Assen: Van Gorcum, 53–69.

(2010), "Beauty and the Good: Situating the *Kalon*," *Classical Philology* 105, 341–357.
Kraut, R. (2008), "Plato on Love," in G. Fine (ed.), *The Oxford Handbook of Plato*. Oxford: Oxford University Press, 268–310.
(forthcoming), "Partiality and Impartiality in Ancient Ethics," in C. Bobonich (ed.), *The Cambridge Companion to Ancient Greek Ethics*. Cambridge: Cambridge University Press.
Krentz, A.A. (1983), "Dramatic Form and Philosophical Content in Plato's Dialogues," *Philosophy and Literature* 7, 32–47.
Kurke, L. (2011), *Aesopic Conversations*. Princeton: Princeton University Press.
Lane, M. (2007), "Virtue as the Love of Knowledge in Plato's *Symposium* and *Republic*," in D. Scott (ed.), *Maieusis: Essays in Ancient Philosophy in Honour of Myles Burnyeat*. Oxford: Oxford University Press, 44–67.
(2013), "Founding as Legislating: The Figure of the Lawgiver in Plato's *Republic*," in B. Notumi and L. Brisson (eds.), *Dialogues on Plato's* Politeia (Republic). *Selected Papers from the Ninth Symposium Platonicum*. Sankt Augustin: Academia Verlag, 104–114.
Lear, J. (1998), *Open Minded: Working Out the Logic of the Soul*. Cambridge (Mass.): Harvard University Press.
Lear, G. (2004), *Happy Lives and the Highest Good: An Essay in Aristotle's Nicomachean Ethics*. Princeton: Princeton University Press.
(2006), "Plato on Learning to Love Beauty," in G. Santas (ed.), *The Blackwell Guide to Plato's Republic*. Boston: Blackwell, 104–125.
(2007), "Permanent Beauty and Becoming Happy in Plato's *Symposium*," in J. Lesher and D. Nails (eds.), *Plato's Symposium: Issues in Interpretation and Reception*. Cambridge (Mass.): Harvard University Press, 96–123.
Leitao, D. (2012), *The Pregnant Male as Myth and Metaphor in Classical Greek Literature*. Cambridge: Cambridge University Press.
Lesher, J., Nails, D. and Sheffield, F. (eds.) (2006), *Plato's Symposium: Issues in Interpretation and Reception*. Cambridge (Mass.): Harvard University Press.
Lévêque, P. (1955), *Agathon*. Paris: Les Belles Lettres.
Levin, S. (2009), "Eryximachus' Tale: The *Symposium*'s Role in Plato's Critique of Medicine," *Apeiron* 42, 275–308.
Linforth, I.M. (1946), "Telestic Madness in Plato, *Phaedrus* 244 DE," *University of California Publications in Classical Philology* 13, 163–172.
Long, A.A. (2004), "*Eudaimonism*, Divinity, and Rationality in Greek Ethics," *Proceedings of the Boston Area Colloquium in Ancient Philosophy* 19, 123–143.
Lowenstam, S. (1985), "Paradoxes in Plato's *Symposium*," *Ramus* 14, 85–104.
Luce, J.V. (1952), "Immortality in Plato's *Symposium*: A Reply," *Classical Review* 66, 137–141.
Ludwig, P. (2002), *Erōs and Polis: Desire and Community in Greek Political Theory*. Cambridge: Cambridge University Press.
MacDowell, D.M. (ed.) (1962), *Andokides: On the Mysteries*. Oxford: Oxford University Press.
(1986), *Spartan Law*. Edinburgh: Scottish Academic Press.

(1990), "The Meaning of ἀλαζών," in E.M. Craik (ed.), *Owls to Athens: Essays on Classical Subjects Presented to Sir Kenneth Dover*. Oxford: Oxford University Press, 287–292.

Mahoney, T. (2008), "Moral virtue and Assimilation to God in Plato's *Timaeus*," *Oxford Studies in Ancient Philosophy* 28, 77–91.

Martin, L.H., and Panayotis, P. (eds.) (2009), *Imagistic Traditions in the Graeco-Roman World: A Cognitive Modeling of History of Religious Research. Acts of the Panel Held During the XIX Congress of the International Association of History of Religions (IAHR), Tokyo, Japan, March 2005*. Thessaloniki: Equinox.

McPherran, D. (2006), "Medicine, Magic, and Religion in Plato's *Symposium*," in J. Lesher, D. Nails, and F. Sheffield (eds.), *Plato's Symposium: Issues in Interpretation and Reception*. Cambridge (Mass.): Harvard University Press, 71–95.

Merki, H. (1952), *ὁμοίωσις θεῷ: Von der platonischen Angleichung an Gott zur Gottähnlichkeit bei Gregor von Nyssa*. Freiburg: Paulusverlag.

Merlan, P. (1946), "Aristotle's Unmoved Mover," *Traditio* 4, 1–30.

Mill, J.S, Gibbs, M., and Lytton, E.B. (eds.) (1897), *Early Essays by John Stuart Mill*. London: G. Bell.

Montiglio, S. (2005), *Wandering in Ancient Greek Culture*. Chicago/London: The University of Chicago Press.

Moravscik, J. (1971), "Reason and Eros in the Ascent passage of the *Symposium*," in J. Anton and G. Kustas (eds.), *Essays in Ancient Greek Philosophy*, Vol. 1. Albany: SUNY Press, 285–303.

Morgan, K.A. (2004), "Plato," in I.J.F. De Jong, R. Nünlist, and A.M. Bowie (eds.), *Narrators, Narratees, and Narratives*. Leiden: Brill, 357–376.

Moss, J. (2008), "Appearances and Calculations: Plato's Division of the Soul," *Oxford Studies in Ancient Philosophy* 34, 35–68.

Murray, O. (1990), "The Affair of the Mysteries: Democracy and the Drinking Group," in O. Murray (ed.), *Sympotica: A Symposium on the Symposion*. Oxford: Clarendon Press, 149–161.

Mylonas, G. (1961), *Eleusis and the Eleusinian Mysteries*. Princeton: Princeton University Press.

Naiden, F.S. (2013), *Smoke Signals for the Gods: Ancient Greek Sacrifice from the Archaic through Roman Periods*. New York: Oxford University Press.

Nails, D. (2006), "Tragedy Off-Stage," in J. Lesher, D. Nails, and F. Sheffield (eds.), *Plato's Symposium: Issues in Interpretation and Reception*. Cambridge (Mass.): Harvard University Press, 179–206.

Nauck, A. (1889), *Tragicorum Graecorum Fragmenta*, 2nd edition Leipzig: Teubner.

Nehamas, A. and Woodruff, P. (transl.) (1989), *Plato: Symposium*. Indianapolis, Hackett.

Nehamas, A. (2007), "Only in the Contemplation of Beauty is Human Life Worth Living (Plato, *Symposium* 211d)," *European Journal of Philosophy* 15, 1–18.

(2007a), "Beauty of Body, Nobility of Soul: The Pursuit of Love in Plato's *Symposium*," in D. Scott (ed.), *Maieusis: Essays in Ancient Philosophy in Honour of Myles Burnyeat*. Oxford: Oxford University Press, 97–135.

Nightingale, A. (1993), "Writing/Reading a Sacred Text: A Literary Interpretation of Plato's *Laws*," *CPh* 88, 279–300.

(1995), *Genres in Dialogue: Plato and the Construct of Philosophy*. Cambridge: Cambridge University Press.

(1999), "Plato's Lawcode in Context: Rule by Written Law in Athens and Magnesia," *Classical Quaterly* 49, 100–122.

Nucci, M. (2009), *Platone: Simposio*. Turin, Einaudi.

Nussbaum, M. (1979), "The Speech of Alcibiades: A Reading of Plato's *Symposium*," *Philosophy and Literature* 3: 131–172.

(1986), *The Fragility of Goodness: Luck and Ethics in Greek Tragedy and Philosophy*. Cambridge: Cambridge University Press.

O'Brien, M.J. (1984), "Becoming Immortal in Plato's *Symposium*," in D.E. Gerber (ed.), *Greek Poetry and Philosophy*. Chico (CA): Scholars Press, 185–205.

Obdrzalek, S. (2010), "Moral Transformation and the Love of Beauty in Plato's *Symposium*," *Journal of the History of Philosophy* 48, 415–44.

(2011), "Next to Godliness: Pleasure and Assimilation to God in the *Philebus*," *Apeiron* 45, 1–31.

Osborne, C. (1994), *Eros Unveiled: Plato and the God of Love*. Oxford: Clarendon Press.

Parker, R. (1998), "Pleasing Thighs: Reciprocity in Greek Religion," in C. Gill, N. Postlethwaite, and R. Seaford (eds.), *Reciprocity in Ancient Greece*. Oxford: Oxford University Press, 105–125.

Penner, T. and Rowe, C. (2005), *Plato's Lysis*. Cambridge: Cambridge University Press.

Peterson, S. (2011), *Socrates and Philosophy in the Dialogues of Plato*. Cambridge: Cambridge University Press.

Prauscello, L. (2014), *Performing Citizenship in Plato's Laws*. Cambridge: Cambridge University Press.

Press, G. (2000), *Who Speaks for Plato? Studies in Platonic Anonymity*. Lanham (Md): Rowman and Littlefield.

Price, A.W. (1989) [1997 extended edition], *Love and Friendship in Plato and Aristotle*. Oxford: Oxford University Press.

(2002), "Plato, Zeno, and the Object of Love," in M.C. Nussbaum and J. Sihvola (eds.), *The Sleep of Reason: Erotic Experience and Sexual Ethics in Ancient Greece and Rome*. Chicago: University of Chicago Press, 170–199.

(2011), *Virtue and Reason in Plato and Aristotle*. Oxford: Clarendon Press.

Prior, W.J. (2006), "The Portrait of Socrates in Plato's Symposium," *Oxford Studies in Ancient Philosophy* XXXI, 137–166.

Pulleyn, S. (1997), *Prayer in Greek Religion*. Oxford/New York: Oxford University Press.

Quispel, G. (1979), "God is Eros," in W.R. Schoedel and R.L. Wilken (eds.), *Early Christian Literature and the Classical Tradition: In Honorem Robert M. Grant*. Paris: Beauchesne, 189–205.

Reeve, C.D.C. (2002), *The Trials of Socrates: Six Classics Texts*, Indianapolis: Hackett.

(2004), "Sôkrates Erôtikos," in V. Karasmanēs (ed.), *Socrates: 2400 Years Since His Death (399 B.C.–2001 A.D.)*. European Cultural Centre of Delphi Publications, 95–110.
(2006), "A Study in Violets: Alcibiades in the *Symposium*," in J.H. Lesher, D. Nails, and F.C.C. Sheffield (eds.), *Plato's Symposium: Issues in Interpretation and Reception*. Cambridge (Mass.): Harvard University Press, 124–146.
(2011), "Plato on Friendship and Eros," in *Stanford Encyclopedia of Philosophy*.
(2012), "Plato on Begetting in Beauty," in Ch. Horn (ed.), *Platon: Symposion*. Berlin: Akademie Verlag, 159–189.
Reeve, M.D. (1971), "Eleven Notes," *Classical Review* 21, 324–329.
Rhodes, J.E. (2003), *Wisdom and Silence: Plato's Erotic Dialogues*. Columbia (MO): The University of Missouri Press.
Richardson, J. (2001), *Vectors: Aphorisms and Ten-Second Essays*. New York: Ausable Press.
Riedweg, C. (1987), *Mysterienterminologie bei Platon, Philon und Klemens von Alexandrien*. Berlin: W. de Gruyter.
Robin, L. (1929), *Platon. Le Banquet*. Paris: Les Belles Lettres.
Robin, L. and Vicaire, P. (1989), *Platon. Le Banquet*. Paris: Les Belles Lettres.
Robinson, S. (2004), "The Contest of Wisdom between Socrates and Agathon in Plato's *Symposium*," *Ancient Philosophy* 24, 81–100.
Rosen, S. (1987), *Plato's Symposium*. New Haven: Yale University Press.
Ross, W.D. (1924), *Aristotle's Metaphysics*. Oxford: Clarendon Press.
Rowe, C. (1998), *Plato: Symposium*. Warminster: Aris and Phillips.
(1998a), "Socrates and Diotima: Eros, Creativity and Immortality," *Proceedings of the Boston Area Colloquium in Ancient Philosophy* 14, 239–259.
(1999), "The Speech of Eryximachus in Plato's *Symposium*", in J.J. Cleary (ed.), *Traditions of Platonism: Essays in Honour of John Dillon*. Brookfield (Vt): Ashgate, 53–64.
(2006), "The *Symposium* as a Socratic Dialogue," in J. Lesher, D. Nails, and F. Sheffield (eds.), *Plato's Symposium: Issues in Interpretation and Reception*. Cambridge (Mass.): Harvard University Press, 9–22.
(2013), "Socrates and his Gods", in V. Harte and M. Lane (eds.), *Politeia in Greek and Roman philosophy*. Cambridge: Cambridge University Press, 313–329.
Russell, D. (2004), "Virtue as 'Likeness to God' in Plato and Seneca," *Journal of the History of Philosophy* 42, 241–260.
Saint-Exupéry, A. de (1939), *Terre des Hommes*. Paris: Gallimard.
Santas, G. (1988), *Plato and Freud*. Oxford: Blackwell.
Sattler, B. (2013), "The Eleusinian Mysteries in Pre-Platonic Thought: Metaphor, Practice, and Imagery for Plato's *Symposium*," in V. Adluri (ed.), *Greek Religion, Philosophy and Salvation*. De Gruyter: Berlin–Boston, 151–190.
Schirlitz, C. (1890), *Beiträge zur Erklärung der Rede des Sokrates in Platons Symposion*. Neustettin: F. Hessenland.
Scott, D. (2000), "Socrates and Alcibiades in the Symposium," *Hermathena* 168, 25–37.

(2007), "*Erōs*, Philosophy, and Tyranny," in D. Scott (ed.), *Maieusis: Essays in Ancient Philosophy in Honour of Myles Burnyeat*. Oxford: Oxford University Press, 136–153.

Sedley, D. (1999), "The Ideal of God-likeness," in Fine (ed.), *Plato: Ethics, Politics Religion and the Soul*. Oxford: Oxford University Press, 309–328.

(2000), "*Metaphysics Lambda* X," in M. Frede and D. Charles (eds.), *Aristotle's Metaphysics Lambda*. Oxford: Oxford University Press, 327–351.

(2006), "The Speech of Agathon in Plato's *Symposium*," in S. Haffmans and B. Reis (eds.), *The Virtuous Life in Greek Ethics*. Cambridge: Cambridge University Press, 47–69.

(2009), "Three Kinds of Platonic Immortality," in D. Frede and B. Reis (eds.), *Body and Soul in Ancient Philosophy*. Berlin: De Gruyter, 145–161.

(forthcoming), "Becoming godlike," in C. Bobonich (ed.), *The Cambridge Companion to Ancient Ethics*. Cambridge.

Sheffield, F. (2001), "Alcibiades' Speech: A Satyric Drama," *Greece and Rome* 48/2, 193–209.

(2006), *Plato's Symposium: The Ethics of Desire*. Oxford: Oxford University Press.

(2006a), "The Role of the Earlier Speeches in the *Symposium*: Plato's Endoxic Method?" in J. Lesher, D. Nails, and F. Sheffield (eds.), *Plato's Symposium: Issues in Interpretation and Reception*. Cambridge (Mass.): Harvard University Press, 23–46.

(2011), "Beyond *eros*: Plato on Friendship in the *Phaedrus*," *Proceedings of the Aristotelian Society* 111, 251–179.

(2012), "The *Symposium* and Platonic Ethics: Plato, Vlastos, and a Misguided Debate," *Phronesis* 57, 117–141.

Sier, K. (1997), Die Rede der Diotima: Untersuchungen zum Platonischen *Symposion*. Stuttgart/Leipzig: Teubner.

Silverman, A. (2010), "Contemplating Divine Mind," in A. Nightingale and D. Sedley (eds.), *Ancient Models of Mind*. Cambridge: Cambridge University Press, 75–96.

Sourvinou-Inwood, C. (2003), "Festival and Mysteries: Aspects of the Eleusinian Cult," in M.B. Cosmopoulos (ed.), *Greek Mysteries: The Archaeology and Ritual of Ancient Greek Secret Cults*. New York: Routledge, 25–49.

Stehle, E. (1997), *Performance and Gender in Ancient Greece: Nondramatic Poetry in its Setting*. Princeton: Princeton University Press.

Steiner, D. (1996), "For Love of a Statue: A Reading of Plato's *Symposium* 215a-b," *Ramus* 25, 89–111.

Stokes, M.C. (1986), *Plato's Socratic Conversations: Drama and Dialectic in Three Dialogues*. Baltimore: The Johns Hopkins University Press.

Taylor, A.E. (1926), *Plato*. London: Methuen.

(1936), *Plato: The Man and His Work*. New York: Dial Press.

Thomas, R. (2003), "Prose Performance Texts: *Epideixis* and Written Publication in the Late Fifth and Early Fourth Centuries," in H. Yunis (ed.), *Written*

Texts and the Rise of Literate Culture in Ancient Greece. Cambridge: Cambridge University Press, 189–212.

Tigerstedt, E.N. (1965), *The Legend of Sparta in Classical Antiquity*, Vol. 1. Stockholm: Almquist and Wiksell.

Trivigno, F. (2009), "Paratragedy in Plato's *Gorgias*," *Oxford Studies in Ancient Philosophy* 36, 73–105.

(2012), "*Technê*, Inspiration and Comedy in Plato's *Ion*," *Apeiron* 45, 283–313.

(2016), "The Moral and the Literary Character of Hippias in the *Hippias Major*," *Oxford Studies in Ancient Philosophy* 50, 31–65.

Usher, M.D. (2002), "Satyr Play in Plato's *Symposium*," *The American Journal of Philology* 123, 205–228.

Vasiliou, I. (2012), "From the *Phaedo* to the *Republic*: Plato's Tripartite Soul and the Possibility of Non-Philosophical Virtue," in R. Barney, T. Brennan, and Ch. Brittain (eds.), *Plato and the Divided Self*. Cambridge: Cambridge University Press, 9–32.

Vlastos, G. (1981) [1973], "The Individual as an Object of Love in Plato," in G. Vlastos (ed.), *Platonic Studies*, 2nd edition. Princeton: Princeton University Press, 3–34.

Walzer, R. (ed.) (1962), "Aristotle, Galen and Palladius on Love," in *Greek into Arabic: Essays on Islamic Philosophy*. Oxford: Oxford University Press.

Waterfield, R. (2009), *Plato:* Symposium. Oxford: Oxford University Press.

Wedgwood, R. (2009), "Diotima's Eudaimonism," *Phronesis* 54, 297–325.

White, F.C. (1989), "Love and Beauty in Plato's *Symposium*," *The Journal of Hellenic Studies* 109, 149–157.

(2004), "Virtue in Plato's *Symposium*," *Classical Quarterly* 54, 366–378.

Whitehouse, H. (2000), *Arguments and Icons: Divergent Modes of Religiosity*. Oxford/New York: Oxford University Press.

Whitehouse, H. and Martin, L.H. (eds.) (2004), *Theorizing Religions Past: Archaeology, History, and Cognition*. Walnut Creek (California): AltaMira Press.

Wilamovitz-Moellendorf, U. von (1929), *Platon I*. Berlin: Weidemann.

Wilburn, J. (2014), "Is Appetite Ever 'Persuaded?' An Alternative Reading of *Republic* 554c-d," *History of Philosophy Quarterly* 31/3, 195–208.

(2015) "The Problem of Alcibiades: Plato on Moral Education and the Many," *Oxford Studies in Ancient Philosophy* 49.

Winkler, J.J. (1990), *The Constraints of Desire: The Anthropology of Sex and Gender in Ancient Greece*. New York: Routledge.

Wohl, V. (1999), "The Eros of Alcibiades," *Classical Antiquity* 18, 349–385.

Index locorum

Symposium

Theaetetus

Timaeus

Index

CAMBRIDGE CRITICAL GUIDES

Titles published in this series:

Hegel's *Phenomenology of Spirit*
EDITED BY DEAN MOYAR and MICHAEL QUANTE

Mill's *On Liberty*
EDITED BY C. L. TEN

Kant's *Idea for a Universal History with a Cosmopolitan Aim*
EDITED BY AMÉLIE OKSENBERG RORTY and JAMES SCHMIDT

Kant's *Groundwork of the Metaphysics of Morals*
EDITED BY JENS TIMMERMANN

Kant's *Critique of Practical Reason*
EDITED BY ANDREWS REATH and JENS TIMMERMANN

Wittgenstein's *Philosophical Investigations*
EDITED BY ARIF AHMED

Kierkegaard's *Concluding Unscientific Postscript*
EDITED BY RICK ANTHONY FURTAK

Plato's *Republic*
EDITED BY MARK L. MCPHERRAN

Plato's *Laws*
EDITED BY CHRISTOPHER BOBONICH

Spinoza's *Theological-Political Treatise*
EDITED BY YITZHAK Y. MELAMED and MICHAEL A. ROSENTHAL

Aristotle's *Nicomachean Ethics*
EDITED BY JON MILLER

Kant's *Metaphysics of Morals*
EDITED BY LARA DENIS

Nietzsche's *On the Genealogy of Morality*
EDITED BY SIMON MAY

Kant's *Observations and Remarks*
EDITED BY RICHARD VELKLEY and SUSAN SHELL

Augustine's *City of God*
EDITED BY JAMES WETZEL

Descartes' *Meditations*
EDITED BY KAREN DETLEFSEN

Kant's *Religion within the Boundaries of Mere Reason*
EDITED BY GORDON MICHALSON

Kant's *Lectures on Anthropology*
EDITED BY ALIX COHEN

Kierkegaard's *Fear and Trembling*
EDITED BY DANIEL CONWAY

Kant's *Lectures on Ethics*
EDITED BY LARA DENIS and OLIVER SENSEN

Aristotle's *Physics*
EDITED BY MARISKA LEUNISSEN
Aristotle's *Politics*
EDITED BY THORNTON LOCKWOOD and THANASSIS SAMARAS
Aquinas's *Disputed Questions on Evil*
EDITED BY M. V. DOUGHERTY

Printed in Great Britain
by Amazon

44918498R00159